MTN is proud to be a sponsor of this remarkable book and its heroine, Alison.

Alison's inner strength, courage and love for life are an inspiration to us all and once she has touched your life through her talks and her book, you will never be the same again. She leaves a footprint in our memory, challenges our beliefs and attitudes and gives us a formula for life that she has used in extraordinary circumstances – her 'ABC' of life.

We trust that you will derive enormous benefit from Alison's story and her life lessons and are confident that she will continue to make a positive impact on the lives of many South Africans and indeed people all over the world.

Your Better Connection

Sam Michel
Group Executive – Marketing
MTN Group (Pty) Ltd

The Better Connection

I Have Life

Alison's Journey

as told to

Marianne Thamm

PENGUIN BOOKS

PENGUIN BOOKS

Published by the Penguin Group
27 Wrights Lane, London W8 5TZ, England
Viking Penguin, a division of Penguin USA Inc, 375 Hudson Street,
New York, New York 10014, USA
Penguin Books Australia Ltd, Ringwood, Victoria, Australia
Penguin Bookd (NZ) Ltd, Cnr Rosedale and Airborne Roads, Albany,
Auckland, New Zealand
Penguin Books (South Africa) (Pty) Ltd, Pallinghurst Road, Parktown,
South Africa 2193

Penguin Books (South Africa) (Pty) Ltd, Registered Offices:
Pallinghurst Road, Parktown, South Africa 2193

First published by Penguin Books (South Africa) (Pty) Ltd 1998
Reprinted 1998 (three times)

Copyright © The Alison Trust 1998
All rights reserved
The moral right of the author has been asserted

ISBN 0 140 28079 0

Typeset in 11/13.5 point Plantin
Cover photograph by Tienie
Printed and bound by Interpak, Natal

Except in the United States of America, this book is sold subject to the
condition that it shall not, by way of trade or otherwise, be lent, resold,
hired out, or otherwise circulated without the publisher's prior consent
in any form of binding or cover other than that in which it is published
and without a similar condition including this condition being
imposed on the subsequent purchaser.

Contents

Message from Alison

This book is for all those people who have felt like a victim at some time in their lives – a victim of circumstances, trauma or crime. I dedicate this book to you and urge you to believe in the strength that is within each one of us – the strength to choose to become victors.

My heartfelt thanks:

To so many wonderful people – my special friends and the many others, some of whom I know and many whom I don't know – who have taken me and my loved ones into their hearts through what happened to me. The collective power of your love has had a profound impact on my life.

To Tiaan – for saving my life. To Doctor Angelov – for repairing my life. To Melvin – for restoring my life. You are the true heroes.

To Penguin Books and MTN – for believing in this project and making this book a reality.

To Marianne – for your commitment to telling my story how I needed it told. For your time, thought and talent in writing this book so beautifully; and to Glynis – your support made it possible.

To my family – to Mom, for teaching me to believe that there is greatness within me; to Dad – for your faith and pride in me, and to Neale and Ronwyn – for your love and your family.

To Tienie – for your quiet strength, your unconditional love and your consistent support. Thank you for reminding and showing me that when we break through the clouds, the sun is always shining up there.

To God – for carrying me when there was only one set of footprints.

Acknowledgements

'In many lives it is the beginnings that are most significant: the first steps, though seemingly effaced, leave their imprint on everything else that follows.' So wrote American philosopher, writer, social commentator and architectural critic Lewis Mumford (1895-1990), one of my favourite authors.

Alison's beginnings start with her mother Claire, both literally and figuratively. When I first met Alison about three years ago I was struck by the close bond between them, so close in fact that it was one of the reasons Alison decided she did not want to die as she lay seriously injured in the bush after the rape and attack. It was love that urged her on, it was love that helped her survive.

I wondered then how many other people who had found themselves in the same situation had loved someone enough, or were loved enough by someone, to do battle with death itself? Such is its power.

I believe much of who Alison is today has to do with Claire, the manner in which she raised both her children and the unconditional love she gave them as they grew up.

Their close bond reminded me of my own beginning and my mother Barbara Maria Thamm, who died on November 3, 1997. I too was blessed to have had a mother who would have fought a bull for me and who believed that I could accomplish anything I set my mind to. Because of her unwavering belief in me, I began to believe in myself. Every child who is privileged to have that sort of beginning will leave an imprint, no matter how small, on everything else that follows. I would like then to honour my mother's memory in dedicating this book to her.

I would also like to thank Alison for allowing me into her life and for being such an inspiration to myself and so many others. Ali, your strength and determination helped me through many nights while writing your remarkable story. Thank you also to Tienie for all your gentle support. Thank you to Jane Raphaely for giving me wings and for planting the seed in the first place. Thanks to the Ponton family for the use of their house where I escaped the bustle of Cape Town to write this book. And lastly, a deep thank you to my partner Glynis for her love, tolerance, support and understanding.

Marianne Thamm

Foreword

IN A TIME and place where violence against women had become pandemic, one woman, still recovering from atrocious wounds to her soul and body, said 'I will not let them take my life away'.

It was as if I had been waiting for someone to say this. The young woman who did was called Alison. She was South African and until that moment had only been remarkable in that when in trouble, other people always reached out to her, a quality inherited from her mother who had instilled in her the need to 'hold your head high' under any circumstances.

Alison's warcry inspired *Femina* to institute a Woman of Courage Award and she became the first recipient. We sent Marianne Thamm to Port Elizabeth to interview her. She was one of the toughest journalists on our team and we knew that not only would she not flinch from a horrific story but that also she had the heart to gain the trust and confidence of someone who was in a shattered and still traumatic state.

This was the beginning of a remarkable relationship between the magazine and a heroine who the whole country would take to its collective heart. The actual award had to take place on a Saturday morning and we anticipated a poor turnout from the rest of the press. They turned out in strength and when she spoke, even the most jaundiced of eyes filled with tears.

Alison's story reflected a triumphant spirit and an unquenched love of life. This set the tone for the journey that would follow as more and more people called on her to comfort and inspire them. She became the symbol of the survival of the human spirit in South Africa. The golden dove of peace which sculptor Stella Magni had given her as part of the award and which she wore everywhere she spoke sent its own message. Like Nelson Mandela, her most impressive attribute was a complete lack of bitterness.

When Alison married Tienie in Knysna, Marianne and I were honoured to be asked and incredibly happy to be there. It was not just that she had found such a good man and that it was such a golden day. It was because when women are violated in their innermost souls it stays with them, sometimes for ever. But on that day, as Alison's remarkable mother said, it wasn't as if it had never happened but it was as if it didn't matter any longer. In fact the brutal attack and rape were hardly referred to.

In the most vital sense Alison's attackers had ceased to exist because she had risen far above them and gone past the darkness they represented.

That meant that it was time for her to write her book. Despite everything, a book remains the most permanent and valuable testament a person can leave for future generations. Alison's message must travel the world and go into the libraries of a new millennium. To find the words which will make it into a great book she needed a partner in the project.

Who better than Marianne who had chronicled the

first in-depth account and, finally, the story of her love and marriage?

Together, Alison, Tienie and Marianne have produced a book which is a beacon and a beautiful read. The story it tells is unforgettable and the hope that it gives is invaluable. It celebrates a life which was reclaimed, which no one could take away. Alison has given us back our courage too.

Jane Raphaely

Part One

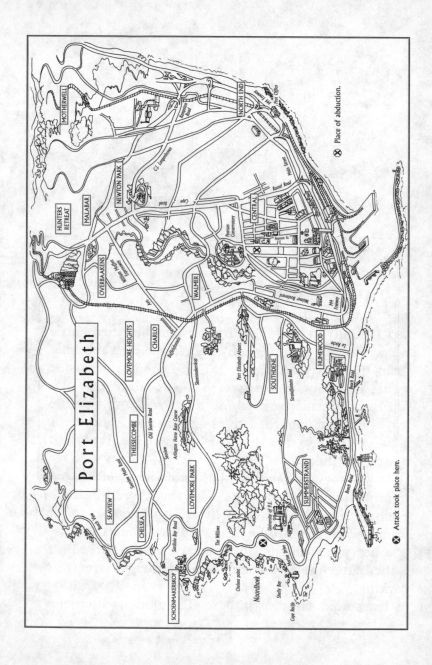

Port Elizabeth

MOTHERWELL

HUNTERS RETREAT

MALABAR

NEWTON PARK

C.J. Langenhoven

NORTH END

Main Road

Russell Road

Cape Road

CENTRAL

Pearson Conservatory

Russell Road

Main Street

Post Office

OVERBAAKENS

William Moffett Expressway

Govan Mbeki St.

WALMER

Walmer Boulevard

M4 Freeway

LOVEMORE HEIGHTS

CHARLO

Baakensriver

THEESCOMBE

Old Seaview Road

SEAVIEW

Seaview Main Road

Buffelsfontein

Steenbokskop

Port Elizabeth Airport

SOUTHDENE

Strandfontein Road

HUMEWOOD

La Roche

Beach Road

CHELSEA

Seaview

Arlington Horse Race Course

LOVEMORE PARK

Sardinia Bay Road

SCHOENMAKERSKOP

Beach Vista

The Willows

Chelsea point

Noordhoek

Shelly Bay

Cape Recife

Marine Drive

University of P.E.

SUMMERSTRAND

Beach Road

⊗ Place of abduction.

⊗ Attack took place here.

1

ALISON

Falling through a crack

———— ◆ ————

AS I TURNED Reginald, my troublesome but trusty little yellow Renault 5, into Deare Street in the early morning hours of Sunday, December 18, 1994 the world outside was as I had always known it. The soft silver light of a full moon brushed everything in its wake, tinting the leaves of tired suburban trees and casting a luminous glow on the few cars that swished past me. It was all quite beautiful.

It was about 1 a.m. and the broad streets of Central were relatively quiet for such a balmy Port Elizabeth evening. The 24-hour, neon-lit café around the corner from my flat was still buzzing, as always, and the pulse of a heavy bass rhythm that pumped from a parked car trailed after me as I scanned the darkened street for parking.

I was tired, but pleasantly so. The glorious afternoon

spent on the beach with my friend Kim and her sons Devon and Jarryd had continued into the night when two mutual friends, Phil and Richard, had arrived unexpectedly at her flat. It had been one of those wonderfully spontaneous evenings and after sitting out on Kim's balcony enjoying the glorious weather and chatting, we all decided, like some happy travelling road show, to return to my flat for a take-away pizza, a game of Balderdash and a bottle of good wine.

I had promised Kim earlier that I would give her a lift home, which I did. Now as I turned back into Deare Street thinking of the cool shower I was about to take, I realised I had lost the convenient parking space I had found earlier almost right outside my front door.

Parking was always a problem this time of night, or should I say, this early in the morning. Most of the people in the blocks of flats bordering my double-storey maisonette, one of six in the charming little complex I had grown to love so much, were probably already tucked up in bed. There isn't that much to draw anyone out of doors at night in Port Elizabeth, which is why we had all chosen to stay at home and enjoy each other's company.

Up ahead I spotted a parking space under a massive old tree. It was about ten metres from my front door, but it would have to do. It wasn't ideal; the pool of light from the street lamp a little way up didn't quite reach there, I remember thinking, but there was no alternative so I backed Reginald into the spot.

Then suddenly he was there. I had just turned off Reginald's engine and flicked off the lights. It was so routine, I did it all in one swift movement. As I reached over to the passenger seat to gather up the pile of clean laundry I had just picked up at Kim's, I felt a gush of warm air as the car door next to me was wrenched open.

Like an apparition, conjured out of the darkness, a scrawny, tallish young man with light blond hair pushed his pinched face into the car. I immediately spotted the knife. It was a long, thin weapon, almost like a letter opener, with a tapering blade. It felt cold and spiny as he pressed it to my neck.

When he spoke, his voice, which was quiet and controlled, sounded as though it emanated from a distant planet. But every word thudded into my skull.

'Move over or I'll kill you,' he almost whispered.

It was a strange, disjointed moment. Until then everything around me had felt so familiar, so predictable and ordinary. Each minute, each second, had merely tumbled into the next. I had taken it all so much for granted that a part of me couldn't quite grasp what was going on.

I shifted on to the passenger seat, clutching the fresh laundry to my chest. A hint of washing powder wafted up my nostrils. It was such a familiar and comforting aroma but it seemed so strangely out of place now. Things started to slow down. I could feel it happening, almost as if my brain was awash with some strange chemical that stalled or muted all outside stimulus. Everything felt uncomfortably unreal, as though I had fallen through a crack in time.

A hollow sense of detachment separated me from this stranger, dressed in a T-shirt and tracksuit pants, as I watched him turn the ignition key. He looked so average, like any number of young men I had seen strolling along the streets and beaches of Port Elizabeth.

And as he jerked my car out into the street I wondered if I would be able to jump out.

'Do it, do it, do it' a voice screamed inside my head. But I couldn't take that chance. I felt strangely immobilised, aware that although this man appeared to be calm and looked so ordinary, there was a menacing edginess brimming below.

He observed me out of the corner of his eye and I could see the knife. It was resting on the seat next to him near the driver's door. We sped off towards the stop sign at the end of my road. While he drove he fumbled around the dashboard looking for the light switch.

'Where do you put the lights on?' he commanded.

The switch was located on the right indicator and I knew he would not find it. I reached over and turned on the lights. He spoke again, his words bouncing off the interior of the car.

'Don't worry, I don't want to hurt you. I just want to use your car for an hour,' he said.

I chose to believe him at that moment.

This is so bizarre, I remember thinking, still not accepting the reality of it all. This doesn't happen. This can't be happening, I repeated to myself like a mantra.

I convinced myself that soon I'd be safely back at home. I couldn't wait to tell Kim what had happened. I really wasn't able to compute the danger of the moment.

'You live in Number One, don't you?' he volunteered quite matter of factly.

So, he'd been watching me. I wondered for how long and how much he really knew. And why was it that I had not seen him? Was I just too absorbed in my own world, or had he hidden in the shadows out of sight?

'What's your name?' the man asked me almost casually as he turned my car right into Pearson Street.

I could not believe his audacity. Here he was abducting me, stealing my car and he wanted to make everyday chit-chat. He already knew where I lived and there was no way I was going to tell him anything more about myself.

'Susan,' I replied. 'And yours?'

He said his name was Clinton.

I wanted to find out more about him. I thought perhaps that way I could play to his sense of fairness, his humanity, and somehow convince him to let me go.

'Where are you from?' I asked.

'I'd rather not tell you anything about me,' he snapped.

I was startled at the sharpness of the reply, the cold edge to his words, but I dared not show him I was afraid.

'So you live there alone,' he picked up the conversation.

'No, my boyfriend's at home waiting for me,' I lied, thinking this might encourage him to let me go.

There was a short silence and I thought I would take the gap.

'Why don't you just let me get out and take the car?' I asked him.

'No,' he said. 'I want company. I have to find this friend of mine who stole my TV. And he owes me money.'

I fought hard to control my thoughts. I'd never felt this helpless before. It was a feeling I didn't like at all. The best way to deal with this, I told myself, was to remain totally calm and not make him angry. I would deal with each moment as it came.

I pressed the bundle of washing to my chest. It was

comforting to have my warm, soft, familiar things so close to me. Soon, I reassured myself, we'd find his friend and this would all be over.

Just then he turned into the traffic circle in Pearson Street. This was still a part of town that was familiar to me. The streets are narrower than others in Central and there are a few quaint little antique and second-hand clothing shops that squat between ordinary businesses. In fact the area reminded me a little of London. Right then though, everything looked so eerie, almost hostile. There was not a soul around.

Then suddenly, up ahead, I spotted it.

A yellow police van was cruising slowly up the street. It was about 15 metres away, but for me it stood out like a beacon. The man sensed this too and my heart sank when he slowed down. I kept my eyes on the back of the vehicle, wishing and willing it to stop.

Now, I thought to myself, jump out now, do something, hoot, lean over, push him.

But just then the police van turned right into a side-street and was gone. My moment of hope vanished as the red tail-lights disappeared around the corner.

There was a crushing, claustrophobic silence in the car. The police van had clearly rattled the man and he appeared to have grown a little irritated.

I looked out of the window at the landscape outside. We were now in a part of Central that had changed completely during my three and a half year stay in London. It was so totally unrecognisable that I felt I had been transported to a foreign place.

The lush gardens that edged on to the cobbled streets and the strange Victorian lamps that glowed quietly seemed like the backdrop to some turn of the century movie. Nothing moved outside and I felt the fear welling up inside me.

Why is he taking me here? I asked myself.

I wanted to speak out, but decided against it. There was no point in trying to reason with him. Strangely, the familiarity of the other streets brought with it a false sense of safety. At least I recognised my surroundings, even though I had no reference point for the situation in which I now found myself.

It felt like hours but it must have taken only a few moments. Soon things began to look familiar again. We were heading towards Main Street, a part of town I knew but seldom visited.

Grey, cold slabs of concrete from the massive highway flyovers cast long shadows across the broad artery with its middle island. The place was humming with people.

They were everywhere. These were the creatures of the night. This was where it all happened while the rest of Port Elizabeth lay asleep. There was a popular club in the area called 'Club Tonite' and it seemed as if the party had spilled out of the venue and on to the street.

Taxis were perched on pavements and double parked in the road. Some had their doors open and music belted out from inside merging with the clatter and noise of the traffic, the hooters, the blur of faces, the colour and neon lights. To me, it was a frightening cacophony.

I stared at it all, feeling quite nauseous. This was not my world and I did not know these people. They scared me. For some reason I felt they were a part of him, this was his turf. I'd be a fool to try anything here. If I jumped out now they would all get me. Besides, I still did not want to let him see that I had begun to panic.

Clinton hunched over the steering wheel and squinted as he scanned the crowd in the street. There were hordes of people loitering everywhere. They were seated on a small wall on one side of the road and just hanging about on the other. He was clearly looking for the man he said had stolen his TV.

'Where the fuck is he?' he muttered under his breath.

I could see he was growing agitated and that was the last thing I wanted. He would, I thought, definitely take it out on me. If I sat quietly enough maybe he would think I had disappeared; maybe, my besieged mind persuaded me, I *would* actually disappear.

Further up Main Street the crowds began to thin out. Just then he turned up a side-street that took us to the darkened lanes of North End. It was a bleak place. There were few street lamps and stray cats scampered through the litter out of the headlights. Rickety fences bordered low crumbling houses in which the occupants lay safely slumbering.

Clinton was growing annoyed. He seemed frustrated and jerked the car up the steep, narrow roads, turning into dark alleyways and small dog-legs behind the closely packed houses.

Next thing I knew we were back on Main Street, except this time we were on the opposite side, heading towards the new post office. The toing and froing was becoming increasing intolerable. I had to fight the compulsive urge to try and put a stop to it all. I had always been in control of my life, or at least had tried to take responsibility for things that affected me. I was totally powerless in this instance. There was really nothing I could do. The best strategy, I decided, was to take each new scenario as it came.

Once again Clinton scanned the crowd, cursing under his breath.

We reached the end of Main Street again and now he was clearly angry. He suddenly slammed his foot down on the accelerator and we sped around a sharp corner, tyres screeching.

'Careful,' I said almost instinctively. 'It's an old car and you'll roll it.'

I was surprised at how calm, how normal, I sounded. He heard me and I was amazed that he even bothered to listen. He slowed down, a response that I found quite comforting in a perverse way. I realised it was the first time I had addressed him before he addressed me.

We were back in Main Street and crawled along it once again. Then suddenly Clinton stopped.

'Ah,' he said. 'There he is.'

A short, sturdy young man, dressed entirely in black, stepped away from a crowd of people who were crouching and sitting on a low wall and strode towards the car.

This must be the friend, I thought, as he approached Clinton at the driver's side. He gave me a cursory glance before Clinton heaved up the driver's seat and our new passenger slid in behind him.

'Have you got any smokes?' was the first thing Clinton said to the man.

I was also dying for a cigarette and when he leaned across offering the driver one I asked if I could have one too.

I puffed nervously on the cigarette as we now headed

out of the city towards Beach Road, one of the main arteries near the beachfront.

'Meet my friend Susan,' Clinton said to the other man and then, turning to me, 'this is Theuns.'

Out of politeness and habit I said, 'Hello.'

The two of them started talking. I couldn't quite follow the thread, but it was some story about the television and somebody called Natalie who lived in the suburb of Overbaakens. My mother, Claire, lives near Overbaakens and when they mentioned they were heading out there I realised that this was not yet over.

Somehow I did not want them to be lying. I wanted to believe that was where we were heading and that once we had got there and they had finished their 'business' they would just dump me somewhere next to the road. I began plotting how I'd walk to my mother's house or a nearby telephone and call someone to fetch me.

There were a number of cars along Beach Road. We stopped at traffic lights and I looked at the stationary vehicles in front of and next to us. I desperately wanted to make contact with someone, anyone, 'out there' and somehow alert them to my predicament.

But each car and its occupants seemed a thousand miles away, in some other universe where everything was safe and normal. They didn't even take in what was going on outside the safe, sealed interiors of their mobile worlds. And what would they have seen had they looked at us anyway? Just two men and a woman heading off somewhere.

How could they possibly know I was being held hostage by these two people, total strangers I had never met before. And besides, even if I did make a face or try to hoot or flick the lights, there wouldn't be enough time for anyone to realise what was going on and to react quickly enough.

When Clinton missed the turn-off to Overbaakens and kept heading along Beach Road towards Summerstrand, a well-known and popular stretch of beaches, I didn't know what to think. In fact, I did not allow myself to think at all. I couldn't afford to.

I wondered about these two men who had dropped into my life from nowhere.

2

ALISON

A waking nightmare

———◆———

I KEPT MY eyes on the black tar ahead of us. No one spoke. The only sound was the high-pitched whirr of Reginald's engine. Theuns puffed away at a cigarette while Clinton stared at the road which was now leading us in the direction of Schoenmakerskop.

For some reason I believed they were taking the long way round to Overbaakens. The route was a popular Sunday afternoon drive. There are many coves and picnic spots dotted along that stretch of the coast. If they carried on driving we could theoretically end up back in town, having gone full circle. I convinced myself that that was what they were planning.

Up ahead I saw the lights of the Holiday Inn. It was the last of the buildings that perched on the city's perimeter. After that the rows of street lights came to an abrupt end. The road was plunged into darkness. We were swallowed by the night. Thick fynbos, willow and Port Jackson flanked either side. There was not a car in sight. I began to feel utterly alone.

Clinton was driving slowly. He kept to the 80 kilometres per hour speed limit and the headlights beamed into the night. The fear inside me was growing. Until then I had somehow managed to keep it at bay, to put my mind in neutral.

But now it welled up from my belly and spread like slow burning lava to my chest. Such a physical sensation. I had never experienced anything like it before. Once again, my mind wrestled for control.

'Theuns doesn't speak good English,' Clinton suddenly announced.

I didn't know why he was telling me this, but at least it was something. Someone was talking and it was an interruption that quietened, if only for a second, my own panicked thoughts.

We were now heading towards the Pine Lodge Holiday resort. There's a caravan park there, a few chalets and a pub. I hoped that this was where we were going. There would be other people there, maybe even a security guard. I would definitely stand a better chance of escaping if that were the case. But we glided past Pine Lodge and I watched the twinkling lights through the thick foliage.

To our right was the University of Port Elizabeth and the Technikon, both of which are situated in a nature reserve. On the opposite side of the road we passed several sandy lanes that trickled their way into clearings. I had never felt safe on this road. This time of night the only people who would dare to come out here were those who wanted to engage in illicit sex.

As we passed the rifle range, the journey began to feel interminable.

What now? I asked myself.

I almost wanted them to complete the story for me. I wanted these men to tell me, 'This is what we are going to do.' At least then I could make a plan, prepare myself. The suspense was unbearable.

Clinton seemed to be looking for something now. He slowed down as we neared a clearing in the bush, peered in, but then carried on. We passed another larger gap in the foliage and a little way on Clinton pulled the car up on to the shoulder of the road, did a U-turn and crawled back towards it.

A canopy of trees hung over the entrance and the car bounced as we hit the white-grey sand. We were heading for some sort of alcove.

Clinton took the left fork that led off to the beach. The car sank into the soft sand and the wheels began to spin as he revved the engine. I could feel the tension in the car.

'*Dis fokken stupid,*'* Theuns growled from the back.

Oh my God, don't make him angry, don't make him angry, I began silently to chant.

Up until that moment I had not feared for my life, but while the wheels spun and the engine whined in protest as Clinton tried to reverse, I thought the moment had come.

An irrational fear overcame me.

*'That's fucking stupid.'

16

They're going to use my body. They are going to put my body under the wheels to get out, I thought in terror.

Just then the tyres found their grip and the car jerked backwards. I was overcome with relief, but managed to reveal nothing. Clinton was reversing like a madman. Turning the wheel this way and that. I could hear him crashing into the foliage. Branches snapped and scraped against the body of the car. Glass and twigs cracked under the wheels.

Eventually he manoeuvred Reginald into a clearing. The ground around us was black with soot. Litter lay strewn everywhere. There were shards of glass from broken bottles, rusted beer cans, empty wine cartons, bits of paper and even a smashed windscreen. The car now faced the road which was some 90 metres away. We were well hidden from any passing vehicles. There was no chance of anyone stumbling across us now.

'How do you turn off the lights?' asked Clinton.

I leaned over and twisted the knob.

Theuns indicated he wanted to get out of the car and Clinton leaned forward to let him out.

Then there was silence. Crushing silence. And darkness.

The two of us sat in the car.

It was time to speak.

'Now what?' I asked, making sure it sounded matter of fact.

I had spent this entire journey wrestling with my thoughts. Now I wanted the truth.

Clinton turned and looked at me. He seemed genuinely surprised.

'But I thought you would have realised we want sex,'

he answered, almost indignantly.

'No,' I replied, disliking the fact that he thought I could have been so stupid. I had actually prevented myself from thinking anything at all.

So this was it, I thought, bracing myself for what was to come.

I looked away at Theuns who was crunching around outside. He strolled over to a clearing at a crossroad about ten metres away. I watched him in the moonlight. I could see him quite clearly. His face was an impassive mask. He seemed bored.

I also realised there was no way he was going to stop Clinton. Theuns lit a cigarette while he surveyed the territory, looking off in the direction of the road and then back at Clinton and me inside the car. Then he crouched down on his haunches and stared at the small glowing coal between his fingers. I latched on to the image as though it was a scene frozen in a film.

'Are you going to fight?' Clinton's voice brought me back.

I kept quiet for what seemed like an eternity. I was calculating the odds and he knew it. I looked at Clinton's hands as they rested on the steering wheel. I had always loved men's hands, but his were hideous. They were small and white. His long, thin fingers tapered off into short, dirty nails. They were weak hands, or so I thought.

What if I *did* fight? Was I going to be able to grab the knife from across his lap, kill him and lock the door before Theuns descended on the car? Could I make a dash into the bush?

I looked out into the pitch black that surrounded us, afraid of what I might find there should I decide to flee.

In the end I realised it was pointless putting up a struggle. I truly believed that they would not hurt me if I did what they asked.

'No,' I replied.

At that stage neither Clinton nor Theuns had said anything that might have led me to suspect that they would physically harm me.

If they wanted to rape me, I thought, then let them do it, I can handle it.

Stay calm, stay calm, that voice in my head kept telling me.

'Take off your clothes,' Clinton ordered.

I was still dressed in my shorts. Underneath I was wearing a full bathing costume over my bikini. I hadn't even thought about changing after the afternoon at the beach. I was also wearing a white vest, a denim shirt and a pair of brown leather sandals.

I felt as if I was undressing someone else's body. As I peeled off each item of clothing I became further and further removed from myself. I sat there naked with this familiar body which now did not belong to me.

Clinton pulled down his tracksuit pants and pushed my head towards his crotch.

'Suck my cock,' he ordered.

My mind went blank. I couldn't think. The only thing I knew was that I should try not to vomit. It was difficult, he was ramming my head down on to his penis. I started to gag.

'If you bite me, I'll kill you,' he threatened.

He held the knife in his hand. It was right next to my head. It was the only thing I could see at that moment.

I don't know how long the whole thing lasted. I found

it degrading, but I didn't want to show any emotion. I would give them no satisfaction. I would be as limp as a rag doll. I would not reveal anything about myself. Clinton suddenly yanked my head up by my hair and pushed me back on to the seat. Next thing I knew his face was between my legs. I don't know how he got there. I couldn't believe this was possible inside such a small car.

'Does your boyfriend do this to you? Do you like it?'

I said no, stupidly hoping that that would stop him.

When he finished he slithered up towards my breast and then he latched on to it like a leech. I stared down at him. It was an oddly disconnected moment. Here was this strange man at my breast. It was such a violation of my body, my personal space. I could see him doing it and it revolted me.

He looked up, smiling at the purple 'love-bite' he had left behind.

Then he moved up and kissed me. There was an overwhelming stench of nicotine. His breath was sour and he probed my mouth with his tongue.

'You have the nicest tasting fanny,' he whispered.

I was disgusted by the intimacy of his remark.

Then he raped me. As it happened I realised that I was moist and I was horrified. I felt that my body had betrayed me completely. I recoiled, pushing my arms up against the roof of the car. I did not want to touch him. He was scrawny like a snake. His skin was white and waxy, like some worm that lived under a dark rock and had never seen the sun.

I felt nothing. I stared over his heaving shoulder at Theuns outside who was bathed in silver light. He just stood there, looking at what was going on in the car.

Ali, he's doing this to your body but not to you, he can't touch you, I chanted silently over and over again.

Clinton groaned as he ejaculated and then he rolled over back on to the driver's seat. I just sat there, dazed.

A moment passed. Clinton must have pulled up his trousers because suddenly he was fully dressed again. He called over to Theuns.

His head lolled to the side as he addressed him through the open window.

'Do you also want to have sex with this lovely lady?' he asked.

'*Nee, ek wil die fokken bitch fok,*'* Theuns replied with a sneer.

'Don't speak to her like that, she's a lady,' said Clinton in a childish singsong.

My God, I thought. How can you say that, you bastard? You've just raped me. You know nothing about me.

But it's bizarre how we look for a lifeline in the most hopeless of situations. I thought that if Clinton thought I was such a lady then maybe he would be able to stop Theuns if he lost it and became violent. He certainly looked capable of it.

Stupidly, I thought he might be the more reasonable of the two. I thought he might be able to influence Theuns and I felt safer because of it.

Theuns walked over to the passenger side of the car. He rummaged through his pockets, emptying the contents on to the roof. I heard a clunking noise and

*'No, I want to fuck the fucking bitch.'

21

imagined it was his cigarettes and his lighter.

'Are you just going to sit there and watch?' I snapped at Clinton.

'Ja, I want to see,' he replied laconically.

Theuns got into the car and kneeled between my legs.

'*Ag nee man, my kom is nog daar*,'* Clinton barked at Theuns.

He kissed me instead. He wasn't really hard enough to penetrate me but he heaved himself on top of me and raped me anyway. I just stared out of the windscreen.

'No,' he said abruptly. 'I can't do this.'

He pulled up his pants, got out of the car and slammed the door.

I was naked and alone, with Clinton starting to doze off in the passenger seat next to me.

Theuns slunk around to the front of the car and hopped up on the bonnet. Then I saw it for the first time. A huge hunting knife with a blade of about 20 centimetres. It was much bigger than the one Clinton had first used to threaten me. Theuns slowly pulled it out of one of his pockets and placed it next to him.

It was the first time that I realised that he too had a knife. It frightened me. I felt vulnerable and wanted to get dressed.

'Can I get dressed?' I pleaded with Clinton.

He didn't answer.

As far as he was concerned I did not really exist. I was not human. I began slowly to rummage around my feet for the clothes that lay strewn on the floor of the

*'No, man, my semen is still there.'

22

car.

Theuns finished his cigarette, hopped off the car and rested on his haunches again. He seemed restless now. He began to pace up and down. I watched him, taking in every detail. I had tried during the entire night to remember little things about them. Their clothes, their hands, their hair, their accents. Now I etched his face into my memory. The dark hair, the lop-sided, sullen face, the small, close-set eyes.

'Frans,' he called out suddenly.

Frans? So that's who you really are. It was the first time I had heard his name and I held on to it.

Frans opened his eyes and turned to me.

'If we take you into town now you are going to go to the police,' he said.

Relief. It was over, or at least almost over.

'No, I won't,' I lied. 'I don't want my parents to find out about this.'

'I don't believe you,' said Frans tauntingly, and then turning to Theuns he asked, 'You think we should leave her here with no clothes on?'

They were speaking in English and I knew they were doing it to scare me, to terrify me. They were clearly enjoying it.

'Ja, maybe,' came the reply.

'What do you think *Oom Nick** would want us to do with her, hey?' one of them called out.

Oom Nick? That was another name for Satan. I remembered that from my early church days.

*Old Nick.

23

'I think he wants us to kill her,' the other replied with a laugh.

I still didn't believe them. I still thought they were just trying to frighten me. They were only bluffing. I hadn't shown them any fear the whole night and now they wanted to play a cruel game. They wanted to torture me, they wanted me to break down, they wanted me to scream and cry, beg for my life. They wanted that power and I was not going to give it to them.

'Take off your clothes,' ordered Frans.

Not again, I thought.

The upside, I thought, if there could be an upside in a moment like this, was that they were definitely planning to leave me there naked. Why else would they be doing this? It would be their final act of humiliation. The little cherry on top of their night of fun. At least I was still alive.

I removed each item again – the vest, the costume, the shorts. I kept my sandals on and hoped Frans wouldn't see. If I was going to walk back to PE, I would need them, I figured.

He didn't see the sandals but he did see my jewellery.

'Hey, Theuns,' he called out, 'here's some rings for you.'

'Take them off,' he ordered.

I removed the three rings. Two were plain silver and the third was a puzzle ring that I deliberately undid. Theuns snatched the rings and slipped them on to his finger. He fiddled with the puzzle ring but couldn't put it back together so he dropped it into his pocket. Then he slipped back behind Frans and flopped on to the back seat.

Now I was convinced they would let me go.

Instead, Frans took me totally off guard. One minute he was sitting there and the next he was on top of me, straddling the seat. His puny hands were like a tourniquet around my neck. I started to choke. I was surprised at how strong he had become. This man knew what he was doing. And he was determined to do it.

That sickly smell of nicotine on his breath caught my nostrils again. Frans's face was millimetres away from mine. I looked into his eyes. They looked cold and cruel and he stared straight back at me. It was a penetrating but vacant gaze. I could not read his expression at all. I had seen nothing like it before. I was clearly making no connection. I could not touch his heart.

'Please don't kill me,' I rasped.

'Sorry,' was all he said.

As he lunged forward and squeezed my neck, I felt my bowels move. The last thing I felt was embarrassment. And then everything went black. It was like clicking off a TV screen and watching the picture fade into a pinpoint.

A rush of cold air filled my lungs and I was suddenly wrenched from unconsciousness. I realised something bad had happened. I was no longer inside the car but outside lying on the sand amongst the broken bottles and beer cans. One of the men knelt over me. I couldn't see his face but I saw his arm moving back and forth in a frenzy. The moon was directly behind his head and formed a surreal halo. It was a horrific sight.

My God, he's slashing my throat.

I could hear the flesh split, it was a sound I had never heard before. I counted eight blows. Back and forth, back and forth, back and forth. But, oddly, I felt no pain. Nothing at all.

This must be a dream, I thought.

It certainly felt unreal. Like one of those nightmares where you want to scream but can't, want to run but your body feels like lead.

But this could not be a dream. I had been with these two men in the car only moments ago. I couldn't deny that. The realisation brought with it an all-consuming terror. It was primal, a feeling I never knew existed. Perhaps this is what a buck feels like when a predator wrenches it from mid-air to the ground before snapping its neck.

This was not an illusion, some horrible hallucination, and I was not going to wake up. I *was* awake.

Then suddenly he stopped and moved away from me.

I was amazed at how sharp my mind was at that moment. I felt supremely conscious and alert.

Every sense, every nerve was alive, like an electric current had shot through me.

I heard mumbling and footsteps and instinctively turned on to my stomach, needing to protect myself. I felt too exposed lying on my back. But had they seen me? I shouldn't have moved. I was sure they'd come back.

But they didn't.

In the distance I heard them talking.

Then I became aware of a low, grumbling sound. It sounded like the rasping of a rabid dog. The leaves in front of me began to rustle. The sound seemed grossly amplified at that moment and I realised it was coming from my throat.

I tried to hold my breath but realised I had no control over my breathing. I moved my hand up to cover my neck. My whole hand disappeared into it but it seemed to have worked. The sound, for now, was silenced.

I knew I had to play dead; it was my only hope now.

These men were killers and they would definitely finish the job if they knew I was still alive.

In the background I heard their footsteps and their voices grow fainter.

I caught snatches of the conversation in Afrikaans.

*'Dink jy sy is dood?'** one asked matter of factly.

'Niemand kan dit oorleef nie,'† the other replied.

I heard fumbling and scratching noises. I gathered that they were inside my car. Then I felt something soft land on my back.

I dared not move.

Sounds around me grew muffled, as if I was listening through a thick wad of cotton wool. Then I heard Reginald's engine roar to life.

It revved a few times before the car began to crackle its way back up the dirt road.

Then they were gone. I was totally alone.

I felt as if I had been sucked into a black void, as if I was the only human being on earth and a part of me then did not want them to leave.

I waited for something to happen. Nothing did.

'This is it,' I thought. 'I'm dying.'

It was terrifying.

---

*'Do you think she's dead?'
†'No one can survive that.'

More than death itself, I feared dying slowly out there on a filthy trash heap.

Who would find me? Would anyone know what had happened?

While I still had some life left in me, I thought, I had better do something. If I didn't make it, then at least I would tell the world who had done this to me. I reached over and began writing their names in the sand.

I forgot how to spell Theuns so I wrote 'Teens' under Frans's name. And then I thought of my mom.

'I love mom' was the last sentence I managed before squaring it all off with a neat border.

And then it happened.

3

ALISON

A moment of choice

———◆———

IT WAS AS if I had cut moorings. I felt a fantastic lightness that lifted me or, should I say, eased my soul from my damaged body. I floated about three metres above the ground and was almost level with a lop-sided tree that formed a sort of protective awning over my physical form.

My mind, in all its clarity, was floating untethered. I was dissolving into a safe, boundless and timeless space. I felt utterly free and peaceful.

As I hovered there, I recognised the person down below. I knew it was me and I felt a strong connection to that bleeding, mangled girl lying on her stomach. She felt like a little girl to me and I knew her so well. I cannot say that it dawned on me that *this* was death itself. How was I to know?

The one thing that was perfectly clear was that this

was a moment of choice. I was being given a second chance. I heard no booming voice, I saw no lights, but I felt a presence with me, within me. I was completely a part of it.

It was a deeply spiritual moment. I was there, but I knew and understood that I was not alone.

Bathed completely in this benevolence, for that is the only word to describe it, and floating on this compassionate plane, I was being asked to decide my fate.

'Do you want to go back? Do you want to go there and fight?' were the questions.

It was so tempting to let go, to surrender to the peace and comfort I was feeling at that moment. I wanted to stay there. There was nothing to fear.

I thought about my life up until that moment and realised that it could not be over yet.

There was still so much I wanted to and needed to do. So much I had done, but could have done better.

I hadn't even begun to explore so many things I had promised myself I would do. As a child I had always had some sense of destiny, that I wanted to do something more with my life.

All of this must have happened in a fraction of a second. I could not grasp time as we know it while I hovered above myself.

But I understood that if I did not make it, if I did not survive, death would be a comfort, it would be painless, it would be glorious. I could always return to this place.

At more or less the same time as these thoughts were forming I spotted, through the bush, the glimmering headlights of a car as it swished past on the road. It definitely seemed closer than I had first thought.

The headlights were enough of an inspiration for me to try to reach a place, away from all this debris, where someone might at least find me, even if I was dead.

And if one car was out on this road this late at night, I figured, there might be others.

Suddenly I was back inside my body. It was like an elastic band that had snapped and returned to its original shape.

The struggle had begun.

I pushed myself up on to my hands and knees.

Then I felt my abdomen and something tepid, wet and slimy.

I looked down and saw my intestines. I realised then that my abdomen had also been very badly injured. It was horrifying, there was just so much of me on the outside. I tried to scoop it all up with my hands but everything just slithered away again.

I had never been seriously injured or hurt before and here I was trying to cradle handfuls of my own warm, moist intestines. There was just so much of it, it was incredible.

Although there was still no pain, I was totally unnerved. I tried to stuff it all back inside me but it was impossible, the pressure had forced out too much through the wound. But I had to do something. I didn't want to have to drag my innards behind me. I could not see the slashes across my neck so it was of secondary concern at that point.

I groped around me, patting the sand. Then my hand felt something soft. It was a denim shirt. This must have been what I felt landing on my back earlier on.

It would have to do. I bundled my intestines inside it

and pressed the gruesome 'parcel' to my stomach. It felt strange and heavy.

My head, at that stage, was in a normal position. It felt odd, sort of loose and unsteady but it was hanging down, resting on my chest.

I began to crawl through the rubbish.

The moonlight flooded the cove, lighting my way. I could see the path to the first open patch in the bushes quite clearly. The sand was fine and tinged jet black from years of outside fires and jagged bits of glass jutted out, cutting into my hands and scraping my knees. But I didn't even notice.

I crept for about 15 metres into the clearing where Theuns had first stood smoking his cigarette while Frans raped me in the car.

Progress, if that is what one could call it, was painstakingly slow. It was awkward crawling with one hand and clutching the shirt with the other. It felt like I was hardly moving, but I must have been.

I was totally exhausted; so, so tired.

By the time I reached the clearing, I was ready to give up. My body felt cumbersome, it had become a burden.

I collapsed on top of a cluster of rocks and just lay there.

The memory of the earlier peace I had felt returned.

'It's OK,' someone or something said. 'If you want to give up now and come it will be all right.'

It was my own voice but it was speaking at me. I certainly wasn't forming the words.

Fight if you want to. Go on if you can, I told myself.

I so badly wanted this all to end. I wanted to surrender

and let go.

If I did, this nightmare would just disappear. I also wouldn't have to hear the awful rasping sound that gurgled from my throat as I involuntarily sucked in and exhaled air through my windpipe. It seemed so loud in the eerie quiet.

I did not want to hear it any more. I lay there thinking that I could not go on.

But still I did not fear death. What frightened me more was the thought of giving up.

Not on life, but on me, Alison. I felt I was too valuable to do that. I loved my life, I liked who I was, and there were still so many important things I had promised myself I would do 'one day'.

I also thought about the people who would find me. And my mother and what she would think and feel.

If I had stayed where I was under the tree and died she would have thought that it had happened quickly, that I could mercifully not have been aware of it.

But if they found me here on the rocks with a trail of blood behind me she would know that I had struggled, that I had suffered. There was no way I could do that to her.

I can't die now. I have to get there to answer all the questions, I thought to myself.

There were no more alternatives or choices. I had to fight. I had to make it.

The crawling was taking far too long and was too exhausting. I realised I had to try to stand up and walk.

With a tremendous effort, I hoisted my body on to my sandalled feet.

And then everything went black.

I was conscious but I could not see. Little wonder. My head, I realised, had flopped backwards and almost rested between my shoulder blades.

With one hand still clutching the shirt, I used the other to wrench my head forward again.

I regained my sight, but only for a split second. I had had fainting spells as a child and knew that I should force my head forward to restore the blood supply to my brain.

My vision faded and then returned to focus as though someone was fiddling with the lens of a camera. I clung desperately to the mental picture of the path in front of me.

With my head now in position I returned my hand to my throat to stop the noise and the blood. I expected to feel something but was completely taken aback when my hand seemed almost to disappear inside my body, as if I had swallowed myself. I could feel the severed flesh, the stickiness and moist warmth of the blood.

Then a tremendous strength that felt more like an unworldly force propelled me forward. It was as if two huge unseen hands were behind me, driving me on.

I plodded on, swinging one foot in front of the other before crashing into an embankment of bush, collapsing to the ground and then struggling back on to my feet.

At some point while I was crawling, my feet slipped out of the front straps of my sandals. Still secured by the ankle straps they flapped, twisted and dragged behind me.

I could think of nothing else but those darned sandals. I knew I had to get rid of them, but stopping to loosen the buckles would waste precious time. I didn't know whether I should risk bending over again; everything seemed to be hanging on a tenuous thread.

Perhaps, I thought, I could use my feet to push them off but the odds were they would not come off that easily. I would probably just lose my balance again and fall.

There was only one solution.

I doubled over, withdrew my hand from my neck, and carefully unbuckled each ankle strap. I stepped out of each sandal and left them lying there. The effort had made me feel dizzy and light-headed and my vision had disappeared again.

For a split second the path snapped back into focus and I managed a few more steps before stumbling and falling again. I must have blacked out like this several times.

There were times when I regained consciousness but couldn't see a thing. I kept moving, guiding myself by feeling the rough branches and leaves of the bushes with one of my hands outstretched, like a blind person who had lost her guide dog. I was astounded that I was still capable of walking but each foot seemed to have a life of its own.

Every now and again I regained my sight. It was like someone was playing with a dimmer switch. At one point I remember looking down and seeing my two filthy feet still plodding along, one in front of the other, like one of those battery-operated stuffed toys.

It felt as if I was on automatic pilot. I certainly was not in control. I was not making them 'walk'.

The journey felt interminable and just as I was about to contemplate giving up for the umpteenth time I saw what I thought was Marine Drive.

It couldn't be. But yes, it was.

I had actually made it.

I had never been so overjoyed to see anything in my entire life.

The sense of accomplishment was tremendous and seemed to give me a fresh burst of energy.

I knew there would be no point in just lying down on the gravel shoulder of the road. If I did, no one would see me unless they were very observant.

I had to make sure that the first person who passed by saw me immediately. I had to get to the middle of the road where I could not be missed.

Clutching my neck I turned and surveyed the area. A few metres away I noticed a huge white painted arrow which seemed to indicate a curve.

If I lay here and someone came speeding around it, I thought, they'd most certainly drive over me. I stumbled a few metres further and eventually found a suitable spot before collapsing horizontally across the white line. My head hit the tar with a thud.

I lay there in the deathly quiet thinking that it was wonderful finally to have a break from all the staggering and falling. I was on my back, my head slack to one side, my eyes level with the tar.

It was an unusual vista. I was amazed that I was still so conscious. I felt utterly alone, helpless and abandoned.

There was only one thing to do now. Wait.

Then, in the distance, I heard the drone of an engine. The car slowed down and then stopped.

For the first time since the whole ordeal had started I felt tremendous relief. I had been fighting all on my own and now someone was going to help me. That epic crawl to the road, I thought, had all been worth it. I had clung on, hoping this would happen and now it had. Despite my exhaustion, I was elated.

But nothing happened. The engine ticked over but no one got out. The headlights shone right on to me, warming me and in a way making me a part of the real world again. They felt like a spotlight. Surely the occupants of the car could see me?

I frantically waved as fast as I could. I wanted whoever it was to see I was alive and needed help.

A long time passed, it felt like 10 to 15 minutes, but was probably much less, and still no one got out.

I simply could not comprehend it.

My earlier sense of elation was replaced with dread as I convinced myself that it was Frans and Theuns and that perhaps they had returned to finish me off.

If it was them, I thought, there was nothing more I could do now. There was no point in panicking. I was already so close to death that it really didn't matter any more. I could actually feel it, feel myself slipping away. If it was them, I resolved, I would not fight any more. I would just let go.

Although death was uppermost in my mind, I still had no fear. But I felt a deep sorrow and disappointment that this time I would not be able to resist. I just did not have the physical strength to fend them off. The choice to live would no longer be mine.

I heard the engine rev and then suddenly the car manoeuvred itself around my body and just sped away. It was a Volkswagen Beetle and I watched the tail-lights become pinpricks in the distance.

Then I started to panic.

What if that was the only car? What if that had been my last chance?

My hopes had been dashed. That tremendous excitement I had first felt evaporated into sadness and a terrible sense of loneliness returned.

I thought about it for a while. Perhaps the person hadn't stopped to help me because she or he was afraid. Perhaps it was a woman on her own who was scared to get out of her car. Maybe the driver sensed danger and thought it was an ambush and that I was some sort of decoy. I was not angry that the person did not stop to help, just sad.

Seconds later I heard more cars. I could tell there was more than one vehicle when I heard several doors slam and lots of voices and shouting.

A woman appeared and stood over me. She began to scream hysterically, the kind of scream you hear in some cheap horror movie, and I realised then how awful I must have looked.

All I could think was 'Get her away, get her away, I don't need this right now.'

More people gathered around me. I couldn't tell how many there were. I could only see their feet. Everyone seemed to be talking at once. First there had been such silence and now so much noise and activity.

Then a handsome young man knelt next to me and took my hand.

He looked straight at me and started talking. At last, someone was connecting with me, someone was helping me and talking directly to me.

I tried to speak but realised my mouth was forming soundless words.

The young man told me to relax. There was just something so reassuring about his demeanour that I knew I was in good hands.

I felt, for the first time that night, total and utter relief.

It was about 2.45 a.m. The whole ordeal, from my abduction to this, had taken all of 90 minutes, although it had felt like an eternity. All in all, I had travelled about 30 kilometres that night. But the real journey was just beginning.

4

TIAAN

A shocking find

———◆———

IT HAD BEEN a long night, but we had enjoyed ourselves. Port Elizabeth was always a good place to come to unwind and about eight of us were trying to make the most of the last few hours of our December holiday in the friendly city before packing up and heading back to Gauteng.

We had spent the evening at a night-club and were heading along Marine Drive, back towards the Willows camping ground around 2.30 in the morning when my friend, who was driving up ahead of me in a BMW, suddenly screeched to a halt and switched on his hazard lights.

I thought that there must have been something in the road. Maybe an injured pedestrian or a buck that had been hit by a car. One of his passengers, a woman, jumped out and then came rushing towards our Combi. She was screaming hysterically and told us that someone had been injured and that I had better come and take a look.

In the headlights of the car I could make out a person lying in the road. As I got closer I could see it was a woman who was naked except for a denim shirt that she held to her stomach. Her head was turned away from our parked cars so I could not really see much from that distance.

As I ran towards her I heard loud, laboured breathing. It was a rasping sound, like someone gasping for their last breath. From that I gathered that she was still alive but I was not sure if she was conscious.

The first thing I noticed as I knelt beside her was the pool of thick, congealed blood that had collected around her head and neck. She was also absolutely filthy, covered in sand and dust. The veins on her forehead bulged, her eyes were open, one was bloodshot and swollen but she seemed to be lucid. She was looking straight at me with fearful eyes.

I realised from the quantity of blood on the road that she was seriously injured. Then I saw the huge gash that circled her neck. It was a slit from ear to ear, almost like a sheep that had been slaughtered.

It was a horrible gaping wound and I could see everything inside it, the veins, the muscles and the severed windpipe. This was no time to panic, I told myself. I had to make a plan and think rationally about what I would have to do.

I did not need any distractions and I told those friends of mine who were too sensitive to move away from the scene and go back to the car.

I had recently completed a year of veterinary technology and had some knowledge of anatomy. Also, I had spent much of my youth in hospital because of my asthma. Now everything in those wards that I had stolen with my eyes, so to speak, came back to me.

I took her pulse. It was extremely faint. I asked her to stick out her tongue, which she did. It was very pale, a sign that she had lost a vast quantity of blood.

Her skin was a deathly pallid colour and she was cold to the touch. But she was alive and that was all that mattered to me at that moment. I was determined to keep it that way.

The most important thing was for me to stop the bleeding. Fluid, mostly blood, was still oozing from the wound in her neck and in the light from the headlights of the car and the weak flicker from the flame of the cigarette lighter that I held near her face, I could see something hanging out of the wound.

I was not sure what it was. It could have been part of her trachea or her thyroid and I decided to tuck it back into the wound to keep it moist, whatever it was. Then I removed my shirt so that I could gently apply pressure to her neck without throttling her.

I was aware of a lot of activity in the road but I had no time to look up and see what was going on. I think two or three other cars might have stopped. Someone began to direct traffic around the young woman and myself and then someone handed me a torch and some gauze which I placed around her neck.

I was grateful for the torch. It would definitely be much more effective in keeping her awake than the cigarette lighter. I had remembered from watching television that it was important to keep an injured person conscious. Once we lost her, I realised, she might never wake up again.

I shone the torch into her beautiful green eyes. She seemed afraid and was starting to breathe irregularly. I tried to calm her by helping her to breathe more rhythmically. I wanted her to know, in no uncertain terms, that I would not let her die.

Who knows what she must have gone through? She seemed like such a fighter and at that moment, for some reason, I had no doubt in my mind that I could keep her alive. I knew she would survive, despite the terrible odds.

One of my friends had already telephoned the police and the ambulance service on his cell phone. I prayed that they were already on their way. This woman was in a very critical condition.

She looked tired and every now and again her eyelids began to droop as if she might be falling asleep. I kept talking to her, telling her to breathe slowly so that she could get oxygen into her body.

While we waited I introduced myself as Tiaan. I spoke Afrikaans and at first she did not seem to respond.

I wondered whether she understood me at all. Maybe she was English-speaking? When she squeezed my hand I realised that she wanted to communicate. With her other hand she pointed to the shirt she held against her stomach.

I noticed a small bruise but didn't think it looked too serious. I tried to get her to straighten her legs but she wouldn't. Then I realised she was trying to tell me something and I leaned over and lifted the shirt.

I was completely shocked when I saw her intestines, covered in twigs and leaves, piled up on top of her stomach. I could not believe it.

Until then I had thought only of her neck. Now I was utterly amazed that this person was still alive, considering this second major injury.

We had to get this woman to hospital immediately. I did not know how long she had been lying there and I grew increasingly irritated that the ambulance had not yet arrived. I tried not to show her my growing sense of panic and carried on as if I knew exactly what was going on.

I called one of my friends over and asked him to massage her legs. It was important to keep her circulation going and to warm her up. The early morning air was chilly and she was cold enough as it was.

I wanted to keep talking to her but I didn't know her name. The first one that sprang to mind for some reason was Carol. It was the only English name I could think of at the time and I decided to call her that. I needed to connect with her and a name somehow made it more personal for me.

Just then another car pulled up. The driver got out, opened the boot and took out a blanket that he said he always carried for emergencies.

I covered her with the blanket and we crouched there in the dark, waiting. Waiting, waiting.

In the mean time I knew I had to keep talking, keep her communicating with me.

I had to find out what had happened. Apart from needing the information to pass on to the police, it would also keep her awake.

I told her I was going to ask her some questions and that if she could, she should squeeze my hand once for yes and twice for no.

In this way, I worked out that two men had done this to her and that they had raped her and stolen her car.

I asked her what make it was. She lifted her hand slowly and wrote an 'R' on her chest. We guessed it was a Renault.

I asked her the colour and she traced out a 'Y'.

'A yellow Renault?'

She squeezed my hand once.

I felt her pulse again. It was getting dangerously weak.

She was still connecting with me. I could tell from her eyes.

We had to keep talking.

I told her that she had the most beautiful green eyes and she gave me an amazing smile. It lifted my spirit for a moment until my mind drifted back to the ambulance that still hadn't arrived.

My ears pricked. I was hoping to hear the sound of that siren in the distance, but it just didn't come.

I kept babbling on, needing to keep her attention. I asked her if she had a boyfriend. She said no and then I said something about the fact that she had to live because we'd go out on a date together when it was all over and she was better and that she'd have to pay because she'd ruined my shirt.

Once again she gave me an incredible smile. She was so brave.

A long time passed. I felt myself getting angry. Where was that ambulance?

At least two interminable hours ground by as I crouched next to her. Two long hours that felt like eternity and still she hung on, she clung on so desperately.

45

She deserved better than this.

Then I heard it in the distance. At last the ambulance pulled up next to us, lights flashing as it disgorged the paramedics. Doors creaked open and I could hear the stretcher being hauled out, its wheels banging as it hit the tar.

Now I was wide awake. The adrenaline was pumping through me.

I told Carol not to worry, that I would accompany her to the hospital. Two paramedics lifted her on to the stretcher while I kept my hand at her throat. One of the medics tried to get a drip running.

I clambered into the ambulance with her and shouted for my friends to follow us to the hospital. The vehicle pulled off.

I wanted it to rush like a bat out of hell, but it seemed as though the driver didn't quite understand the emergency. At one stage he pulled over while a medic tried to find a vein for the drip. Eventually we hitched it up to her hand and then I just couldn't contain myself any more. I growled at the driver to put foot and to at least turn on the damn siren.

All the way I kept on talking to the woman. I told her to hang on. We were almost there. We were going to make it.

Eventually we screeched into the parking bay outside the Casualty Unit. Carol was still awake and holding my hand. We lifted her out of the belly of the ambulance and wheeled her into a pre-op theatre. Staff were rushing all over the place and I shouted that we needed a doctor urgently and that someone should call one immediately.

There didn't seem to be one around and I hoped that

somewhere, someone was rushing to get there.

Finally a doctor appeared. I squeezed Carol's hand.

Then suddenly I was ushered away. I was no longer needed. I did not want to leave but I knew I had to. I had to believe that she was in safe hands now. I had to believe that she would make it.

I leaned over and whispered to her that I would be there when she woke up. I watched as the hospital staff drew the curtain around her, secure in the knowledge that we would soon be seeing each other again.

I looked down at my watch. It was 4.30 a.m. While people in white coats and green overalls rushed around me I realised I was standing there, in the middle of it all, still shirtless.

I had to get back to the camping ground. I needed to shower and change and come straight back to the hospital to wait for Carol to come out of theatre.

I would be there, no matter what.

As we drove back to the Willows I replayed the strange twist our last night in Port Elizabeth had taken. Who could have imagined that any human being could do this to another? Who would have thought that our holiday would end this way and that I would have met this very special human being in these bizarre circumstances.

5

ALISON

A roadside angel

THE YOUNG MAN knelt next to me and calmly examined my neck. He leaned closer and seemed to be working on the wound. I couldn't quite tell what he was doing. Perhaps he was trying to stop the bleeding.

His demeanour immediately relaxed me. He seemed so confident and in control that I wondered if he had some kind of medical background. He certainly knew exactly what to do and how to deal with me. I felt an immediate and incredible bond with this stranger.

For the first time that night I felt that someone else was really with me. He focused on me completely, seemingly oblivious to anything else.

He made me feel I was the most important person at the scene, and I suppose I was. It was exactly what I needed right then.

I was so grateful. I knew I would not have coped with

someone who was out of control or who did not know what to do.

I heard him calling out to someone to get the ambulance on the line again and to tell them it was urgent.

I could still hear that awful breathing coming from my throat. As I tried to communicate it grew faster and more erratic. I was trying to force something to happen now. I wanted the ambulance to be there.

I also wanted the man to see the wound on my abdomen. I was worried about that more than anything else. I pointed to the denim shirt with my left hand.

'Breathe slowly,' he instructed me gently.

I did as he asked and a calmness returned. His voice was so reassuring.

He told me his name was Tiaan and moved over me to lift the shirt. I don't know how he reacted but when he came back into my field of vision he seemed as calm as before. Then he took off his shirt and placed it over my body.

A while later another car pulled up. It stopped just behind me and I heard the driver get out. Then I felt a blanket being placed over me. I was grateful; I had felt so vulnerable lying there naked.

The only problem was the driver of the car left the engine running. I could taste the exhaust fumes and hoped he would move quickly. The last thing I needed in my state was to breathe in pure carbon monoxide. I tried to stay calm but was extremely frustrated at not being able to tell anyone. Eventually he drove off. Relief.

'You're going to be all right. Don't worry. You are not going to die on this road. I won't let you,' Tiaan said.

He continued: 'I'm going to ask you some questions.

Squeeze my hand. Once for yes and twice for no. Do you understand?'

I squeezed his hand once.

'Are you English or Afrikaans? English?' he asked.

I squeezed his hand once.

'Have you been raped?'

One squeeze.

'How many men?'

I gripped his hand twice. I knew he would understand.

We carried on communicating this way. At one stage I became aware of a cluster of people standing around me. Tiaan asked me what kind of car I had driven.

I traced out an 'R' on my chest. Someone in the group guessed 'Rover'. I squeezed Tiaan's hand twice. Then someone else said 'Renault' and I pointed at him. It was a little like a game of charades.

Then he asked me what colour it was and I wrote a 'Y'.

'A yellow Renault?' Tiaan asked.

One squeeze.

I presumed they wanted the information for the police.

I felt so exhausted and just wanted to close my eyes now that Tiaan was with me. I felt safe and I knew that he would fight for me. I just wanted to sleep. I played a little game with Tiaan. Each time he looked up or away to address someone else I closed my eyes.

'Hey,' he said gently nudging me. 'Don't close your eyes.'

He flicked a lighter and asked me to look at the flame. He kept on talking, asking me questions. He told me I had beautiful eyes.

'Have you got a boyfriend?' he asked with a smile.

Two squeezes.

'Would you like one?' he cajoled.

One squeeze.

I was flattered that he thought I had such beautiful eyes. I obligingly tried to keep them open just for him. In between the delightful small talk which kept my mind off things, Tiaan kept reassuring me that the ambulance was on its way.

'Five more minutes,' he would repeat every now and again.

Time lost its meaning. I couldn't keep track of it any more but I realised that we must have been waiting for a while when Tiaan began to get agitated and shouted out for someone to call the ambulance again.

Another vehicle stopped. I gathered it was some sort of medical van but the occupants couldn't do much except prop my head up and place some sort of dressing on my neck.

I could barely keep my eyes open now but I was hanging on for Tiaan. I also knew if the ambulance did not arrive soon I would have to give in to the oppressive fatigue.

Then I heard the siren. I could see the relief on Tiaan's face.

Suddenly men in uniform were scurrying around. I felt myself being lifted on to a stretcher.

I could see only the right side of the interior of the vehicle with its tubes, pumps and shiny metal gadgets.

Tiaan clambered in with me. I was so grateful. He was my lifeline. We had connected. He knew how to talk to me, how to keep me alive.

The ambulance suddenly pulled over. One of the paramedics was trying to find a vein to insert a drip. I had lost so much blood that they needed to hydrate me.

'I'm going to let go of your hand for minute,' Tiaan said.

All the time he kept reassuring me, kept telling me to 'hang on, we're nearly there'.

The ambulance felt as though it was going quite slowly and I knew I was right when I heard Tiaan shout out, 'Hurry up, man, and put on the siren!'

It wailed into life. As I lay there I remembered how a school friend of mine had always said 'touch my head, touch my toes, hope I never go in one of those' each time an ambulance passed us in the street. I had thought she was silly, but now I wondered whether I should have done it too.

Eventually we pulled into the Casualty Unit at the Port Elizabeth Provincial Hospital. The ambulance doors were wrenched open. There was a blur of lights, activity and noise. I was lowered out of the belly of the ambulance and across the threshold of the double wooden doors.

Yes, I thought to myself. I'm nearly there. It's almost over.

But I was growing weaker each moment. I tried to keep my eyes open by looking at the lights in the ceiling. Tiaan was still at my side, holding my hand, talking to me.

I wanted him to stay with me. I wanted him to sit with me in the theatre. He felt like a part of me now, a part of this battle. He was my comrade, he was the only one who understood that I knew what was going on around me.

But the Casualty nurses asked him politely to leave.

He leaned over and whispered, 'You're going to be OK. Don't worry, I'll be here when you get out.'

I was wheeled into a pre-op casualty room, Tiaan following a few steps behind.

The stretcher came to a halt and I kept looking at his kind, concerned face until they closed the curtain. Being separated from him now was awful. I really wanted him to stay.

Strange people in hospital outfits buzzed around me. They seemed to be working on my abdomen and between my legs. I couldn't see what they were doing and still could not feel any pain.

My breathing grew heavy again and that frightening rasping sound had returned. I realised I was choking and that blood was seeping into my windpipe. There was no one near my head so that I could make eye contact and I could not speak.

No, no, please, I thought. I'm going to choke and die here while they're fiddling with my stomach.

It can't be! We'd come all this way only for this to happen! I could not let Tiaan down. He had worked so hard to keep me alive. I had to do it for him. I had to live. I had come this far.

I waved frantically. It took a while before anyone noticed. I pointed to my throat and a nurse quickly realised what was happening. She switched on the suction pipe that was attached to a pump on the wall. It was a cool and refreshing sensation and I felt immediate relief.

Then she suddenly stopped and went back and joined the others at the bottom of the bed.

The gurgling sound returned.

I'm going to die, I thought.

I was extremely agitated and I could hear my breathing had become erratic.

I thought of Tiaan and his soothing voice and calmed myself.

No point in getting upset now when it was almost over.

I waved like a mad person. This time the nurse kept the suction pump at my neck. She stroked my shoulder and told me everything would be OK.

I could tell she felt awkward and didn't really know what to say. I missed Tiaan so badly. His calmness had really soothed me and I held on to the memory of it. I kept hearing his gentle voice echoing in my mind.

Eventually I felt the stretcher jerk forward gently and start to move. At last I was getting away from this place and all the eyes that couldn't quite meet mine. Away from them and, it dawned on me, my much-needed suction pump.

We tore down corridors, the ceiling lights flashing. It was like a scene from some television series set in a hospital, where the camera tries to angle itself from the patient's point of view.

There were so many passages, twists and turns that it felt as though they were wheeling me to another part of town. I concentrated on my breathing, remembering Tiaan's words.

Breathe, breathe, I repeated to myself, over and over.

Eventually I came to a halt under a massive set of lights. I presumed I was now in the theatre. I was lifted on to the operating table and then suddenly everyone left. I was alone.

What's going on here? I wondered. Where's the suction pump? Come on, come on, I can't have come this far only to die now.

A man in a white coat appeared next to the operating table.

I was certain he was now going to begin surgery but no, he leaned over and explained that the doctors were soon going to operate and that he needed me to sign the consent form.

'Do you understand?' he asked.

I smiled at him and took the pen. I wrote down my name, relieved that someone would at last be able to get hold of my mom. I wrote down her telephone number and 'Mom' next to it.

I became aware of someone else next to me. He was an extremely kind-looking man and had the gentlest eyes. He spoke reassuringly to me and I realised that he was a doctor.

Another man came in. He was shorter and had a confident energy about him.

The first doctor spoke.

'I think we're going to need a specialist here,' he said.

Oh no, I thought. I can't wait any longer. Either these guys get on with it or I give up right now.

The other doctor quietly examined my wounds and then announced in a foreign accent: 'I'm a thoracic surgeon. It's OK,' he said, turning towards me. 'I can do it.'

The first doctor, who I now realised was the anaesthetist, stroked my head.

'Don't worry now,' his voice sounded reassuring. 'We

are going to take care of your breathing. When you wake up everything will be over. You can relax now.'

And I did.

For the second time that day, I slipped into a black unconsciousness.

6

DR VOLODIA ANGELOV

Miracle worker

———◆———

I WAS AT home when the phone rang around 4.30 a.m. on December 18. Early morning wake-ups like this are routine for doctors on call at busy provincial hospitals.

I threw on some clothes, grabbed my keys, jumped into my car and sped off. I was quite accustomed to performing surgery at this hour and at such short notice, so I braced myself for a long morning ahead.

I arrived at the hospital ready to work, but for some reason the ambulance transporting the expected patient was nowhere to be seen. We were anticipating a seriously injured assault victim. We had no idea of the extent of the damage or whether the patient would even be alive when she got here.

My anaesthetist colleague, Dr Comyn, and I prepared ourselves for theatre. We waited for about 20 minutes before we were told that the ambulance had arrived at

Casualty. I was informed that the patient was in a critical condition and that her head had been almost severed from her body. She also had multiple lacerations to her abdomen and her entire small intestine had ruptured through the wound.

The porters wheeled the patient into the operating theatre. As I got to the door I saw an orderly with a clipboard talking to her. I couldn't believe that the wheels of bureaucracy continued to turn in such an emergency. There was no way this woman could give consent right now! Well, at least that's what I thought until, to my utter amazement, I saw her take the pen from him and sign the form.

The orderly brought it to me.

It was incredible. The patient had managed to write down her name 'Alison', her surname and her mother's telephone number. The handwriting on the typed sheet was deliberate and legible. Most people forget their own telephone numbers when they're in a state of shock but this patient was clearly quite lucid.

The formalities over, I quickly checked the results of the blood test that had been done in Casualty. Alison's blood pressure was extremely low at 90/50. Her pulse rate was 125 which was very high and indicative of the fact that she was in a state of compensated shock.

In medical terms, shock occurs when a patient has lost a large quantity of blood and the body compensates by constricting the vessels in the veins and arteries. The heart races to enable the remaining blood to be pumped through the body.

Her sodium count was 137, her potassium 3,8; chloride 101 and her urea 6,3. Alison was severely dehydrated and if we did not move quickly she would go into early renal failure. There had clearly been significant blood loss, or she was in a state of terror.

Then I got my first good look at the young woman. In my 16 years as a doctor I had never seen a patient like this. There, lying on the white sheet, was a creature straight out of a Dickens novel. She looked like a corpse.

She was filthy, black as a coal miner. Her entire body was covered in a fine layer of black sand. Her eyes had haemorrhaged and were blood red, her hair was matted with sand, twigs, leaves and dried blood, her knees were cut and scraped, her feet were lacerated and her finger nails were black.

I moved closer to inspect the wound at her throat.

I was shocked but I didn't let her see this. She had green, intelligent eyes and was looking directly at me. Although she was deathly pale, cold to the touch, had clearly lost a huge amount of blood and could not speak, I knew she was fully conscious.

Her head flopped to her right and I could see the muscle there had been completely severed. From that angle I could also see her spinal column quite clearly.

Her neck had been split open almost from ear to ear. It was as if she had been cut by a sharp razor.

It was an angry, violent and cruel wound and I wondered what kind of savages had done this to her.

I had seen many injuries as a doctor, but the severe cruelty of these wounds really shocked me.

The thyroid, usually situated at the front of the neck, had been sliced in two and was tucked inside the wound. Someone, I reasoned, had thought quickly and placed it there so that it would remain moist. She should have died from that wound alone. A prick or a nick to the thyroid during surgery can lead to substantial blood loss and even death.

I made the assessment while Dr Comyn looked on.

Her anterior muscles and the trachea had been cut in half. Because of the severing, the muscles had retracted into the base of the skull. Her larynx was also completely separated from the lower part of the trachea. All the main veins had been cut and it was a miracle that whatever brute had done this to her had missed the most important main arteries and her voice box.

To tell the truth, I was surprised that she had survived at all. Theoretically, it was impossible for her not to have aspirated or breathed in the copious amount of blood that must have poured from the gash. She should have choked on it, but for some reason she had not. I could not explain it.

I then examined the wound in the pubic area. There were mounds of innards piled up on her abdomen. In fact the entire small intestine was exposed. It was covered in dirt, sand, leaves and various other foreign objects. The intestine had also been ruptured by multiple stab wounds. Luckily the patient's bowels were empty, a common reaction to strangulation. In this case it was a good sign because of the strong likelihood of infection if the bowels had been full.

Dr Comyn suggested we call in several specialists. He must have realised that this was going to be difficult. Luckily, I am a specialist in general and thoracic surgery.

'I can do it,' I said, looking at the young woman.

I could see the relief in her eyes.

This, I realised, was going to be one of the biggest

challenges of my life, but I was determined to try.

We had to get to work. Time was crucial. The patient had already lost so much blood and her pulse was weak.

Around 5 a.m. Dr Comyn administered the anaesthetic and we began to work. I needed to start stitching the various injuries on the neck wound first. It was the most critical and I knew that if she could breathe, she would survive.

I retrieved the anterior muscle that had completely retracted into her skull, just behind her ear, and reconnected it to the severed part near her collar bone. To prevent later scarring I carefully stitched the layers of flesh from the inside out. It took about two hours to perform the delicate surgery.

The countless lacerations to her abdomen had caused the muscle to collapse completely. Also, the skin had totally disintegrated. But we'd have to deal with that later.

I had to physically wash the patient's intestines twice in a saline solution to get rid of the debris. Parts of the lower bowel had also been ruptured during the attack but I noticed that her uterus had only been nicked by the knife. There were two small stab wounds that I sutured immediately.

I had to examine every inch of her intestine looking for cuts and ruptures. I found many and stitched them up. Then I returned her intestines into the abdominal cavity.

I had to make absolutely sure that there were no leaks in this region. There was a strong chance that this wound would become infected so, just to make sure, I removed her intestines again and checked for anything

I might have missed. Everything seemed in order.

I stitched up some of the smaller, isolated injuries on her abdomen and tried, with much difficulty, to close the bigger wound in the centre. There wasn't much left to work on. I hoped the stitches would hold, otherwise this wound would have to heal from the inside.

I knew I would be seeing Alison again. There would have to be plastic surgery later, but for now she was almost out of danger.

And then we were done.

At 8.35 a.m., three hours later, we wheeled Alison out of the theatre and to the High Care Unit. There was a possibility that she still might not make it and I requested the nurses to monitor her around the clock.

I said goodbye to this brave person. How she had survived, I did not know. I am a scientist, but this case, I had to admit to myself, was truly a miracle.

7

CLAIRE

In the hands of God

———◆———

PHONE CALLS IN the night, and especially early in the morning, are not the kind one wants to get. When I heard the phone in my passage ring at 5 a.m. on the morning of December 18, I prayed that it was the wrong number. But it was not. It was the thing that every mother, from the moment a child is born, dreads more than anything.

I picked up the phone, still three-quarters asleep, my heart pounding.

'This is the provincial hospital,' a man's voice announced politely.

I braced myself. The worst was going to hit me now and I immediately called on the Lord. I just said his name, 'Jesus', and I felt a peace and calm come over me like still water.

'We've got your daughter here,' he continued.

'What's wrong with her?' I asked.

'She's had her neck cut and she's been stabbed in the stomach.'

I was stunned. I could not conjure up a real picture in my mind. Neck cut? Stabbed in the stomach?

'But how did this happen?' I demanded.

'We don't know. She was picked up in Summerstrand.'

Summerstrand? What on earth was Ali doing there? She had called me earlier to say she and Kim and a few other friends were going to the beach. I thought maybe they had gone to a club or a pub and some brawl had broken out and Ali had got in the way of someone else's knife.

'Can you fix her?' I wanted to know.

'We'll try. We're going into theatre now,' he said.

'What shall I do?' I asked him.

'Well, you can come over here or you can wait at the phone. I will call you and tell you when she's out of surgery,' he offered.

'I'll stay here. Thank you,' I said and replaced the receiver.

The first person I called was my friend Mercia. I told her what had happened and asked her to come to my house so that we could begin to pray for Ali.

While I waited I called Kim. I needed to know what they had been doing in Summerstrand and what had happened to Ali. She answered the phone in a sleepy voice. I told her that Ali was in hospital and that she had been stabbed. She had no idea what was going on. The last she had seen of Ali, she said, was when she had dropped her off at home around 1 a.m. Then she went to pieces. I tried to calm her down and promised to talk to her later.

My friend arrived and we made a few more phone calls. I called my son Neale and his wife Ronwyn and asked them to pray as well. Then I called my sister and other friends. I asked them all to start a prayer chain.

So while Ali lay in theatre more than a thousand people, some as far away as England, were praying for her.

Mercia and I stood in the lounge praying. Suddenly she said the Lord had given her a scripture. It was an obscure piece and we took out the Bible to look it up.

'Do not fear the King of Babylon for he is a mere man whereas I am the all-wise, all-powerful, ever-present God and I am with you to save you and deliver you from his hand.'

I knew then that Ali would pull through. Out of all the verses in the Bible, God had given us that one. He had made a promise. We started to thank him.

About three hours later the phone rang. It was a nurse at the hospital. She had called to tell me that the first part of the operation to Ali's throat had been completed and that the doctor was now starting on her stomach.

'Sister,' I asked, 'is she going to be all right?'

'She's going to be fine,' she reassured me.

We went back to praying. At about 9.15 a.m. the hospital called again. Ali was out of surgery. We could come now and see her.

I raced to the hospital and the High Care Unit.

A doctor, a short man with greying hair and dark eyes, stepped through the doors of the unit. He looked exhausted.

'I'm Alison's mother,' I introduced myself.

'I'm Dr Angelov,' he said shaking my hand.

Then he looked at me for a long while before he spoke.

'Such brutality, I have never seen such brutality,' he shook his head before walking off.

Brutality? What did he mean? That was not how I had understood it when I spoke to the other doctor earlier. I thought she had only superficial stab wounds.

I pushed open the door to High Care and moved quickly towards the ward in which Ali was lying. I was shocked and nervous, extremely anxious about her.

She looked frightening. She was filthy, her face was swollen, her eyes were filled with blood and bulged out of her head which was propped between two sandbags. She had tubes and pipes everywhere. There was a cage over her lower body, keeping the blankets off her, and there was this massive bandage across her throat.

As I stared at my beautiful child my insides were caught in an icy grip of terror and agony that only a mother knows when her child is suffering. But I knew she needed me to be strong now. I lifted my spirit and concentrated on the promise God had given me.

She was awake and conscious and I took her hand.

'Hello, my baba,' I leaned over and whispered to her.

'Hello, my mommy,' she replied.

I could not believe that she was actually capable of speaking. I instantly realised that this was much more serious than I had originally thought but I still had no idea of how it had happened. I did not want to burden Ali now by asking her. All I focused on at that moment was the fact that she was alive.

Inwardly, I said 'Thank you Lord. Thank you for keeping your promise.'

She started to speak. Her voice, I noticed, was a little hoarse.

'The police must get the people who did this to me,' she said.

People? What people?

'They will, my darling, they will,' I said with utter confidence.

Before I left I slipped a piece of paper on which I had written out the verse we had been given earlier under Ali's pillow. I wanted His promise to be with her every minute of every day.

Ali clearly needed to be left alone to recover. Outside a group of her friends had gathered. Everyone was shocked and numbed by the news.

There was also a young man there, a very good-looking chap who held a little cactus in his hand. He introduced himself as Tiaan Eilerd and I learned that he had been the one who had rescued Ali and brought her to the hospital.

'Thank you,' I said, hugging him.

The two words were all I could manage to convey my huge gratitude and my immense thankfulness that God had placed this special young man in the right place at the right time.

At noon Dr Comyn, the anaesthetist, called Ali's dad Brian, who had flown down from Johannesburg, and me into his office.

We were now going to be told the truth and the full extent of her injuries and the doctors' opinion of it all. Dr Comyn spelt out, in graphic detail, what had happened

He did not mince his words and gave it to us straight. He told us her head had almost been severed from her body. He also told us she had been raped. It was the first time that I had heard that and my heart broke.

At least she is alive, I comforted myself.

At that point I wanted rather to focus my attention on the fact that she was going to recover because God had promised it. I did not want to dwell on the details of the attack or my own anguish.

'I fought in the Rhodesian bush war,' Dr Comyn continued, 'and I have never seen anyone with injuries like this survive. These wounds were gross beyond belief.'

The prognosis, he went on, was not good. Ali stood the risk of getting septicaemia because of the debris that clung to her intestines. Although they had washed almost all of it out there was a good chance that she would become infected.

The outcome for the throat injury was equally poor, he told us. It was such a severe injury that there was a strong possibility that the wound would thicken and constrict the trachea. If this happened, Ali could choke and nurses were watching her every breath in the event that this might happen.

The more I heard how bad everything was, the more I thought, 'This is incredible. She survived all this, my brave, brave child.' I thanked the Lord again.

I suppose Dr Comyn was puzzled by my composure. He stopped talking and turned to me.

'Do you understand what I am telling you?' he asked.

'Yes,' I replied calmly. 'I understand perfectly. But none of those things you say might happen will happen.'

'And why not?' he sounded a little indignant now.

'Because God has told me so,' I answered with confidence. 'Because God has said He will deliver her and I believe Him.'

Dr Comyn looked at me with a pitying expression, as if I was a total idiot. But it didn't worry me much at all. I would have looked at someone the same way if they had said that to me before I had been saved. I, too, would have thought they were stupid.

Meanwhile, doctors from all over the hospital came to look at Ali. They stood there over her bed, flipping through her chart. Some of them just shook their heads. A woman doctor came and spoke to me.

'If I had not seen this with my own eyes,' she said, 'I would not have believed it.'

The thing that amazed them all, apparently, was the fact that her thyroid had been cut in half and that she had survived more than four hours. Staff who had been in Casualty when Ali was admitted also stopped by, amazed that she had pulled through. Everyone who had seen her seemed completely flabbergasted by it all.

Dr Comyn, I suspected, also felt a bond with Ali. Something about her had touched him deeply. He did say that as he was about to anaesthetise her he had looked down and said, 'It's OK, we'll breathe for you now' and she had flashed him the most incredible smile that just tore at his heart.

More and more people poured into the hospital wanting to see Ali. Dr Comyn thought visitors would be good for her and Ali agreed. She saw almost everyone and talked to all of them. The nurses were beside themselves. They could not cope with the constant throng and asked me to vet some of the visitors. Many people who did not even know who she was came to see her. It seemed that she had already touched some kind of universal chord.

Then the flowers started to arrive. On the hour, every hour, another basket or bunch would arrive. Soon there was nowhere left in High Care to put them all. Every single available surface was filled with bursts of beautiful colour. Eventually they filled the entire corridor outside her room as well as another around the corner.

About three days later, while I was at home, Dr Comyn called me from High Care.

'We're approaching our most critical time now,' he said sounding quite grave.

'That's fine, doctor,' I said. 'Don't worry, God is in control.'

I heard him sigh.

The next day I saw him at the hospital again. He walked towards me with a smile on his face. Although I must have exasperated him at times, he was an extra-ordinarily compassionate and gentle man.

'Everything's fine now. She's out of danger,' he declared.

'But I knew that from the beginning and I told you so,' I replied, returning his kind smile.

He looked at me tenderly and a tear rolled down his cheek.

8

BRIAN

A father's rage

———◆———

MY WIFE SALLY and I were virtually ready to leave for a church service in Johannesburg when the phone rang around 6.30 a.m. that Sunday morning. It was my son Neale who, while doing his best to sound contained, could scarcely disguise the fact that he was upset. He told me that Claire had called.

Alison, he said, had been involved in some kind of attack and had been admitted to the provincial hospital for surgery. I tried to extract more information from Neale, but he had nothing more to go on than that.

It was a long weekend and I had spoken to Alison some time during the week. She had told me that she had been invited to spend it out of town with some guy. She didn't say who he was, but she did say she wasn't quite sure of his intentions. My immediate thoughts were that this man had done something terrible to her.

I knew Claire would be at the hospital so there was no point trying to phone her. I was left with a feeling of helplessness which only a parent can experience in these circumstances. After speaking to Neale, I put down the phone and immediately flew into a blind rage. I was totally overwhelmed with feelings of anger, horror, fear, panic and revenge. I felt like a man possessed. I lost it completely and wanted to smash everything around me.

My wife at the time, Sally, tried to calm me down and when the initial shock was over we made immediate plans for me to get to Port Elizabeth. I was due to fly to Durban on business that evening, but I just had to get on the next plane and be with Alison.

In the mean time, Sally's daughter Anita called an airline and got me a seat, the last one, on a 10.30 a.m. flight to Port Elizabeth.

The world disappeared around me as we raced to the airport. Everything seemed to be happening so slowly. I wanted to be physically there right then. Sally and Anita went off to organise the ticket while I stood at the check-in queue. The wait seemed interminable.

Anita and Sally appeared. They seemed grave and drawn. Anita had phoned the hospital and had been told that Alison had been raped. I felt a blow to my chest and could not come to grips with what they had told me. Just then I had to check in my bags and rush through the security check.

I hugged Sally and Anita and left them. Now I was alone with this news. Somehow in moments like that, when you are helpless, your soul builds a callus to protect you. I calmed myself, knowing that it would be useless to try to do anything now.

I boarded flight SA 409 and realised that I had an hour and a half with only myself now. I had a copy of the *Sunday Times* and tried to distract myself reading it. It didn't work. I could think only of Alison.

I got out my diary and started writing on a blank page. I wrote the word 'Why?' over and over. 'Why Ali? She doesn't deserve this.' The anger and helplessness spilled out on to the diary pages as I battled to come to grips with the horror of what had happened.

I wrote: 'I just pray to God and his Son Jesus Christ that my darling daughter will be able to recover from this ghastly ordeal. I pray – although I know I shouldn't – for vengeance and retribution on the perpetrators of this dastardly act of cowardice.'

There were many other scribbles in the diary before we touched down in Port Elizabeth, but I suppose it did help to pass the time and see me through the most traumatic journey of my life.

On arrival, I hired a car and raced to the hospital. It was after midday when I met Claire in the corridor outside the High Care Unit.

She gave me an update. Alison had pulled through surgery and was conscious. I went in to see her, fearful of what I might find and not knowing what to expect.

At first I could not handle it. She looked terrible. Her eyes were bloodshot and her nails were full of soil. Her face was swollen and she had this bandage across her neck. There were tubes and pipes everywhere.

Ali must have sensed my feeling of helplessness. The first thing she said to me was, 'Daddy, please don't worry about me.'

I was overcome. Here she was in this state and she

was thinking about *me* and not herself. Ali had always tried to protect me. I had always been the more emotional parent.

Her calmness and strength soothed me. She talked some more, holding my hand. She was a little incoherent. She pointed to a little cactus on the cabinet next to her and said that someone called Tiaan had given it to her. I gathered that he must have done something to help her.

I left her needing to know more about what had happened. As I walked out of the ward the reality of the situation really hit me. I was shell-shocked.

Claire and I went to the duty room where we met with Dr Comyn. He had been the doctor on duty the night before. He told us about the surgery, how intricate and difficult the procedure had been. He clearly had deep admiration for Ali and for Dr Angelov. He said he had never seen anyone perform such delicate surgery so professionally.

Dr Comyn said Ali was not out of danger yet. The wounds might still become infected and there could be complications. I received this information with dread. I wished I could somehow make it better for Ali, make it all go away, but the reality was we just had to wait.

I went back to the waiting-room where a few people had gathered. Two police officers arrived. One of them was a woman who introduced herself as Nadia Swanepoel. She told us she had a good idea of who could have been responsible for Ali's attack and that she needed an ID.

She had apparently seen one of the suspects in a shopping mall the day before. If Ali was able to pick him out of an album of photographs, she was quite confident that she would know who the other attacker was as both of them were apparently out on bail on another charge of rape.

She went in to see Ali and a short while later was back with a smile on her face.

After that I realised there was nothing more I could do at the hospital. It was after 3 p.m. and I needed to sort out accommodation. Dear friends, Willy and Jill, rallied around and gave me a bed for the night. They were wonderful, caring and loving. They knew exactly when to leave me to be on my own.

I needed to get out and think. I have always tended to bottle up my feelings. In the past I had always found comfort near the sea, and I made my way to Schoenmaker's Kop at the start of the Sacramento Trail.

I started walking. It was so beautiful but I couldn't appreciate it. My feelings overwhelmed me again, so I shouted out at the top of my voice. I screamed at the sea and at the sky. 'Why? Why my daughter?' I could find no answer.

I carried on walking up as far as the shells, which is about a two-kilometre stretch.

As dusk gently descended I turned around and headed back. I felt more composed and in that moment I believe God gave an answer.

I just knew that Ali would not die. That she had been saved for a purpose. I did not know how bad she'd be or how the injuries would affect her. But there and then I decided to pull myself together. I promised that I would be there for her no matter what, even if it meant I had to change my life.

I was in awe of my beautiful daughter.

The next day news of the attack was all over the papers. The headlines were huge; the event had clearly shocked and outraged everyone in the city. There was a tremendous feeling of joy and relief that the suspects had been apprehended.

Ali seemed genuinely surprised at all the attention her case had attracted. That, and the heaps of flowers and cards and the well-wishers who streamed in to see her.

Her strength and bravery had clearly got to everyone. There was a sense of pride in those who knew her and I understood exactly what they were feeling.

When I got back to Johannesburg a couple of days later, I sat down and wrote a letter to the editor of the *Eastern Province Herald*. For me, it was an outpouring of my anger at a justice or law enforcement system that allowed known perpetrators of heinous crimes such as rape to be out on bail and free to carry on with their evil business. I called on people, through the letter, to say that enough is enough and to stand up and voice their anger. I faxed this letter off and to my surprise it was published, unedited, on the front page the very next day.

I also sent a submission to the Constitutional Court which was in the process of drawing up our new constitution. Unfortunately my plea did not have the desired effect, but I suppose I can say that at least I tried.

Every father will handle his rage in a different way and it can turn to revenge, or it can turn to retribution, but at the end of the day it is his love for his child which will determine the outcome. Blind rage is self-destructive and will usually turn out to be very harmful to the very person you are trying to protect. I am thankful that I was able to consider my course of action and remain relatively calm, under the circumstances. I believe that we can all overcome the temptation to do something rash if we step back from the situation and think it through, before rushing headlong into what could be the worst mistake of our lives.

9

KIM KARP

My beautiful friend

———◆———

CLAIRE SOUNDED CALM and controlled at the other end of the line. I was still half asleep when she called around 6.30 a.m. on that Sunday morning. I suppose it was the tone of her voice and the nature of the information that she was conveying that initially confused me.

She told me Alison was at the Port Elizabeth Provincial Hospital and that she'd been involved in some kind of attack. Her neck had been cut and she had been stabbed in the stomach.

It just didn't gel but I knew she was serious. Claire is not someone prone to wild emotional displays. But I knew that she and Ali shared a particularly close bond and that although she could not show it, deep inside, Claire was devastated. Her utter faith in God was what was probably keeping her together at that moment.

She wanted to know what had happened the night

before, where we had been. I told her the last I had seen of Ali was when she had waved a cheery goodbye after dropping me off at my flat around 12.45 a.m. Earlier we had played a game of Balderdash at her flat and that was about it. We hadn't been out anywhere else.

I could not understand what had happened. Claire said Ali had been found at Summerstrand. I tried to put the puzzle together, but the pieces just didn't fit. When you hear something like that it takes time for things to click, for it all to really sink in.

I said goodbye to Claire, pulled on an old pair of shorts and T-shirt, not bothering to brush my hair or my teeth or even take off the previous night's make-up. I rushed over to Ali's flat which was just around the corner.

Her car wasn't there, so I burst into the nearby all-night café. I thought they would know what had happened. Outside on the pavement I saw something that looked like blood. I totally freaked out and shouted at the Greek owner, 'What's happened to Ali, what's happened to Ali?'

He must have thought I was mental. I then realised the stuff on the pavement was tomato sauce from someone's take-away burger.

The only people who would really be able to answer my questions were the cops. I drove downtown to the police headquarters. There was no one around except for a few uniformed police officers behind a counter. I asked them if they had heard anything about an attack and they said yes, a woman whose name at that stage they thought was Carol, had been picked up on Marine Drive near Noordhoek.

She had been brutally assaulted, but they didn't know

much else at that stage. They had a black plastic bag behind the counter with some items that had been taken from the scene. I asked if I could look at it.

I opened the bag and immediately saw a blue and white denim shirt that belonged to me. It was covered in blood. Inside was Ali's kikhoi that she had used at the beach earlier, a book and a few other bits of clothing. Everything was soiled and bloodied.

I went into a state of complete shock. I felt lame. What could have happened to my dear, sweet, beautiful friend? Who on earth would have done this to such a good person?

I asked the police if they had found Ali's car and offered to collect the registration papers from her flat. Ali's a perfectionist and I knew I would find all the documents filed in alphabetical order in some cupboard or desk.

A young constable drove me to Claire's house. I needed to get a spare set of keys so that I could get into Ali's flat. En route I asked him if she had been raped.

'Yes,' he answered. 'By both of them.'

I was horrified. Being raped is any woman's worst nightmare. I could only pray that they hadn't hurt her although from the sound of things, they had.

Claire and her friend Mercia were praying when I arrived at the complex where she lived. They were waiting for the doctors to call when the operation was over. I told her I needed Ali's keys and she fetched them. I left, telling her we'd meet up at the hospital later on.

The keys turned out to be Ali's spare car keys so eventually the police called the fire brigade who arrived, sirens blaring. They stretched a ladder up to one of the first floor windows and opened it. No one was sure whether Ali's attackers might be inside, so a policeman climbed in. The place was deserted and he unlatched the front door for me.

The scene inside was so weird. It was exactly as I had left it the night before. Frozen in time.

The lights were still on and the candles were burning. The game of Balderdash we had played was still unpacked and a few plates with left-over pizza lay on the table.

Nothing had been touched. Ali had clearly not been home. If she had, all this would have been cleared up. The flat would have been spotless.

I went upstairs and, sure enough, there in a lever arch file were all the papers for her car, from the notice advertising it in the local paper to all the licence and registration documents. I handed it over to the police before blowing out the candles and turning out the lights.

I needed to get to the hospital and find out what was really going on.

Coincidentally, seconds after I arrived and stepped into the lift Ali was wheeled in on a gurney. She was semi-conscious and had obviously just come out of theatre. Her eyes were open but I don't think she saw me. They were terribly bloodshot and swollen. I wanted to burst into tears but controlled myself in case she was aware of me. She looked so vulnerable, so bruised and battered. If there was one person who did not deserve this, I thought, it was Ali.

The porter accompanying her turned to me and said: 'Shame, are you her mother?'

I thought I must have looked a sight with my shorts,

crumpled T-shirt, uncombed hair and unwashed face.

'No,' I replied softly. 'I'm a good friend.'

Ali was wheeled into High Care and I hung around the waiting-room. There were two young men there, people I did not know. They introduced themselves as two of the group who had come across Ali in the road. One of the men, who introduced himself as Tiaan, said she had been very brave and that he had been with her in the ambulance. We speculated about what could have happened.

I did not want to go home. I would not rest until I had spoken to Ali myself. We had known each other for close on ten years. We had met when Ali joined the travel agency where I worked.

She was young then, in her early twenties, but she was one of the most wonderful people I had ever met. She was also an exceptional receptionist and a fantastic colleague to work with.

We became friends over the years. I felt truly blessed to know her. She was very special, not only to me but to many people. Ali was one of the most loyal, considerate and honest people I had ever known.

She was one of those people you could ask for advice and you knew she would always be truthful. She might not have told you what you wanted to hear, but she was always willing to listen and offer a valid and carefully thought through opinion. She also never forgot a birthday or other important date and a little card or bunch of flowers would always arrive unexpectedly on the day.

I thought back to when I visited her in London while she was living there. I remembered arriving one winter, depressed, overweight and generally unhappy. I was to spend two weeks with her and pitched up at her flat while she was at work.

In the guest room she had left me a basket overflowing with wonderful things. There were clean towels, little bars of soaps, aromatherapy oils, peppermint lotion for my feet, lots of small, delicious things to make me feel better. She had even put out a pair of long johns in case I had not packed enough warm clothes.

That was Ali. Always considering others. She was utterly constant in that way.

Everything was important to her. She was one of those people who inspired others, she made me want to do more with my life. She made me realise there was more to life than work, sleep and eat.

I couldn't understand why anyone would want to hurt a person like her, and in such a ruthless way. Obviously they didn't know her.

What strange forces of nature had brought these brutal people into her space, I wondered?

Claire and Mercia arrived shortly afterwards. Claire was still in control and went in to see Ali. Afterwards I went to talk to her.

I was surprised at how alert she was. But that was typical of Ali. Couldn't wait to communicate. She told me everything. I stood there listening to this incredible tale. From the beginning she told me that she had been raped. It was important that she did that. It brought it out into the open. There was nothing for her to be ashamed of. If it had happened to me I might not have talked about it so openly.

But I realised this was Ali's way of dealing with it. She did not want people to avoid the subject as so many victims are prone to do.

As I walked wearily down the corridor back to my car I wondered if this might all not have happened if she had not given me a lift home. If only I had gone home with Richard or Phillip, or even used my own car. But then, I thought, this could have happened to anyone. It was one of those random, senseless crimes that we have grown so accustomed to. It could have been me.

But if there was one person who had the strength and the character to get over this, it was Ali. I knew it would be a long struggle and I had no idea how it would affect her life later. At that moment I was simply overjoyed that my wonderful friend was alive.

10

ALISON

Safe and almost sound

———

I OPENED MY eyes. I was being wheeled along a beige corridor. I felt groggy but my heart sang. I had made it! I had actually survived! The last thing I could remember thinking was 'keep breathing and you'll make it' and now I had.

I was certain then that I would not die.

I was taken to the P4 High Care Unit and attached to various monitors and bleeping instruments.

It was morning and bright sunlight streamed into the room through the large aluminium-framed windows.

I couldn't move my head, it was trapped between two very sturdy sandbags, but the light in the room was beautiful, almost brilliant, and even lit up the ceiling which was just about all I could see from that angle.

Every single part of my body ached. It was a solid pain from my toes to my head. But the fact that I had survived overshadowed it all at that point. It made it all bearable somehow.

I was overwhelmed with the urge to speak and did as soon as I opened my eyes. The nurses were very concerned about it but nothing could stop me. They'd have to gag or sedate me to shut me up.

I had lived through the nightmare completely alone until then, unable to tell anyone because I could not speak. There was just so much I wanted to say now.

It was as if I had been on this incredible trip or had seen an amazing movie that I wanted to share with everyone. I felt as though I had survived the sinking of the Titanic.

The first person I saw after the doctors and the nurses was my mom. She appeared at my bedside like a guardian angel. I was so overwhelmed to see her. I had thought about her so much while I struggled to live and now here she was.

Her face was drawn and pale and I knew she was trying to look cheerful for my sake. I felt such sorrow for her at that moment. Sorrow because she had to stand there and see me in that state. But I knew she was strong.

I wanted to tell her that the outward injuries she saw were nothing compared to what I had gone through. But it was not the right time then. It was all behind me now, gone, over.

One of the first things I remembered when I came to was that my good friend Helena, whom I had met in London, was due to have visited me from Cape Town that weekend. I knew she would be arriving that morning and that she would go directly to my flat. I worried that she would think I had let her down and told mom to get someone to put a note up on the door to tell her to call my mom. I had always boasted to Helena that Port Elizabeth was a safe city and now this had happened. How was I to explain it to her?

Mom assured me she would get the message to Helena. I was relieved.

I held on to her hand, thrilled to be alive, thrilled to feel the warmth of life that coursed through her and myself.

We spoke a little. I told her that I wanted the guys who had done this to me to be caught. They were still out there somewhere. But I knew their names and I would not forget their faces.

I must have drifted in and out of sleep several times that morning after she left. When I was awake, I was very awake, but I do remember feeling so, so tired.

When Tiaan popped in I was elated, so much so that I began to cry. My leading man!

He had promised he would be there when I woke up and he was. He was so much a part of what had happened the night before and I was proud that I had survived and that he hadn't done it all for nothing.

Of all the people who came to see me, I felt that he understood what I was feeling because he had been there, he knew just how close I had come to dying.

Besides, now I could talk to him, tell him my name was Alison and not Carol and thank him, in my own words, for saving my life.

Some of the other people who were also at the scene dropped by as well. I thanked them for everything they had done. Even though I did not know or remember their faces, I thought it was sweet of them to come. We shared a bond; they knew what I had gone through.

Tiaan didn't linger for too long. He looked exhausted. He had not slept at all but had gone straight back to the holiday resort to shower, change his clothes and pack his bags. He was leaving for Kempton Park the same day. I was very sad that he had to leave, but he promised he'd pop in again on his way out of town and that he would phone every day.

A few more of my friends trickled in. Kim and Jan, two of my closest girlfriends, came. I could see the shock register on their faces when they saw me. It must have been terrible for them. I realised that I had already gone through the trauma, but that they were hearing about it and seeing me for the first time. I had to remind myself that some people were not able to cope with it.

I told everyone about the rape and everything else that had happened. It seemed quite natural to talk about it immediately. I was not ashamed. There was nothing to hide.

Flowers began to fill the room. Bunches and bunches of them. Who on earth were they from? Did I know that many people?

They were absolutely lovely, and such a manifestation of life in all its beauty. I was quite frustrated that I could not see them all. My mom would hold up a basket or a bunch and read out the card. So many cards already. I was touched and humbled by all the love and good wishes that poured in.

My father Brian arrived from Johannesburg. He looked ashen, totally distraught. I know how sensitive he is and how difficult it must have been for him to see me that way. I told him not to worry about me, that I was sure I would be fine. I was pleased he was there.

My brother Neale and his wife Ronwyn also flew from Johannesburg to be with me and my family. Their first child, Jenali, was four months old and was not allowed into the High Care Unit, but Neale 'smuggled' her in under his jacket. It wasn't perhaps under the best of circumstances, but it was a joy to get to meet her.

Helena finally made it to the hospital as well, completely distraught and utterly shocked at what had happened to me. I told her that next time she visited PE I would be well enough to show her just how beautiful it was and that I was sorry that this had to be her introduction to my home town.

Later that afternoon two police officers arrived at my bedside. One was a young woman who introduced herself as Nadia Swanepoel. The other was Jacques van Rensburg.

Nadia hauled out a thick book of police head and shoulder shots they had on record.

'Do you think you will be able to identify them?' she asked.

'Without a doubt,' I replied.

This was the moment I had been waiting for.

Then she opened the first page of the catalogue. There was blur of photographs, so many on one page. I could not move my head and could only scan the rows of faces with my eyes.

I swivelled my eyes back and forth across the page. I could not see Frans, he was not there.

Nadia held the book up over me.

'I can't see them,' I told her.

She turned to a double-page spread.

It was quite overwhelming. Too many faces. I couldn't focus on them at all and actually felt quite nauseous. It was impossible.

'I can't,' I groaned.

'Just try,' she urged me gently.

I wasn't really looking any more, it was all too much. But I pretended for Nadia's sake.

I started to doubt whether I would recognise them at all. Looking at all these faces now, I was afraid the images I had so carefully captured would just dissolve into generic features.

She turned the page slowly.

And then I saw him.

Towards the bottom of the page, Frans stared out at me. I felt a jolt as my eyes met his staring out of the photograph. It was almost as if his picture was in colour or had a different background. But it was black and white and the same size as all the others. His hair was longer, but it was him. I sighed with relief.

'That's him,' I said to Nadia. 'There, near the bottom of the page.'

She did a little jig.

'I knew it,' she said excitedly.

I didn't understand what she meant, but surmised that he had had a brush with the police before.

They left almost immediately, telling me they would be back later to take a statement.

Around 3 p.m. the district surgeon arrived. He needed to do a vaginal swab and a smear for the police forensic tests. It didn't matter much to me at that stage. I didn't find it uncomfortable because the overall pain was so bad I could barely feel what he was doing.

Later Tiaan stopped by again with a tiny cactus. He was on his way back to Kempton Park. He said he was reluctant to leave, but felt better about it now that I had pulled through and was surrounded by so many people who loved me.

He placed the little plant on the stainless steel cabinet next to me and squeezed my hand before saying goodbye.

'You're the bravest person I have ever met,' was the message he had written inside the card he left behind.

I knew I would see him again.

That night more visitors arrived. My boss, Ettienne, an insurance broker, came. He was very concerned and angry about what had happened. He had heard a news bulletin about the attack and the rape and was worried that the men would hear it and know that I had survived. He wanted to station himself at the hospital door and protect me should they decide to return and finish me off.

On the Monday morning another policeman strode into the room. He looked like the quintessential cop, thickset, with a broad Eastern Cape accent. He introduced himself as Melvin Humpel and said he would be heading the investigation. I didn't quite know what to make of him at that stage, but I was reassured by his confident manner. He was also extremely polite and gentle.

'We've got them and we've found your car. They're in custody now for questioning. Don't worry, they won't get bail,' he said.

Triumph and relief. Apparently both Frans and Theuns were already out on bail for two other rape charges. Now they were finally behind bars.

My mom arrived and told me that the press were hounding her. She had taken endless calls from reporters from all over the country who had wanted to interview her or me.

I wanted to talk, I had nothing to hide, but at that stage I was too tired and too sore to think of speaking to the press. I would deal with it all later. I needed to rest more than anything else.

I was kept in High Care for eight days. Between the visits, the sleeping, the nausea and the pain, I began to think about what had happened.

The first thing I needed to come to terms with was that Frans and Theuns had actually tried to kill me. I could not compute it. How? How could two human beings do this to another? And so callously. Why did they want to take my life? I could find no answer. At that time the rape was a secondary issue compared with the attack.

I was comforted so often by the tremendous goodness that surrounded me in High Care. The staff were exemplary and everyone went out of their way to do things for me, even though I tried to be as little trouble as possible. A physiotherapist visited me and taught me how to get rid of the phlegm that collected in my chest. My stomach was too sore and weak to cough.

Once while Kim was visiting, I began to choke. A nurse rushed over and it seemed as though she was lunging at my bloated stomach. I let out a penetrating scream. Even the blanket seemed like a heavy weight on the wound and I couldn't imagine anyone touching me there.

The nurse was clearly irritated with me and said that

I was emotional because I was receiving too many visitors. That one admonishment really threw me. I realised how fragile I was. I knew she was probably right, but I was stung by her remark. I wanted to sob, but I couldn't. It would have been too painful.

There were lots of moments like that in High Care, when the pain in my body and the fact that I couldn't do simple things like cough, laugh or sob, scared me and made me feel vulnerable.

Sometimes the nurses would tell me that I had cried out, mumbled in my sleep or had had a restless night. I didn't realise they were watching me that closely, but it was comforting to know that they were.

There were still stories in the paper every day. One report claimed that Frans and Theuns had been threatened by a bystander when they appeared in the magistrate's court. The journalist had described them as looking 'dishevelled'. Frans was dressed entirely in black and had seemed 'terrified' when the member of the public shouted at them as they were led back to the cells. Actually many of those members of the public were my friends, my boss and former boyfriends.

I wondered what Frans and Theuns thought about it all.

The regular visitors kept my mind off things. That, and the excruciating, mind-blowing pain, even though my wounds seemed to be healing well at that stage.

I dreaded the early morning washes when the nurses had to turn me over in the bed. The pain was more than overwhelming. It was agonising. I tried to make the best of it. At least I could look at the flowers as they heaved me over and my head faced the window sill where they perched. I hung on long enough, knowing they'd soon be finished. The flowers always looked so wonderful.

Every day the nurses or Dr Angelov or Dr Comyn would check up on me. Dressings were changed, pipes were removed, new dressings were applied.

I was getting to know the doctors and the hospital staff so well now that they almost felt like new family.

Four days after the attack I sat up in bed and the new perspective was refreshing even if it meant more pain.

A few days before Christmas I got up out of bed for the first time. I had been flat on my back until then and it took ages before I actually managed to lift myself slowly up out of the bed. I felt faint as my feet touched the floor.

I looked down and was quite startled to see them. They didn't look as though they belonged to me. They seemed smaller somehow.

The sensation of touching the floor was also strange. Nothing felt familiar to me. My body seemed not to be my own any more.

I had to prop myself up against the bed for a few minutes as the blood rushed to my abdomen. My neck ached even when I did not move it. Eventually I manoeuvred myself, like an old person, into a chair.

I clutched a towel to my abdomen for security more than anything else. The wound felt as though it might burst open at any time. The doctors had told me that it was quite a common feeling after one's intestines had been 'handled'. It was extremely uncomfortable sitting up, but I didn't mind. I could see the world around me and not just stare up at the ceiling.

The next day I got up again and was determined to

walk a few steps even if it was just to the door. I plodded across the ward like some ancient, tired person. I managed to peek around the door and look down the corridor, much to the surprise of some of my friends.

Eventually, I managed to shuffle down the corridor to the loo all by myself. I felt triumphant. It was the breakthrough I had been waiting for. Soon I would be moved to a general ward.

On Christmas Day, Kim and her two sons brought a small tree and decorated it with little shiny ornaments. They were all so excited and it warmed my heart.

Mom and Dad popped in and so did my boss Ettienne and his wife Hanlie. It was the first time Hanlie had come to see me. I think she had been too traumatised before that. She sat down on one of the chairs and the first thing she said was 'But look at your knees, they're all cut up and terrible.' I hadn't had the opportunity to examine my knees and it seemed funny that they would concern her when my other injuries were so much more severe. We chuckled together about it.

Although everyone who visited that day made me feel so loved and special, I felt lonely. Sad and lonely. As each one left to join their loved ones for Christmas dinner I too longed to be with my family.

My treat for the day was fish soup which I had for lunch and dinner. It was the first 'solid' I had been allowed to eat and after a few spoonfuls I felt full. Still, it was the best thing I had tasted in a long while. I had this craving for some custard and had mentioned it to someone. Soon everyone arrived with bowls or cartons of the stuff.

The next day I was moved from High Care to M3, a

general ward. One step closer to the exit, I thought. By now I regularly took myself off to the toilet on my own. It was so liberating to be mobile, even if I did hobble along trailing a drip. I felt I was gaining back more control.

My room filled up with flowers and cards again. There were so many bouquets and baskets the nurses had to wheel in a multi-tiered trolley to accommodate them all. I couldn't keep them all, so each time someone visited I asked them to take a bunch home to enjoy.

I had more time to think in the general ward. I had a private room and was left alone more often.

What was I going to do with this experience? How was I going to integrate it into the rest of my life – a life that until now had been so carefree, so uncomplicated and so happy.

There was one thing I did know. I would never let Frans and Theuns take more than they already had. They had no power over me and I would not allow them to destroy my positive mind, my love for life.

I had always believed that nothing happened to anyone who didn't have the capacity to overcome it. We are never given more than we can bear. It was up to me now to have faith in my own power and believe that this would not set me back or change my life. Time would tell.

The first time I cried was while listening to a CD Ettienne had brought me. Before the attack Kim and I were out one night when we heard a song that had really touched us.

It was a beautiful soothing melody sung by a woman. The ever-inventive Ettienne had managed to find out what it was and track down the album.

It was a song by Phoebe Snow and the chorus went something like this: 'If I can just get through the night, I'll give it all up tomorrow.'

I lay in bed in the dark with the earphones on, listening to the words. They reached a place deep inside me, comforting me and opening me up. The tears just streamed down my face.

I remembered the intense feeling I had had the night of the attack. The feeling of refusing to give up and die because I knew I was capable of so much more, but had accepted mediocrity from myself so many times. The song reminded me that I now had the chance to live my life and do my best, always. I would never take my life for granted again.

I was recovering well. Dr Angelov said I might even be ready to go home in a couple of days' time. Joy of joys, to get out from behind these walls and get back to my life.

My mom visited one afternoon and told me that a journalist from the *Eastern Province Herald*, Brett Adkins, had called to say he wanted to interview me. She said she had liked him because, of all the reporters, he had not been pushy and had always been polite.

I felt stronger and agreed to talk to him because I had grown tired of regurgitating the story over and over again. I asked my mom if she thought it would be of any benefit, if I could help anyone by telling the story. She assured me she thought I could and I trusted her opinion.

I had no thoughts at that stage about my privacy and it never crossed my mind that I had any reason to feel guilt or shame about what had happened, but I was advised by the police not to reveal my identity. I also had no idea just how big the story would become.

Mom and Mercia sat in on the interview. Brett seemed shocked when he first saw me. He was very polite, gentle and unobtrusive but I could see he was surprised at my appearance. I think he couldn't believe how well I looked after such a savage attack.

I was healing well, and quickly, much to my delight.

Although I loved being in the private room it was lonelier than High Care where I had the constant attention of the nurses.

I did have the use of a cell phone someone had kindly lent me so I was able to call my friends, including Tiaan. But still I felt cut off.

I wanted desperately to go home now and every day when Dr Angelov came to check up on me, I would try to convince him that I was ready and well enough to leave. He kept saying, 'Well, maybe tomorrow.'

Then there was a slight setback. The wound on my neck, now that the drains had been removed, had started to go septic. It was the one thing Dr Angelov had feared most of all.

I could not believe it. The wound was swollen, red and angry and bulged like an egg at one end. I told the sister about it and was surprised when she prodded at the protrusion with the ink tip of her ballpoint pen. I tried to get her to call Dr Angelov but she said it would not be necessary. I should have spoken up, but I didn't. I wanted to be a model patient.

The next morning Dr Angelov arrived. He was furious that he had not been summoned earlier. He left the room and I could hear him shouting down the corridor. He had stitched the gash so beautifully and now all his work stood to be ruined. They inserted another drain and cleared up the fluid.

On the morning of December 31 he removed the drain and changed the dressing. The swelling had gone down. Then, with a large smile cracking his face, he told me that it was time to go home.

I actually couldn't believe it. It was such an anti-climax. I suppose I expected I would hear music or a dramatic drumroll in the background.

At 11.35 a.m. a porter brought a wheelchair to the room. My mom had helped me pack up my belongings. I had noted that over 300 people had visited or sent messages and flowers. I carefully placed all their cards and letters in a folder. They were so dear to me and one of the first things I intended to do was place them all in a scrapbook.

As I was wheeled out of the room I did not say goodbye. I knew this would not be the last time I would see this hospital, these walls, these kind people in their uniforms.

I was so excited that I wanted to walk out of there on my own feet.

But everyone insisted I get into the chair. When we got to the threshold I asked the porter to stop. I stood up and walked into the warm sunlight.

Tomorrow the new year would begin.

11

MELVIN HUMPEL

The suspects

———————◆———————

I WAS OFF duty on the long weekend of December 16, 1994. On the Monday morning, December 19, around 7 a.m., the phone rang. It was a colleague from the Port Elizabeth Murder and Robbery Squad. She said I had better get down there as there had been this savage attack and rape of a young woman at Noordhoek. They needed my help with the investigation.

Two other officers, Nadia Swanepoel and Jacques van Rensburg had arrested the suspects, Frans du Toit and Theuns Kruger, at 5 a.m. that morning. They found the victim's car with the keys still in the ignition abandoned near the breweries in North End.

These guys were still asleep when Nadia and Jacques got to their flat, which was literally around the corner from where they had dumped the car. They took them both in. Apparently they hadn't put up a struggle.

It was Nadia who had actually suspected that Frans might have been involved in Alison's attack.

At that stage she had been investigating two other rape cases, one involving only Frans and the other both Frans and Theuns. I was with Nadia when we first caught Frans in February that year after he had abducted and raped and sexually assaulted a 20-year-old woman at gunpoint in Central.

He was released on bail on that occasion. The victim had only reported the rape a week later. There was no medical evidence. It was his word against hers. At that stage he had a stable job as a driver with a stationery supply company. He also had a fixed address so the court had to let him go.

On December 4, Frans and Theuns struck again. This time they accosted, raped and sexually assaulted a 21-year-old pregnant woman who was walking to a nearby café to buy cigarettes. The attack happened in the same suburb, but the suspects were arrested by the Flying Squad and taken to the Humewood police station.

They appeared in the magistrate's court the next morning before the case had been assigned to a specific investigating officer and before anyone could make a connection to the previous rape.

The prosecutor could not have known about the other case and so both were let out on bail again. By the time Nadia had put two and two together it was too late, Frans and Theuns had already ambushed their third victim, Alison.

I had been called in ostensibly to head the investigation into Alison's case. But, I was told, there were strings attached. It looked as though the men were connected with the other rapes so in the end I got all three dockets.

I had been with the police service for over 16 years and was one of their most experienced officers. In all my years I had never, ever before heard of such a savage, premeditated and callous attack. If they were guilty, I wanted these guys behind bars for the rest of their lives.

Nadia told me that Alison had made a very positive ID earlier that morning. She had picked Frans du Toit out from hundreds of other photographs in the police identity catalogue.

Both men were being kept in holding cells at the Darling Street headquarters of the Murder and Robbery Unit in North End and it was my job to interview them.

After our usual morning lecture I went down and introduced myself. I told them that I would be the investigating officer. They were still quite arrogant at that stage. They did not know that Alison was alive. They had only been told they were being arrested for rape when they were picked up.

I decided to haul Theuns out first. He was 19, the younger of the two and I had already had dealings with Du Toit before.

I escorted him to my office. He looked as though he didn't give a damn. I sat him down and read him his rights. Then I told him that I was investigating two charges against him. One of rape and one of attempted murder.

He was semi-slouched in the chair and he looked up at me when I said this.

'Attempted murder? Why attempted murder?' he asked.

I could see he was surprised.

'I have news for you,' I answered. 'Your last victim, Alison, the lady you left for dead at Noordhoek, survived. She's talking and remembers everything.'

It was as if I had thrown a bucket of ice water over him. He got the fright of his life.

'*O fok, dan help dit nie eers as ek vir jou lieg nie,*'* he said.

Then he took some rings off his finger and flung them on the table.

'*De, hier's haar ringe,*'† he said.

He told me exactly how it happened. How he and Frans had been drinking and barbecuing that afternoon and that at one stage they decided to go out and look for a 'beautiful girl to rape and kill with a nice car'.

They had hung around Central area but he had got '*gatvol*' and told Frans he was going to Club Tonite and that he should come and look for him if he found someone.

He said Du Toit had arrived later with this woman in a Renault and that they had spun some bullshit story about a TV. He told me how they had driven to the scene and how Frans had raped and sexually assaulted her before he did the same thing.

He said Du Toit had then strangled the woman and he had helped him to drag her out of the car. Then he told me exactly how the stabbing took place.

I realised then that this man was giving me a con-

---

*'Oh fuck, then it won't even help if I lie.'
†'There, here are her rings.'

fession, so I stopped him. I told him he should be making a statement to a magistrate, but he wanted to carry on. I made notes in my pocketbook.

After they dragged her from the car Theuns said he asked Du Toit if he thought she was dead. Du Toit said 'let's find out' and started stabbing Alison's abdomen and her private parts.

Then he said he heard a '*roggel*', or rasping sound, coming from her and he took out his knife and slashed her throat. Du Toit shoved him aside after he had made the first cut with his knife and then started slashing at the woman's throat with the smaller knife.

After that, he said, they ransacked her car, tossed out things they thought were of no value and drove home where they had a couple of beers before going to sleep.

I told him he should tell all this to a magistrate, which he agreed to do. During that confession he admitted to the other rape, the one that had taken place on December 4. It was as if he knew his time was up. Then he agreed to go with another police officer and point out the scene of Alison's attack. When he came back a little while later he had his knife with him.

'Here's the knife I used to cut her throat,' he said to me.

It was a huge thing with a blade of about 20 centimetres and it had the name 'Frik' quite crudely engraved on it.

He told me they had used it to prepare food that morning. That he hadn't even bothered to wipe the blood off the blade.

Then it was Du Toit's turn.

When I told him one of the charges was attempted

murder he said, '*Dit is onmoontlik, sy kan nie leef nie.*'*

He, too, seemed quite surprised.

'*Wel dan sal ek maar die hele waarheid moet vertel,*'† he said quite calmly.

He told me the same story. I felt he was somehow enjoying reliving it all. It was just something else that had happened to them. He showed no remorse whatsoever. There were times during that interview when my hands really itched. I would have loved to have punched him, but obviously I couldn't.

He also told me that the next day, before their arrest, they had planned to abduct and murder another woman. This time they wanted to throw her off the Van Staden's bridge.

I was thrilled that we had caught them both and that they had confessed to it all.

Later that morning I headed off for the hospital. I wanted to tell Alison that we had the savages who had done this to her and that she needn't worry.

But before I could meet her I first had to deal with her mother, Claire. She was outside the ward when I arrived and quite correctly asked me what I was doing there. She was very protective and I understood what she felt. I don't think she liked the look of me initially, but I made it clear that I was not there to disturb Alison. I knew she had been through a terrible ordeal and needed to rest, but I wanted to inform her that the suspects were safely behind bars.

---

*'That's impossible, she couldn't have survived.'
†'Well then, I have to tell the whole truth.'

Alison looked absolutely terrible. She was black and blue, her eyes were swollen and red with blood and she had this huge bandage on her neck. I felt so angry with those guys. I told her not to worry and that we would be taking a statement from her once she had been discharged. I was looking forward to getting to know this remarkable person.

Part Two

12

ALISON

Finding the threads

———◆———

IT WAS FANTASTIC to be out of hospital. Just stepping through the doors in my own clothes made me feel I was a tiny bit closer to gathering the threads of my life again.

Everything had come to a standstill during those two weeks I had been trapped behind the beige walls of the wards and corridors. I felt as though I had been pencilled into someone else's story, as if I had boarded the wrong plane to a destination I hadn't chosen.

As mom drove me through the streets of PE I felt exhilarated, so happy to be alive. The sunshine, the people, the cars and the bustle filled me with a sense of wonderment.

I realised I might never have seen it all again. I might have died. Everything that I had always taken for granted and sometimes had not really seen, the grubby, familiar shops and streets, all looked quite beautiful.

While I lay in hospital fighting for my life this had simply gone on, had continued as before. All these people, these cars moving to and fro, had gone about their business as if nothing had happened, while my life had changed irrevocably.

That's the thing about life. Only we can intensely experience each moment. Although it is connected in some esoteric way to the greater cosmos, only we live in it, through it, totally alone.

I was tired. It was a tiredness beyond exhaustion and my body sank into the contours of the car seat. It was a painful journey. I could feel every bump in the road, every pot-hole. Searing arrows of pain shot through me and even the slightest movement of my head tore at my neck.

But the journey was sweet, none the less. I let it all wash over me. I took in everything, or rather it took me in, a little like when you need to close your eyes to sleep but can't because you're enjoying something too much.

I was not ready to go back to my flat in Deare Street. My entire body hurt. There had not been a day in the last two weeks when I had not felt pain. The medication had helped to relieve it somewhat and I supposed I was also getting used to it, learning to live with it.

The wound on my abdomen had still not healed and wept into the dressing. I'd have to go back to the hospital daily to have it cleaned, changed, checked up on. Sometimes when I moved the most excruciating pain wrenched through me. I tried to relax through it and the worst was always followed by a brief, less painful respite.

My neck also ached constantly. It felt as if it were

wedged in a tight brace. I could not turn my head or even angle my body to look anywhere but straight ahead.

There was no way I could care for myself in that state so I went where I knew I would get the love, comfort and safety I needed. I went home to mom.

It was New Year's Eve and the excitement of leaving the hospital had exhausted me. I crawled into bed immediately. A few friends called to wish me well and tell me about the parties they planned to go to.

I was just so happy to be home. I didn't need to stay awake to see the New Year in. That night I fell into a deep, contented sleep. It was one of the first nights I did not dream.

The next day mom arranged a little barbecue. There were only a few people: mom, Mercia and her daughter and son-in-law. I was looking forward to doing something quite ordinary again. A lounger and a chair were carried outside and I could choose which of the two was the most comfortable.

It was a wonderful, sunny day. Just perfect. We ate, we talked, we laughed and we celebrated.

I felt like a queen, everyone wanted to do everything for me. I only had to lift my arm and beckon.

The next day, a Monday, my good friend Jan called. I had said something the day before about wanting to go back to the place where it had all happened. I wanted to reclaim it. We had talked about how I should never be afraid to drive along that road again and that Frans and Theuns did not have the power to stop me from enjoying my city.

I was keen to go. I wanted to get back to my old life as soon as possible and this would be one way, I thought, of doing that. I was also curious. I had not had time to piece the whole attack together and I felt I needed to see where it had happened.

I also wanted to see the place in daylight and measure the distances that had felt so endless to me that night.

My mom was against my going. I think she was afraid of what it might open up and that it might upset me. But she didn't try to stop me. I think she understood that it was something I had to do.

Jan and her boyfriend Gary collected me. I sat in the passenger seat hugging my stomach as we drove out to Noordhoek. I wasn't sure I'd find it again. I saw a clearing and we turned in, but I immediately knew it was not the place. Further on I spotted another parting in the bush. We pulled off, I peered in and recognised it.

It looked different in the daylight but there was no doubt this was it. We parked the car and crunched around. It looked a little cleaner than it had that night. I thought that the police or someone must have removed some of the debris. I don't think I was really ready for the experience and knew it was bravado more than anything else that had spurred me on. I suppose I wanted to show everyone and myself that I was strong and tough enough.

I was surprised that I felt nothing. It was a neutral, ordinary picnic spot. I tried to connect with something that I knew must be lurking somewhere in my subconscious, but it didn't happen. I didn't cry, I didn't panic. It was a very clinical experience. All I gained at that stage was a mental map of the area.

Gary paced out the distance from the clearing where they had left me to Marine Drive. It was about 90 metres.

I must have gabbled a bit but I don't remember much of that day. We did take a photograph as a reminder. I posed like a triumphant boxer, one foot on a log, my arm flexed, showing off a non-existent muscle.

I felt a bit silly, but convinced myself that it had not been a pointless exercise. At least I had a clear picture now of where to begin.

We stopped off for some lunch on the way back. Of course we talked about the attack, I couldn't stop talking about it and my friends were just as engrossed as I was.

I knew mom would be worried that it might have upset me. But when I got home I told her I had felt nothing and that she needn't be concerned.

I contemplated what I had thought I might find there. Maybe I was looking for myself, my old self. Perhaps I just wanted to make sure that this was not a dream and that once I had found the physical location the entire incident would be given a real form and shape.

It is my nature to want as much information as possible in any given situation. The more I know the easier it is to evaluate, compute and interpret whatever it is.

Frans and Theuns had caught me by surprise. I did not want any more surprises. I wanted to own as much information about the attack as possible.

Someone else had exactly the same mission. The police.

A few days after I had settled in, Nadia Swanepoel visited me to take a statement. It was one of the first times that I retold the story in detail. I wanted to be able to give them as much information as possible. She sat opposite me quietly writing it all down. Afterwards she asked me to accompany her to the police pound to 'identify' Reginald.

I couldn't miss him. He was covered in the silver dust detectives use to lift fingerprints and looked so forlorn there next to a few other wrecks parked in the fenced-off courtyard.

I couldn't face driving him again and as I left I felt I had abandoned him. A friend kindly offered to take him to be cleaned before he was returned to me.

The media were still trying to contact my mom and me. The phone had not stopped ringing since the attack. I was quite surprised at the interest my case had attracted, but I understood that people were amazed that I had survived. Also, the whole thing had tapped into a collective anger about crime. That and the fact that both Frans and Theuns were out on bail when they attacked me. My father had written a letter to the local newspaper about that issue and they had published it on the front page, apparently a first. The letter later led to a campaign by a local resident, Charmaine Holder, to collect a million signatures for a petition to be sent to the Minister of Justice, Mr Dullah Omar, expressing outrage at the lax bail laws.

I had told Melvin Humpel, the investigating officer on my case, that I wanted to speak out and that I had nothing to hide. I was not ashamed to talk about the rape or identify myself. Why should I hide my face?

He advised me not to say too much until after the Supreme Court trial. Anything I said, he told me, could be used in court or could jeopardise the entire case. I did agree to let Brett Adkins do a short interview about the fact that I was back home and on the mend. I also wrote an open letter to the *Herald* thanking everyone, my family, my friends and the hospital staff for their love, support, flowers and gifts.

I wrote: 'For fear of omitting any one of you from my heartfelt thanks, I have decided to attempt to thank you all collectively . . . Each one who sent flowers, gifts, cards, wishes, thoughts, prayers and love should know how they brought a smile to my face and an added warmth to my heart . . . I HAVE LIFE . . . Beautiful people – you have my heart.'

I was really deeply moved by everyone's response. It had strengthened and carried me when I had needed it most. Even strangers as far away as Johannesburg sent me little gifts and the Mayor of Port Elizabeth, Nceba Faku, visited me at home clutching a beautiful bunch of flowers in one hand and a pot plant in the other. I was touched that he had taken time out to visit me personally. He apologised for not coming to see me sooner.

The initial thrill of being home faded as my body began to demand rest. I tired easily. By mid afternoon I would find myself exhausted, unable to think or do anything except lie down to try and restore my energy.

The days passed and soon everyone went back to their lives. I assured all concerned that I was fine and as long as I told them that, I knew they wouldn't worry. I had always tended to do that, to reassure others that I was in control. I almost felt it was expected of me, even though I had created those expectations myself. In most cases I had lived up to them, in others not.

The first time I realised that I had created this aura was after I had matriculated from Collegiate High School in 1985. I had been the head girl that year and I must say

I was a little surprised at the time as I was not particularly academically conscientious.

I was always considered bright, but I knew I did not apply myself to the fullest in my last few years at school. Also, I wasn't good at any sport and I didn't really shine in any one area so I guess I thought I wouldn't be good enough to be head girl.

I was well behaved and I think I was a good head girl, but I had always believed people saw me as a bit of a nerd. I was one of those children who always wanted to please.

I often thought it was a weakness but later came to realise that it was a quality which, if balanced with enough self-knowledge and confidence, was not a bad one.

'Alison is a mature young woman of the utmost integrity and sound moral values,' our headmistress, Miss Cameron Ellis, waxed lyrical in my school testimonial.

'Outgoing with a quiet confidence, she has a strong personality and as head girl has proved to be a sound and effective leader. She has dignity and poise and is unfailingly neat and well groomed. Her loyalty and trust-worthiness are above question. Friendly and cheerful, she is courteous and considerate and relates very well to others.'

No wonder then, once I had matriculated, that every-one expected me to study law or become a doctor. The truth was I had no idea what I wanted to do with my life. Mom suggested I do a secretarial course. 'It will stand you in good stead,' she said like so many other mothers, and of course it did.

Now I found myself back in the home I had come to

every day as a school girl. Mom's little knick-knacks on the walls, the carpets, the chairs, the garden and the gurgling sound of the pool cleaner were all so familiar. But at the same time it felt different.

This was where I had grown up, this was the place I had always felt safe and welcome. In this house I plotted what I would do with my life (becoming an air hostess was an early option), wrote poetry, and dreamed of some or other boy I fancied at school.

They were good memories but there were times in those first few weeks when they felt as if they belonged to someone else. A lifetime had somehow passed between me and the little girl who had once lived here.

The rhythm of my life had changed now. I was not yet ready to return to my job as an insurance broker, but I was growing impatient. I wanted to shake off this state.

My mom had given me the telephone number of one of her friends who was a trained counsellor and who had kindly offered herself and her time to talk to me if I needed it.

She didn't pressure me to contact her, but said I should call her if I needed to talk.

Mom could tell I needed help. Although I showed everyone else my brave face, she bore the brunt of my mood swings and the bouts of irritation that seemed to come from nowhere. I snapped and snarled at her. At times I just wanted to curl up and be left alone, but I also wanted her to be there. I hated hurting her but I couldn't stop myself. I knew she would forgive me, she had always loved me unconditionally and I felt safe enough to be my wretched self with her.

At first I resisted the idea of talking to a stranger. I

would have preferred to discuss things with Melvin or Nadia, but I realised that they were busy and, besides, I could not expect them to play therapist.

I made an appointment and went to see the woman more for my mom's sake than my own. I had only planned to go that once, but afterwards I realised I had really benefited from talking to someone who gently listened and reassured me that I was handling everything. I saw her quite often in the first few months and my gratitude to her knows no bounds.

The only thing stopping me from going back to work was my injuries. Every day mom took me down to the hospital to have the wounds dressed. Without my own car, I had to rely on other people to get around. Besides, even if I had had access to a car I would not have been able to drive it. The injuries were still far too painful and the muscles in my stomach were not strong enough yet for me to move about.

I enjoyed my visits to Dr Angelov. He was always so reassuring and he belonged, like Tiaan, Melvin and a few others, to a new circle that had formed around my life.

Also, Dr Angelov did not pity me. He was a doctor and quite at ease around people in pain. I always tried to be brave but sometimes it really hurt when he scraped away the dead tissue from my still-septic wounds. When I mentioned to him that it hurt he would shrug and say, 'I can't feel anything.'

It was exactly this unemotional bedside manner and dry sense of humour that so endeared him to me. He knew what I had already gone through. I did not need to explain it.

We laughed a lot together and he made the frustration of it all disappear. I knew I would miss my visits to him when I was well again.

I didn't think much in the beginning. It was almost impossible to find a still place inside me to reflect on anything profound. Even during the counselling sessions I found myself merely retelling the story as if it had happened to someone else.

The only thing I could do was feel, not emotion, but pain, raw physical pain. Sometimes just being alive hurt.

Simple, routine tasks seemed to take ages. Walking was difficult, it took effort to breathe and bathing was impossible. How I longed to soak in a hot bath. I had not had one since the attack. I was not allowed to get water into any of the wounds so I had to kneel in the bath and splash myself like a bird.

One evening as I squatted in the bath I stared at my new body. The scars on my stomach were red and raw. They were hideous. I had been cut open from my belly button during the operation to replace my intestines. At the end of that flat, wide scar was the wound that was struggling to heal. A suppurating reminder that, even when it did heal, I was sure would never go away.

I did not recognise myself and I felt a tremendous sadness. I wanted to shed that skin and emerge glistening and whole. I wanted it all to go away. I felt very sorry for myself and began to sob. I called my mom and told her to look at me.

'Who will love me this way?' I asked her.

'One day you will find someone who will. Someone who will be capable of seeing beyond the scars to the beautiful person you are,' she tried to reassure me calmly.

I could not hear her. There was nothing anyone could say at that moment to take away the hurt. Mom loved me and it didn't matter to her. She was just thrilled I was alive.

The incident in the bathroom left me feeling tired and vulnerable. Mom tucked me in and kissed me good-night. She told me to call if I needed anything.

I wondered where Frans and Theuns were at that very moment. What were they thinking? What if they got bail and came back to finish me off now? What if they haunted me for the rest of my life, even if they did go to jail? What if they came back to seek revenge in years to come? Why wasn't I angry?

I lay in bed petrified, thinking of them. At the end of January, the *Evening Post* ran an article revealing that Theuns had told a Port Elizabeth district surgeon that he was a Satanist and had claimed that he 'believed in the devil'. He had also told the doctor that he 'had no feeling for his victim' (who I presumed was me), 'or any other person' and that 'he had had no feeling for his mother because she had never given him any material things'.

What was I to make of this? It was the first time I had learned that he might use Satanism as a defence. The journalist, Raymond Hill, had gleaned this from documents submitted to the court at a hearing post-ponement. But could he use his Satanism as an excuse? A murder is a murder, whether it is committed by some-one who claims to be a Christian or someone who says he is a Satanist. The Satanism defence, I thought, was a ploy, an attempt to lessen the severity and the calculated manner in which they had deliberately hunted me down that night. Frans and Theuns were not in court that day to shed any light on the issue; they were undergoing psychiatric evaluations at Valkenberg Hospital in Cape Town.

I had feared Theuns more than Frans that night. He was disturbingly quiet. But in the end it was Frans, the 'smooth-talker', who had put his hands around my throat and looked me in the eye as he tried to take my life.

Each time the court date was postponed another story appeared. 'Sons of Satan' screamed one headline. In this article Frans, a policeman's son, had 'admitted' to an 'evil side with a desire to kill during sex'.

I tossed the newspaper aside. But thinking about them now took me away from myself and my own recovery. There was no point, I reckoned, in wasting my precious energy trying to make sense of it yet.

I would never know what they had really thought, if indeed they thought anything at all. Maybe I would gain more insight at the Supreme Court trial when they testified. Until then I vowed to try not to think about them and to concentrate on myself.

After all, I had fought for my life in the dark, alone and frightened beyond belief. I had done that because I had wanted to live. What would that be worth if I now lived in fear? I had almost died, I had almost been there anyway.

My mind cleared and calmed. I was safe for now, here in my mom's double bed.

Even with these scars, I told myself, I would live again. Life was more precious to me now than it had ever been. As I drifted off to sleep I tried to recapture that first feeling of liberation and marvel I had felt driving home.

Sure I was a victim, but that didn't mean I had to live like one. But how I would accomplish that I did not know.

13

ALISON

Back on the horse

———— ◆ ————

I CLOSED THE door on Deare Street for the last time. I did not feel safe there any more and during February we moved dribs and drabs of my furniture and belongings to the new home that I had rented in a secure complex in South End.

A PE resident who had heard about my attack kindly offered to put up a sturdy security gate. It was just one of so many little gestures that meant so much to me at that time. I was grateful. I wanted to make sure all the windows and other possible entry points were inaccessible to outsiders. I was going to live alone for a while before I considered the possibility of a house mate and I wanted to feel utterly safe.

The injuries still hurt but I was much more mobile now. My friend returned Reginald, gleaming and freshly cleaned and vacuumed of the evidence from that night, but I couldn't keep him. He looked better than he had ever done but I knew that every time I got behind the steering wheel I would be reminded of what had happened inside that car.

I was sad to part with him and hoped his new owners would treat him well. We traded him in for a burgundy Mazda and I drove out of the showroom with a growing sense of independence.

I filled those first days with endless appointments and meetings with friends. I had always enjoyed going out and I would not stop now.

It was hard though. I always felt nervy. In the beginning I drove through many red traffic lights. I would slow down, check if anyone was around and just carry on. I couldn't deal with the vulnerability and fear that overwhelmed me sitting alone at a red light. I hoped that if a policeman ever stopped me he would recognise who I was and understand why I was flaunting the traffic code.

Getting out and confronting those fears made me feel I was a little closer to the slipstream of ordinary life again. But things had changed.

At every turn the conversation revolved around the rape and the attack. At that stage I wanted to talk about it and did not mind answering questions.

I would often return home, exhausted, and think about what people had asked. One friend wanted to know how the fear had felt. I could not answer him then, but as I lay in bed I realised that in my case the fear was relative to my will to survive. The fear that night was not of dying. It was of not surviving. I had had a total peace about death. I suppose I was spiritually ready for it, but I knew it was not my time.

But fear is not a one-off occurrence. Just because I had lived through a nightmare didn't mean I didn't fear anything any more. I didn't have the desire – as some people who have survived aeroplane crashes or other near-death encounters sometimes do – to test the limits or place myself in danger once again.

At night when I returned home after going out, I constantly reassured myself that there was nothing to fear, that I was safe and that the chances of something happening again at that stage were remote. I did not want to be consumed by it all the time. It was exhausting enough trying to be rational about it.

I was still not really thinking about the attack. I knew I was supposed to, but I just couldn't seem to concentrate long enough to access my deepest thoughts. Every morning I would wake up and for a split second everything would be wonderful. Then it would dawn on me. Something huge had happened and I was not dealing with it.

I was keen to get to work and away from trying to reflect. Maybe there was nothing to think about or to resolve anyway? Was I in denial? I didn't think so. I had no trouble talking about the rape and the assault, but I knew there would come a time when I might have to seek in-depth therapy.

There was little else I could do at that moment except get back on the horse. Two months after the attack I returned to work. I got a tremendous welcome from my boss Ettienne and the rest of the staff. It felt really good to be back. There were cards and flowers and calls from clients who were thrilled I was up and about again.

I was buoyed by their enthusiasm and felt a burst of new-found energy.

By then the bandage had been removed from my neck. The scar, I could tell, shocked people. Their eyes would linger there before they met my own, but I didn't mind. It was so obvious you could hardly not notice it.

Someone had mentioned that I should wear a scarf to cover it up but I didn't want to. There was no need to hide it from anyone. Besides, I could not stand anything around my neck. It made me feel claustrophobic and covering it up would only make me more aware of it.

If people saw the scar and asked about it I would tell them. Some didn't ask, they just stared. Eventually, I reckoned, they would get used to it. And so would I.

The abdominal injury was also starting to heal but it felt uncomfortable. I was aware of it all the time and I noticed that it had started to bulge out like a huge orange. I had been to see Dr Angelov regularly and we discussed the fact that I would need reconstructive and plastic surgery later. The muscles had collapsed completely and there was nothing to keep my tummy in. He said they would be able to reconstruct using muscles from my leg at a much later stage. We also talked about doing plastic surgery on my neck so that the scar would be less obvious in years to come.

A few days after I had returned to work Melvin called. We needed to go through the finer details of the case and to talk about the ID parade that was going to take place in about a week's time.

I had never dealt with the police before and was a little apprehensive about him at first. They see so much in their jobs that I wondered if my case would be any different from the thousands of others they had to investigate?

But Melvin never made me feel like I was intruding or interrupting him. He was always welcoming and his manner was confident but reassuring. He made me feel safe and I knew if there was one man who would put Frans and Theuns behind bars it was him.

Melvin carefully explained the course the rest of the investigation would take. I would be required to give pubic hair samples, he told me, and then I would have to pick Frans and Theuns out at an ID parade. After that there would be months of preparation for the trial. I told Melvin I was willing to do anything to help the investigation.

I tried to make late afternoon appointments so that my meetings with him would not clash with my work. Our relationship had grown over the past weeks. There were many times, late at night when I would remember a detail or something I knew I had forgotten to make in my statement and I would call him. He was always there, ready to talk and to listen.

The ID parade began to intrude on everything. It was OK at work when my mind was occupied, but at night I dreaded having to face Frans and Theuns again.

At first Melvin told me that the police did not have a one-way glass facility in Port Elizabeth and that I would therefore have to go through the 'standard' procedure which meant going into a room with all the men who were taking part in the parade.

I would then have to stand in front of Frans or Theuns once I had identified them and place my hand on their shoulder while a photographer captured the moment.

I didn't think I would be able to do it, but I gritted my teeth and convinced myself that I could, that as was the case with everything else that had happened to me, I could 'handle' it.

But the thought of touching either of them filled me with fear and disgust.

After talking to my mother about it and hearing a terrible tale of a man who had had a really bad experience identifying a burglar in this outdated manner, I thought I would tell Melvin that I was not prepared to go through with it.

Mom agreed with my sentiments, saying although she had no doubt I could do it, I shouldn't have to under those circumstances.

I was told that the parade would have to be moved to East London or Grahamstown where one-way facilities were in place. Although I felt guilty about creating this 'inconvenience' I was not prepared to compromise. I was not prepared to face those two men again.

Melvin then informed me that they had a one-way partition at the offices in Port Elizabeth and although I would still be in the same room as them I would be shielded to some extent.

Still, I wondered if Frans and Theuns would recognise me?

I also worried that Frans and Theuns might have friends who would find out where I lived and threaten me before the trial. It is not uncommon for rape victims to be intimidated either by the rapist himself or his friends and family. So many women withdraw charges because of that. I could understand it. Why risk your life if no one can protect you?

By then the defence legal team had received a complete copy of the investigation docket with all my personal information. I asked Melvin if my name could be withheld but he told me that they already knew who I was. I felt vulnerable. I had used a false name that night because I didn't want them to know anything about me.

But Melvin reassured me that nothing would happen. Frans and Theuns were not going to go anywhere and, anyway, if I did receive any threats, he said he would immediately tap my phone line and provide police protection.

Still, I didn't feel very safe about it.

The case began to consume my life. There were hair samples that needed to be taken at the district surgeon's office. Melvin accompanied me. I needed his moral support. I didn't want to go through such an intimate experience, but I knew they needed the evidence. It was strange going back to work after having your pubic hair plucked out by a stranger.

Ettienne and my colleagues were understanding. They realised there was no way I could get away from it until the court case. Maybe by then I would have had some kind of catharsis and be able to put the entire ordeal behind me.

I lay awake at night wondering if I would be able to recognise them. I don't know why I thought that – their faces were etched into my brain. Would I faint when I saw them?

I felt physically ill thinking about it. I called Melvin and asked him if the other men who would be used in the parade would have an opportunity to talk to Frans and Theuns. I was concerned that they might influence them and get them to intimidate me afterwards. Once again, Melvin patiently listened and assured me that it wouldn't happen.

The ID parade took place at 10.30 a.m. on the morning of March 3. I drove down to the offices of the Murder and Robbery Squad a bundle of nerves, totally strung out. Mom came with me and reminded me of the person I had been in hospital and that selfsame person who had fought to survive, partly so that I could live to identify them. This was the day.

'You know you will triumph over this. Remember that, my darling,' she said.

Melvin ushered me into a small, drab waiting-room while mom waited in some sort of boardroom.

The three other women, one who had been raped two weeks prior to me and the two others Frans and Theuns had tried to abduct on the Saturday before my attack and the Sunday afterwards, were also shown into the waiting-room.

We were not allowed to speak or have any contact with each other but I felt a bond between us, even though they were strangers.

I wanted it all to be over as we sat there in silence, waiting for our names to be called. My mind drifted back to the night of the attack and specifically the long journey back to the road.

One of the reasons I had fought to live was because I wanted to get these guys. I didn't want them to get away with what they had done. And being there was what I had been fighting for.

Be strong, I told myself. Be as strong as you were that

night.

About an hour later someone called out my name. I was surprised. I did not expect to go in first.

I was ushered from the waiting-room into an ordinary office that had been turned into a makeshift ID room. Immediately to my right was a half-wood, half-glass partition and I turned my back to it. I was glad it was there. I would not have been able to face them. Although it was a relatively flimsy panel, it provided a sense of separateness.

I did not want any distractions. A policeman briefed me but I could not hear what he was saying. I was trembling inside.

Be strong, be calm, be still, I told myself.

Then I turned around and looked at the men through the strips of reflective glass. There was a long row of about 14 of them but I immediately spotted Frans.

He was number six in the line-up, but I didn't say anything. Then I saw Theuns.

The number 13 hung around his neck like a price tag. Both had changed their appearances considerably. Frans had grown his hair and had it parted in the middle. He had a scraggly goatee and was wearing a checked sweat shirt.

Theuns had cut his hair. It was close-cropped and he looked even more of a thug. Both stared vacantly ahead, their hands clasped in front of them.

I wanted to sound confident when I answered.

'They look different, but it's number six and number thirteen,' I announced loud enough for them to hear me.

And then it was over.

I was escorted back to another room where I waited while the other women went in to make their IDs. The entire procedure was very strictly monitored and none of the victims was allowed to have any contact with the others.

Later, one of the women joined me in the room. She looked pale and shaky and I wanted to hug her or say something, but I couldn't.

I hung around waiting to talk to Melvin. Although I was certain I had made a positive ID I still needed to be reassured.

One of the women they had tried to abduct came out looking very dejected. She said she felt devastated because she hadn't been able to identify them and felt it would be 'bad for my case'.

But Melvin soon appeared and wrapped an arm around my shoulder, saying 'Spot on, sweetheart, and in only 30 seconds.'

Mom was chatting to a young man when we re-connected again. I didn't recognise him but she told me that he had been one of the men in the parade.

He had ended up standing next to Frans and had said he could feel his 'evilness' and had had to stop himself from lunging at him.

I couldn't go back to work at that stage. I felt very shaky and mom drove me home. I was exhausted from the fear and the nerves that had consumed me that morning.

I wondered what they had thought, but I doubted whether anything had gone through their minds. But it was over now; well, at least until the trial began.

I called Jan to tell her about the ID parade. I

mentioned that the other women seemed so young, small and frightened and that my heart had ached for them. I said, without really thinking, that I was glad, if that was the right word, that the worst had happened to me because I somehow knew I had the strength to survive it and to push forward with the case.

Now that the ID parade was behind me I wondered if I was going to crack, whether the whole thing would start to take some shape and form in my mind and crash in and crush me.

I wanted to be psychologically ready for the court case so that I knew exactly where I was coming from and why I was doing it.

I had been keeping myself together for my work and the ID parade and now, for a brief moment, I felt no responsibility to stay sane. I wanted to just give up, but I couldn't.

I felt like a sponge that had taken everything in and wondered when I would reach a saturation point when it would all pour out again.

But I seemed to be getting on with my life. There were lots of arrangements that had to be taken care of. Before the attack I had connected with some old school friends and we had talked of planning a reunion. I joined the committee and at the first planning meeting got the whole issue of the attack out of the way. There were those who said they could not believe that it had happened to someone like me but, they added, they knew I would cope.

I wanted everyone to feel comfortable about it. I did not want to be a freak that everyone pitied. But deep down I began to feel the rumblings.

In conversation one night someone asked me if I was angry. It was a difficult question to answer because there were several things I could have been angry about and yet was not.

The guy who asked me the question was amazed at that. I had spent a long time contemplating my life and the way I wanted to live it. I had spent more than three years in London exploring myself, the world and my place in it. It was an experience that had opened me up in so many ways.

I realised I had an immense capacity to be positive and that I naturally looked for the answers to issues that presented themselves as problems.

I had needed to leave Port Elizabeth to learn that. I was so comfortable there, but it was also very parochial. I knew I would not be challenged. I was young and looking for something more. I could have survived there then, just merrily chugging along doing jobs I didn't really want to do. I always tried my best no matter how dreary the work was, but it was not where I saw myself going.

People in PE knew me too well. Everyone had a fixed idea of who I was. Alison who didn't smoke, Alison who didn't drink. Alison who would become the doctor or the lawyer. I felt stifled. I wanted to get away from it all.

In London I would be stripped of all my usual support systems. I wanted to find out who I was, what I was capable of doing without those familiar props. I had many characteristics that had been nurtured and appreciated, but were they really mine? Would they pass the test? Would *I* pass the test?

Away from it all and coping quite well, I came to the realisation that I lived my life not by chance but by choice. My most significant realisation was that no one could make me be or do anything that I did not want, unless I gave them the power to do so.

The same applied to Frans and Theuns. I could surrender my life to those total strangers who had tried to kill me or I could honour myself and find a new meaning to life.

I was determined not to let them take my sanity, my confidence, my character, my personality. These were things that were precious to me, more so now than before, and I would never give them the power to destroy it all. If I remained angry at Frans and Theuns, I would be giving them power over my life.

Driving home from work a few weeks later, I could not miss the *Evening Post* posters lining the streets. 'PE Rape Pair Plead Guilty', they announced in huge black letters.

Frans and Theuns had made a statement admitting that they had kidnapped and raped the first woman at gunpoint on December 4, and to my kidnapping, rape and attack 14 days later.

I learned that the first woman had been pregnant at the time and that she had pleaded with them not to do it. They had also threatened to leave her naked and to kill her, but Frans was quoted as saying 'the urge had passed' once he had raped her.

Then I read, for the first time, the events that led to them crossing my path that night. After a barbecue that afternoon, during which they consumed nine bottles of beer and a 2,5 litre jug of sherry, the report said, Frans and Theuns had decided they wanted to rape someone. They had stalked the streets of Central 'looking for the right woman to rape'.

Theuns was quoted as saying, 'We wanted a nice car and a nice woman. Our goal was to find the woman, take her car, kidnap her, rape her and then kill her.'

So, Frans had known from the start that they had wanted to kill me. The news chilled me. I was astounded at the cold-bloodedness and the randomness of it all. They didn't even know me, but it did not seem to matter, I was at the right place at the wrong time.

Theuns had then apparently become 'bored' while they hunted their prey that night and Frans had told him to go on and that he would find a woman within five minutes and follow him.

And then I pulled into that parking spot. And now I was reading about myself – 'the 27-year-old Noordhoek rape victim'.

The next morning there were huge colour photographs of the two of them in the *Herald*. Both looked straight at the camera. They seemed smug, arrogant, even confident. Their eyes disturbed me the most. They were cold and cruel, as I had remembered them.

Theuns had shaved his head completely and was actually beginning to look demonic.

In this story, which was more extensive than the one I had read the previous evening, it was reported that they had told the magistrate that they had gone home to drink after leaving me for dead.

'We planned again that same morning to take another victim, to kill her and then flee. We were, however, arrested at a later stage the same day,' Theuns had told the court.

They had obviously tasted blood after they had tried

to kill me and were clearly planning to embark on a killing spree that would have taken more innocent lives.

I thought then that if what I had suffered had stopped them from doing just that it would all have been worth while. I had made it to the road and, because I had, someone else's life had been spared.

Theuns also made a public apology in his statement.

'I am sorry for what I did. As I stand here I have great remorse for my deeds. I apologise for what I did to her [me, in other words]. Further, I just ask for mercy,' he said.

I tried to reconcile the words with the photographs on the opposite page. They didn't quite fit. Not only that, but another story had reported that they had posed calmly for the pictures (in one they were leaning casually against a wall sipping soft drinks) immediately after the plea and that they had walked away smiling and laughing. They clearly had no shame and took everyone for fools.

The story went on about how Frans had told the magistrate that he was a 'good husband and father to his child'.

'My wife and child, however, only know my good properties. I know I have a problem. When the bad side comes into me, then it is as if a supernatural power takes over my body.'

I was learning more and more about my tormentors daily, but it still all seemed so surreal.

Of course every time a story appeared in the paper there would be endless discussions between my colleagues, friends and myself. People were outraged at their statements and the obvious discrepancy between their words and their deeds. They were only saying sorry to save their own skins, we all agreed.

One night when I was out with friends someone asked me if I had been traumatised. I said no, although I clearly had been. It was my way of letting him know that I was 'handling' it.

I suppose it was difficult to talk about because trauma is not something you can describe, like an illness. It is a very personal thing and each individual will respond to, handle and react to it differently.

Sure, there are common, clinical symptoms, but each person will have a unique set of responses to a particular trauma. And, generally, we do have a choice as to how we will integrate the experience. I didn't quite know how I would do that, but I did know I had the capacity to turn it into something worth while. I wasn't really thinking about it then, I was merely coping.

What enabled me to do so, I realised, was that I had such a strong sense of self. This was partly to do with my upbringing and my mother's parenting. She had always told both Neale and me that we were special, unique and different. It instilled in me a deep sense of value which was one of the primary reasons I fought to live that night.

I knew I had not really even begun to integrate the rape and the attack into my life and looked forward to a three-week break in Zimbabwe with three friends at the end of March.

I felt guilty about asking for time off again and even more so when Ettienne agreed. But my need for it was far greater than the guilt.

I hoped that I would find space in the unfamiliar surroundings to feel carefree again, as if none of this had happened.

Maybe it would be possible, by getting away physically, to 'pretend' I was as I had been before.

14

ALISON

Rumblings

❖

DIARY ENTRY – NYANGA, Eastern Highlands, Zimbabwe, March 20:

I can smell the smoke of fire and pine needles. It's very quiet. I am surrounded by the sound of crickets and the wind in the trees. I don't know if I am happy, content, or what I really feel.

Right now, I'm just here. I can see stars. They're pretty.

I'm a bit down today. Thinking, but not too much, about what happened to me. The fact that I cannot walk up a little hill without gasping for air really scares me. My stomach is painful all the time. ALL the time. The pain never goes away. I'm so tired of it. So tired of being someone who has to deal with this. I just want to be normal, like I was before.

But I know it is impossible. It makes me want to cry but I can't. I'm tired of this weight of knowing every minute that I should actually be thinking about something more serious. Something big. I can't get away from it, the feeling that I should not just be getting on with my life as if nothing has happened. I'm trying but it is hard. I feel different from everyone else and they treat me that way. Everyone is careful around me.

On the one hand I want to get away from everything and everyone but at the same time I want them around me. I want them to understand and let me know that they care but I also want it to be as if it did not happen. It's not at all easy.

It's so beautiful here.

March 31, Sinamatela Camp, Hwange Game Park:

I still don't know how I feel. I want more attention. I don't know if I am just used to it now or if it is what I really need. Maybe I'm just being self-centred. Behaving like someone who has been thoroughly spoilt.

It has started to dawn on me that what has happened was very traumatic and difficult. The trip has been OK but also frustrating because I don't feel like I belong. I'm just a tag-along. There are times when I wish I could go away and be by myself. I really want to enjoy being here but it is so hard.

In a week I will be home. I wonder what that will be like?

Right now I don't know what it is I am looking

for. I really don't know, at the end of it all, how I am going to cope with this.

Even out here there is no time to be alone and think. I actually need to talk, thinking just turns in on itself, spiralling down or up. I never seem to come up with any conclusion, any decision.

I need to find someone who can listen. I don't know who that is. Maybe Jan.

I haven't really thought much about the trial because every time it pops into my mind I shift it out again. I am expecting it to be horrendous. I am not looking forward to it but a part of me is.

It will be the culmination of it all. I will probably never be able to put an end to it but the court case will be like finishing one race. I'll just have to go on from there.

It's going to be hard and sometimes I don't feel I have the strength to go the distance. What if I just gave up and said to Melvin, drop the charges, I can't go through with it?

But where would that leave me? As long as I am alive I will have to deal with this thing so I might as well face up to it.

I don't think I am capable of suicide. I fought too hard to live. I don't know where that leaves me, though. But the fact that I fought to survive leaves me no choice now. I can't give up now. I just can't.

But where will the strength come from? Must I turn to God? Right now I just feel so weak that I can't deal with it.

Throw my hands in the air saying 'I can't'. But that's not me. I am a fighter, dammit. I must carry on regardless. I wish I could actually break down, that I could cry. I really want to cry. I want to cry for the Ali that is lost for ever. I want to cry for the emotional heartache and torment that I have gone through and that I will go through for the rest of my life.

I want to cry for my body. I want to cry for the carefree life that I had that I did not appreciate enough when it was there.

I did appreciate it but I never thought it was not always going to be that way. I always believed tomorrow is another day, never once stopping to contemplate that this day could be my last.

We talk about living each day as if it is your last but how many of us do that or really believe it?

Still now after this has happened to me I have this insane idea that it can never happen again.

Rubbish. Of course it can. As much as it could happen before it can happen again.

* * *

Zimbabwe had rattled me. Instead of coming home refreshed and with renewed vigour I felt vulnerable and confused. I badly needed a therapist. I had seen one briefly in February and I knew it was time to go back. I also accepted that I needed medication, tranquillisers or anti-depressants, so that I could focus my mind.

I was not coping with my work. I was going through the motions but my performance was nothing compared to what it had been before. I was capable of an enormous work load and had often stayed at the office until 10 p.m. at night. My work had always been important to me and

143

I did not want to let things slide. I was starting to feel guilty that I was not performing.

By now I had come to accept that I would not be able to just pick up my old life. That Alison was no more. Who she was now I still did not know, but I needed to find out.

I called the counsellor I had seen originally. She had been quite unobtrusive and just listened when I spoke. I needed advice now.

In the mean time I contacted my family doctor about medication and she prescribed an anti-depressant. It didn't take away the pain but it helped me to function, to get up every morning and go to work.

I had had one or two nightmares in the early days, but now they returned almost every night. I woke up often, paralysed with fear or in a complete sweat. Either that or I could not sleep at all, afraid that if I closed my eyes I'd give the visions a chance to come alive.

They were extremely vivid dreams. In one of them I was inside my house, in my bedroom. I kept telling myself in the dream that I was dreaming and that I should wake up. Then the scene changed and although I thought I was awake the dream continued with a different scenario.

In the dream I cannot lift my head from the pillow. I feel drugged, heavy, scared. I cannot move. Next door the neighbours are having a party on their balcony, which overlooks my bedroom. I know they are there, but I am paralysed. Suddenly it's daytime and the room is very bright. I know I am not awake yet. I get out of bed and go to the door. I open it and there's another door directly behind it. I open that and there's a sliding door. Door after door. I eventually get through. I have a cell phone and a friend of mine is on the other end. He says 'Hello honey, what's up?' but I do not trust that it is him and tell him I will call back.

I get to the phone, but it's a pay phone and I have no money. I eventually wake up shaking and sweating.

A few nights later I have another dream. This time I'm walking along a country road. There are fields and cottages. I feel danger but try not to appear afraid. I must get home to the other side of the river. A woman befriends me. She is sophisticated, wearing smart clothes. She wears her dark hair in a bob. I trust her. I know she will help me across the river. Once I am on the other side she turns, and I realise she is evil. I cannot run away. A black car pulls up. There are several men inside. I do not fight. There is nothing I can do to get away.

The therapy sessions helped. It was the only space I could find to connect what was in my head to the rest of me. I needed to find a way to link my subconscious with my conscious mind. The dreams were clearly a manifestation of that.

What I needed to do somehow was find a grip, or a way of stopping that overwhelming, paralysing fear. There was always fear, never anger.

It was frustrating trying to fit in the therapy sessions around my work. I would always try to make early morning, lunch time or late afternoon appointments. Sometimes I would get to work at 9 a.m. after a particularly debilitating session and have to deal with clients as if nothing was wrong.

I had trouble trying to keep it all together.

I had this need to see Melvin all the time. He was so cool and level-headed and he wanted to talk about the case. I suspected other people were getting a little tired of it all now. I was obviously trying to pretend that I was coping. I understood that unless someone had personally experienced a trauma of this nature they would not be able to understand the underlying turmoil I felt. And why should they?

I dashed out of the office at odd times to see Melvin. Sometimes it was just to have a cigarette or some coffee. I always felt better afterwards. He was incredibly kind and caring and never ever said he couldn't see me.

Later in the month I heard news that cheered me up considerably. Tiaan was to be given a special citation by the Port Elizabeth Municipality and the SAPS and would be flying to PE to receive the award. I called him immediately to congratulate him. We had telephoned each other regularly. I felt a very close bond with this shy, brave young man and couldn't think of a more deserving person.

He asked me how I was and I told him about my ups and downs. He told me it was only natural that I would see-saw between exhaustion and confusion and that it would take time. We ended our conversation thrilled that we would be reunited.

I started going out less and when I did go out I felt odd, as if I had a secret no one else knew about.

I had always found it easy to mix socially. I liked the company of people, the connection, the swapping of little bits of irrelevant information. But I couldn't do it any more.

There were times when I felt small. I wanted to be a

little girl whom someone protected. I wanted to be looked after and not have to make decisions by myself. I didn't want to worry, plan or concentrate on anything.

As the trial date loomed on June 12 it began to become the entire focus of my life. Before then I had had a preliminary meeting with Melvin at the attorney general's office. Melvin wanted to acquaint me with the procedures, who sat where, where I would sit, where Frans and Theuns would be seated in relation to me. He showed me the witness box and told me that I should address all my answers to the judge and not the lawyers who would be asking the questions.

I was sent to a psychologist for an assessment that would later be handed to the court. It was all so tiring. But the one thing I wanted to do was be utterly ready for the trial. Several people kept reassuring me that when that was over it would all be behind me. I almost looked forward to it because of that. This, I thought, would be the last lap in the race.

15

ALISON

My Day in Court

———————◆———————

CASE NUMBER CC15/95, otherwise known as 'the Noordhoek ripper' trial, kicked off in the Supreme Court in Port Elizabeth on the mild winter's morning of June 12, 1995. Ten days had been set aside for the hearing and once again Ettienne had given me time off to attend the proceedings.

I felt guilty about taking so much time off work but I wanted to sit in every day. I did not want to miss a single word or nuance and was determined to see it through until the end, until I saw Frans and Theuns being sentenced and sent down the stairs to the prison cells.

I woke that morning feeling quite composed. A few months earlier I had dreaded this day, but now I was a little excited. More apprehensive than excited, I should say. It was the same feeling one gets before going in to write an exam or start a long race. But it was a contest I had been preparing for for months. I had lived it, breathed it, dreamed it. And now it was about to begin.

The previous week Frans had called some sort of press conference at the offices of the Murder and Robbery Squad. Every weekend paper had carried a photograph of him with his hair shaved at the sides and the rest swept up into a minuscule, mushroom-like pony tail at the top of his head. I couldn't believe it. He sat there at a table, a cup of coffee casually in front of him, talking confidently to the journalists who seemed to have lapped it all up.

He had had a 'change of heart', he told the press, and was calling the conference to 'denounce Satanism and explain how he was possessed by demons'. He now regarded himself as an 'apostle Paul who killed Christians and people in synagogues but managed to change and turn to Jesus'.

That weekend, he said, he would be undergoing some sort of exorcism in the cells. His wife Natalie and his two-year-old son Joshua would also be 'freed' of the demons he had brought into their lives.

The whole thing smacked of a crude and cheap publicity stunt and I was amazed that the police had allowed him to talk to the press while he was still in custody and especially so close to the start of the court case.

I doubted that his so-called conversion had happened at all, although I would not have begrudged him his salvation, if it had been true. The timing was so wrong and it was all so obvious. I thought it was a clear last-ditch attempt on his part to gain favour with the authorities and the people of Port Elizabeth.

I noticed that Theuns was not there and wondered

why. Perhaps it wouldn't have looked 'good' if both of them had suddenly 'found the Lord' and 'seen the light'. It would have made the entire bizarre circus even more improbable.

Frans was shrewder than I had thought. He was clearly a skilled manipulator and enjoyed all the attention that I felt he certainly did not deserve. Still, no one bought it.

Everyone agreed there was nothing sincere about this sudden turn-around, this miraculous change of heart.

My dad collected me from my home and drove me to the Supreme Court. It is an austere and grand building with grey marble floors, plush maroon carpets and imposing columns. Melvin had already shown me around so I did not feel unfamiliar in the surroundings. There was an incredible buzz inside and outside the court. The place was overrun with journalists, photographers, news cameramen and curious members of the public. Melvin escorted us through a back entrance so that we could escape the crush. As we snaked our way through the corridors I was afraid that we might bump into Frans and Theuns somewhere. Luckily it didn't happen.

Everyone was clearly expecting a sensational trial and I felt as if all eyes were on me as I walked in.

The big news in the paper that morning was the sudden and mysterious withdrawal 'for ethical reasons' of Frans's attorney, Henry Lerm. Mr Lerm had sat in on Frans's 'press conference' on the Friday and I wondered whether something had happened there that had triggered his decision. He was keeping mum about it though.

Criminal Court A had started filling up with people

quite early in the morning. It was a small, wood-panelled room, plush but claustrophobic with no view of the outside world. It felt like a sealed pod or a quarantine station cut off from everything else.

The first day was taken up with the testimony of the first woman, the young Technikon student Frans had raped in February. Frans was charged separately with that case but Theuns remained next to him in the dock.

I was not allowed into the court until I had given my testimony so I spent the morning in a small waiting-room smoking cigarettes, chatting to various friends and drinking endless cups of coffee.

Mom, dad and friends were inside the court and I wished I could have been there.

The woman's evidence made the front page of the afternoon newspapers. Apparently she had broken down while giving testimony and I wondered if it would happen to me too.

It was the first time I had read the details of the case and they were horrific. Frans had abducted the woman while she was doing a survey on a pizza parlour in Central. She had been employed by a rival company to 'spy' on the business. She was a sitting duck. Frans had pounced on her and shoved a gun to her head before telling her to move over.

He then drove her out towards Noordhoek where he sexually assaulted her and then raped her. As the story unfolded in newsprint I sympathised with the woman. I knew what she must have felt.

After raping the terrified girl, Frans drove her to a roadhouse and bought her a sandwich and a rose.

His sick gesture nauseated me. The arrogance and

audacity of it.

Frans had raped her again after that, all the while chatting to her as if she was a long-lost girlfriend. After that he dropped her off, telling her that she was 'an amazing person' and that he hoped he could 'make it up to her some time'.

She had been so traumatised by the three-hour ordeal that she had not told anyone. She had gone home to her parents too petrified to speak. A week later she had told a friend who had urged her to report it to the police. It had affected her so badly, she said, that at times she had gone out at night, deliberately placing herself in dangerous situations. It is apparently a common reaction in a victim who is suffering from post-traumatic shock.

June 13. Today I would get my day in court, but only after Frans and Theuns's second victim, the young pregnant woman, had testified during the morning session. Once again the trial dominated the morning's papers. Frans had been convicted the previous day of two charges of rape, abduction and indecent assault. Sentencing for those charges would come later at the end of the trial when the judge handed down a final verdict on all the charges.

That day I wore an outfit a good friend, Nicki, had designed for the occasion. It was a light blue trouser suit. I wanted to look good. I wanted Frans and Theuns to see I was strong and that I was holding it all together. The suit was like armour, it protected me and made me feel confident. I also thought about the many meetings I had had with the prosecution advocates Grant Buchner and Hannelie Bakker before the trial. They had taken me through how they would lead the evidence and had prepared me for questions the defence might ask. I was nervous but ready.

A surprise witness was called by the state that morning. The woman, Dane de Bruyn, had called the police after reading about my attack and reported that two men fitting the descriptions of Frans and Theuns had tried to accost her while she was parking her car, in broad daylight, in Humewood that same day.

It was 12.30 p.m. on the afternoon of my attack when they had tried to wrench open her car door. They had fled when she managed to lock the doors after Frans had looked away for 'a split second'.

That split second had saved her life.

I had watched as the second young victim had arrived at the court that morning. She looked so vulnerable with her beautiful pregnant belly. She was close to term and I hoped that testifying would not be too much of an ordeal for her.

Although I wanted to, I didn't feel that I could talk to her. We had only one thing in common. Both of us had been raped by Frans and Theuns. I caught her eye and hoped that she could see my empathy and that I felt strongly for her.

I would have to sit it out in the waiting-room while she testified. I knew I would feel safe there, away from all the eyes that watched me so intently. I was thrilled as I stepped inside to see Tiaan perched on a bench, grinning from ear to ear. We gave each other huge hugs. I was so pleased to see him. He is so special, so quiet and self-effacing. My special hero. We were not allowed to talk to each other about the case that morning which was, of course, hugely frustrating.

Instead we caught up with other news and talked about the award he was going to receive for saving my life. A glittering ceremony had been arranged in the City Hall where the award, given jointly by the South African Police and the City of Port Elizabeth, was to be handed over.

I felt most comfortable around him and Melvin, my two new friends. They were in this with me.

The court adjourned for lunch before I was called. I was growing tense; I wanted it to all begin now.

Mom, dad, a few friends and I remained in the waiting-room munching our take-away food.

There was an almost festive air in the room. Everyone talked around the court case, trying to relax, but I knew they couldn't. They were just as nervous as I was.

I didn't really want to be there. Actually I didn't feel as if I was there at all.

I could hardly eat and felt totally detached from it all.

I actually wanted to be with Melvin and Tiaan. They knew exactly how I felt.

After lunch everyone else disappeared into the court again, including Frans's wife, Natalie who had come with her father David Naidoo each day to hear evidence. She was a pretty young woman with short hair and striking oriental features. She looked such a child and I wondered how she could still support Frans knowing everything she knew now.

She was clearly under his spell and I don't mean that in a demonic sense. Frans was an arch manipulator and a supremely confident liar who had convinced her several times, even after he had been arrested, that everyone else was to blame and not him.

I waited for my name to be called out and when it was it sounded so weird. It felt as if they were summoning someone else.

The same odd feeling of detachment I had felt the night of the attack returned as I stepped through the side door a young policeman held open.

I saw them immediately. Frans and Theuns were sitting in the dock, right in my field of vision. Melvin had warned me that I would see them first and that I should not look at them. I looked away. There was a blur of faces and I caught a glimpse of one or two familiar smiles. Everyone kept their eyes on me as I stepped into the wooden witness stand.

I was acutely aware of Frans and Theuns sitting there. I could feel their presence. Grant, Hannelie and Melvin sat in front of them and smiled at me as I took up my position.

I looked at Judge Chris Jansen and he too gave me a little smile. He was a handsome, fit-looking, distinguished man with a kind face and a calm demeanour and he immediately made me feel at ease.

Grant stood up and led me through my evidence. It took two hours to get through my testimony. Throughout it all I felt disconnected, apart from myself. There was total silence in the court as I recounted the events of that night.

I could hear my own voice, it sounded clear and confident. Every now and again, after a particularly gruesome bit in the story, I would hear a gasp from the gallery.

As I relayed some of the smaller details of the night, I wondered what Frans and Theuns were thinking. I

155

hoped that they were shocked and amazed that I had remembered everything so clearly. It was very tempting, but I stopped myself from looking at them.

When it was finally over I felt a tremendous sense of accomplishment. I felt triumphant and very proud of myself. I did not cry, I did not break down. I told it as it had happened.

When I had finished the defence lawyers cross-questioned me. Frans's counsel, an Advocate Frost, seemed lost. He had been appointed to defend Frans after Henry Lerm had stepped down. He was clearly not enjoying it.

He could not really defend Frans and at times I felt he was grasping at straws, quibbling about minor details as if he had to pretend to be putting up some semblance of an argument.

Theuns's advocate irritated me. He, too, felt he had to try and poke holes in a watertight case. The judge admonished him several times as he badgered me over and over again on some minor detail, like whether Theuns was actually in the car when Frans had leaned over to strangle me. I could see where he was going. He was trying to suggest that Theuns was not in the car, and that if he had been he might have been able to stop Frans.

He didn't listen to my answers and hammered away at the same pointless question until the judge stopped him. I stuck to my guns. I was proud of how vividly and clearly I recalled things.

And then suddenly it was all over. I had wanted to say so much more and could not believe I had covered so much ground. I left the courtroom through a side entrance and re-entered through the back to take my seat between my mom and dad afterwards. Mom squeezed my hand and dad stroked my back.

'You were wonderful,' mom leaned over and whispered.

Frans and Theuns had their backs to me now and I found Frans's water fountain hairstyle ridiculous. I was pleased I did not have to see their faces.

Then Tiaan took the stand. He strode confidently into the court. He was a wonderful witness.

He was soft-spoken but totally poised. I was so touched that he had flown down from Johannesburg to do this. I was proud of him.

There were more gasps and shaking of heads in the public gallery as Tiaan told the judge about my injuries and that we had waited more than 90 minutes for the ambulance to arrive.

As Dr Angelov took the stand Tiaan moved in next to me in the public gallery. People were riveted by the medical evidence, and so was I. It was the first time I had heard, in such detail, about my injuries and what Dr Angelov had had to do in surgery. I was so proud of him too.

He ended his testimony by saying that he could not explain medically how I had survived.

'It was a miracle,' he told the judge.

And that was the end of the State's case. What was left now was for Judge Jansen to convict or acquit Frans and Theuns of the charges. After that each legal team would have the opportunity to present evidence 'in mitigation of sentence'.

Judge Jansen spoke quickly and deliberately. He convicted Frans on two counts of rape, two charges of indecent assault and two of abduction and further charges of attempted murder and theft. Theuns was convicted on the same charges. I wondered what sentence would be handed down later.

I was relieved, but it was not an unexpected finding. There was no way they could not have been convicted. Judge Jansen cleared the public gallery and the press bench when Gillian Smale, a psychologist who had interviewed me and the two other women, was called to testify. Melvin asked me if I wanted to sit outside while she presented her psychological evaluation of me.

Gillian had actually requested that I not be present. She had thought that her testimony of my condition might actually impact on my future handling of the trauma, but I stubbornly insisted on being there. Only my mom and dad were allowed to remain and I was comforted by their presence.

I was ready to hear it all.

16

DR GILLIAN SMALE

Inside Alison's mind

———◆———

VERBATIM REPORT FROM COURT RECORDS

In my eight years as a clinical psychologist I have often been asked to prepare reports on the psychological state of rape victims for the ensuing court cases. I developed a special interest in Rape Trauma Syndrome after I began training counsellors for Rape Crisis and Life Line's crisis branch.

Rape Trauma Syndrome (RTS) and Post Traumatic Stress Disorder (PTSD) are reactions to the ordeal of rape or a traumatic, usually violent experience, and follow a particular course, although this varies from individual to individual.

Generally, most rape survivors experience an initial state of shock. This can be expressed in a controlled manner during which feelings are suppressed, or in a very chaotic way where emotions are vented and the survivor disintegrates emotionally and struggles outwardly.

There is no specific duration to this state of shock. For some women it can last only days, others months or even years. It can also be delayed or immediate.

After the initial shock a period – the 'recoil' stage – generally follows. This is when the survivor appears to be functioning and coping with the trauma but remains inwardly in crisis. After recoil comes re-integration or a re-organisational state when the trauma will resurface and manifest in feelings of anger, apathy, fear, depression, fear of death, shame, self-loathing and guilt.

These feelings can result in various types of stress-related behaviour. Although not common, there are survivors who may respond by deliberately exposing themselves to dangerous situations in an attempt to undo feelings of powerlessness. Other manifestations include social withdrawal, irritability, a fear of intimacy, uncontrollable rage and even suicidal thoughts. Many women may re-experience the trauma years later when a specific event or set of circumstances triggers the memory.

I was approached by the State to evaluate the three women who had been raped by Frans du Toit and Theuns Kruger. The women were given a personality and psychological test known as the MMPI and this was followed up with more extensive interviews with the survivors themselves, members of their families and close friends.

Alison has been exposed to a trauma that is considered 'beyond the normal range of human experience'. She has been raped, violently assaulted and has experienced near death.

In such a case, the more severe the physical violence and the near death experience, the deeper the psychological trauma. Because of Alison's personality, which is typically emotionally over-controlled, she tended to show a lot of concern for others' feelings and initially appeared composed after the attack.

She did not display feelings such as fear, anger, shame, helplessness and emotional disintegration that are typically expressed by rape survivors. During my interviews with those who knew her she was frequently described as 'coping very well'.

However, in psychological terms and in terms of RTS, she was in fact in a prolonged state of shock and the coping that had been described by the press and by friends was a manifestation of emotional shock.

This period of shock and outward coping was necessitated by Alison's need to minimise worry to her friends and family and also her need to feel that she could cope professionally and emotionally. It has, nevertheless, led to the development and the exacerbation of PTSD.

At the time of my assessment of her, PTSD was becoming chronic and had already lasted six months. As far as I could tell, her symptoms were worsening.

Alison's experience could be considered to have been comprised of three separate traumas (rape, assault and near death) and she exhibited specific symptoms of PTSD at the time of our interview.

She often re-experienced the trauma through nightmares, had recurrent and intrusive episodes of reliving of the event as well as sudden recollections. This happened particularly when her breathing was impaired and she relived the memories and the sensations of having her throat cut.

She also experienced constricted or numb emotions accompanied by feelings of social detachment. This is a typical reaction to trauma when the feelings were too painful or too overwhelming to experience. The numbness develops as a defence against those feelings.

All of these reactions impaired Alison's general sense of well-being and are potentially disruptive to intimate relationships. She was also hyper alert and jumpy and exhibited sleep disturbance that in turn impaired her energy and her work performance. She also had trouble with her memory and concentration.

At the time of the assessment I felt that Alison had symptoms of a Major Depression and even though she was on strong anti-depressant medication she continued to experience these symptoms which affected her work and her social interaction. Even though she did socialise extremely well, Alison felt and probably will always feel different to others because of this bizarre experience.

It could continue to make her feel emotionally isolated as it was an experience with which few people she would ever mix with could truly identify.

I learned during the interview that Alison was nervous about sexual relationships. Before the attack she had enjoyed men's company but since then she had avoided intimate relationships and had, on one occasion, become anxious when she was kissed on a date. She was also self-conscious about her physical scars and felt they inhibited her sexually.

Alison was a former head girl and was used to being popular and supportive of others. She was accustomed to being seen by her friends and her family as a strong and independent individual.

Living up to these expectations meant that she had to suppress much of the horror she had experienced in order to maintain that strong image for other people.

This, I concluded, was ultimately exacerbating her depression and her feelings of alienation, helplessness and loneliness. Although she had regained much of her outward independence since the attack, Alison remained hyper vigilant and was nervous about being alone. She was constantly on her guard and felt anxious, which of course contributed to her feeling continually exhausted.

My opinion at the time was that Alison was suffering from chronic, as opposed to acute, PTSD. Her prognosis was not good and I felt that her characteristic over-control and inability to let go presented a strong likelihood that her condition could deteriorate further.

She might well reach a point of emotional exhaustion where she could no longer ward off her psychological turmoil and she would then risk emotional breakdown. What counted in Alison's favour, though, was her family and her network of friends and the fact that she had been extremely well adjusted emotionally before the attack.

Because of this she has found meaning in the incident and her attempts to help others by talking about her suffering had also helped her to make sense of it.

I felt that Alison might lapse into a severe depression if she discontinued her anti-depressant medication which was controlling the physical symptoms of depression.

17

ALISON

My tormentor becomes real

———◆———

I LISTENED TO Gillian's testimony of my psychological state quite dispassionately. Was this the detachment she was talking about? Everything she said had made rational sense to me. Yes, I did feel hyper vigilant, I was anxious and knew I was different to everyone else now.

It was so strange being able to grasp intellectually what she was saying but not be able to connect with the underlying feelings. I knew they lurked there, simmering away like a volcano. I wondered whether I would ever break down, fall in on myself and become a gibbering wreck? It was still too early to tell.

I was sure also that Gillian was presenting the court with the worst case scenario. It was important for the judge to hear what was going on or not going on inside my head and that what Frans and Theuns had done would affect me for the rest of my life.

I did not think it was necessarily true that I would slip into a severe major depression later. What I did know was that the one per cent of me that had kept going that night would keep me from slipping over the edge. If I had had the strength to ignore what 99 per cent of me had wanted to do, which was just to die, then I could access that again when I needed to. I wanted to live then and I still wanted to live now.

Like that night in the car when they drove me around, I knew I would take each new set of circumstances as they manifested. It was the one per cent that had got me to the road. Tiaan would have driven past there anyway, but if I had not made the effort to get there he would not have been able to save my life. The lifelines were thrown out for me to grasp many times that night, but I too had had to make an effort to reach out for them.

No matter how long or how difficult my recovery, I was at least determined to try. I wondered how much the anti-depressants were helping.

At first I was against taking pills, but mom reminded me that I had been through a severe physical and mental shock and that the anti-depressants would help my body to cope chemically with that.

I supposed she was right. At that stage I think the medication helped me to get up in the morning and at least try and get on with it all, but I was determined to get off it as soon as I could.

After Gillian's testimony the court started to fill up again. On less dramatic days people would trickle in and out, but on the major days, like today, everyone wanted a ringside seat. I sat with mom and dad in the front row with a rear view of Frans and Theuns.

I was fascinated by the machinations of the law and the court. It was really like watching an episode of *LA Law*, except that I was startled every now and again when I heard my name spoken.

That afternoon Grant Buchner asked the court to declare both men 'dangerous criminals' under a new section of the Criminal Procedures Act. I suspect he made the request because the death penalty had just been abolished in South Africa and he wanted to make sure that if they were sentenced to life imprisonment they would never be eligible for parole. They would have to spend the rest of their lives in jail.

Grant also suggested they be sent to the Elizabeth Donkin Hospital for psychiatric observation and evaluation to strengthen his application. The judge said he would consider Grant's request after he heard evidence in mitigation.

It was a Friday and I thought it unlikely that Frans or Theuns would be called to take the stand to speak out on their own behalf so late in the day. At that stage we also had no idea whether they would actually be testifying, whether I would ever hear the story from their own mouths.

It would be better for their case if they did not testify, I thought. If they opened their mouths they would definitely ruin any remote chance that the court might be more lenient.

Still, I thought, Frans at least might not be able to resist the temptation to turn the spotlight on himself.

On the Monday we would all find out.

I left court that Friday knowing that we were nearing the end of this episode. It was all moving on, but I was not ready yet to let it go. After the sentencing I'd be able to sit down and decide what I really wanted to do. I didn't know what I'd feel or whether I would experience some epiphany when the judge handed down his ruling.

I had a busy weekend ahead and I was pleased. I needed a break from the routine of the court.

That night, my boss Ettienne and his wife Hanlie hosted a bash for 'Ali's Support Group' – all the friends who had supported my family and me – at their house.

It was a real party with ribbons and balloons, tables laden with food and two very special and huge bouquets of long-stemmed, coloured roses festooned with cards with messages from my old friends, my new friends and my family.

I was deeply touched by everyone's support and this was my way of thanking them all for bolstering me over the months. I felt so privileged and spoilt. Melvin and his wife were there and so was Tiaan, my mom and all my special friends. I forgot about everything and simply enjoyed myself. I had always believed that you could tell someone's worth by their friends and that night I was overwhelmed with emotion and gratitude for the collection of people, some of whom had travelled from Cape Town and Johannesburg, who considered themselves to be my friends. I felt truly blessed.

On the Monday morning I was back at the court, not knowing what to expect.

We learned that Frans would be taking the stand to testify in his own defence. Theuns's lawyer told the court he would not be saying anything.

By now I had become an objective observer, a mere onlooker.

Frans shuffled out from the dock and stepped up into the witness box. It was the first time that I could observe him at such close proximity and in such safe circumstances. I was fascinated.

I also knew the press would be watching my every move. So often in reports I had read descriptions of my body language and what it was supposed to have signified. Leaning over to ask my mom where we should have lunch could be interpreted as something entirely different. I did not want anyone to read my thoughts so I looked at Frans through a mask.

He was thin and drawn and still had that silly pony tail on top of his head. But to me he was no longer Frans who had tried to kill me. He was just another criminal who was standing trial for attempted murder and rape. I was watching my own movie.

When he first spoke I was surprised at how vocal he was. He began by apologising for his hairstyle, telling the judge that he did not have the 'adequate facilities' in prison to get a 'decent' haircut.

He started at the beginning, telling the court that he was the son of an Aliwal North policeman and that he had once had a good relationship with the members of his family. They were devout Christians, 'churchgoing people', and respected members of the community.

He too had been a good Christian and as a child had gone to church regularly although he had never been confirmed. It was some time during his youth that he first began to dabble in Satanism and he didn't consider it appropriate 'to stand in front of a dominee and lie about my beliefs'.

At school, he said, he had fallen in with a bad crowd,

'dagga smokers, hippies and surfers', although he didn't think he was the kind of person who was easily influenced by others.

He was asked to leave school after a mysterious fire in one of the hostels. He burnt the building, he said, because he had listened to heavy metal music and the 'backtracking' had inspired him. The music had harboured hidden messages, like subliminal advertising, that subconsciously urged the listener to commit various criminal deeds.

For someone who claimed not to be easily influenced I thought it quite ridiculous that he was so susceptible to the music.

When he began to unravel the mysteries of Satanism, the rituals and the rites, I became even more fascinated with him as a person. Suddenly Frans du Toit was fleshed out, given form and substance. He was a real human being.

He was opening a window into an underworld I had never known and doubted even existed. It was so far from ordinary life I could not help but be gripped by it all. Maybe I would now find an answer to the one question I could not fathom. Why had he tried to kill me? What purpose would the taking of my life have served in his life?

There were those who said I should be angry with him. This man had tried to murder me and here he was calmly trying to excuse his deeds. But I could not be angry; he meant nothing to me. He became less and less human as I watched him display no outward sign of emotion or any remorse.

The detachment was what was helping me to go to

court each day and watch the spectacle unfold.

Frans said he had begun seriously to explore Satanism after moving to a school in Adelaide. There he had met a young woman on a train one afternoon. She was a matric pupil at the same school and they had been mysteriously drawn to each other. She was the head witch of a coven and he had believed she possessed 'supernatural powers'.

He had seen her casting spells on people, hoping to bring ill fortune in their lives. She had shown him the secrets of black magic and had even summoned demons that spoke through her in gruff, manly voices.

He claimed he could feel the presence of a demon in a room. After making itself heard, he said, the physical environment would grow cold and a stench would permeate everything. He had become convinced then that demonic forces existed and he began to believe and trust in them.

From there, Frans's life began the downward spiral that led him ultimately to this court. He had never finished school and had failed standard 7 twice. In an attempt to help him, his parents sent him off to the army. He was stationed in Kimberley and had fought on the border in the then South West Africa for 19 months. Even there the Satanists had sniffed each other out and had formed a 'cell'.

After his national service he took a menial job at a mine in Welkom where his father had persuaded someone to give his son a chance. He failed at that also. In Welkom he had met and married a young woman who had no idea of his Satanist beliefs. They had had a child, a daughter, before the relationship ended 18 months later.

He abandoned her and headed back to Port Elizabeth and 'the sea' around 1990. The only job on offer was another menial one, driving a delivery truck for a stationery company. He lost that job after it was discovered that he had stolen money, but the company later dropped the charges.

Frans continued his itinerant lifestyle, heading for Johannesburg where he found work in a night-club and then returning to Port Elizabeth where he married his second wife, Natalie, in 1993.

During that time, he said, he had performed some sort of ritual asking the devil to give him a son who would be born on his birthday. He also asked that Natalie become so spellbound by him that she would never have the strength to leave.

The request, he said, was 'honoured' when his son Joshua was indeed born on his birthday, July 6, and Natalie had stood by him throughout the trial. This was proof, he maintained, of the power of Satan and his demons.

The crimes he had committed, he told the court, could be blamed on a demon called Incubus that he had accepted into his life when he was 15. This demon, he said, made him sexually insatiable but also highly attractive to women. It gave him 'telekinetic' powers that enabled him to move objects using only his eyes.

I wondered then, if women had found him so desirable, why it was that he needed to take sex by force. Surely he would not have needed to rape women if they were lining up for him?

He had met Theuns, he said, in June 1994 when he moved in with an aunt who lived across the street from his flat. Frans had run a shebeen and Theuns had regularly bought liquor from him.

At the time, Theuns was recovering from a shotgun wound. He had accidentally shot himself in the foot. I wanted to laugh out loud when I heard that. Such a cliché. It must be quite difficult to shoot yourself in the foot with a shotgun.

Frans said that at first he did not realise that Theuns was only 19 but their friendship grew and Theuns often confided in him, told him his problems, his life story, and the fact that he felt unwelcome in his aunt's home. He had slowly begun to introduce him to Satanism, he said, taking Theuns on a midnight jaunt to the St Mary's graveyard.

They had talked about the power of demons and Theuns had said that he too wanted that power.

Frans had started calling him 'Damien' which apparently meant 'son of the devil'. He did this, he said, to help Theuns with his 'low self-esteem' and 'to cheer him up'.

The night he abducted me, he said, he was 'under the influence' of his own demon, Incubus. Earlier, while he and Theuns had been barbecuing and drinking in his backyard, Incubus had spoken to him and told him to 'rape and kill a pretty woman'.

One of the lawyers asked Frans if he knew me and he said he had seen me before that night.

I admonished myself for being so unobservant. When and how had he seen me? Was it while I worked in my garden at the weekends? The little patch was quite exposed to Russel Road.

Advocate Frost asked him how he knew me and he

replied that he had often seen me park my car and walk into my house.

It was quite coincidental, he added, that I had pulled my car into the parking space that night.

He had not planned it that way.

'Alison just happened to be in the wrong place at the wrong time,' he said.

When he used my first name I felt a physical shock ripple through me. It was so personal. I felt he had no right to utter my name.

He went on, saying he had shoved the knife into my ribs and not my neck. I disagreed. I remembered it at my neck. He wasn't thrilled with my car, he said. It was old and not quite what he had had in mind.

He had wanted a reliable car because he knew he would not be able to rape me in the city and needed to drive quite a distance. He was worried that the car might break down.

Pity, I thought to myself, that I had looked after Reginald so carefully. He was a temperamental car and often gave me trouble but not, unfortunately, that night.

He claimed that Theuns had been under the impression that I was actually a friend of his as he had introduced me as such. That, and the fact that the car wasn't a 'good' one.

I knew he was lying. Both of them had been out 'looking for a girl to abduct' and when Frans arrived with me in the car Theuns was more than aware that I was their next victim.

Frans said that Incubus had controlled everything that night. It was the demon that had told him to rape me, it was the demon that had called Theuns and exhorted him to rape me as well, it was the demon that had told him to kill me. It was a loud, stern voice in his head, he said, a voice he simply could not ignore.

Then he described how he felt at my response to his throttling me. I was riveted.

He said he had been surprised at how 'peaceful' – that was the exact word he used – I had been when he had gripped my neck and I had asked him not to kill me.

For a split second, he said, he had wanted to let go, but Incubus had cheered him on.

He had said he was sorry because 'his hands were tied' and it was 'outside my power'.

'I strangled her until I thought she was dead,' he said. The words just spewed from his mouth, they rolled off his tongue, undramatically, clinically.

Theuns, he added, had been shocked that he had strangled me. I doubted that somehow; he seemed to be protecting him all the time, intimating that Theuns did not know what was going on.

After I had passed out they both dragged me from the car and flung me down on the ground outside. It was Theuns who had asked him if he thought I was dead.

'Let's find out,' he had replied, drawing the knife and stabbing my stomach and abdomen.

He had aimed for that region because he had wanted to rupture my kidneys and my liver, but Incubus had told him to destroy 'her private parts'.

Theuns, he said, had been sitting a little way off calmly watching all of this, but he suddenly jumped up and joined in, slashing me across my neck with his large knife.

The first cut, said Frans, was only superficial although

it bled. It was the sight of the blood, he claimed, that drove him 'berserk'. He elbowed Theuns out of the way and began to cut wildly at my throat with the smaller knife.

When he had finished, he said, he felt an 'extremely strange feeling' like 'God was looking at me and was asking me "What have you done? Now you have gone too far." ' The feeling, he said, unsettled him.

They had discussed whether I could have survived and decided that it was impossible. Theuns then rummaged through everything in the car, tossing out what he did not want.

Why, Advocate Frost asked, did Theuns go through the clothes in the car?

Frans replied that he thought he might be looking for more information on me, perhaps an address, an identity book to find out 'who she really was' or 'where she worked'.

Why did he need to know, I wondered? I was supposedly dead to him. What perverse urge was this to learn my identity? Would I only have become real to him once I was dead?

They drove home after 'finishing her off'. They did not speak en route, he said. I had always wondered about that. He also said he had tossed his weapon, the smaller knife, out into the bushes, which is why the police never found it.

After abandoning the car they had sat down to drink their last beer before going to sleep. While they were doing that, I was crawling and crashing my way back to the road.

They slept late the next morning, until 11 a.m., said

Frans, and then they got up and made breakfast with the knife Theuns had used.

It still had my blood on it, he said, and Theuns was 'very chuffed with it'.

An audible gasp rose from the public gallery. People could just not hide their shock at the callousness of these two men. I also noticed that several times while he was testifying, Frans would glance away from the judge and look at the public gallery. Occasionally I would hear a sharp intake of breath as if people were afraid of the evil that hid behind those cold and steely eyes, afraid that if he looked at them it would somehow touch and contaminate them.

Once I did catch his eye and a chill ran through me. I feared him with every cell in my body.

Frans said he and Theuns had planned to kill someone else the day after 'killing' me and that he was actually 'relieved' that he had been arrested.

Throughout his testimony it was clear that Frans was trying to protect Theuns. But lies will out.

If Theuns was merely a misguided innocent, why was he so 'chuffed' with the bloodied knife?

I would find out more about Theuns later after he had been examined by a psychologist. I was curious to learn about his life and what had gone so horribly wrong.

Frans stepped down from the witness stand and I looked away. I did it every time he and Theuns were led back to the cells in the afternoons. I did not want to catch their eyes. I did not want to deal with that.

After Frans, Colonel Kobus Jonker of the police's occult-related crime unit testified. He said he was convinced that Frans had not been possessed by the demon at the time as he had claimed. He said he had had years of experience with Satanists and people who were possessed, and that Frans was most certainly responsible for his own actions.

'Although following Satan is not a crime in itself, any person who chooses to do so does it knowing that they will be required, at some time, to commit a crime.'

Colonel Jonker said if Frans had really been possessed he would have raped his own wife when the demon was awakened. He would also not have had the presence of mind, as he did in one of the rapes, to wear a condom to 'prevent the woman from falling pregnant'.

Also, Frans's very clear recollection of all the rapes and my attempted murder was proof that he had not been possessed. Colonel Jonker firmly believed that Satanism existed and that there were people who were possessed.

But, he added, the person had a choice as to whether or not he would obey the demon.

'If a demon merely instigates a crime by suggesting it, the person can refuse to obey,' he said. 'The person has that choice. If he commits a crime under the influence of a demon, he will not know about it or remember it afterwards.'

He added that people who were genuinely possessed often showed tremendous remorse and guilt for their deeds after an exorcism. This was something that had never happened with Frans.

Frans's wife Natalie and his parents also testified that day. I felt sorry for all of them. His parents in particular. They seemed so bewildered by what their son had done. Frans hung his head when his mother testified; he was clearly ashamed of himself.

Natalie looked like the young girl she still was. I felt sorry that she was so in love with Frans that she could not see him for what he was.

At the end of a very long day the Judge postponed the trial to July 31. I would have a welcome two-week break from it all.

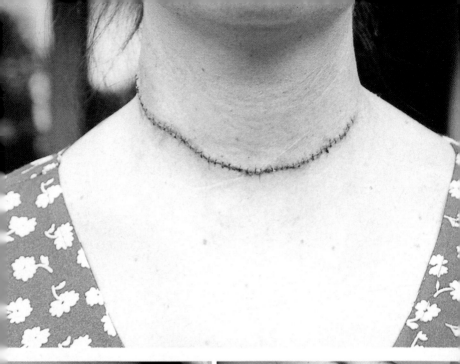

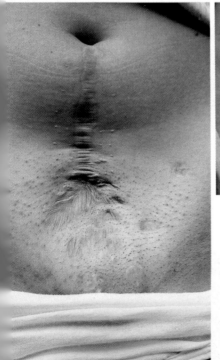

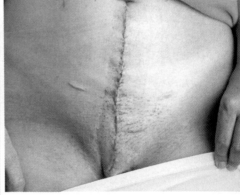

Top: Neck wound after plastic surgery (January 1996)

Below left: Stomach scarring before the second operation to repair a hernia (January 1996)

Below right: Stomach after reparative surgery (January 1996)

Above left: Tiaan Eilerd with some of the awards he received for saving my life (Photo: Jack Cooper, *Eastern Province Herald*)

Above right: With Dr Angelov in the same casualty room to which I was admitted on the night of the attack (Photo: Tienie)

Below: Court evidence: Theuns's knife

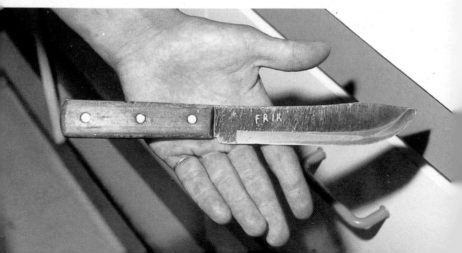

Above: Frans du Toit and Theuns Kruger outside the magistrate's court in Port Elizabeth (Photo: *Eastern Province Herald*)

Below left: Frans du Toit holding a press conference (Photo: *Eastern Province Herald*)

Below right: The newspaper coverage of the case was overwhelming (Photo: Tienie)

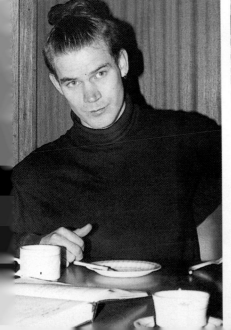

Above: Receiving the first *Femina* Woman of Courage Award. Pictured with my mom, Marianne Thamm and Jane Raphaely, February 1996 (Photo: courtesy of *Femina* magazine/Karina Turok)

Below left: Some of the many magazines that covered my story (Photo: Tienie)

Below right: With Inspector Melvin Humpel, the officer in charge of my case, with the award he received for the way in which he conducted the investigation, September 1995 (Photo: *Die Burger* Oos-Kaap)

Above: Marrying my prince, February 1997 (Photo: Courtesy of *Femina* magazine/Neil Hermann)

Below: With mom and dad on my wedding day (Photo: courtesy of *Femina* magazine/Neil Hermann)

Left: Addressing 500 people at an MTN Mega-Breakfast event in Johannesburg, July 1998 (Photo: Shawn Benjamin)

Below: Signing autographs at the same event

Below left: With Tienie at the opening of a trauma centre in Margate which was named the 'Alison Trauma Room' (Photo: *South Coast Fever*)

Below right: Opening of NCEDO Care Centre, PE. *(l to r):* General Gerrie Bezuidenhout, Minister Jay Naidoo and Inspector Melvin Humpel

Left: Preparing to burn my blood-soaked beach bag (Photo: Tienie)

Below: Putting the past to rest (Photo: Marianne Thamm)

Marianne and I creating the book (Photos: Tienie)

18

ALISON

Judgment day

───────◆───────

DURING THE TIME off I made the decision to go public. The trial was nearly over and it was something I had wanted to do from the beginning. Now that I had testified I felt that the time was right. There had already been so much publicity around the case, what harm could there be in people knowing that the 27-year-old 'insurance broker' had a name and a face?

It was clear that my survival and the way I had coped with the rape and the attack had captured popular imagination. Here, for once, was a 'good news' story about someone who had fought back and won. I think I came to embody something that inspired every South African who had felt paralysed in the face of crime. At that time it was also rare for a rape survivor to show her face and, I believe, only one other woman in Cape Town had done so before.

Although I understood why women were reluctant to speak out and be identified, I also felt it was about time someone shattered the myths. Why did women so often feel responsible for what had happened to them? Why were they reluctant to talk openly about it or show their faces?

If I had been hijacked or robbed no one would have blamed me for it or expected me to keep quiet, to suffer in silence and hide my face.

The notion that women are somehow to blame for a rape is a deep-seated one in most societies. But I realised that society would not change until we, the rape survivors, facilitated it. How could attitudes be adjusted if no one came out and challenged them?

I realised I had been fortunate to have had the personal resources and the unconditional support of my family and friends. So many women do not have that security and comfort. I felt that if I spoke about my ordeal, some of those women might not feel so alone and maybe they would find something to latch on to.

If I could help just one rape survivor to come to terms with what had happened to her, to free her of the pain, break the crushing silence and enable her to find the pieces of her own life, it would be worth it.

So many victims crumble and surrender the rest of their lives to the ordeal. In doing that, they give the men who do this so much more power than they deserve. Rapists thrive on the fact that their victims will remain faceless and silent, that they are terrified to be identified because it might destroy their 'reputation' or 'standing' in life. If we could remove that sting, if we could remove that double or even triple jeopardy that a rape survivor faces after the crime and in court, thousands of women could begin to be released.

At the time I had no idea of the impact my story would have. I thought that it would be a one-off and so I chose to talk to a popular, mass-circulation national magazine because I thought it would reach the greatest number of people.

Carol Coetzee of *You* magazine flew down to PE to interview me. I wasn't nervous; she was easy to talk to. I found it difficult to pose for the camera though. Not because I didn't want to. I had always been self-conscious in situations like that.

I arranged with the magazine to publish the interview only after the sentence had been handed down.

On July 31 the court case resumed. By now I had grown accustomed to it all and felt quite at home back in the wood-panelled courtroom. It had been a long recess, more than two weeks, and I had to admit I was growing tired of it all. Things seemed to drag on endlessly but I knew we were reaching some sort of closure.

During this leg of the trial we heard evidence in mitigation of sentence. Various people, including Melvin, a police chaplain and a psychologist, testified on Theuns and Frans's behalf.

Until then Theuns had been a formless shadow to me. He had not said much that night and also had not testified in court.

There was something sad about him. He seemed lost, confused and deeply troubled. Frans was clearly the one who enjoyed the limelight and being the centre of attention. Theuns was an enigma. No one quite knew what went on inside his mind.

The first person to testify that morning was the Reverend Jacobus Kruger, a police chaplain who had been contacted by Frans's parents after their son's arrest. They had obviously thought he needed counselling and spiritual guidance.

Rev. Kruger said when he first met Frans in the cells he had carried a Bible with him. Frans had underlined many verses and had quoted a passage from Hebrews. He clearly knew the Christian doctrine but had somehow struggled to embrace it.

Frans, he said, had acknowledged his guilt but his main concern was 'how he would escape the wrath of God' should he be sentenced to death. Rev. Kruger also said he had been present during the 'exorcism' that had taken place at police headquarters in which Frans had apparently yelled and screamed and had had difficulty saying the word 'Christ'. He concluded his evidence by saying that he thought that Frans was still possessed.

The clergyman's testimony made little difference to Frans's case except for the fact that at the end of it all it was clear that Frans, and Frans only, was responsible for his deeds. This whole demon thing, was, I thought, a ploy, a way of exonerating himself and distracting the court from the real issues.

Clinical psychologist Ian Meyer then took the stand. He had done extensive interviews with Theuns during the two-week observation at the Elizabeth Donkin Hospital.

I listened to his lengthy evidence carefully. Perhaps it would give me some clue to understanding Theuns.

A sorry tale of a poverty-stricken, loveless life emerged. It was such an extreme story that it almost belonged to the realms of fiction.

Theuns's real father, a Mr van der Westhuizen, who Dr Meyer described as 'a drug-addicted philanderer', had disappeared shortly after his mother had fallen pregnant with Theuns. He was later arrested and was currently serving a sentence in Pretoria Central Prison.

The cycle had come full circle, I thought to myself. Even though he did not know his real father, Theuns was walking in his footsteps and they would inevitably lead him to the same place.

Theuns's mother had then married a Mr Kruger who registered Theuns in his name. But Kruger Senior also turned out to be a 'very unsavoury character' and Theuns's mother also divorced him.

Afterwards, in desperation, she had placed an advertisement in the 'Lonely Hearts' section of a magazine. A Mr Steyn had responded and after a brief courtship, which consisted of a couple of letters, she had married him.

She moved with her small son, who was nine months old at the time, to Tsitsikamma Forest where Mr Steyn worked as a labourer for the forestry department.

Steyn, Dr Meyer said, was known as 'the village idiot', but was also a brutish, unpredictable man who was prone to violent outbursts that he often took out on Theuns.

Theuns, he said, had tried to escape his wretched family life by fleeing into the forest and connecting with the 'coloured' community in Sandrif where he had been made to feel welcome. This had earned him the wrath of the small white community in which he lived. He had also been mocked by his peers because of his third nipple and had been called *'drie tiet'*. He had the nipple surgically removed when he was in the army.

Theuns had learned at the age of six that Steyn was not his biological father and had confronted his mother about it but she had refused to discuss the matter. Dr Meyer said Theuns had only learned his true father's identity since his own arrest.

It was really a tragic story of a wasted, meaningless life that lurched from one disaster to the next. Theuns completed standard 8 before leaving school and going to the army. While doing his national service, he claimed he had 'blown off a woman's head' during the township unrest in 1993 because she had sworn at the police.

Theuns laughed when this evidence was given and Judge Jansen interjected suddenly, asking Dr Meyer why he thought Theuns would find it funny.

'I can't say, Your Honour,' he replied.

Dr Meyer said it was his opinion that Theuns had extremely low self-esteem and suffered from borderline personality disorder which made him susceptible to other people's influences.

I can't say I felt anything for Theuns the adult, but I did feel sorry for the little boy who never really quite found a home or people who loved him.

In a way everyone, including Theuns himself, had to take responsibility for the person he had become. I realised how vital it was for children to feel they were loved and wanted and how much that affected the way someone moved through life.

It seemed like such a simple thing but there are so many complexities to human relationships, so many shades of grey.

If Theuns had been loved and nurtured, would he

have ended up here now?

There was no point trying to speculate. It was too late, the damage had been done and was, in his case, clearly irreparable.

The day of the sentencing on August 7, I decided to drive myself to the court building. Until then I had always gone with someone else, either my dad or mom or one of my friends.

I felt disjointed and a little panicky that morning. I found myself hauling several outfits from my cupboard, unable to make decision about what to wear.

Was I somehow stalling? I knew I was going to be late and I irritated myself flinging combinations of skirts, dresses and blouses on to my bed. Nothing felt comfortable, not even my shoes. I had put on weight eating junk food and fast lunches during the trial.

It was getting late, so eventually I settled on a pair of comfortable, roomy pants and a top that didn't feel right at all.

Everyone had already gone inside when I pulled up outside the courthouse. I knew my mom would be concerned that I was not there. It was unlike me to be late for anything.

Outside in the road the television camera crews had set up their equipment and photographers stood in clusters, cameras dangling from their necks.

As I hopped up the steps I saw Melvin standing nervously outside the court.

'I thought you weren't going to show,' he said guiding me towards the door.

'I wouldn't miss this for anything,' I replied.

I crept into the packed courtroom and took up a seat

my mom had kept for me. There were people everywhere. I glanced around quickly and spotted the familiar faces of several of my friends. I was glad they were there with me.

The rest of the 'audience' spilled over into every available space. People were leaning against the walls, sitting in the aisles and perched on the extra chairs that had been brought in.

Once again, all eyes were on me. I wondered if anyone could tell I felt so strange in my skin.

There was an edge to everything that day and inside the court the tension was palpable, more so than the first day. This was, after all, the grande finale.

Judge Jansen stepped through the back door of Court A for the last time. There was a whooshing sound as everyone rose. He carried a thick pile of papers which he set out before him before adjusting the microphone.

Frans and Theuns were asked to remain standing for the judgment. Frans was wearing a lurid pink and blue tracksuit and Theuns was dressed in a pair of jeans and a black sweater.

I wished I could have seen their faces. They stood quite still and didn't look around them. I noticed Frans's wife in the gallery and I was also aware that the press, who had their pens poised, were closely watching the key players in the trial. They were especially interested in me.

There was utter silence as Judge Jansen spoke. His voice was calm and deliberate. I was frustrated that he gave the sentence in Afrikaans and strained to catch every word.

It was a lengthy sentence and about half way through

it I could feel a restlessness in the crowd.

Essentially, Judge Jansen said he did not accept the defence that Incubus had driven Frans to commit the crimes. Frans had voluntarily and deliberately dabbled in Satanism. It was he who had made that choice and it would be a 'sad day', he added, if a belief in Satanism was regarded as a mitigating factor.

Theuns, he said, might have been influenced by Frans but he was not merely a 'slavish follower'.

He was the one who had made the first cut to my neck and later, after he had been caught, had shown no remorse for his deeds. In fact he was proud of what he had done and even went as far as using the bloodied knife to prepare food. It was also clear, the Judge said, that both men had carefully planned and executed their 'dastardly deeds'.

'I have come to the conclusion that they wanted to kill Alison simply because they felt like it – like little boys shooting birds for the enjoyment thereof,' he said.

This lack of conscience and the cold-blooded manner in which they had tortured both myself and the other victims was indicative of their 'inherent evilness'.

Frans and Theuns, he said, were clearly a great danger to society.

'I would be shirking my duties if I did not remove them from society for ever.'

Judge Jansen said he had watched Frans and Theuns carefully during the trial.

'Accused number one (Frans) gave his testimony in a challenging manner. While he sat in the dock I looked at him several times while witnesses testified. Even when the complainants broke down and cried and stutteringly told the court about their nightmare experiences, there was no vague sign of emotion on their faces.'

Theuns, he said, was often amused when witnesses testified.

There was a short pause before he pronounced the sentence. Everyone seemed to lean forward, eager to hear every word. He looked directly at Frans as he spoke.

'Frans du Toit. In the case CC21/95 (the first rape in February) I will take all the charges together for one sentence. In this case you are sentenced to life imprisonment.'

There was a gasp from the gallery. Natalie, Frans's wife, began to weep uncontrollably and lay slumped in the arms of a companion.

Another of Frans's friends said, 'Oh God, what's this man up to.' Everyone craned to see who had spoken out. The eyes of the gallery swept over Natalie and then swivelled back towards me. I was still determined to show nothing.

Judge Jansen went on. He grouped together the following eight charges against Frans and the four against Theuns for sentencing.

'Accused number one, I sentence you to life imprisonment on charges one, two and three (the second rape). Theuns Kruger, on charges one, two and three, I sentence you to 25 years. Frans du Toit, on charges four, five, six, seven and eight (my case) you are sentenced to a further term of life imprisonment. Theuns Kruger, on charges four, six, seven and eight (my case) you are sentenced to life imprisonment.'

There was an audible buzz in the court now. Everyone

was trying to work out what this all meant. Essentially, Frans had been sentenced to three terms of life imprisonment. Theuns got 25 years and one life term.

The judge waited for the court to settle.

'I also make the following order. I insist that this judgment be typed up and two copies sent to the relevant authorities at the Department of Correctional Services to be placed on the files of the two accused. It must be clear that, if at any time in the future, there is any consideration for parole, it was my intention that these two men be removed from society for the rest of their natural lives and that they should spend it behind bars.'

A collective and spontaneous cheer rippled through the gallery as Judge Jansen packed up his papers and left through the back door with the assessor.

It was all over.

I was grateful to the judge. I had admired him from the beginning and I could not have wished for a more balanced and fair summing up.

Justice, I felt, had been done.

But I wasn't sure what I really felt. I did feel relief, but there was still too much going on inside the courtroom. Frans and Theuns still stood in the dock looking a little bewildered.

Natalie was ushered out by her friends, still sobbing. An orderly moved quickly across to escort Frans and Theuns down the stairway towards the cells.

I wanted to look at them both now. As emotional as I was, I knew it would be the last time that I saw them and I wanted that image to remain inside my head.

I forced myself to look as their heads bobbed down the stairs. Then suddenly there was a loud bang and a shout rose from the stairwell. It was Theuns. He had hit the side of the wood panelling with his hand, shouting: 'Here we go. Fuck you all.'

It was a pathetic display of machismo. I suppose it was all that was left for him to do now that he would never be a part of normal society again.

Suddenly I no longer wanted to be there. I wished I could have been whisked away without any fuss but there was no way out. People milled around inside and outside Court A. It was as if they could not leave, as if they had been to the première of a play or a movie and needed to stand around and talk about it.

Melvin had warned me about the bank of photographers gathered outside and someone suggested that I cover my head. But there was no way I would slink out of there like some criminal. Although I had promised *You* magazine an exclusive on the story, there was no way I was going to dodge the cameras outside.

People would misunderstand the gesture, thinking that I was trying to hide my face. I heard the whirring and the clicking as soon as I stepped into the sunlight. A few journalists shouted out questions. One asked me if I was satisfied with the sentence.

I replied that I was very happy but somehow, at that stage, could think of nothing more to say. I needed to digest it all. I still felt tense.

Our little group – mom, dad, Melvin and my friends – didn't quite know what to do next so we headed for a little pub. I did not really feel like celebrating. This was not like getting a degree or winning an award.

This was a milestone of another sort. Up ahead was a new road I would have to walk and I knew I had no map. Deep down I knew that I was heading now for the most difficult part of my healing process. With the court case over there would be nothing to distract me from myself.

I had come this far, but would I be able to go the whole distance?

19

ALISON

The wheels come off

———◆———

I RETURNED TO work on the Tuesday after the sentencing hoping that the constant edginess I had felt would finally go away. Everyone was pleased with the outcome and, of course, now that Frans and Theuns were behind bars, there was theoretically no excuse for me to be consumed by it all any more.

That first week I kept waiting for my life to snap back into focus, but somehow it didn't.

I would go into work in the morning and dread being there. I just could not seem to get out of the starting gates. It was so unlike me. I wondered when, if ever, I would feel like myself again.

I missed the carefree person I used to be, but I also knew that the lessons I would learn from this would be life-altering. There would be, could be, no going back.

Time, I realised, would be the only balm. Time and

space to collect my thoughts and to heal. What I really needed and wanted most then was to withdraw into myself, but I could not.

There just didn't seem to be a single moment in the day when something was not vying for my attention. The media interest had not yet died down. Now that the trial was over everyone wanted to know what I felt, how I was coping.

I realised I had unwittingly brought the attention on myself and that I would have to see it through until all the questions had been answered. I owed it to everyone who had rallied around to support me.

I had been somewhere few had gone before and people were clearly intrigued by what I had found there. By going public I had opened a window into the world of the rape survivor that had been jammed tightly shut until then.

A local radio presenter, Neil Pienaar, invited me to be a guest on his show on Radio Algoa.

Much of Port Elizabeth was still talking about the case, discussing its merits and my miraculous survival.

I agreed to go on air, firstly to thank everyone in the city for their love and support, but mostly so that I could reach other rape survivors and their families and perhaps offer some succour, and so that I could tell the story and how I felt about it in my own words.

I was quite tense about going on air, but Neil guided me through it and made me feel quite at home. He was a little taken aback in the beginning when, after saying that he felt honoured to be talking to a rape survivor as he had never done so before, I shot back with 'You don't know that. So many women are silent about it.'

He didn't pick up on the issue again until much later in the programme when we discussed the frightening rape statistics in this country. If one woman is raped every 28 seconds, then I knew that many were listening that night and that for some it was the first time they had heard another woman talk so openly about it.

It is the living with the silent burden of guilt that ruins so many women's lives. I felt it was important for them to realise that they needed to deal with it and not to be silent, to accept it as a part of their life that would never go away but that did not have to destroy them.

My heart aches for those women who are not able to come to terms with rape and in so doing waste their precious lives.

I was lucky that I had not for one moment felt guilty about what had happened to me and it was a liberating feeling. I wanted to share that.

I was alarmed at first to discover that many rape survivors did not seek counselling and did not press charges. The ordeal of the investigation and the court case was too much for many women and their fragile sense of self could just not withstand the detached bureaucracy of the system. I said that there was no way this would change if we did not force it, if we did not speak out as rape survivors and as a community.

The switchboard lit up when Neil opened the phone lines.

People called in from everywhere and all of them poured out their hearts. Some seemed overwhelmed by my 'strength', describing me as 'an angel' and 'an inspiration'. I realised just how much we need everyday heroes and that I had unwittingly become one.

One caller offered to fix my car any time it was needed, another said he wanted to cast me in bronze and put me on the mantelpiece. There was an outpouring of love and once again I was buoyed by it. I was deeply humbled and touched by everyone's incredible generosity of spirit.

There were many callers too, both men and women, who were angry with men 'as a species' and enraged that they were capable of so much destruction and hurt.

I reminded the listeners that there were many good men who were as appalled and shocked at what had happened to me and what is happening to the women of this country. Besides, I would not be alive today if it were not for those brave and wonderful men who had helped me to hold on to my life.

I felt great the next morning. The programme had reaffirmed my commitment to make something more of this experience. It was usually not easy for people to talk about trauma, but I seemed to be able to do it quite naturally.

I don't know how or why; at that stage I never questioned it.

There was more publicity after the radio broadcast and the following week I set up a press conference at the Murder and Robbery Headquarters so that any remaining questions could be answered. I was nervous and it was actually the last thing I felt like doing, but it had to be done.

I felt that if I could speak to them all at the same time the media attention would finally die down.

It went well, everyone was kind, considerate, respectful and gentle and I told myself I would answer all questions truthfully. I also wanted to clear up the perception that there was anything extraordinary or 'special' about me. I was just an ordinary girl who had endured something out of the ordinary.

Back at work things were not going well at all. Although I could admit it to myself I could not do so to Ettienne who had been so patient and supportive throughout it all.

I felt guilty about letting him down now, but there was nothing I could do. I had lost interest in my work completely. My heart was not in it. I just didn't care any more.

It all seemed so irrelevant to me now. Some mornings I would get to work, sit behind my desk, open a file and then just shut it again. Other mornings I could not lift myself out of bed at all.

I started arriving late at the office. I stopped making appointments with clients except for those that I knew were absolutely vital. I had no desire to talk to people.

I also didn't follow up phone calls and just shuffled paper around my desk. I was waiting for something to happen, but I wasn't going to make it happen by myself. What it was, I didn't quite know.

No one said anything. For nine months my colleagues had gone through this with me. I felt I could no longer burden them with my problems.

I was, I suppose, waiting for Ettienne to explode and pull me up on my lacklustre performance. Subconsciously I was egging him on. I wanted him to ask me to leave, to fire me.

I was clearly in the beginning stages of what was to become a severe and debilitating depression. I did not recognise the signs at first although now they seem so obvious.

I hated the way I felt, I hated the fact that I was letting other people down and that I had this indifferent attitude to everything. It was completely new to me. I had never felt this way before and it was so contrary to my personality, my very being.

Before, I had been able to make the best of my worst moments. I had always looked for the jewels in the rubble, but now nothing glinted, nothing shone. Everything appeared pallid and grey. Sounds and colours became muted, as if viewed through a veil or heard through a wad of wet cotton wool. Inside me there was a heavy stillness, like a deserted factory.

It would have been fine if I had at least felt pain or sadness, but I felt nothing at all. The nothingness was frightening.

One day at work the producers of a television actuality programme, Carte Blanche, called to say they wanted to do an insert. I agreed to it, although in retrospect I feel I shouldn't have.

I tried to fit the interview in between working hours but had to leave work early to meet the television crew. I knew I had to be lucid and strong. Luckily, my mom was interviewed with me.

Having her around made me feel stronger. I had to be strong for her.

Looking at the tapes now I am amazed at how 'normal' and together I sounded and looked. The truth was I was falling apart, but I couldn't tell anyone about it.

Immediately after the interview my mom and I left for Cape Town with Ettienne and Hanlie. We had some business to do there, but it was also another way he thought he would treat me and give me a weekend away with some close friends who live in Stellenbosch. His kindness only compounded my feelings of guilt.

More than anything else I yearned for my old life. I knew things had changed but I was not yet really prepared to accept that.

I had always looked for meaning in life and had spent three years in London doing some serious soul searching. Over and over again I had asked myself why I was here, what we as human beings are meant to be doing? Now I had survived a trauma I could never have imagined would have befallen me.

There must be some meaning in it, but what was it? Surely I should now be ready to accept the miraculous gift that is life and hold it in my hands and heart like a precious, rare thing.

But my mind was empty. There were no more magical thoughts about wonderful possibilities.

All I could do at times was sit, my mind totally empty, like a shell. I could not watch TV or read. I could not go out for a walk or even write a thank you note.

I was crouching behind a wall I had built, or that had built itself around me, and I did not know how to smash it down.

There were times when I hated feeling that way. The strange changes frightened me. The minute I allowed myself to feel something, I'd trip the switch again and make sure I didn't.

At that time I must admit that I embraced my depression. I thought I owed it to myself.

I managed to pull on a mask in public, but in private

I wallowed in it. It was easier that way. I did not have to make any decisions at all. I surrendered to the nothingness and nothing came of it. It was the way I wanted it.

My body felt heavy and I was incapacitated by an overwhelming urge to sleep. Sometimes I slept for days, amazed that this was possible.

I still managed to drag myself off to the office, but it was all a sham. I made an appointment with a psychologist and she made me punch a pillow to access my anger.

It didn't work; I just did not have the inner reserves.

One of the first invitations to give a public talk came in the middle of this depression. For some reason I accepted, although I had never spoken publicly before and had always dreaded the idea.

My only experience had been at school as head girl and the memory of how I had felt then filled me with fear.

But, I thought, the talk would be a challenge. At least it would force me to think about the rape and the attack.

The night before I was due to speak I tossed and turned in bed. I began to dread the entire thing. I lay awake trying to think of a way out, imagining an illness I could suddenly contract to get me out of the engagement.

But then, as the sun rose and the birds began to chirp, I realised that nothing could ever be as frightening as that night in Noordhoek. What harm could a group of Rotarians possibly do me?

If I had survived that night because a small part of me believed enough that I could, there was nothing that I couldn't do now if I believed in myself that way again.

I was very nervous about the talk but it seemed to go

down well.

I did a few more talks, mostly to small groups, and the more I got out, the closer I moved towards finding some sort of resolution. Because of the talks I was forced to examine what I had learned so that I could share this with the audiences.

Although I was still depressed, I knew I was feeling better. In those moments I knew I would never allow myself to slip over the edge. I had fought too hard to live and there was no point just giving up.

Towards the end of the year it became clear to me that I would have to resign. I had always told friends who had asked my advice about situations like this to hang on to a job until they found another one.

I took no heed of my own words. There was just no way I could carry on. It was a major decision for me. I had worked so hard at it. I was a good insurance broker and Ettienne had even offered me a partnership in the firm.

But deep down I knew that if I stayed I would be doing it for him, not for me. Besides, what would all of this have been about if I just tried to continue with my old life?

Never again, I promised myself, would I simply coast along taking things for granted. I wanted to live life fully, even if it meant I had to be penniless. I realised I had been given a second chance. That essentially every day was a bonus, a gift, and I had to make the best of it.

I finally made the decision to leave while Ettienne was away on a family holiday. He had left the office in my 'capable' hands and I made a last attempt at making it work for me. I always remained responsible, but it became painfully obvious that I had to make a break. I had to leave.

I cried many times on the shoulders of my friends and my mom as I wrestled with the decision. I looked at it from every possible angle and came to the conclusion that the only possible solution was to tell Ettienne, upon his return, that I was going to leave.

As soon as he got back he knew something was up. I had wanted to wait a few days before informing him of my decision but he dragged it out of me. Understandably he was disappointed and upset, but there was no turning back for me.

I left that December with no clue about how I was going to live. I had some savings, but none of that seemed to matter.

On January 14, 1996, I returned to the provincial hospital for further plastic surgery. The scar on my neck, although it had healed, had left a few thick keloid scars and a hernia in my abdominal wound had caused it to bulge out quite badly. I couldn't stand upright without it protruding like a small ball. It looked terrible, but everyone assured me that the surgery would correct it.

I wasn't looking forward to going back. I was still in so much pain and the thought of opening up those wounds again frightened me. It was odd going back, and I checked in a day before the operation. Mom went with me and we entered through the front door this time and not the Casualty Unit. It was strange spending the night in the same hospital again and I wondered how long it would take me to heal from this round of surgery. It had to be done though, and there was no point in delaying it.

The next day I was wheeled into theatre at around 8 a.m. Dr Angelov was there to repair the hernia, and a plastic surgeon, Dr Solomons, who would be working on my neck and abdomen. The second operation lasted about two hours and I awoke that morning at around 11 a.m. That searing pain that I had first remembered was back. Once again I had a dressing around my neck and my stomach. The first day was awful, but within four days my body regained its strength. The surgery had been successful and everything was healing well.

I was discharged on January 18. Mom walked alongside the wheelchair and as we got to the entrance, I lifted myself up and walked to the car.

I returned two days later to have the stitches removed. The wounds looked red and raw, especially the one on my stomach. I had been cut open from my navel to my pubic area so that a piece of muscle from my leg could be stretched up and sewn into place. Dr Angelov assured me that the scar would eventually improve, but at that moment it looked quite horrific.

I took it easy for a week or two, and just as I had begun to wonder what I was going to do, requests for me to make speeches began to trickle in. And the more I went out and spoke, the more things began to make sense to me.

At first I was surprised at how many people would talk to me afterwards and thank me for helping them. I had no idea what it was I had done, but clearly there was something in my message that was universal and healing.

Also, I began receiving letters from all over the country. Every single one of them was positive and reassuring.

I remember one evening as I was paying my bill in a Johannesburg restaurant a young woman came up to me and pressed a tiny folded note into my hand.

She had written my name and drawn a little flower on the outside and I opened it carefully in the car.

It was such a heartfelt note. She wrote that as a child she had been abused by her stepfather and that it had recently come to a head again when her mother found out that another of her boyfriends had been molesting her younger sister.

She said that just seeing me had given her the strength to cope with it all. Until then, she had felt like giving up.

Somehow letters like these, and the many others, made it all worth it and set me on a new path. I could feel that the healing had begun.

Finally, I had found a way of giving back something to the world and of finding a meaning in what had happened to me. If I could outweigh the bad with good, I could turn the experience into something positive and meaningful.

One of the greatest honours for me that year was being named a Rotary Foundation Paul Harris Fellow, one of the highest awards in recognition of 'the furtherance of better understanding and friendly relations between peoples of the world' and 'for courage beyond the norm'.

Mom and I flew up to Johannesburg where we were both treated like royalty. I was extremely moved by the award ceremony. Tiaan was also honoured by the Rotarians. He received the Paul Harris award for Humanitarianism.

Later, when a member of the public nominated me for the Port Elizabeth Citizen of the Year Award in the Community Service category I was quite uncomfortable with it. All the other nominees seemed to have actively done so much more than I.

'But I haven't really done anything,' I told a good friend.

'Ali,' she replied, 'it's not what you've done, it's the effect that you've had.'

There were other awards and accolades that meant so much to me, including *Femina* magazine's first Woman of Courage award.

A few months into my newfound career as a public speaker someone called and asked how much I charged to speak. I was quite surprised at that. I had never thought of charging people; in fact I felt quite uncomfortable about it at first.

But in essence this was becoming a new career for me and there was no way I could begin to turn down the ongoing requests to make public appearances.

At the end of my first year I had spoken to about 75 people and now, more than three years later, I have been privileged to have reached over 100 000.

And each time I get up to speak I am reminded of the collective power of good, how so many people in this country, like me, have managed to turn a tragedy into a triumph and that we all essentially have the capacity to do so.

Part Three

20

ALISON

Counting miracles

―――――――◆―――――――

WAS IT DESTINY or fate that brought Frans du Toit and Theuns Kruger into my life that night?

Is there a great plan or scheme to life and do we just have to accept that a path has already been laid out, that the story has already been written somewhere up there in the stars?

These are questions I am often asked and I have pondered them myself.

Although I consider myself to be a spiritual person, I am not religious. I am convinced there is a higher power, God, a divine essence, whatever you personally choose to call it, that makes up a greater consciousness and which resides within every living being.

I also believe in the concept of good and evil but they are not 'qualities', if that is the correct way of describing them, that reside outside us, that are foisted upon us by some unseen benevolent or malevolent hand.

The capacity for good and bad lies within us. The choice is ours. Sometimes we have no control over how we come into the world and the events that will shape and affect the way we see this glorious gift that is life.

There are so many factors that determine what we will make of it and how we will influence others but, in the end, we all have a personal responsibility. Although I don't believe in destiny, I do believe that we create our own successes or failures as we move through the world. Realising this brings with it a tremendous sense of liberation, but also much trepidation and fear.

It also brings with it a responsibility about who we are and where we find ourselves in our lives.

It is scary to be the captain of your own ship and often it just seems so much easier to simply take orders from someone else, to let them do the worrying or take the initiative and responsibility.

But as long as you surrender your life to someone else or to outside forces, you will be a little boat tossed upon a choppy sea.

I do not believe that Frans and Theuns were 'sent' to me so that I could learn something. Essentially, they came into my life because I was unconscious, unaware, and wrapped up in a world of my own.

I lived then, like so many of us still do, in a bubble, a safe little cocoon, blissfully ignorant of what was going on around me.

Sure, I had all these life philosophies and theories that I had worked on and explored for as long as I could remember, but in retrospect I realise I did not appreciate life as much as I could and should have. I did not take it as seriously as I thought I did.

I had always wanted to live by my own rules, to be a good person and do no harm. I constantly searched for growth and meaning, for new experiences that would open me up to the world around me.

Although I do not blame myself for what happened that night and I could not have controlled events, I must share the responsibility for not being vigilant.

Back then I did not read newspapers and I had never, ever thought about the possibility that I could be raped and attacked. I should have. These crimes are so much a part of everyday South African life, but for some reason I chose not to know, not to be aware. I took my freedom for granted.

I certainly did not choose for this to happen to me and it was certainly not preordained, but I acknowledge my role in it. Instead of believing it would never happen to me, I should have been thinking of what I could have done to have stopped it from happening to me.

Not everyone can or will feel this way about adversity. There are times, even when we have taken every possible precaution to prevent upset and trauma, that adversity comes crashing in, wreaking havoc and displacing us.

In essence, life is chaos and the only thing that is consistent is inconsistency. Random acts of tragedy and triumph, of pain and glory, occur independently of each other all the time. That is the way life is and the only way to deal with it is to understand the unpredictable nature of things, prepare yourself for that, and accept it.

The one thing I do have control over, and it is this that has helped and is still helping me to deal with this trauma, is choice. I have the freedom to choose how I will respond to it, I have the choice to make of it what I must and to learn from it.

Frans and Theuns were not 'sent'. They were there already and if it had not been I that they had 'chosen' that evening, it would have been someone else. The fact remains that I crossed Frans's path like a new-born lamb wobbling its way across an open field while a hungry predator crouched in the bush.

I did ask the question, 'Why me?' We all do when things go wrong, when we lose something precious, when our lives are thrown off kilter by forces beyond our control. It is natural to presume that there is something 'personal' about the things that happen so personally to us.

But we may as well ask 'why *not* me?' and I believe that so many people are drawn to my case because they do think exactly that, especially in this country where we live with so much senseless violence and crime.

Each day we read of another horrific case, we see another photograph of a dead body, we hear of someone else's nightmare and we ask ourselves, 'How will that person cope? How can they ever get over what has happened to them or their loved ones?'

We hear horror story after horror story at the Truth and Reconciliation Commission hearings and some of the accounts are so chilling one wonders whether the people who committed the deeds are even human.

But the wonderful thing is that we are able to cope, if we can only believe it. Somewhere deep inside us, we all have the capacity, even if we have not yet needed to access it.

There is ample proof of this in the lives of Holocaust

survivors and those people in this country who have been able to forgive torturers and murderers for what they have done. These people and many, many others have been through a living hell that is beyond the normal realm of human experience, and they have survived.

Not only survived, but changed their lives, liberated themselves and found something of value.

The truth is we do not all have to wait for a life-altering experience to come along before we make changes to our lives. You don't have to go where I went in order to see the value of your life, the value of other people's lives.

We can all begin by trying to become more conscious of the world around us, of what life has to offer and what other people can mean to us.

How many of us are caught up in the whirlwind of everyday life, just living from moment to moment, taking care of basic needs and doing crisis management?

We rush to and from work, we try to fit everything into 12 hours, we try to take care of our families, our loved ones, and sometimes it feels as if there is no time left to do anything else.

When we are caught up and ensnared in this perpetual state of motion we cannot absorb or integrate some of the lessons we are given and need to learn.

We only grow when things go wrong. The 'no pain, no gain' maxim exists because it is true. Whether it is a small setback or a major catastrophe, we need to find a quiet space to think about it, to find the meaning or the message.

Sometimes it is easy to see and know what must be done or what it is we need to change but so often, once life 'gets back to normal', we fall back into old patterns.

We forget or are too lazy to put those lessons into practice and seem surprised when it happens again and again, until we are forced to look at it and learn.

The lessons will keep coming, they are unstoppable, and we can either choose to ignore them or we can heed the wake-up call and open ourselves to them.

Frans did not choose me personally. I just happened to cross his path at that moment. I wasn't looking for trouble. Perhaps if I had, I would have seen it coming.

And if you asked me today if I could go back in time and make that night in Noordhoek 'unhappen', I would have to answer you that I would not – because I have learned so much from it.

I have been given so many gifts that I believe it was worth going through that terror, pain and heartache.

People often look at the lives of others and say 'he or she is so lucky'. You may even think that about me.

That I am lucky to have survived the ordeal, that I am lucky that I had the personality, the resources, the friends and the support to overcome this terrible thing and not allow it to ruin my life.

But I do not believe in luck.

Those people who we think are lucky actually work very hard at creating that good fortune. And it does not come easily. There will be many failures along the way, but we can choose to allow them to defeat us or we can, as I said earlier, look at the lessons learned and try again.

We can create luck by taking personal responsibility, by working hard at changing old habits and attitudes, basically by reprogramming ourselves to accept that we have the choice to surrender to life, but not to be crushed by it.

We must learn to live not in our skin, but through it. When we live through our skin we connect with the world outside, open ourselves to it without judgement or expectation. We will see the signs along the way, we will notice the little hints that come along and help to guide us. If we are self-absorbed we can not take in the vista outside.

We must learn to embrace the chaos, but never allow it to embrace us. Knowing it is there is half the battle won and you will not be surprised when it strikes.

There are so many things in life that cause despair and disappointment. On the surface it often appears as if everything bad and negative has gained the upper hand in the world.

We hear only the bad news and see only the horror, but the truth is there are many more good people in the world than there are bad. Yes, one drop of poison can contaminate the entire well, but it is important to remember that we are surrounded by many positive, life-giving things that make it all worth while.

Every day and all around us there are small and great miracles that take place unseen, unheard of and un-heralded. They are there if we only stop to look.

The young boy helping the old lady across the road, the motorist who stops and smiles and waves you across, the woman who takes in unwanted children, the poor person who gives his last pennies to someone else. And if we look for them and believe they are there, miracles appear everywhere.

I have been amazed at the miracles that have occurred in my own life. From the moment Frans abducted me a series of events carried me through the nightmare and helped me to survive.

Seeing those miracles or those miraculous acts has, to a certain extent, counteracted the damage and destruction Frans and Theuns sowed.

Firstly, it was a warm evening, unusually so for Port Elizabeth. If it had been any cooler I would most certainly have died of exposure after lying naked in the road for so many hours. The full moon enabled me to find my way back to the road. Without that light I might never have done so.

I remained calm and wasted no energy fighting them off, and because of that I had extra reserves later on. When Frans strangled me, I evacuated my bowels. If that had not happened, the doctors have told me, my intestines would have 'exploded' when they were repeatedly stabbed and the chances of a serious and fatal infection would have been much higher.

During the more than 35 times they lunged and stabbed at my stomach they missed all my vital organs. They were aiming for my liver, Frans had said during the court case, and they had also wanted to 'destroy' my reproductive organs. None of that happened.

When they slashed my throat over 16 times they also missed the vital arteries and my voice box. The irony was that it was the cutting of my throat that led to my regaining consciousness.

If Frans had not cut through my windpipe and inadvertently enabled me to breathe and regain consciousness, I would have remained unconscious and bled to death.

Frans and Theuns threw my clothing out of the car.

If they had not, I would not have been able to move from the spot where I lay. The shirt that landed on my back enabled me to wrap up my intestines and get on to my feet.

Tiaan Eilerd would have driven along Marine Drive that night, but if I had not made the effort to get there he would not have found me. He had medical experience and did not panic. He knew what to do and what was needed to keep me alive.

Dr Angelov, a thoracic specialist, just happened to be on call that evening. I might have been taken to a private hospital where they might not have been able to deal with my injuries in the same way.

Many people have asked me whether I am angry at what happened to me, angry at Frans and Theuns, angry at the person who first stopped when I lay in the road and then just drove off.

Anger is one of the most destructive of emotions. Guilt is one of the most incapacitating.

I can honestly say I have never felt any anger towards Frans or Theuns, nor towards the person or persons who didn't stop to help me as I realise it was probably because of their own fear.

Being angry with Frans or Theuns would be giving them too much. Anger tears you up and eats away at the very core of your soul.

Anger does not promote healing; it does the opposite. It allows a wound to fester and bleed over and over again.

By being angry one gives power to people who do not deserve it. Frans and Theuns are nothing to me. I think about them only because it is they who did this to me, but nothing else.

I have also often been asked whether I would have felt that justice would have been better served if Frans and Theuns had been sentenced to death. My answer to that question is that I am satisfied with the sentence they received. Although it does not in any way diminish or alleviate the pain and trauma that I still live with today, and which is my own life sentence, they are where they deserve to be. It would have made no difference if they had been put to death. For me, the fact that they received life sentences and were not let off on some legal technicality or sentenced to a short jail term, is good enough. Their punishment is that they will have to live with themselves behind bars for the rest of their lives.

When I first started to speak publicly I noticed that most people were interested in my amazing survival and physical recovery, but as the years have gone by, I have found more and more people have become interested in my mental and spiritual rejuvenation.

They want to know how I, an ordinary PE girl, could get to the point in my life where I could say that I am better now than I have ever been before, I am happier now than I have ever been before – not necessarily in spite of what has happened, but because of it.

I did not do it alone. Apart from all the hands, both known and unknown, that reached out and buoyed me through my bleakest moments, there was one person who helped me to make the final breakthrough. His name is Tienie and he was an old acquaintance that I met again one night at a party while he was sitting on the roof, of all places, gazing at the stars and contemplating the meaning of life.

21

ALISON

Finding my prince

———◆———

ONE AFTERNOON MY mom and I were out having coffee somewhere in PE when we began to talk about relationships. At that stage I was still concerned that I might not be able to form romantic attachments. I knew that if and when I fell in love he would have to be an exceptional man. I had always been choosy and now I worried that the rape and the attack would make me so discriminating that almost no one would fit the profile of what I perceived to be my ideal man.

I had gone on a few 'dates' since the rape and attack and although there were several wonderful men who appeared in my life at that time, I was not ready for any of them. I just did not feel comfortable yet.

I did not dwell on the issue. There were far larger concerns in my life – like coming to terms with what had happened to me and adjusting to the fact that I had given up my full-time job.

That afternoon my mom guiltily reminded me of an incident that took place in the garden of our family home many years ago.

I was about thirteen or so, she said, and had obviously been sitting in my bedroom daydreaming, wondering about the future and the 'prince' who would eventually become my husband.

It was a typical little girl fantasy and, as we reminisced, I recalled those moments clearly. That particular day I was so caught up in it all that I wanted an immediate answer.

I ventured outside to find mom. She was crouching in the flower beds planting seedlings and I hovered for a while before asking, 'Mommy, when can I have a boyfriend?'

It's amazing how at that age we believe our parents have all the solutions to our problems. Mom, of course, was quite accustomed to my flights of fantasy and she always indulged them. She once even went as far as making a little air hostess uniform for me when I proudly announced that that was my career of choice.

That afternoon in the garden she looked up at me, slightly bemused by my question.

'Oh Alison, when you're 27,' she answered with her usual confidence and I suppose to quieten my sudden interest in boys.

It was all I needed to hear. Satisfied, I returned to my bedroom and counted the years, convinced somehow that my mom had a special way of seeing into the future.

Now mom confided in me that she had talked to God about my future since the attack and that He had reminded her of the incident in the garden and reassured her that I *would* be 27. He had added that it would be someone I had already met.

We sat there like two young girls going through names of a few possible candidates. We drew up a list and ended up scratching off every single name. Once again, I would just have to wait and see if her prediction came true.

On February 15, 1997 I walked down the aisle of the tiny stone Holy Trinity Church that nestles in the Belvedere Valley in Knysna with the man of my dreams, Tienie.

I was 30, so my mother wasn't that far off the mark all those years ago and, believe it or not, I had actually met him long before we fell in love.

It was several years before the attack and both of us were out walking our dogs with friends on the beach. We saw each other but at that time I was involved with someone else so I thought nothing more of this tanned, strapping, rather shy Afrikaans surfer boy.

Port Elizabeth is a small town and it is easy to see a face for many years without ever really getting to know the person behind it. Tienie knew some of my friends and I often saw him around. But he was just there, part of a larger group. I didn't see him again until a year after the attack.

At that time I was able to go out and interact socially although I knew I was deeply depressed. I was surprised to find that I was even able to stand up in front of an audience and talk confidently when actually I was far from finding any sense of inner tranquillity and peace.

When people complimented me or came up to me to

tell me how 'wonderful' they thought I was, I would outwardly acknowledge their compliments but it hardly touched me. At times I felt such a fraud. Here I was surrounded by and showered with all this love and care, but it made no difference. I felt cold and grey and alone.

I tried to connect with people but inside I still felt strangely removed from it all and often, when I went out, the conversation would inevitably revolve around me and the trauma. Although I did not mind talking about it, there were times when I just longed to be like everyone else and chat about nothing in particular.

One evening my friend Nicki invited me to a party at her house. Shortly after I arrived and started to mingle, I noticed Tienie in the crowd. There was something about him that intrigued me. He seemed sad and a little aloof. I had never once, during the times I had encountered him recently, seen him smile.

He seemed almost to glide about, quite separate from everyone else. He came over and said hello. We exchanged a few pleasantries before he melted back into the sea of faces.

A lot of people came over to chat to me that evening. Everyone was concerned about me, how I was doing, how my wounds were healing, what my life was like now. After a while I grew quite tired of it all. For some reason I looked around for Tienie, but couldn't see him anywhere.

I asked Nicki what had happened to him and she said she'd show me. She took me by the hand and led me upstairs and told me to look out of the window that opened up on to the roof.

I stuck my head out and spotted him sitting alone on

the roof, a glass of wine cupped in his hand. He sat motionless, staring straight ahead. I was drawn to this stranger and I wanted to talk and connect with him but I was shy. When Nicki egged me on I hesitated, saying that I didn't really need the company. She looked at me and said knowingly, 'It's not *you* I'm worried about.'

Nicki clearly thought I would 'be good for him' in some way. I clambered up on to the roof and perched next to him.

He seemed quite vulnerable and sad. We started chatting and I decided to ask him outright why he never smiled.

It was as if I had pressed the button that opened a sluice gate. Suddenly he just opened up to me and started telling me about his life. It was obvious he was close to breaking point and that he had reached a crossroads. He told me about his childhood and about his current problems.

Tienie's father, a farmer in the George district, had died tragically in a motor accident near Riversdale. Tienie was only three months old at the time and his mother, Rykie, was left to raise him and his sister Belinda alone. The young widow left the farmstead and took her two children to Port Elizabeth where she started a new life.

His father's death had left a lingering void in Tienie's life. With no father figure to guide him he had to find his own way through the world. As a young boy he had been molested and abused by a close member of the family, someone he had always looked up to and trusted. I could tell he was a survivor, he had an edge to him that other men who had not known misfortune or tragedy seldom display.

But beneath that tough exterior, I could see an incredibly vulnerable and complex person. After travelling and working at various jobs in the country Tienie eventually settled in Port Elizabeth with his mom. He had opened a very successful night-club but was later forced to close it down. There were complaints about noise and other municipal and legal wrangles.

It was just one blow too many in his short life. The loss of the business, as far as he was concerned, was the last straw. Suddenly he could see no future ahead.

I recognised the depression that lurked there.

I wanted to know more about him and we talked about his hopes and his dreams. He was talking eagerly now that he had broken the silence he had kept for so long.

I really liked what he said and how he saw the world. Tienie is an unpretentious man who loves the earth, farming, the sea and the simple beautiful things in life. I too love those things.

He did not need to brag or boast about himself; he was gentle and sensitive and I began to like him more and more. We talked deep into the night as the stars twinkled overhead and the music from the party drifted up around us. But we were in our own little world and I felt safe and normal for the first time in a long while.

In the mean time the party had almost petered out and the crowd was thinning. We were enjoying each other's company so much we decided to go for a stroll on the beach.

The more Tienie spoke the more I realised what a special man he was. He was definitely extremely depressed at the time and had lost interest in almost everything he had previously enjoyed.

After that we went for coffee and when we parted I realised that for the first time since the attack I had not spoken about it. I wasn't even sure if Tienie knew who I was or that it had even happened.

But one thing I knew was that I wanted to see this man again.

At the time I didn't realise that I was falling in love with him. I saw him as an interesting person who I wanted to get to know a little better.

Besides, I was so switched off to romantic signs that if he had shown any interest I would not have noticed. But he began to occupy my thoughts more and more. There had to be a way, I thought, of restoring some balance in his life. He had so much potential and all he needed was something to break the back of this terrible depression.

What he really needed, I thought, was a break from PE and everything that was dragging him down. Perhaps a working holiday overseas would do the trick.

I checked my savings account and decided that I would lend him the money to go somewhere else in the world. Somewhere where he could collect his thoughts and find himself again.

I told him what I thought and although he seemed quite surprised at first, he began to get excited about the idea. He promised he would pay me back as soon as he could and off the two of us went to a travel agent. We sat there flipping through brochures on Greece and Turkey.

We didn't buy a ticket that day but decided to think it through properly before booking the flights.

Every time Tienie and I parted I began to miss him.

I began to feel the need to see him and we kept making 'excuses' to link up with each other again.

We sneaked off for a coffee here and a long walk on the beach there. When I think back to it now it was so obvious that we were falling in love. We often behaved like two children, laughing, giggling and doing silly things.

The first time I saw Tienie smile was at a party at his friend John's house in Cape St Francis. He had offered to go up ahead of a group of friends to prepare the house. When he asked me to go with him I said yes immediately.

We went in separate cars and en route we sort of chased each other along the road. Tienie would pull up to me and hoot and then I would pull over. We really were behaving strangely, come to think of it. It was a fantastic weekend. I didn't think about anything and simply enjoyed myself. I even sang again at the top of my voice in a boat bobbing about in the pouring rain. I felt very close to Tienie that weekend. It was as if his aura enveloped me. It was like a healing balm.

And as he gradually thawed and opened up I began to see the spirit inside. And I liked what I saw.

I met Tienie's mom for the first time after that weekend. As soon as we had a moment alone she grabbed my hand and said, 'What have you done to my son?'

I wasn't sure what she meant until she finished her sentence.

'He's smiling again,' she said.

A while later I was invited to give a talk in Knysna. I told Tienie about it and he offered to accompany me. I was thrilled to have the company and I felt extraordinarily comfortable and safe around him. I trusted him implicitly.

In many ways, when I think of it now, we were already behaving like a married couple. Everything we did seemed so right, so natural and so without stress or pretence.

That weekend we packed the Combi and off we went. It was a wonderful trip. We talked, we laughed, we listened to music and we enjoyed the spectacular views.

In between, we touched on what had happened to me and I could tell that Tienie understood. He was one of the few people, I felt, who did not view me as Alison the Noordhoek rape victim. He was concerned and had many questions, but he was much more interested in *me*, Alison, the person.

In Knysna that first night Tienie cooked a meal and we opened a bottle of red wine.

When he kissed me it all seemed so natural and right. I was actually waiting for him to do it but certainly wasn't going to say so. He just knew when to choose the right moment.

I had worried that I would have flashbacks or that it would be difficult for me to be physical with a man, but what happened on that beautiful evening with Tienie was so far removed from it all that it never entered my mind.

It was so exhilarating to feel that way again. I looked at Tienie and for the first time it actually dawned on me that I had fallen deeply in love.

It was such an uncomplicated feeling. There were no games being played and we had hidden nothing from each other.

Once we acknowledged our love for each other there

was no stopping us. We got back to Port Elizabeth a few days later and it must have been so obvious that something had happened between us.

Soon we were the talk of the town and everyone tried to extract more information, but we still didn't want to talk about it. It was so new to us there was no way we could explain it to other people.

In June 1996, we both went to Sedgefield to visit family. Tienie and I went out to dinner one evening and while we were enjoying a delicious candle-lit meal, he suddenly got up and went down on his knee in front of me.

I was quite astounded. It was incredibly romantic and was exactly how I'd always dreamed that moment would be.

Then he asked me to marry him. Of course I said yes immediately.

At the time he didn't have a ring but promised to get me one later. We also decided to keep our 'engagement' a secret until we had told our respective parents and until we set an official date later in the year.

But that night I was so excited I just had to tell someone. On our way out of the restaurant I blurted it out to the manager. His faced broke into a smile and he wished us well.

The following day we drove back to Port Elizabeth and Tienie told my mom. She was ecstatic. And his mom told me she thought I was the best thing that had ever happened to her son. She still tells me that regularly. Tienie also telephoned my dad in Johannesburg to ask for his blessing.

In the mean time the local papers had somehow found

out about it and started pressuring us to make it public. We really didn't want to as most of our friends didn't know yet, but eventually we gave in and gave an interview making an unofficial, official announcement.

I wasn't sure when Tienie would choose a special moment to make the official announcement with the ring which we had designed together.

As my birthday approached on September 22 I wondered whether he would do it that night. But it seemed too obvious and I put the thought out of my mind. But when I stepped out of the bathroom that night, all dressed up to go out, I found the lounge filled with flowers, the lights down low and romantic music wafting through the air. I knew what was about to happen.

Tienie asked me to dance and then afterwards sat me down and gave me the ring. Yes, when we left to join the rest of my friends I did feel as though I was floating on air.

Four months later we got married. It might seem that it was a very short time between his proposal and the marriage date, but we did not feel we were rushing it. We were meant for each other and there was no point wasting any time. We were so sure.

We spent the next month planning the marriage. Tienie plunged himself into the arrangements. He's a great organiser and comes to life when he has to pull things together.

On Valentine's Day the storm clouds started packing over the skies at Knysna but the next morning the sky was a brilliant blue and the sun beat down. It was, as *Femina* magazine described it, a perfect day for a wedding. It was one of the most beautiful days in my life, never mind the fact that it was swelteringly hot in the tiny church. It was everything I had dreamed it would be.

Tienie whisked me off for our surprise honeymoon in Mombasa, which was wonderful, and then we returned to Knysna where we had decided to settle.

For the first time in a long while I felt real again. I felt alive and a little more like my old self. I looked at my wonderful husband and realised that he was the person who had helped me to do it.

With his calm, deliberate manner and his secure presence he had helped me to find myself again, to put that last piece of the new puzzle into place.

22

TIENIE

Woman of my dreams

———◆———

THE NIGHT ALISON scrambled into my life I was on the point of sliding into a deep, dark depression. I had been clinging to the edge for quite some time and, as I sat there on the roof that night looking up at the stars, I knew that very soon something had to give.

For most of my life I had taken one knock after the other both in business and my personal life. Nothing I tried had seemed to work out. I felt thwarted at every turn and life, to me, had begun to lose all meaning.

It was so bad that I had reached a stage where I had lost faith in all humanity. Once I had been a carefree and happy boy who enjoyed so many things. Now I hated the way I had turned out. I had forgotten what it felt like to be happy, to love.

At that time, a good friend of mine, John, often tossed me a couple of lifelines and gave me the odd job to do here and there. I was grateful for his interest and for the little bits of money it brought in.

In retrospect, I should have sought help sooner. All the classic symptoms of depression were there.

I had given up my own apartment and was living with my mother. I would sleep through the day, awake at dusk and aimlessly roam the streets of Port Elizabeth until dawn.

I became a person of the night and I must have looked that way. I was trapped in a vicious circle and there seemed to be no end to it all. I was crying out for help, but didn't know how to ask for it.

Although outwardly I appeared to be holding it all together, I was abusing myself. I experimented with all sorts of drugs and drank far too much. I had lost all interest in sport and surfing. I did no physical exercise. Basically, I didn't care about anything any more.

I had read about Alison in the newspapers and knew that she was somehow connected with a good friend of mine, Nicki.

I didn't know Alison, although I remembered seeing her on the beach sometimes. She had also, at one stage, dated a neighbour of mine.

My first 'encounter' with her was via a little hand-made card she had given to Nicki to thank her for designing a dress for some occasion. I often used to visit Nicki and sometimes, when I just could not face going home, I would sleep over. She was one of the few people I could talk to and who hadn't grown tired of my sorry tale. Everyone else was losing patience with me and seemed to have grown accustomed to the new Tienie who mooched about with a sullen face and who had nothing of value to contribute to any conversation.

That night after she had gone to bed I pottered around and saw the beautiful garment and the note.

The next morning I asked Nicki about it and she told me that Alison, 'the Noordhoek girl', had written it.

We left it at that.

A few days later I went to a party at Nicki's. I remember seeing Ali arrive that night. I didn't think anything in particular, I was too caught up in my own depression to really care about anyone else.

At some stage we connected briefly. We said 'hello' to each other and chatted about mundane things.

As the party progressed I noticed everyone wanted a piece of her. She was surrounded by people, they were drawn to her like a magnet. She did exude an incredible, calm presence and she was exquisite but I had no 'romantic' intentions at the time. I could hardly feel anything for myself, never mind anyone else.

I felt out of place and went up on to the roof. When I owned the club I often did that. The noise and the crush would get to me and I yearned to be somewhere quiet where the sky stretched over me and where I could find an uncluttered space in my own head.

I scrambled up on to Nicki's roof. I didn't think anyone would miss me. I wasn't exactly the most scintillating person to be with at the time. It was standard behaviour for me. I'd go to a party and then just simply disappear.

I don't know how long I sat there but suddenly I noticed Nicki and Alison peering out of a window that looked out on to the roof. Alison had to navigate a precarious pitch and I was quite surprised to see her negotiating it.

'I've come to join you,' she said settling down next to me.

I wondered why she wanted to be with me. I really had nothing to offer, but it felt quite good to have some company.

I don't know how it happened but there was something about Ali that quietened my inner turmoil. She was so gentle and caring and was the first person in a long time who bothered to ask questions.

Then suddenly I felt a tremendous welling up of emotion inside me and I just opened up. I must have babbled on like a mad man. It all just flowed out of me like a raging torrent.

Up above us were the stars and down below were the people at the party. It felt as though Ali and I were on some plane in the middle, in a world of our own.

Ali just sat there, listening attentively to me.

We talked deep into the night and went out for some coffee later. When we parted I felt as light as a soap bubble. I didn't think I would ever feel that way again, but the unburdening had somehow flushed something out of my system.

Ali and I didn't exchange numbers that night. I didn't think she would care for such a wretched creature and was just grateful for the time she had spent with me.

A few weeks later the Citizen of the Year Award ceremony took place. Ali was one of the people who had been nominated and my friend John had booked an entire table. He persuaded me to come with him and even hired a tuxedo for me.

I offered to drive everyone there in the Combi, hoping

that by having something to do I would melt into the background. When I saw Ali, I noticed she was wearing the dress that Nicki had designed for her. It was the same one I had seen earlier with the note attached to it. She looked stunning when she went up on stage to collect the award for Citizen of the Year.

Later she joined us at our table. Everyone seemed to be dazzled by her and although I could tell she was special I didn't think, 'Wow, this is Alison.' I just thought, 'Wow, what a beautiful girl.'

Afterwards we all went out for coffee again. I was hoping she'd come with us. I really wanted to connect with her again and throughout that evening I felt as if we were both 'looking for each other'.

I was thrilled when she agreed. We went to a restaurant and gradually everyone left. Alison, I noticed, had stayed behind and eventually the two of us ended up chatting again until four in the morning.

Once again I opened up to her. At that stage she never spoke about her experience at all. She concentrated on me exclusively and I wondered why.

The next day we met again. I felt we were growing closer and that Ali could see where I was coming from. She allowed me to delve into myself and find those special places I had forgotten or neglected for so long.

I was quite surprised when she suggested that we go to a travel agent. She told me she had thought about me and felt that what I needed was a break away from it all.

Next thing we were sitting in a travel agency discussing where I would go. I thought it was a good idea. At least it was something concrete and it would hopefully break the awful cycle in which I had become trapped.

I was so touched that someone had enough faith in me to, first, lend me money and, secondly, to take the time and make the effort to help me. I was adamant that I would pay her back the money as soon as I could.

We didn't book the tickets that day and decided we would both think it over. As we parted that afternoon I realised that I missed her. Actually I hated leaving her. I had felt so comfortable with her it was quite weird. We hadn't even held hands and at that stage it had not entered my mind that we might be able to have a relationship.

She was one of the most remarkable people I had met in a long time. She was so beautiful, loving, sincere and caring and I realised that she was someone really special.

The overseas trip sort of began to fade into the background as we made excuses to see each other. I would call her in the morning saying I was going to be in the vicinity running some errand. Oddly enough she'd always be available.

Ali was also in a state of limbo at that stage. She had resigned from her job and was seeing doctors almost every day.

One weekend my friend John asked me to arrange a party at his house in Cape St Francis. I was planning to go out ahead of everyone else to air the house and organise everything. I told Ali that I was going ahead and asked her to come with me. She agreed and we went off in separate cars. We behaved like two kids on the way, stopping on the side of the road and passing each other all the time.

I set up the house and every time I looked for Ali she

was out somewhere on her bicycle. The other guests arrived and the weekend started to turn into a party.

Some of the guests broke off into separate groups but Ali and I stayed together all the time.

We had a fantastic time walking, lying on the lawn talking about poetry, sitting in the dunes, making a huge bonfire on the beach. I did not really want to acknowledge it at the time, but we were falling in love. I felt alive again and Ali too seemed happy. At one stage we sat in a boat in the pouring rain while she sang her heart out. The next day she was completely hoarse.

Later we went to visit some friends of Ali's who lived in the area. The atmosphere at that house was completely different from the party energy at John's. We spent a calm and peaceful afternoon with Ali's friends and at one stage took a walk through their spectacular indigenous garden that had been made into a garden of remembrance.

Then something strange happened to me. Ali was up front strolling with her friends and I lagged behind just enjoying the scenery. I saw a bench and sat down on it and then suddenly I just began to cry. I was mildly embarrassed about it and hoped that Ali wouldn't turn around and see me. As I sat there sobbing I felt the rest of the weight that had burdened me quietly lift.

I felt, for the first time in many years, that I had found myself again and I knew that Ali had been a big part of that. She had somehow seen the real me, believed in the real me, and that in turn helped me to find and believe in myself again.

That was a very special day for me and when Ali and I connected later on I didn't feel like leaving and going back to the more rowdy crowd at John's house.

There was an incredible energy between us that weekend. Occasionally we would brush against each other and I would feel an electric current rushing through my body. I still wasn't sure whether Ali felt the same way so I decided not to rush things.

I was born in the George area so a few weeks later when Ali told me she had been asked to give a talk there, I volunteered to accompany her. This was my world and I wanted to show her around.

I also thought it would be great for both of us to get out of PE for a while.

To my delight she agreed. For the first time in many years I grew excited about something. I had suddenly begun to feel connected to the real world again.

We packed the Combi with food and wine and our mountain bikes and off we went. The journey down the Garden Route was wonderful. We listened to music and just talked. We both felt like ordinary people again, unfettered by our respective demons.

On that journey I realised I had fallen in love with this most special woman. Ali, it dawned on me, was everything I had ever dreamed of in a woman.

She was my ultimate partner and I knew then and there that I wanted to spend the rest of my life with her. Everything about her, the way she viewed the world, the way she interacted with people and the value she saw in life, were qualities I respected and admired.

I didn't think there were many people like her in the world and I felt blessed that I had found her.

My emotions were in complete turmoil that weekend in Knysna. One evening I cooked a meal for us. It was something I enjoyed doing but had not done in a long while.

It was so romantic. Just the two of us. I cooked pasta and we opened a bottle of red wine. Everything was just so right and I wanted the moment to last for ever.

I wanted to savour it all, I was afraid it would all just disappear, that it was all just a beautiful dream.

When I leaned over to kiss her the first time it felt so natural. It was as if I was meant to be with her, that she was the other half of my soul, and that I had been looking for her for all these years.

Now, I had come home. Things felt complete.

Of course I thought about the rape and the attack but it was never a problem as far as I was concerned. I never held back intentionally. I was reticent at first because I was so afraid I would lose this beautiful person. From the first day I met her, she was just Ali. Not Ali the rape victim, or Ali this amazing person.

We have talked at length about Ali's trauma. It happened, it will never, ever go away but we have put it in its place. We know it is there, we are comfortable with the way we have dealt and are still dealing with it.

I have always said to Ali that if I ever do anything that bugs her or that she needs to talk about she must tell me. The stigma that is attached to rape and that cripples so many women is something that can be worked through with a loving partner.

Why should Ali feel any shame about being raped? It doesn't make her less of a person and the trauma is not all that there is in our lives.

Ali was and is the first person I have met in many years who feels completely real to me. It is as if I had known her in a previous lifetime.

Soon after our Knysna weekend I asked her to marry me. We were on another trip to Sedgefield and there was no point in delaying it. I had absolutely no doubts about her.

Ali is my ultimate friend. It's amazing how similar our dreams and interests are. We see and want the same things from life.

Our wedding day was amazing and I was so proud to be walking down the aisle with her at my side. I am so proud she is my wife.

Ali and I have been married for close on two years now. Her work often takes her away from home and from me. Often she is completely exhausted when she gets back to our house in Knysna. The talks, I can see, take so much out of her. Ali always gives 100 per cent of herself and we have agreed to make sure that the time we spend together is always restorative.

I know how important these talks are to Ali and I have seen, as I have sat in the audience, how much it means to the people who come to hear her speak. She seems to open people up and so many of them come up to her afterwards to talk about their own traumas. She is very affected by other people's stories, more so than anyone else I know. When you've been there yourself you are able to feel another person's pain.

I see how some people view Ali as this exceptional human being and of course she is, but I also get to see the private Ali, the vulnerable Ali, who sometimes just needs to be nurtured and cared for.

We complement each other that way. I will for ever be grateful to Ali for giving me back my life, for helping me to understand that you write your own ticket and that life is what you make of it.

We're in the process of building our dream home. It is everything I have always wanted and very soon I would like us to start a family. Although Ali's uterus was slightly scarred during the attack it appears as if no major damage was done. We'll just have to see, although I must confess I can't wait to see my beautiful wife pregnant with our first child.

23

ALISON

From victim to victor

———◆———

RECENTLY, WHILE SORTING through boxes in my office, I came across a file of letters and various other cards and notes I had written and received over the years. I am a great letter writer. I love sitting down and putting my thoughts on paper without distraction or interruption.

I bombarded my friends in South Africa with my correspondence when I was in London. Writing, for me, has always been a way of making sense of things, a way of communicating intimately.

Often when we write things down, be it a poem, a letter or a diary entry, we create a record of our past, although that might not have been the primary motivation at the time. Sometimes the stuff that spills out is merely self-indulgent and really cringe-worthy, but in between we may find little gems or nuggets of wisdom and profundity that relate to moments when we have had some kind of personal epiphany or realisation.

The writing on the page can bring those moments back to life so vividly. Memory can often fail us. We can bluff ourselves, framing only certain incidents and neglecting or forgetting many subtle nuances that flavoured a particularly poignant experience.

My collection of letters and other writings are part of my history now. Perhaps if the attack had never happened to me I might not have gone back to them to track my life up until that moment when it changed so irrevocably.

It is always wonderful to rummage through old photographs and letters and the day I found my boxes I sat on the floor for hours lost in a journey through my past.

I suppose you could say that in some way I was looking for answers and evidence of change. I wanted to see how much of the old Ali was still part of the new Ali. I was heartened to discover that so much of her is still alive and perfectly intact, but a part of her has been lost.

What is missing now from my life is a feeling of innocence and youth and the belief that everything is good, but most of us lose that with the natural passage of time, although I might have been jolted from that blissful state a little earlier and much more traumatically than most people.

Still, sifting through the records of my past I was struck by some of the things I said and believed at the time.

There was one letter that particularly caught my attention. I had written it to a dear friend in November

1990, four years before my attack.

It went:

I was thinking about how much emphasis we place on how we should live our lives that sometimes we forget how just to BE.

When we have dreams and expectations we make ourselves vulnerable because so much is beyond our control. One incident can shatter lifelong dreams (a death, an accident, a financial set-back, a break-up with a loved one) and unforeseeable circumstances can scupper all our plans.

I could not have known then that it would be me who would experience and survive the very 'one incident' I had referred to in the letter.

I read on.

I am not saying that we should stop dreaming or stop setting goals for ourselves, but instead of placing so much importance on the things that bring us happiness, we should live each moment with joy, a passionate fervour and a contentment of being. Our dreams and our plans are only that. They are not necessarily what the future will be or where we will find ourselves in that future.

In other words, we cannot foretell the future but we can choose how to live each day.

Looking back and reading those letters I realise that so much of who I was then has helped me to cope with this trauma. Without realising it, I had created for myself a set of ideas and beliefs, a life code if you like, that has helped me to become a victor and not remain a victim.

I had unknowingly been preparing myself to survive and cope with my trauma and when these philosophies and beliefs were tested they stood their ground and came through for me with flying colours.

So many times people have said to me, 'You are such an extraordinary person. You are so amazing.'

I do not think so at all. The way I have coped with the attack and the rape and the way I live my life now is actually all common sense. We all have the capacity to be 'extraordinary' but we don't have to wait until something traumatic happens to discover this.

The difference between the Ali who wrote that letter in 1990 and the Ali today is that I have been forced to live out my own code, to take it seriously and to incorporate it into every waking moment.

To make it easier to explain and to share it with my audiences as an inspirational speaker, I have called it my ABC.

The A is for attitude, the B for belief and the C for choice. These three elements, I have come to realise, have had a tremendous effect and have made a difference in my recovery.

Although I have experienced what could be viewed as a personal cataclysm, I do believe that these principles can be applied to everyone's life. They have worked for me and I am convinced that they can work for you.

They will, I am sure, with the correct amount of discipline and dedication, enable you to deal with whatever it is that you feel is holding you back in your life and preventing you from achieving your personal best, whatever that may be.

But before I get to the core of my ABC, I would like to tell you a story. This is something I share with some of my audiences and it usually results in an interesting but common response.

I ask people to imagine that they have wandered into an antique shop where they have found an exquisite old lamp. You've guessed it, after rubbing it, a genie pops out, but instead of the proverbial three wishes he tells you that you only have one wish and that is to be turned into any person you wish to be. Who would it be?

Think about it for a moment. What would your answer be?

The most common response from my audiences and those who feel they want to answer the question is that they would like to be someone else. A lot want to be Mel Gibson or someone famous and one gentleman even said he would like to be his mother-in-law.

The vast majority, sadly, say they would like to be someone else. Only a handful say they are happy to be themselves.

I find this sad.

Why?

Because it indicates that a large number of people live with à wish, a hope, that can and will never be realised. It is an impossible dream. It doesn't matter how much you wish you were someone else, you never will be. You will always be you – who you were when you were born and who you will be when you die.

There are those who are fortunate enough to have loads of money who have spent fortunes trying to change themselves. For example, celebrities who try to change their appearance with plastic surgery.

Money can perhaps buy you a new face and body but it cannot buy a new soul, or peace and contentment for that matter. Our attitude towards ourselves is one of the foundations of our lives, the rock on which we build everything else and from which all things grow.

What is your attitude towards yourself and do you see yourself as someone of worth?

If you do not value yourself, how can you ever begin to convince anyone else that you are of value?

There are so many people who have said that it is difficult for them to find any value in their lives or in themselves. They suffer from low self-esteem for many reasons, many of them beginning with their early childhood experiences.

I was fortunate. I grew up with parents, my mother in particular, who gave me unconditional love. My parents divorced when I was ten and although my father is precious and dear to me, my brother Neale and I lived with my mom so she exerted the greatest influence on our lives.

Often, as we were growing up, she would take us aside and tell us how special we were. She would always add, though, that this did not mean we were better than or above others, but that we had our own inner value. It made me realise and appreciate that I was different, that each of us is different and totally unique.

I knew that my mother would support whatever it was I chose to do with my life. She always encouraged us to achieve our personal best, even if that didn't meet the standards or notions of anyone else.

So, from an early age I was instilled with a wonderful sense of self-worth that I have been able to take with me throughout my life. Such a sense of value is unshakeable and I believe it had a lot to do with my need to survive that night and my emotional and physical healing afterwards.

And so we must begin by valuing ourselves and cultivating a sense of self-worth. If it comes naturally, continue to work on it. If it doesn't, I believe it is something that can be developed, even if you find it difficult at first.

To me, something valuable is something that is impossible to replace, and we are all impossible to replace. It is also in valuing others that we find greater meaning in our own lives. Understanding that allows us to begin to see beyond ourselves and to realise that everything is interconnected.

Each person that you meet, each person you interact with in business or your personal life, be it a child or an adult, has as much value as you do. That person is as unique as you are and what is going on in that person's life is as important to him or her as the ebb and flow of your own life.

Treat people with an attitude that shows that you value them. It is amazing how we can change the outcome of a situation by simply remembering and applying that.

We may feel irritated by someone or we may be angry at the way they behave. It doesn't mean we don't have to express those feelings, but if we do we need to remember that each person has dignity. Treating someone with respect and value, even if we vehemently disagree with him or her, can produce miraculous results.

For example, the young democracy we now enjoy in

South Africa came about when those in power began to realise that each of us has value and a point of view and that suppressing that point of view or treating people as if they had no value could have disastrous consequences.

But it is not only our attitude to ourselves and others that is important, it is also our attitude towards particular problems, dilemmas and difficulties that determines possible outcomes.

I would like to recount a story from the Bible that sums up for me the meaning and the power of positive thought when viewing problems.

It is the story of David and Goliath the giant.

When the Israelites faced Goliath they looked at him and said, 'Oh, he's so big, we can't possibly kill him.'

But little David, armed only with a slingshot and a handful of stones, looked at the same giant and said, 'Ah, but he's so big, I can't possibly miss.'

If only we could see all our problems that way it would be so much easier to solve them.

Every problem has a weak spot and every problem has a solution.

We tend to approach problems with the notion that there is only one solution. We look at our problem, we think about it, and often we decide what the solution is without considering other options.

At first I thought the only solution to my situation would be to carry on as if the whole trauma had not happened. I wanted to undo the damage by getting on with my life and ignoring it.

Because I was so determined to believe this, at first, I missed all the other options that were available to me. I could not see them because I focused too closely on the problem and because I did not look for alternative answers.

Another story I enjoy retelling to illustrate this point is the one about a man who is caught with his family in a flash flood. As the waters rise around him, he manages to get everyone, including the dog, up on to the roof of his house.

He stands there praying silently, asking God to save them all. Just then a neighbour passes by in a boat. He calls out to the family and urges them to get in with him and his family and leave while they still can.

But the man waves his neighbour off, stubbornly insisting that God will take care of them all.

Torrential rain falls and the waters rise even higher. Still the man keeps praying. A while later a rescue boat cruises up alongside the house and the crew urge the man and his family to get in and save themselves.

Once again he waves them on, saying the Lord will take care of them.

The water inches up and reaches dangerous levels. All around him the man sees a vast sea of brown, bubbling, cold water. Even the rooftops have disappeared.

He hears the sound of a helicopter and looks up as it hovers above his home and his wretched family trapped on the last bit of roofing that is left exposed.

'Take the rope ladder,' one of the men shouts down through the din. 'Save yourself and your family. It is your last chance.'

The man looks up and shouts, 'I have placed my faith in God. He will save us. Go away.'

Eventually the flood waters break and wash over the

house. The man and his entire family, including the dog, drown.

Luckily they find themselves at heaven's gate and the man, now highly disappointed and in the throes of a crisis of faith, confronts God.

'Listen,' he says in a confrontational tone, 'I don't understand it. All my life I've learned to put my faith in you and here was a moment of crisis when I needed you most and you failed me. You did not answer my prayers.'

God looks at the man, his family and the dog and despairingly shakes his head.

Then he speaks: 'First I sent your neighbour, then I sent the rescue boat and then the helicopter. What else did you expect me to do?'

The man's stubborn belief in only one solution had blinded him to all the other possibilities.

Like me, who just wanted it all to go away.

I had not, at that time, looked back at the miracles that had been sent to help me heal and make sense of it all.

Remember this story when you are dealing with a problem of your own.

Be open to all solutions. You might be surprised to find that one may immediately present itself. If it does, think about it, ponder other avenues. But once you have found a solution to a problem, implement it immediately.

Many of us carry our problems around with us for much longer than we need to. They become an intrinsic part of who we are and we can become perversely attached to them. If that happens we actually burden ourselves with things we don't need to.

I see life as a journey. On this magical journey it is

inevitable that we will gather baggage.

Imagine that we all carry a rucksack and that each problem we encounter is translated into something tangible, say a rock or a stone, depending on the size of the problem or trauma.

What we do is pick up that rock or stone and place it in the rucksack. Eventually it will become too heavy for us to carry. It becomes a burden that stops our progress. We may fall along the wayside, too tired to carry on.

But if we stop sometimes and make the time to open that rucksack and examine what is inside it, we will find many things lurking there that we no longer need and that we can happily discard.

The point is, all of us need an emotional and mental spring-clean occasionally. We need to throw out some of those stones and rocks we have been carrying with us. It might be a terrible divorce or childhood trauma that has filled you with bitterness, resentment and hatred towards someone.

It might be a minor or major betrayal or even a financial set-back, but the question to ask yourself is: Why have you decided to keep that burden?

Sometimes it is a very traumatic issue in our lives and we may find it very hard to put it down or discard.

Yet it can be done.

I made a conscious decision to put down the burden of the trauma that had happened to me and all the negative emotions it brought. I vowed that I would make an effort not to carry it with me for the rest of my life.

That doesn't mean I must forget it and pretend it didn't happen. But I have lightened the burden by looking for the meaning and the lessons that are held within it and by not carrying the burdens of bitterness, anger and hatred.

So often a problem can become such a part of us that it is all that there is. We brood on it, we talk about it constantly. It gets us the attention we need from others.

People are generally sympathetic to someone with a problem. If you find yourself amongst friends and bring up your problem you will get them to take notice.

Most will feel sorry for you and indulge you. Eventually you convince yourself and others that your problem is the worst and deserving of much scrutiny and dissection.

By getting their undivided attention and focus, the problem is reaffirmed. In turn, we hold on to it for much longer than we need to.

Ultimately it can become a security blanket, something familiar and the very thing by which we define ourselves. And whenever we feel down or out of control, we blame and curse the problem.

By refusing to deal with and let go of it you are actually holding yourself back. You have no one to blame but yourself.

My advice in these circumstances is to learn from your problem, take from it instead of letting it take from you, and then move on.

I have been asked if I have moved on from my trauma, if I have taken that huge rock out of my own personal rucksack.

At this stage I can answer that I have located the rock, placed it outside on the grass and am looking at it, still working with it.

I am a different person today. I can never be the same

Alison. I can never make what happened to me go away but I have, by adopting a positive attitude, not allowed it to remain a burden.

It is not holding me back.

I sometimes shudder to think of what I might have missed out on if I still carried the burden of bitterness and hatred towards the perpetrators of the crime or towards the system that allowed it to happen.

There were times when I was momentarily overwhelmed with anger, but I knew that if I allowed myself to be consumed by the anger I would never again be able to see the magic in life or even to love again.

You might think it has been easier for me because of my naturally positive nature, but I believe that this is an attribute that can be cultivated even in the most barren of emotional and mental landscapes.

Just as we cultivate bad habits, so can we cultivate good ones.

We can reshape and repattern life experiences and find something positive in them. It is an exercise in discipline but eventually, if you are committed enough and work at it, positivism will become a part of your nature.

Let's look at a very simple hypothetical situation where negativity can cascade and permeate everything.

You wake up one morning and your spouse or your children irritate you or make you angry.

Without thinking, you leave the house carrying that anger with you.

It simmers inside as you get into the car and drive to work. By the time you've turned the corner you've convinced yourself the world is a foul, mean place and that you'll probably encounter red traffic lights all along your route.

You pass through one green light and there are few red ones along the way. But those are the only ones you remember. Sitting there in the gridlock, you fume even more.

You get to the office and everything now becomes an irritation. Someone may even remark that it appears that you have 'got up on the wrong side of the bed'.

As the day wears on your mood deteriorates. A colleague tries to cheer you up but you fob him off, enveloped in your own anger and misery.

On the way home you get caught in another heavy traffic jam and of course all the traffic lights are red. You pull up in the driveway and the first thing you say when you see your spouse is, 'Thanks to you, I've had the most awful day.'

The truth of the matter is that your spouse had nothing to do with the events that have plagued your day.

You, and you alone, were responsible for holding that anger, that petty feeling of irritation, inside you the moment you stepped into your car. It was your choice to hold on to it and let it tinge everything in your wake.

Your attitude towards the minor and inevitable irritations of life determined how you would experience everything else that day. You did not have to be angry. Perhaps your spouse did trigger something or was at fault at first, but it was your own attitude towards it that prolonged it all unnecessarily.

If we can learn to step back for just a moment, catch our breath and think about what is going on, we give ourselves the space to change our attitude towards something, we give ourselves a small gap in which we can make a choice.

It's like driving in the fast lane which can, in a city like Johannesburg, be an extremely stressful experience. You have to watch out for those people behind you who are determined to go faster than you. They pull up behind you, red in the face, gesticulating and cursing and flashing their lights.

Becoming absorbed or consumed by a mood is akin to that.

That driver in the fast lane is so consumed and single-minded that he can think of nothing else and sometimes this can lead to tragedy.

Try driving in the slow lane, put on a cassette with your favourite soothing music, and watch how in a little while the feelings of irritation begin to subside. You stop thinking about the cars in front of or next to you.

I don't mean that you must become reckless, but that all your senses should not merely be focused on driving and getting to your destination.

You can take in the countryside that flashes by, you can linger on a particularly beautiful note in a song.

You will get to your destination in a much better mood than the person who has rushed there like a bat out of hell.

With a change of attitude comes a new perspective on belief and belief is the B part of my ABC.

How many of us really believe in ourselves?

So many of us stop ourselves at the starting gates, convincing ourselves that we cannot do something, that it is too difficult or impossible to achieve.

It is easier to believe when we value ourselves but it is also amazing to learn that only a tiny ounce of belief can accomplish incredible things.

It was so in my case. Only one per cent of me believed that night that I would make it to the road. The rest of me, every fibre in my being, did not believe it. Yet it was that tiny percentage of hope and belief that enabled me to try and crawl another centimetre, to take just one more step.

That one per cent of me overrode the rest and miracles happened, the seemingly impossible was accomplished. I survived.

That belief in ourselves is a potential we all possess but rarely use. It is at our disposal every day and it is amazing what it enables us to achieve.

Another example of the power of belief was brought to my attention during one of my talks in Knysna.

When I had finished speaking, a woman whose son had been seriously injured after he was caught and dumped by a freak wave told me of his incredible strength and amazing belief in himself.

After the accident, she told the crowd, her son had been washed up on the remote beach. He realised that he could not move. His limbs felt like lead and the messages from his brain did not seem to go anywhere.

For some reason, she said, her son had thought of me.

He said to himself, 'If she could do it, then so can I.'

He decided that he would not give up and just lie there, hoping someone would find him. So he gathered all his strength and will and got up.

He managed to walk for about two kilometres over

hills, rocks and bushes before he found help and was taken to the nearest hospital where, like me, he was rushed into surgery.

Afterwards the doctor asked him where the accident had happened and the young man told him the name of the beach and the fact that he had walked to find help.

The doctor was astounded. He told the young man that he must have been mistaken because the nature and extent of his injuries were such that it would have been impossible for him to walk.

But he did it. His belief in himself gave him the extraordinary strength to accomplish what he did.

No one had told him he could not do it and because he believed he made the miracle happen.

So, if you believe in yourself, if you have faith in whatever talents you have inside you, you will make something of nothing.

You do not always have to be *the* best. Just do *your* best.

A perfect example of what I'm referring to happens during another little test I often do on my audiences.

I ask everyone who can sing to raise their hand. Inevitably only a few shoot up. I always thank those who are brave enough to admit their talent, but I usually tell the rest of the crowd that they are lying.

The point is, if you can talk, you can sing. You don't have to sing beautifully or even in tune.

My question to the audience was not if they could sing *well*, but if they could simply *sing*.

When I ask an audience of children the same question, something remarkable happens.

Each and every one of them puts up their hands.

Sometimes there's a veritable stampede to the front of the stage as everyone eagerly offers to come up and sing.

The difference between the children and the adults is that the children haven't yet been told that they cannot do something.

They still believe in themselves. They have not been told to worry about what the person next to them may think or that they will make fools of themselves.

We should remember that we were all children once and maybe we should work at recapturing that open-mindedness and belief that anything is possible, even flying.

The first battering of our sense of belief often comes at high school where a competitive edge creeps into everything. Only the best make it to the team, only the brightest and the cleverest are rewarded.

If you don't shine in some way you are expected to languish in the shadow of someone else, wishing you were them.

I used to love to play hockey. I adored the outfits, the shin guards and being part of the team. But I was not good at it as a sport. I was hopeless, actually.

One day the coach called me over and told me that they couldn't use me any more and that I shouldn't worry to attend practice.

I was mortified. And since that day I have carried the belief that I am not good at sport.

Each time I am asked to participate in some sort of sporty thing, even throwing the frisbee on the beach, I think I can't do it. So naturally, I can't.

We allow ourselves to stop doing the things we love because we think we are not the *best* at it.

Believe in your personal best and make use of the talent that you have, no matter how great or small.

I always urge parents to do this with their children. To encourage them to do whatever it is they get pleasure from, even if they are not the best.

I take some comfort from this saying: 'The woods would be silent if the only birds that sang there were the ones who sang best.'

Be a bird, sing to whatever ability you have. The world would most certainly be a dull place if the only people who ever did anything were the ones who knew that they would excel.

Remember whether you think you can, or you think you can't, you're right.

If you have a task in front of you and you think 'I can't, I can't I can't', then you will not.

But if you think 'I can, I can, I can', you will, and in so doing amaze yourself.

I urge you in life, wherever you find yourself, whether in a business presentation or a confrontation with a friend, to turn it around whenever you begin to feel those nagging doubts.

Believe in yourself, convince yourself beforehand that you are confident, that you can do it. Believe in the results you want and you will find yourself convinced before you convince anyone else. Try it. It really works.

And when you are grappling with a problem, believe in the bigger picture.

In our modern, rushed society today everything seems so stressful. We juggle so many balls trying desperately to keep them all in the air at the same time. We see only those balls then and nothing else.

When I worked in an office I would often lie awake at night worrying about something on my desk. At the time there was nothing I could do about it. It just had to wait until the next day, yet I wasted time and energy thinking about something that had no solution at the time.

I cluttered my mind with things that were so unnecessary and ended up being unproductive when I could have focused my energies on something more worth while.

The point is, we must learn not to worry about things if there is nothing we can do about them at that very moment. That does not mean we must simply forget that a problem exists; it means we must acknowledge that the best thing to do at that moment is to let it go and to pick it up again when it is appropriate.

Do not allow your problems to become larger than they really are.

Imagine your problem is a glass on a table. Now imagine a camera that zooms in and focuses only on the glass. Suddenly it fills the frame, it becomes huge and we can see nothing else.

Now, imagine the camera zooming out again. Suddenly we see the glass on the table, we see a hand clutching at the stem, we see a group of people sitting around that table. Suddenly the glass no longer looks so huge, as if it is the only thing that exists.

Step back even more and you see that the room is full of people. It is in a context and so much more is going on around it. The glass – the problem, in other words – is just a small part of a bigger picture.

Do the same with a problem. Step back from it. Look

at your life in perspective. See what other hardships you have already overcome.

And if you can't find anything in your own life, look at the lives of others and what they have managed to overcome. Look at my life, or the life of someone else who has experienced a traumatic event and was able to overcome it.

Do not allow your problems to make your life a misery. All we have is a short space of time in which to live our lives and we really need to make conscious choices to be happy as much as we can.

This leads into the most important part of my three-step solution – the C which stands for choice.

The instant I realised I had a choice in the manner in which I dealt with what had happened to me I reached a turning point.

It lifted me out of my depression and gave me back a sense of control.

It was one of the most difficult things I needed to learn and it was not easy to accept. I had to realise that although it hadn't been my choice to be attacked and raped, everything after that was within my control.

I remember sitting alone at home one day in the depths of a terrible depression.

I asked myself: 'Is this what you want your life to be? Did you fight so hard to live so that you can sit here feeling sorry for yourself? Is this what it is going to be like for the rest of your life?'

Instinctively, I knew that if I was ever going to be happy again, if I was ever going to enjoy my life again, I was going to have to choose to do so.

None of my friends or my family blamed me for being

depressed. They all said, 'A terrible thing has happened to Alison, of course she is going to be depressed.'

No one blamed me for my condition.

You might want to blame the situation that you find yourself in. You might want to blame the economy, you might want to blame the 'new' South Africa. You might want to blame your husband or your wife. But you cannot. You, and you alone, are responsible for choosing to be happy, sad or angry.

I realised that I had to choose to be happy again, no matter how difficult it may have seemed.

Be proactive in life. Do not wait for something to happen before you realise how important these things are.

I just love Oprah Winfrey's idea of the gratitude journal. In the beginning she said she had trouble writing or remembering five good things that had happened to her or that she had seen that day. But with time, and as her attitude adjusted and she became more positive, she found many more than five things to be grateful for.

I suggest you start such a journal. What it does is force you to look for the good in each moment. It is always there. We can see the world only through our own eyes. If we are angry and bitter, it will feel like an angry and bitter place to be.

Our days are numbered from the moment we are born. There are only two things in life we can be sure of – one is that we are born and the other is that we will die. We do not know how much time each of us has here. We don't get to choose when we will die or how we will die, but we always have the choice about how we will live. No matter what circumstances you may find yourself in, and no matter if a situation is out of your control, you always have control over your attitude, your belief and what you choose to do.

Please choose wisely. Choose to be happy. It can be done.

24

ALISON

Surviving rape

————◆————

IF ONE CONSIDERS the shocking rape statistics in South Africa it is highly likely that many of you who have chosen to read my book have been raped yourself or know of someone who has. I find it utterly tragic that rape has reached such epidemic proportions in our country.

It is a violent crime that not only causes physical damage, but can result in lasting psychological, emotional and spiritual pain in survivors.

I was surprised to find, after I had been raped, just how insensitive many people are. One evening the topic came up during a discussion and one man in the group actually voiced an opinion that I believe is shared by many unenlightened men.

He actually said, 'What's the big fuss? It's only sex.'

At the time I reeled from the shock. I could not believe

that someone would view rape that way. But there are still many people who, despite the ongoing work by various organisations and groups, do not understand the nature of rape.

Rape is never about sex. It is about power and it is about violence. To a woman it is the ultimate personal invasion.

When I first spoke out and showed my face, I did not realise how much it would mean and the storm of publicity it would create. Until then, it seemed, women bore the frightening stigma of rape in silence. They were faceless and nameless victims, a situation that, I believe, exacerbated the burden that these women carry and that somehow sent a message to the rapist that he could continue his crimes as women were too 'ashamed' to report it or speak out.

This perpetuated the myth that a woman who is raped is somehow responsible for the deed.

I am lucky that I never once felt that way about what Frans and Theuns did to me. As far as I am concerned they committed a crime. If they had broken into my home or had hijacked me I would not have kept quiet about it. If someone breaks into your car, no one asks why you parked it in a certain place or why you didn't make sure you had a better alarm or whatever.

So why should we, as rape survivors, have to bear the added pain of being made to think we have some responsibility for the violent acts of others?

But attitudes in this country are changing, albeit slowly. Many women come up to me after my talks and tell me of their own ordeals at the hands of rapists. Some of them have lived with the pain for many years and have never been able to speak about it. Many have been raped by people they knew and trusted, and in some cases the scars have never healed.

But the first step in the healing process, I believe, is to tell people that you have been raped. You should never hide it from anyone. I am not suggesting that you raise it all the time or that you get up on a soapbox, although if that's what you need to do then do it.

People should be made aware of the fact that there are many more rape survivors in their midst than they realise. The statistics alone, if we look at only those rapes that are reported to the police, are proof of this.

Many times when I have been out socially, people have made insensitive and crude comments. Once in a bar, a man said he found someone so attractive that he could rape her. I was about to explode when Tienie gently put his hand on my shoulder. There was no point, I realised, in confronting him at that time and in that place. It would have served no purpose.

My advice to rape survivors is that they report the crime to the police. You might be afraid to do so, or you might believe there is no point when the rapist will simply be granted bail and be back on the streets the next day.

That was exactly the case with Frans and Theuns. At one stage I was advised by a lawyer to sue the Minister of Justice and the South African Police Service because my attack and rape had occurred because of the lax bail laws at the time and insufficient evidence led regarding their previous crimes.

Tienie and I explored the issue but eventually realised we could not take it any further as our costs would have been exorbitant. I do believe it is the duty of the government to protect its citizens from criminals such as Frans and Theuns.

In the mean time, bail laws have been tightened and other anti-crime legislation has been passed but we are still reeling, as a nation, from an unacceptably high level of crime.

If we want to see more action we must continue to lobby, protest, organise petitions and place pressure on the relevant authorities to enact more changes to the law that will eventually ensure our safety as South Africans.

There are women in Parliament who have raised this issue continuously and who have tirelessly highlighted the shocking level of violence in this country. They have correctly pointed out that women and children bear the full brunt of it.

Communities are growing tired of excuses and in some cases are taking the law into their own hands. We have seen many reports of angry residents across the country parading rapists and child molesters naked through the streets. There is just so much we can take.

But we must not lose hope. In the mean time I have seen concrete evidence that the attitudes in the SAPS towards rape and rape survivors has started to change. Policemen are much more sensitive to the issue and public awareness has been heightened.

There is a special court for sexual offences that is up and running in Wynberg, Cape Town. Recently I was delighted and honoured to learn that a trauma room had been added to the Margate police station in KwaZulu-Natal and that it had been named after me.

It is also vitally important for rape survivors to seek some form of counselling. You cannot handle the trauma alone and there are many organisations, like Rape Crisis and POWA, that have offices or branches in every town in the country and that give advice free of charge.

To the families and loved ones of a rape survivor I can only say, let her deal with the rape in her own way. Do not displace your own feelings on to her. Often when a woman is raped her husband or her boyfriend flies into a fit of rage and wants to go out and kill the rapist. Although you might believe this is a noble sentiment, it does not help the survivor. What she needs most at that time is your care, your love and, most of all, your support.

Families of rape survivors often feel helpless and this comes across in their behaviour towards the survivor. The most important thing to remember is that although you are hurt and enraged, the rape survivor is the person you need to think about. If it is at all possible do not lose your cool when you are dealing with her.

Every woman will have her own way of dealing with a rape. Some will want to withdraw, others will want to talk. Let her do it her way.

Do not try and lift a survivor out of her depression or tell her to pull herself together. There will be days when the survivor will be able to get on with her life but there will also be times, and sometimes it creeps up from nowhere, when the ordeal will play itself out in her mind over and over again.

But the most important thing to know is that rape no longer needs to remain your secret and your pain.

Something I also discovered after my rape is that very few people openly discuss the physiological response, or one's body's reaction, in a physical trauma like rape.

In Chapter 2, *A Waking Nightmare*, I describe the moment that Frans raped me.

You might have been startled to read the lines: 'I realised that I was moist and I was horrified. I felt that my body had betrayed me completely.'

Many rape survivors I have spoken to say they experienced the same thing. It was something that confused them at the time and because of that many have been embarrassed to talk or even think about. I, too, was embarrassed by it.

Survivors feel ashamed that, by telling someone about it, it might be thought that they actually 'enjoyed' the rape. The vagina lubricates during a rape because it is the body's natural response to a trauma of this nature. The adrenaline that is released enables the body to prepare itself for this violation. Your body does this to minimise the potential damage.

I have also been told that the ability of a rapist to maintain an erection in a violent situation such as a rape is also as a result of adrenaline. Sexual desire has nothing to do with it.

I am determined to continue to speak out about rape and its consequences for victims, their family and everyone close to them.

The violent crime of rape is one that every woman fears and dreads. After my attack I did a self-defence course. I found it a very empowering experience and realised that if I had done the training before I might have been able to fight Frans off the moment he got into my car.

I cannot stress how important it is for women to do

some form of self-defence training. It is a valuable tool, not just in fighting off a potential attacker, but also because it prepares you psychologically for the eventuality. You will not be taken by surprise as I was that night.

Self-defence training teaches you to become more aware of your circumstances, how to read them and how to manage your 'fear'.

Fear is a valuable instinct and we should learn to harness it productively. Fear need not paralyse you. It can be turned into a powerful weapon.

I have found that many people think I am an extraordinary person. I am not. I am an ordinary girl who had an extraordinary thing happen to her.

I do not claim to be an expert on rape and I do not want other rape survivors to look at me and compare themselves with me. I do not want you to think that you have to deal with your rape the same way I did with mine.

Go through it your own way and at your own pace. Many people tell me that they could not have survived if what happened to me had happened to them, but the truth is we don't know what we are capable of unless we are put to the test.

I am proud of the fact that I have handled the trauma the way I have. I found that hard to say at first, but now I can.

25

ALISON

Tiring but inspiring

———————◆———————

IN THE FOUR years or so since my attack I have criss-crossed the country giving my talks. I have spent countless hours in airports (staff at some even greet me now), at baggage carousels and checking in and out of hotels.

I could not have dreamed that the people of South Africa would have taken me to heart the way that they have. The love and support that I encounter at every talk keeps me going and inspires me to continue with the direction my life has taken.

They have shown me that my decision to make something more of my ordeal and to use it for the greater good and to help others was the right one. I do believe that everything in the world conspires to help us when we have made the right choice.

My work, which consists of my public speaking

appearances, often takes me away from my home and my husband. There are times when I do not spend a single day in the week at home, but it is all worth it.

Now that I feel almost whole again I am really able to appreciate and absorb the love and friendship I have found in so many small towns as well as the larger cities. I am touched by the gifts, cards and letters that people still send me.

Earlier this year, 1998, for the first time I felt it was time to begin the in-depth therapy I had put off for so long. I think it was because I had not connected with quite the right person.

I made the decision, not because I was or am depressed, but because I need to determine just how far I have or have not moved in the years since the attack.

Recently I had the privilege of connecting with Professor Lawrence Schlebusch in Durban. Because of my hectic travelling schedule I am only able to see him when I am in the city. But already, after only a few sessions with him, I feel I am closer to understanding some of the issues that still trouble me.

He has also helped me to understand what motivated and drove Frans and Theuns to do what they did. Although I will never really know what went on in their minds, Professor Schlebusch has been able to help me understand their actions.

Although it is not difficult for me to talk about my rape and attack, I am not certain that I have completely integrated the trauma. I need to find out if there are still any issues that I am avoiding.

Most days I feel I am coping with it but I am aware, every day, that it is there. I still have nightmares occasionally and wake up drenched in my own sweat.

I have not cried much at all and at times this worries me. At times I long to be able to sob, to break down and really have a good cry. But something is holding me back and I need to know what it is. Perhaps I am afraid that if I go there I might never return to my 'normal' self. Professor Schlebusch has reassured me that, judging from my personality and character, it will not happen.

While writing this book, Marianne, Tienie and I went back to the bushes in Noordhoek to perform what I thought would be a ritual that would purge and cleanse me of the experience.

After the court case, Melvin handed me a small cardboard box that contained the evidence they found at the scene. He asked me if I wanted it and somehow I couldn't think of it just being tossed away on a trash heap.

I took it, and it moved with me from Port Elizabeth to Knysna where I stuffed it at the back of a cupboard, unopened. In some way it was as if I wanted or needed to keep a physical part of the experience. I could not let it go at that time. Maybe I also kept it because the clothes and other personal belongings were part of an Alison that no longer exists. By getting rid of it, I was afraid that I might lose her.

The sealed box travelled in the boot of the car and Marianne, Tienie and I drove the same route that Frans and Theuns had taken that night. It was more or less the same time as well. I had not been back to the spot at night and although Marianne and Tienie were with me I could not help but feel frightened.

At first we could not find the spot. I began to panic. I

needed it to be there so that I could go through with the ritual. But eventually we found it.

It looked more or less the same except for the fact that a recent veld fire had destroyed some of the foliage and the entrance had been almost covered by the re-growth.

But once we turned into the clearing and I spotted the tree that overhung it I knew it was the right place. I had hovered above that very same tree when I had my near death experience.

We parked the car and I asked Tienie to keep the headlights on at first.

I did not know what to expect from myself. I suppose I wanted some sort of catharsis. I wanted, for once, to break down and *feel*.

I was extremely edgy and even the slightest noise in the bush made me nervous. We lifted the box out of the boot and broke the seal. It was quiet and cold and I realised I was shivering. Inside, my blood-stained belongings were all individually packed in neat little plastic bags.

I took each one out and unwrapped it. There was my beautiful white shirt, my little knapsack I had bought in London. There was a lot of blood on it. My blood. There was the book I had read on the beach that afternoon, my bikini top and various bits of the laundry I had collected from Kim.

There was the duvet cover I had loved so much.

Tienie piled the clothes more or less on the spot where I had lain when they dragged me, unconscious, from the car. He packed fire lighters underneath and then struck a match.

It went up in a whoosh and as I stood there watching I wanted, for a split second, to stop it. I wanted to extinguish the flames. For some reason I didn't want to lose this part of myself.

I realised that this was a big rock in my personal rucksack and that it was time to put it down.

We watched the flames in silence. The heat from the fire warmed me up.

As it burned and I stared into the flames I suddenly felt totally exhausted. I began to yawn uncontrollably. Tienie put his arms around me and we all three stood there, each with our private thoughts.

It was Tienie's warm and strong embrace that reminded me that I was grateful to be alive and that I was ready to leave it there and move on.

Later as the little heap began to fizzle out a strange calm overcame me. I felt relieved.

I let it go. I let that Ali go.

I have found a measure of blissful happiness in my life. I appreciate it more because I have had this trauma. I might not have lived and learned how precious and wondrous life is.

Tienie and I are building a home in an idyllic setting in the country. He has always dreamed of it but didn't think he would find someone who would share that dream. Together we are both able to live out our personal dreams and I couldn't ask for anything more.

If it were up to Tienie we would have ten children, but we've settled for two at this stage.

Although there might be complications I am still able to have children. I am prepared for any eventuality and will take each day as it comes.

We make our own happiness. We can only see the world through our own eyes and our own state of mind affects everything. It is truly a beautiful place with bountiful gifts if only we choose to see them.

Like the butterfly.

Choose to believe in miracles.

I certainly do.

KU-157-109

Kinsale

JOHN J. SILKE

The occupation of the Irish port of Kinsale by a Spanish force in 1601 and its surrender to an English army early in 1602 is an event of both European and Irish significance. This work, based mainly on research in the Archivo General de Simancas, has since its first publication in 1970 remained the standard treatment of the invasion and its outcome. That invasion marked the last attempt by Spain to force a decision in the long sea war with England which had lasted since 1585.

The prolonged Tudor attempt to reconquer Ireland met its strongest opposition from Hugh O'Neill. The records of Spanish and Roman archives show O'Neill's diplomacy at work, clear in its aims and far-reaching in extent, but finally unable to overcome deep-seated prejudices. The anarchy of the Gaelic system and the mistrust between Gael and Gall were the factors that most contributed towards the decisive English victory at Kinsale. This was a milestone on the way towards general disengagement on the Atlantic front, and was followed by the Peace of London in 1604 between Spain and England which enabled the papacy to take up with James I the question of toleration towards his Catholic subjects, forced O'Neill to retire to Ulster and ended, for a generation, serious resistance to English rule.

Kinsale has been extensively written on from the Irish side and it is treated in most histories of Spain and some of Europe, but it has never been examined systematically from the Spanish side. Dr Silke has consulted the Spanish records which provide a full account of the inception of the Irish invasion project, its political setting, the logistics of the despatch of the expedition and the story of its fortunes in Ireland. He answers a great many questions which have hitherto remained obscure and places the episode properly in both its European and Irish setting.

'He sets out to do something which was not seriously attempted before, that is, to give an adequate account from the Spanish side of Don Juan del Águila's attempt to assist Hugh O'Neill and the Irish Catholic malcontents by invading Queen Elizabeth's Ireland. In this he has been commendably succcessful', G.A.Hayes-McCoy, *Studia Hibernica*.

John J. Silke, a priest of the diocese of Raphoe, taught history in Letterkenny, New York and Rome, where he was also archivist of the Irish College. Before retiring he was parish priest of Glenswilly.

FOUR COURTS HISTORY CLASSICS

Irish Kings and High Kings
F.J. Byrne

The Old English in Ireland, 1625-42
Aidan Clarke

Priests and People in Pre-Famine Ireland, 1780-1845
S.J. Connolly

*Kinsale: The Spanish Intervention in Ireland
at the End of the Elizabethan Wars*
John J. Silke

Jacobite Ireland, 1685-91
J.G. Simms

JOHN J. SILKE

Kinsale

*The Spanish Intervention
in Ireland at the End of the
Elizabethan Wars*

FOUR COURTS PRESS

Published by
FOUR COURTS PRESS
Fumbally Lane, Dublin 8, Ireland
email: info@four-courts-press.ie
http://www.four-courts-press.ie
and in North America by
FOUR COURTS PRESS
c/o ISBS, 5804 N.E. Hassalo Street, Portland, OR 97213.

© John J. Silke 2000

First published 1970 by Liverpool University Press
First paperback edition 2000

ISBN 1-85182-551-7

A catalogue record for this title
is available from the British Library.

All rights reserved. No part of this publication may be
reproduced, stored in or introduced into a retrieval system,
or transmitted, in any form or by any means (electronic,
mechanical, photocopying, recording or otherwise), without
the prior written permission of both the copyright owner and
publisher of this book.

Note: This new paperback edition of *Kinsale* does not
include the ten illustrations which appeared in the original printing.

The cover design, by Terry Foley, incorporates a detail
from a contemporary copy of a map of the siege of Kinsale,
probably made by Paul Ivye, at the end of November 1601.

Printed in Ireland
by Colour Books Ltd, Dublin.

IN MEMORIAM MATRIS ET PATRIS

ERRATA

Page 1, line 5: for Day *read* Eve

Page 11, last paragraph becomes:

> England, across the Channel from France and the Netherlands, was courted by both Habsburg and Valois. Surrey's crushing defeat of James IV at Flodden (1513) meant that for the next twenty years England need not fear attack from Scotland. England, too [*etc.*]

Page 28, line 4: insert a full stop after Spain.

Page 55, line 2: after footnote trigger 1 insert the following sentence:

> It is likely, although we have no clear information on this, that O'Donnell trained his *buannachadha* in like manner. Beside the bonnaghts, drawn from the unfree classes, the Irish armies included the traditional rising out of aristocracy and freemen, as well as the *gallóglaigh* families.

Page 55, second paragraph: delete first sentence O'Neill and his allies ... raw levies.

Page 55, second last paragraph: delete sentence O'Neill and O'Donnell had ... moderately well-armed.

> *and replace with*
>
> The combined confederate forces numbered probably less than half the 20,000 men of some English estimates.

Page 63, note 2: for 27 Feb. 1599 *read* 22 Feb. 1599

Page 82, note 1: for AGS Estado 2053 *read* AGS, Estado 2023

Page 82, note 1: for 5 Aug. 1601 *read* 5 Aug. 1600

Page 116, note 1: for E.M. Jones *read* F.M. Jones

Page 125, line 29: for 6 December *read* 5 December

Page 129, line 7: for 3 December *read* 4 December

FOREWORD

by

D. B. QUINN

*Professor of Modern History
in the University of Liverpool*

THE OCCUPATION of the Irish port of Kinsale by a Spanish force in 1601 and its surrender to an English army early in 1602 is an event of both European and Irish significance. It marked the last attempt by Spain to force a decision in the long sea war with England which had lasted since 1585. It was intended to demonstrate that the Spanish fleet, wounded in 1588 and subsequently suffering rather more rebuffs than successes, was still a formidable threat to English security. It was a reminder, too, though rather a tardy one, that while England could aid the United Provinces to the detriment of Spain, Spain could retaliate by assisting Irish opponents of English authority. Perhaps, also, the taking of San Juan de Puerto Rico by Cumberland in 1598, the first of a series of damaging sackings of Caribbean towns, had something to do with this counter-attack against an English dependency.

The failure at Kinsale was not, in itself, a serious blow to anything except Spanish prestige, but it was the last aggressive thrust at England before the death of Elizabeth I enabled effective peace negotiations to take place. On the Irish side the nature and result of Spanish intervention had more far-reaching consequences. Promises of Spanish aid from 1596 onwards had helped to sustain Hugh O'Neill's lengthy struggle for autonomy in Ulster and had been a factor in spreading over two-thirds of Ireland what had begun as a provincial revolt, so that it became the nearest approach in the sixteenth century to an all-Ireland attempt to eliminate English rule. The English military build-up after 1598 had converted Ireland into a major theatre of war, but the fiasco of Essex's campaign in 1599 aroused serious apprehension in England so that immense responsibilities were laid on Mountjoy when he succeeded Essex in Ireland in 1600. Up to the time of the Spanish arrival at Kinsale, Mountjoy had had very substantial though not decisive successes and could reasonably hope to finish off the insurgents in another campaign.

The Spanish force, once installed in Kinsale, changed all this. It presented the English commander with a challenge to which he must rise. It gave O'Neill a chance—though a difficult one—to break the siege and open up a way of using the Spanish infantry in mobile warfare, and so of having the opportunity to defeat Mountjoy in the field. The failure of the Irish attack, and no less the absence of effective coordination with the Spaniards, forced the latter to capitulate and O'Neill to retire to Ulster. For Ireland the battle of Kinsale and the year 1602 marked the end of serious resistance to English rule, though O'Neill was able to hold out until he obtained not inglorious terms in 1603. But Ireland, at the accession of James I, was fully at the disposal of the king of Great Britain and Ireland.

Kinsale has been extensively written on from the Irish side and it is treated in most histories of Spain and some of Europe, but it has never been examined systematically from the Spanish side. Father Silke, already known for his more specialized studies of the period, has been able to consult the Spanish records which provide a full account of the inception of the Irish-invasion project, its political setting, and the logistics of the dispatch of the expedition as well as the story of its fortunes in Ireland. He answers a great many questions which have hitherto remained obscure and places the episode squarely in its European and its Irish setting. His book will take its place as a standard treatment of the subject for students of Irish and of European history alike.

CONTENTS

PREFACE

The present work has been written in the hope that a treatment based on Spanish sources, of the Kinsale episode may fill a gap in Irish (and to some slight extent, perhaps, in European) historiography. Among those to whom I am indebted for assistance in preparing the work mention must be made of the Directors and staffs of the Archivo General, Simancas; of the Biblioteca Nacional, Madrid; of the National Library of Ireland; and of the British Museum. I gratefully acknowledge the permission of the Director to quote from the documents in the Archivo General, Simancas.

I must also thank Mr Michael Mulcahy, Cork, who very generously made his unpublished researches into the battle of Kinsale available to me; Mr S.P. Ó Mórdha, Dublin, for the stimulation of his conversation on Irish history; Mr A.N. Ryan, of the School of History, University of Liverpool, for his advice on Chapter I; and above all Professor David Quinn, who gave me the encouragement without which the book might never have been written. In drawing up the index, I benefited from the expert advice given me by Mrs Alison Quinn. Any faults that remain in the book are my sole responsibility.

New York, January 1970

Reviewers of *Kinsale* on both sides of the Atlantic gave a generally warm welcome to the book and it is gratifying that after a generation there is a demand for its reprinting. I take the opportunity in this edition issued as preparations are being made to commemorate the quatercentenary of the battle, to make a few minor corrections, which in one or two cases reflect criticisms made. In one or two other cases there was, it seemed to me, a misreading either of the evidence or of what I had written, or both. To an objection that I painted too broad a canvas in the beginning of the book, I would reply that from as early as 1520 Ireland was a pawn in the power game between Habsburg, Valois and Tudor (see my *Ireland and Europe, 1559-1607*) and that this, despite the efforts of a few scholars, Hogan, Hume, Kelso and Fr Murphy, had not been sufficiently appreciated by historians of the period.

J.J.S.
Portnablagh, June 2000

ABBREVIATIONS

PRINCIPAL SOURCES are described and listed in the bibliography under the headings: I. Spanish sources, pp. 182–6, and II. Other sources, pp. 186–91. The following abbreviations are used in the footnotes, and in the bibliography.

A.F.M.	Annals of the Four Masters (Annála Ríoghachta Éireann)
AGS	Archivo General de Simancas
AGS, Estado	AGS, fondo Estado, sección Secretaría de Estado
AGS, Guerra Antigua	AGS, fondo Guerra y Marina, sección Guerra Antigua
Anal. Hib.	Analecta Hibernica (IMC, 1930–)
Archiv. Hib.	Archivium Hibernicum (Catholic Record Society of Ireland, 1912–)
Archiv. Hist. Soc. Iesu	Archivium Historicum Societatis Iesu
BM	British Museum
Cal. Carew MSS.	Calendar of Carew papers in the Lambeth library
Cal. S.P. Ire.	Calendar of state papers relating to Ireland
Cal. S.P. Spain	The letters and state papers relating to English affairs . . . in . . . Simancas
Cal. S.P. Venice	Calendar of state papers and manuscripts relating to English affairs . . . in . . . Venice
CRS	Catholic Record Society, Publications
CSIC	Consejo Superior de Investigaciones Científicas
Codoin	Colección de documentos inéditos para la historia de España
D.H.E.	Diccionario de historia de España
D.N.B.	Dictionary of National Biography
E.H.R.	English Historical Review
Galway Arch. Soc. J.	Galway Archaeological Society, Journal
HMC	Historical Manuscripts Commission
I.C.H.S. Bull.	Irish Committee for Historical Sciences, Bulletin (1939–)
I.E.R.	Irish Ecclesiastical Record
I.H.S.	Irish Historical Studies
IMC	Irish Manuscripts Commission
Inst. Hist. Res. Bull.	Institute of Historical Research, Bulletin
Ir. Sword	Irish Sword
Ir. Theol. Quart.	Irish Theological Quarterly
NLI	National Library of Ireland
NUI	National University of Ireland

Pac. Hib.	[Stafford, Thomas], *Pacata Hibernia*
PROL	Public Record Office, London
RAH	Real Academia de Historia
R.E.	*Revista de España* (149 vols., Madrid, 1869–1904)
Rep. Nov.	*Reportorium Novum*
Rév. d'Hist. Dipl.	*Révue d'Histoire Diplomatique*
RHS	Royal Historical Society
VA, Borghese III	Vatican Archives, Borghese, series III
Vallid.	Valladolid

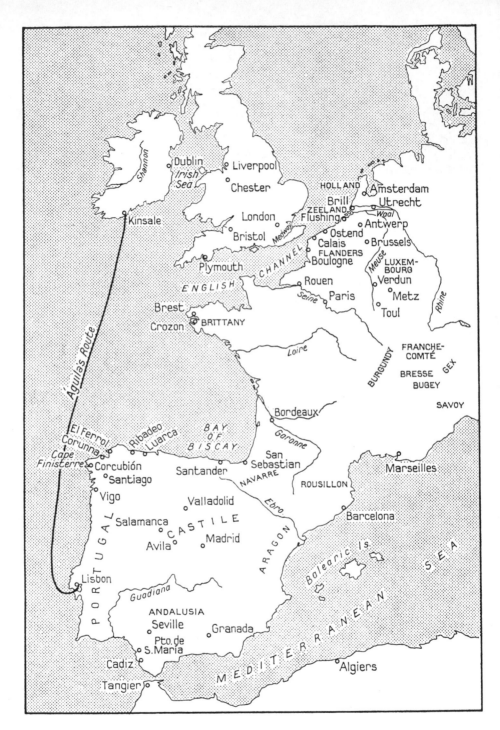

THE ELIZABETHAN WARS: I. THE EUROPEAN THEATRE

THE ELIZABETHAN WARS: II. THE IRISH THEATRE

RÓISÍN DUBH

Hugh O'Donnell addresses Ireland

A Róisín, na bíodh brón ort fár éirigh dhuit:
tá na bráithre ag teacht thar sáile 's ag triall ar muir;
tiochfaidh do phárdún on bPapa 's on Róimh anoir
's ní spárálfar fíon Spáinneach ar mo Róisín Dubh.
Mhairbh tú mé, a bhrídeach, is nár ba fearrde duit,
is go bhuil m'anam istigh i ngean ort, 's ní hinné ná inniu;
d' fhág tú lag anbhann mé i ngné 's i gcruth —
ná feall orm is mé i ngean ort, a Róisín Dubh.

Anon (sixteenth century)

O, My Dark Rosaleen,
  Do not sigh, do not weep!
The priests are on the ocean green,
  They march along the deep.
There's wine from the royal pope
  Upon the ocean green,
And Spanish ale shall give you hope,
    My Dark Rosaleen!
    My own Rosaleen!
Shall glad your heart, shall give you hope,
Shall give you health, and help, and hope,
    My Dark Rosaleen!

All day long, in unrest.
  To and fro, do I move.
The very soul within my breast
  Is wasted for you, love!
The heart in my bosom faints
  To think of you, my queen,
My life of life, my saint of saints,
    My Dark Rosaleen!
    My own Rosaleen!
To hear your sweet and sad complaints,
My life, my love, my saint of saints,
    My Dark Rosaleen!

James Clarence Mangan (1803–49)

INTRODUCTION

Éigceart na nÉireannach féin
Do threascair iad d'aoinbhéim
Ag spairn fa ceart ghearr chorrach
Ní neart airm na n-eachtrannach.[1]
    Fr. Geoffrey Keating (1570–1645)

ON A MORNING in midwinter towards the close of the reign of Queen Elizabeth I one of the decisive battles in Irish history was fought, outside the walled town of Kinsale, in the extreme south of Ireland. There, as the night mists gave way before the dawn of 3 January 1602 (Christmas Day, 1601, with the English, who thought that the revised Gregorian calendar smacked too much of popery), a small English force under Lord Mountjoy, the queen's general and lord deputy in Ireland, routed with the greatest dispatch the entire Irish army, led by Hugh O'Neill. By this singular victory the old queen had virtually achieved an aim cherished by the Tudor monarchy during the century and more of its existence. Ireland, the victim alike of its anarchic, if heroic, Gaelic past and of the fatal mistrust between Gael and Gall, between the 'old Irish' and 'old English', went down before the superior discipline of a modern state. The effect of the great victory gained by O'Neill at the Yellow Ford was now annulled, and although the war, with its benumbing horrors for the native population, was to drag on for over another year the final reduction of the country was now in sight.

While the English victory at Kinsale made certain at last the conquest of Ireland, it was not without effect on the outcome of the Atlantic conflict between Spain and her enemies, now, with France out of the war, reduced to two: England and the Northern Provinces of the Netherlands. Hugh O'Neill had been drawn from the security

---

1. It was the fault of the Irish themselves—wrangling over petty, worthless claims—which destroyed them at one stroke, and not the armed might of the foreigners.

of his Ulster fastness southwards to give battle at Kinsale by a Spanish occupation of the town. His defeat, followed by the capitulation of the Spanish invaders, prepared the way for the treaty of London (in 1604) between Spain, the Netherlands, and England. Spain had made her peace with France in 1598 (treaty of Vervins); after 1604 there remained for her only the Dutch to deal with. In her eyes the Dutch were rebels; but peacemaking had its own momentum, and in 1609 she concluded a truce of twelve years with them.

The Irish defeat and the Spanish withdrawal from Ireland also provided the Papacy with an opportunity to explore the possibility of gaining from Elizabeth's successor, James I, some amelioration of the disabilities under which his Catholic subjects laboured. The morning's fight, then, at Kinsale had more than local consequences.

Ireland had played a minor but definite role in European politics ever since the Tudors had begun first to assert and then to extend their authority over their colony to the west. The Irish lords in opposing the Tudor attack on their independence had turned for aid to the Catholic powers—first to the empire, then to France, and finally to Spain. The peace of Cateau-Cambrésis (1559) established Spain as the leading power in Europe. At the same time France began to be torn internally by religious strife. It was natural, therefore, that from now on Irish hopes for foreign intervention against the crown rested mainly on Spain. These hopes increased when, by the Spanish annexation of Portugal in 1580, conflict between Elizabeth and Philip II became more open. The Spanish response to Irish appeals is viewed as a rule by Irish writers in the context of their country's struggle against England and by English historians in that of the colonial administration in Ireland. A few writers, however, Professor Manuel Fernández Álvarez in a brief article on Shane O'Neill,[1] and Major Hume and J. B. Kelso at more length,[2] view Spanish intervention in Ireland from the wider perspective of European politics. Both Hume and Kelso, who base their researches on documents in the Spanish state archives at Simancas, concentrate on the period between the 'invincible' armada and the death of Elizabeth. But Hume's contributions and

1. Fernández Álvarez, 'La sublevación de Shane O'Neill contra Isabel de Inglaterra', in *Simancas*, i (1950), 327–33.
2. Hume, 'Españoles e irlandeses', in *Españoles e ingleses en el siglo xvi*, ch. VI; *Treason and plot* (in which Hume relates the Irish opposition to Elizabeth to that of the English and Scottish Catholics); 'Spain under Philip III', *Camb. mod. hist.*, vol. iii, ch. XVI; Kelso, *Die Spanier in Irland 1588–1603*.

Kelso's monograph, however compendious, are not full-scale works; furthermore, they need to be brought up to date in their treatment of both the international and Irish backgrounds to the Spanish intervention. The findings of two generations of research workers since Hume and Kelso have left us in a better position than they were to appreciate the complexity of the factors—political, economic, religious, even geographical and logistical—that determined the nature and extent of Spanish aid to Ireland, just as they have given us a clearer understanding than was possible for scholars of sixty-odd years ago of the changing shifts in royal policy towards Ireland and of the internal Irish political, religious, and military situations.

The present work aims at setting the Spanish invasion of Munster against a backcloth of the contemporary international, colonial, and Irish scenes. It is, surely, owing to the lack of such a study that Irish historiography has not gone beyond a superficial view of Don Juan del Águila's invasion. That invasion is seen as the simple and necessary intervention of Catholic Spain in the Irish struggle for faith and fatherland, almost a fact of nature which could be taken for granted. That the sending of the armada by Spain might not have been such a simple matter, or that, once sent, it might have had difficulty in landing at the port of its choice, or, indeed, in landing at all, are considerations which have not been adverted to.

In fact, the controversies which Águila's expedition has aroused in the past, controversies about his destination and about his conduct of the defence of Kinsale, simply show that the available source-material has not been properly studied. Besides, these disputes overlook the difficulties of raising such an expedition as Águila's and of landing it in Ireland at all, as they overlook the poverty of his resources and the lack of support accorded him. Ignacio Olagüe wrote to the point when he observed that it would have been a miracle if the 'invincible' armada and the two later expeditions (one against England and the other against Ireland) sent by Philip II had succeeded. Olagüe (who wrote thus in 1938) compared the launching of these expeditions to the sending of a squadron of planes from Europe to cross the Atlantic in one flight and bombard New York.[1]

Águila's expedition, it may then be agreed, is mainly of interest, not for the issues around which the controversies alluded to above have raged, but for more fundamental reasons, namely why was it sent at

1. Olagüe, *La decadencia española*, i. 355.

all? need it necessarily have been sent? and what light does a study of it throw on the nature of the struggle in Ireland and on the place of Ireland in contemporary power politics?

Fault is found by historians with the Spanish expedition to Munster on four standard counts: it was too little, it was too late, it came to the wrong place, and it was incompetently led by Águila. The first three charges, or the first and third at any rate, may be readily admitted. But if we are to guard against the danger of making facile judgements, it would be well for us here to recall the warning sounded by Fernand Braudel, in connection with the duke of Alba's movement of troops to the Netherlands in 1567. The recruiting of infantry, the mobilization and victualling of round ships, the movement of troops from far-away Andalusia, and the navigation, 'continental' in extent, that was demanded by the operation, presented, Braudel points out, a tremendous problem in logistics in the sixteenth century.[1] And granted that Águila's little force was far less calculated to strain the resources of the Spanish empire (even in decline) than was Alba's army of 25,000 men, yet the movement (directed at times from Madrid, at times from Valladolid) of 4,000 infantry (camp-followers do not appear on the official list of those going to Ireland) from Guipúzcoa, Andalusia, and the remote Azores by way of Lisbon to Ireland was not achieved without considerable difficulty.

But the sending of the expedition was determined by considerations not merely of logistics but also of the political objectives to be gained. Contemporary Irish leaders were realistic enough to see that they could not secure Spanish aid on the plea of Irish need alone; the Spaniards, however altruistic they were, however Catholic, naturally considered their own interests, and these interests were primary in their calculations. Accustomed as Irish historians are to seeing the nine years' war as the game on the board and the Spanish intervention as the moving of one piece (however important) by Hugh O'Neill, it might be salutary for them to realize that the Spanish outlook was not necessarily so restricted; Spanish friendship for Ireland and Spanish concern at the threat to Catholicism in Ireland did not blind Spaniards to Ireland's importance as the English 'Netherlands' and to Hugh O'Neill's value as a pawn to be used in the game against Elizabeth. As his advisers, in a key-statement, put it to Philip III:

1. Braudel, *Méditeranée et monde méditerranéen*, p. 883.

Spanish aid to Ireland will save our holy faith in that country. Besides, by aiding Ireland His Majesty will at very little cost achieve the same effect as Queen Elizabeth does by aiding the Dutch rebels. This is a matter whose importance we ought to rate very highly and to which we ought to attend with great care and diligence . . .[1]

What Braudel has said of Philip II after 1559 is true also of Philip III: it is from Spain that the king views and judges events; it is within a climate morally Spanish that his policy is elaborated, because Spanish interests and Spanish statesmen are closest to him.[2]

This is not to say that Philip III was hypocritical in his attitude towards Ireland; the justice and the utility of intervention in Ireland could very easily be reconciled. Ideally, of course, Spain was committed to the defence of Catholicism, and her obligations as Catholic champion were a too-continually recurring theme on the lips of her statesmen to be dismissed as mere platitudes. But however much they sought in theory the restoration of the old Christian unity of Europe, and however much the crusade remained an aspiration for them, the policy of the Spanish Habsburgs was in practice determined rather by reasons of state than by the crusading ideal. It is perhaps necessary to stress this in an age which has seen a secular and professedly more liberal society wage total war on an 'evil' enemy, offering him no choice but unconditional surrender.

The succouring of the persecuted Irish Catholics appealed to the piety of the young Philip III, as the honouring of his father's promise made in 1596 to the Irish appealed to his pride. But the invasion of Munster resulted not so much from Philip's wish as from the decision of the duke of Lerma, the king's first minister, to favour it. Lerma's decision, in turn, was consequent on the fact that the accident of peace between France and Savoy had made available two thousand men in Lisbon to become the nucleus of the invading force. A study of the expedition illustrates, as to certain vital elements, the working of the Spanish administration, for the councils of state, of war, and of finance were all engaged in its direction. The difficulties which the preparation of the invasion encountered reveal in turn the administrative chaos of Spain, the weakness of the naval arm, and Philip III's

1. . . . *demas de que dello resulterá conservasse allá nuestra sancta fe por aquella mano podrá su magestad hazer el mesmo effecto que la reyna haze por la de los rebeldes a muy poca costa, que es cosa de tanta consideración que se deve stimar en mucho, y acudir a ella con extraordinario cuydado y diligencia* . . . AGS, Estado 840, f. 288: Council of state to Philip III, 8 June 1600.
2. Braudel, *Méditerranée et monde méditerranéen*, pp. 773-4.

inability to meet the demands of such a comparatively modest expedition at a time when money was being squandered on frivolities; just as the efforts made by a dedicated few to surmount these difficulties reveal the concern of individuals for Spain and for her mission. The story of the expedition makes clear also the essential subordination by Spain of Irish interests to her own, at a time when her chief concern was to make England yield good peace terms.

Spain, when in 1601 she sent an army to Ireland, was paradoxically really interested in disengagement. But while she had concluded peace with France, had sent out overtures to England, was seeking to extricate herself from the costly Dutch war, and was conducting negotiations even with Constantinople, she yet maintained a jealous care for her greatness. Thus she prepared herself for war with France, if that country should attack Savoy; she continued to aid Archduke Albert, sovereign of the Netherlands, in his struggle against the United Provinces; she sought to support the emperor's eastern war against the Turk by attacking the Berbers in the western Mediterranean; and she tried by creating a diversion in Ireland to extract better peace terms from England.

For the English and Spaniards had already in 1600 come to the conference table. But the peace-talks at Boulogne, at which the archduke, who in fact had taken the initiative on the discussions, was also represented, had proved to be premature. There were at least two good reasons why Elizabeth saw more to be gained from a continuation of the war than from peace. In the first place France was threatening to attack Savoy; such an attack would endanger Spanish possession of Milan and probably lead to a renewal of hostilities between France and Spain. Secondly, the Dutch inflicted a crushing defeat on Albert at Nieuport on 2 July, providing Sir Francis Vere, the English general, with an opportunity to strengthen Ostend. With the Spaniards and the archduke so hard pressed the English envoys at Boulogne proved unyielding, and the negotiations broke off, *re infecta*, in August.

Then in January 1601 France and Savoy made peace, and the French threat to the Milanese lifted. Spain had intended to transport troops from Lisbon to the relief of Albert; she now could send men overland from Milan instead, and the 2,000 infantry assembled at Lisbon were made ready for call. The Spaniards decided to raise this force, by the addition of further levies, to 6,000 men to go to the aid of Hugh

O'Neill. Philip III also decided to send the Genoese brothers Fedérico and Ambrosio Spínola with another army of 6,000 men to invade England. Elizabeth was to be brought to her knees.

The army which sailed from Belém for Ireland on 3 September 1601 numbered only 4,432 men, far short of the expected 6,000. It was too small therefore to take the field and attack the Munster towns, and its immediate aim should have been to join forces with the Irish. Its destination for that reason should have been Killybegs or Teelin or, at the very furthest south, Limerick. But owing to a combination of inexpert advice and ill-chance it landed at Kinsale instead. The Spaniards were thus at the furthest remove in Ireland from O'Neill and his ally, Hugh O'Donnell, who were now taken in the rear at Loch Foyle and Lifford and had lost again the allegiance of Leinster and Munster. The chances that the Spanish and Irish forces might effect a junction were thus very remote. Moreover, by sending their ships home the Spaniards gave up control of Kinsale harbour and thereby considerably reduced their ability to stand siege against a well-armed, well-provisioned, and determined enemy. Pope Clement VIII finally refused to make it a matter of conscience for Catholics to support the invasion, so that the Munster lords (apart from a number in the south-west) and townsmen did not come out in support of the Spaniards.

The reasons why many (but not all) of the lords of the south-west did declare for the Spaniards were these: a further small force of Spanish infantry occupied the ports of Castlehaven, Baltimore, and Berehaven in December, and O'Neill and O'Donnell against all probability broke through the encircling enemy and reached the neighbourhood of Kinsale and cut off the besiegers' land-approaches.

O'Neill sensibly wished to avoid an engagement with the English on open ground, and to let starvation and exposure defeat them instead. However, he was forced to attack by Águila, the Spanish general, and by O'Donnell. In the ensuing fight, which does not merit the name of battle, the Irish were utterly routed. Nine days later the Spaniards in Kinsale capitulated. Spain withdrew from the Irish theatre of war, and Philip's plan of invading England was defeated by the exigencies of the war in Flanders. Spain in any case was now dedicating her energies to peacemaking. Philip had ratified the treaty of Vervins in 1601. When Elizabeth died and O'Neill had submitted, it was easy to come to terms with the peacefully inclined James I. The peace of London of 1604 together with the truce of 1609 between Spain and the Dutch brought about a general disengagement in Europe. Irish hopes of further Spanish aid faded to become a dream of the poets, 'the tellers of the tale and myth'.

I · THE EMPEROR CHARLES V AND PHILIP II OF SPAIN

> Now for reasons of state there was armed intervention in France and in Brittany. In spite of the considerable loss suffered, this was very proper. It follows that some intervention in Ireland would be of no less value.
>
> Don Martín de la Cerdá, 1600[1]

CHARLES I OF SPAIN (1516–56) outbid his competitors and secured election as Holy Roman Emperor in 1519. Charles V (his imperial title) now united under his personal rule a vast number of heterogeneous dominions sprawling over Europe and the New World. His maternal grandfather Ferdinand had bequeathed to him the kingship of Aragon, with Naples, Sicily, Sardinia, and Corsica, and a claim to the duchy of Milan, which was in 1519 held by the French but was technically a fief of the empire. Ferdinand had also left to his grandson certain stations in North Africa, together with Cerdagne and Rousillon; these latter were two Catalan counties which lay on the French side of the Pyrenees and were claimed by France. With his imbecile mother Joanna, Charles was joint ruler of Castile, to which was annexed Navarre and the rapidly growing American empire. As heir to his father, Philip the handsome, he was duke of Burgundy; this title made him lord of Artois and Flanders (both of them French fiefs), the Netherlands, Luxembourg, and Franche-Comté, and claimant to the duchy of Burgundy, which had reverted to the crown of France. Finally, as head of the house of Habsburg, Charles ruled over the five duchies of Austria, Tyrol, Styria, Carinthia, and Carniola, together with Alsace and expected the reversions of the other Habsburg hereditary lands, the kingdoms of Bohemia and Hungary.

---

1. *Pues, por razón destado se metió la guerra en Francia, siendo muy acertado, y en Bretaña, donde se ha perdido tanto. De donde se sigue no ser de menos conveniencia meter alguna en esta isla* ... AGS, Estado 185.

Each of these varied and extensive dominions had its own problems, and their interests were often in conflict and were indeed irreconcilable. Castile, for instance, now needed to establish her power in North Africa and to make secure possession of her Atlantic discoveries. But her partner Aragon had designs on Italy, so that Castile was distracted by the demands of her alliance from serving her real interests. Italy was a battle-ground between Aragon and France. The Italian peninsula, with its rich cities, developed economy, and political weakness, invited conquest, and the struggle between France and Spain for its possession was the central issue on which Europe divided between the years 1494 and 1559. In order to maintain the Spanish hold on Italy and to keep the French out of the country, Charles V like Ferdinand before him sought to contain France within a system of alliances embracing chiefly Spain, England, and Austria.[1]

If Spanish policy was at odds with itself, Germany was now presented with a great opportunity to achieve her goal of unification, for her king could draw on the resources of Germany's borderlands, the Burgundian Netherlands and Austria, to impose centralization on the Reich. But unfortunately Charles had too many other preoccupations to be able to devote himself single-mindedly to this task, and the favourable moment was lost.

Unappalled, however, by the magnitude of the problems of his far-spreading empire, and undeterred by the tensions from within and without which constantly threatened to rend it asunder, Charles worked steadily and patiently for almost forty years to keep his dominions together and to transmit them intact to his heir. His strategy was essentially conservative, his outlook that of the medieval emperors, of whom in fact he was the last. As Caesar, as Charlemagne, he saw it as his sacred charge to maintain the unity of Catholic and feudal Europe and to defend it against its external foes, the Ottoman Turks, and later against its internal enemies, the Lutheran princes.[2]

If the strategy of Charles V was to maintain the politico-religious unity of Europe under pope and emperor, his tactics were, in the first place and in true medieval fashion, to form dynastic alliances, and only when danger threatened the security of the Habsburg possessions to resort to war with other Christian powers. In the second place

1. Lynch, *Spain under the Habsburgs*, i. 34.
2. Cf. Koenigsberger, in *New Camb. mod. hist.*, ii. 302–3.

Charles sought to isolate his problems and to deal with them one at a time, to find a compromise solution for one problem which would leave him free to deal with another; thus he hoped eventually to settle them all.

But the enemies of the emperor's design were too numerous for these tactics to succeed. Islam, France, the Lutherans, England, and even the Papacy: his opponents were a Hydra who grew heads faster than he could cut them off. To put the matter in another way: Europe was now in a ferment, seething with new nationalism and old dynasticism, novel heresies and old Guelph notions, and it would not be contained within the mould which Charles sought to impose upon it.

Already, indeed, western Europe had taken on a new mould, in which four major territorial units were engaged in a struggle for power, a struggle which was now complicated by the religious divisions which followed upon the Lutheran revolt. These four units were France, England, and, united under the Habsburg rule of Charles V, the two power-aggregates of Burgundy–Austria and Castile–Aragon. Between these two power-aggregates lay, as has been said, the German empire.

France, even if she could not compare in extent with the Habsburg empire, was undoubtedly first and greatest of the new powers. With a coastline bordering the Mediterranean, the Atlantic, the English Channel, and the North Sea, she outshone even Spain as a maritime power. Her developed urban life, her wealth of corn and vines, her great waterways, all ensured her commercial strength. The crown of France was hereditary in the male line, a factor which gave stability. The crown had secured control over all the great fiefs and had at command a standing army, which it could support by imposing taxation without reference to the States-General. France occupied a central position in Europe, with internal communications, and with England, Italy, and Spain arranged symmetrically around her. Her population of perhaps fifteen million was twice that of Spain, four times that of England.

England was a small nation indeed, but her people were well-endowed with the requisite qualities of daring for making the most of the great opportunities that were now offered them for advancement in political and commercial strength. England, too, was well-placed for developing her ocean trade and she could exploit the fact that her

friendship was eagerly sought by both the emperor and the king of
France.

The imperial objective was to maintain the *status quo*, that of the
other powers to disrupt it; and the advantage lay with them. Luther-
anism found strong support from the princes and cities of Germany,
who wished to guard their autonomy against the emperor and to
emulate the autocracy of the 'new' monarchies, in England, France,
and Spain. Civil and religious disobedience thus combined against
Charles in Germany. The French, in order to escape from Habsburg
encirclement and to win back control of Italy, turned this situation to
their own advantage, as they did also the fears of the Papacy. Rome,
seeing in the growth of Charles's influence in Italy the greatest threat
to her independence of action, resisted that growth by whatever
means she could; but in so doing she gave aid to the forces of disintegration within the universal church. The Holy See thus found itself
in the unpleasant dilemma of either losing its independence or
assisting in the disruption of Christianity.

England saw in a balance between Habsburg imperialism and
France the best guarantee of her own liberty, and in order to
maintain this equilibrium sometimes supported the emperor in his
war with France, sometimes opposed him. Europe was dividing
politically into the two great masses of the Habsburg empire and
France, which attracted within their orbits all the lesser powers, and
England wavered between the two. Then in the mid 1530s Henry
VIII, fearful of losing his independence to the emperor, sought to
build up alliances with Charles's enemies in Germany. This policy
proved a failure, and Henry in the end threw in his lot with Charles
against Francis I, the Valois king of France. It was difficult for England
to avoid committing her support to one or other of the giant powers.
In the reign of Edward VI she patched up a truce with France, but
under Mary she was again drawn into the imperial orbit.

It was essential for Henry VIII, seeking as he did from the 1520s to
arbitrate between Habsburg and Valois, that he should not be open
to attack from the European enemy of the moment through Ireland.
To reduce the independence of the Irish lords, both Norman and
Gaelic, therefore became his policy across the Irish Sea. It was a policy
which naturally provoked resistance. But Ireland's success in ob-
structing Henry's policy of political and religious centralization
depended on two factors, namely, a positive response of the European

powers to Ireland's appeals for help and a measure of political unity among the princes. Unfortunately, both of these factors were missing.

The Geraldines, greatest of the Anglo-Norman houses and dominant power in Ireland, were the first victims of Henry's new policy of centralization; and under attack James Fitzmaurice Fitzgerald, tenth earl of Desmond, 'Silken' Thomas, and the lords of the Geraldine League[1] all in turn appealed to the continental powers for help. James of Desmond sought aid first, in 1523, from Francis I and then, in 1527, from Charles V. Unfortunately for the success of Desmond's intrigues, Habsburg and Valois were engaged in the Italian wars, and Desmond died in the year in which peace between the two was signed (1529). When in 1534 the rebel 'Silken' Thomas, Lord Offaly, appealed to the emperor for support, the latter was too busy fighting with the corsairs in the Mediterranean to think of going to his assistance; then the Habsburg–Valois conflict drew on once more and two years afterwards, in 1536, the emperor was at war again with his great enemy Francis, in Italy. Henry VIII was thus left free to destroy the power of the once-great house of the Leinster Geraldines.

The stern lesson taught by the king, who executed together Thomas of Offaly and his five uncles, was not lost on the Irish lords. To both Gael and Norman it was now apparent that Henry no longer intended to tolerate any independent power in Ireland. A number of the lords, therefore, drew together in the Geraldine League, organized by Manus O'Donnell, lord of Tyrconnell. But the League's attempts to secure foreign intervention also failed. The year 1538 saw Francis signing a truce with Charles, but it was recognized as only a temporary cessation of hostilities; there was no possibility that the two monarchs would co-operate in any action against Henry. The latter placated Charles by dropping Cromwell's policies of protestantizing England and of forming alliances with the emperor's German opponents. He then felt secure enough to deal with Ireland in a more conciliatory fashion. His moderate policy of 'surrender and regrant' which he followed between 1540 and his death in 1547 secured acceptance. The Irish lords received their lands by feudal tenure from the Crown and in return acknowledged Henry as king of Ireland. The monarch could feel well content with the success of his new colonial policy, which had secured

1. On the Geraldine revolts cf. Read (ed.), *Bibliog. Br. hist., Tudor Period*, for sources. *Ir. hist. documents 1172–1922*, eds. Curtis and McDowell, pp. 77–125, gives a representative selection of documents.

on paper at least, and for the moment, the submission of Ireland.

It was easy for the king to out-manœuvre the Irish nobility, as Ireland was a jungle of inter-sept and inter-racial rivalries. The lords of this jungle were unable to set aside their feuds in favour of combined action against the king. Their inability to present a common front also made it impossible for them to exploit either Habsburg or Valois against England. Their lack of political sophistication allowed the crown to isolate them one after the other, and the outcome of their revolts was only to secure more firmly royal control of Ireland.

With the west divided against itself the emperor was prevented from meeting, with the united forces of Europe, the Turkish attack in the east and south. The Turks had made Constantinople their new capital, renaming it Istanbul, and from there as base they advanced into Europe in a crescent-shaped attack. One horn of the crescent moved up the Danube valley into Hungary and in the direction of Vienna, while the other penetrated into the central and western Mediterranean, the preserve of the Aragonese.

Thus harassed on all sides the emperor failed to realize his grand design for Europe: the formation of a front by France, the Empire, and the Papacy aimed at the crushing of Protestantism and the conquest of England, the liberation of Hungary from the Turk, and the transmission to his son Philip of the imperial dignity in addition to the kingship of Spain, which Philip had enjoyed since 1542.[1]

Charles V abdicated in 1556, dividing his territories. Philip II, already king of Spain and since 1554 joint ruler with Mary of England, received the Netherlands; his uncle, Ferdinand, added Germany and the imperial title to his dominions of Austria, Bohemia, and Hungary. The death of Mary Tudor in 1558 dissolved the union of England and Spain and shattered another Habsburg dream, that of an Anglo-Flemish state based on the North Sea. France might have lost Milan for good,[2] but with the incorporation of Calais, Metz, Toul, and Verdun into the state she was more unified and powerful than ever.

But Spain had gained from her release from the union with Germany, which in any case was still in the possession of the junior branch of the Habsburg family. Philip was ruler of a more compact empire than his father: made up of the Mediterranean lands and the Americas,

1. Lynch, *Spain under the Habsburgs*, i. 68–100.
2. Francesco, the last Sforza duke of Milan, died in 1535, and the duchy reverted to the emperor as an imperial fief. Charles invested his son, Prince Philip, with the duchy in 1540, and thereafter it remained a Spanish possession.

with the Netherlands, its composition was now more logical, and its opportunities for development could be realized. Spaniards, at first antipathetic towards Charles V, and frustrated by seeing the Reconquest checked, had eventually under his rule come to accept their 'destiny' as leaders of the Christian world-empire. Now with Philip II began their great century of military, intellectual, and artistic predominance. The movement towards unification in Iberia received a new impetus, which had effect in the annexation of Portugal and the Portuguese maritime empire. Ruler of the whole peninsula and of a vast empire, both in the old world and the new, the Catholic king could believe that it was his mission to shape the destinies of the globe. And this belief was shared by Spaniards in general.

But Spanish hegemony did not go undisputed. If the two power blocs which for forty years had sundered Europe between them had now broken up, the continent was dividing even more sharply into two new hostile camps, at issue with each other on the question of religion. Reluctantly Spain was driven to become champion of Catholicism, and, just as reluctantly, England, facing Spain across the Atlantic, was forced to become the upholder of the Protestant challenge to Catholicism. The fires of religious conflict were fed by other fuel: the growing Spanish preponderance, commercial rivalry, the struggle for control in France, and the efforts by the Dutch and Irish to gain independence. For a hundred years the fires blazed throughout Europe, until the peace of Westphalia in 1648 at last officially acknowledged the passing of the old medieval unity. Even then the confessional passion was not spent, but continued to smoulder for many years to come, making the air of Europe and the world foul with the intolerance shown by most temporal and spiritual authorities at a national level towards dissident minorities.

At war on the Atlantic front, Spain had to maintain a vigilant guard against the Turk in the south as well. Philip II had to bear the brunt of the infidel assault on the western Mediterranean. Inheriting bankruptcy and heresy from the previous reign, her attention diverted from the more pressing and rewarding task of putting her own house in order, the Spain of Philip II found herself unhappily engaged with both north and south in fateful hostility. In the south she checked the advance of Islam, but France, England, and the United Provinces successfully contested her supremacy in the north and established themselves as her rivals.

Philip won the victory of Saint Quentin and forced the French to sign the definitive peace of Cateau-Cambrésis in 1559. With peace established in the north, the king of Spain used the opportunity afforded him to launch a counter-attack against the Turks, whose Berber allies had taken possession of Algiers and Tripoli. But the expedition which Philip sent against Tripoli in 1560 was defeated with heavy loss. Philip, however, built up his fleet and at Lepanto (1571) endangered Turkish supremacy in the Mediterranean.

Forced to meet the challenge from the Turks and bankrupted, Philip had other preoccupations as well. He feared that Spain was to be the victim of the next attack from Protestantism, now again on the march in its Calvinist form. He was concerned too, since Mary Stuart was queen of France, that the French might gain control of England and Scotland, a control that would endanger Spanish possession of the Netherlands. Apart from his many concerns Philip's outlook was conservative. He made no response therefore in 1559 to an offer of the throne of Ireland to a king of his choice, in return for a Spanish force sent to liberate the country. This offer did not in any case come from any national confederacy, and Philip was shrewd enough to realize this. In fact, it is doubtful if the alleged national league of bishops and nobles which made it had any existence other than in the perfervid imagination of James Fitzmaurice Fitzgerald, cousin of the earl of Desmond.[1]

To the appeals which continued to come from Ireland during the early sixties Philip turned a deaf ear.[2] These appeals now came from Shane O'Neill, who had made himself master of Ulster and then had sought Spain's assistance against the crown. Philip did not find Shane's suggestions 'desirable' and instructed his ambassador in England to 'cut them short gently'. Disappointed in Spain, O'Neill in his later years turned to the Guises and their cousin, Mary Stuart, for help in driving out the English. But the Guise party was no longer in the ascendancy in France, and in the period of calm (1559–65) that succeeded the great series of wars in Europe, the waters were too untroubled for Irish malcontents to fish in. Death found Shane in 1567 with nothing to show for his overtures to France.

Shane O'Neill, essentially provincial rather than national in outlook, was typical of the Irish nobility, who gave no serious indication that

1. Cf. Silke, *Ireland and Europe 1559–1607*, pp. 5–8.
2. *Cal. S.P. Spain, 1558–67*, p. 370: Philip to Silva, 6 Aug. 1564.

they would rally to support any Spanish or French force sent to liberate the country from English rule. This was demonstrated once more when, as a result of the expropriations which followed upon the earl of Desmond's forced surrender of his palatinate into the queen's hands (February 1568), James Fitzmaurice Fitzgerald dispatched the archbishop of Cashel, Maurice Fitzgibbon, to Spain as his envoy in 1569[1]. The archbishop presented a memorial to Philip II, which declared that Elizabeth, against the wishes of all the Irish leaders and people, was seeking to impose heresy on the country. The memorial went on to ask that Philip nominate a Spanish or Burgundian prince as king of Ireland, whose appointment would be confirmed by the pope, suzerain of Ireland. There followed a list of bishops and nobles who, it was claimed, favoured this request. The list contained the names of the four archbishops and of eight bishops, as well as of every leading lord, old English and old Irish.

There are striking similarities between Fitzgibbon's appeal to Philip and that made in 1559. Both refer to a vast Irish confederacy, in which Desmond's name takes first place; in both Philip is asked to appoint a prince of his blood as king of Ireland; and in both the motive for the Irish appeal is stated to be religious alone. But in each case the list of supporters is less that of an actual confederacy than of one that, it was felt, the arrival of Spanish aid would bring into being. Fitzmaurice, whose aims were transparent enough, sought to rally all Ireland in the cause of religion, but with little success.

Philip in any case returned no favourable answer to the appeal of Archbishop Fitzgibbon. A Spanish victory at Malta (1565), the death of Sultan Sulaiman, and Turkish losses in Hungary (1566) had caused a relaxation of Ottoman pressure in the Mediterranean in 1567. Philip was therefore free to turn his attention to the northern front. He sent the duke of Alba with 25,000 men into the Netherlands to reduce them to obedience. They were in a state of unrest, owing among other things to Philip's foreign origin and his policies of high taxation and religious uniformity and to the growth of militant Calvinism. It was essential for Philip to pacify the Low Countries, as they provided him with a considerable part of his revenue and were of great strategic importance to Spain and the emperor in any war with France.

1. Cf. Binchy, 'An Irish Ambassador at the Spanish court, 1569–74', in *Studies*, x–xiv (1921–5).

The following year, 1568, Mary Queen of Scots fled to England and
was kept prisoner by Elizabeth. Now the main threat to England came
from the Low Countries, rather than from France through Scotland.
The danger was that the main Spanish army under Alba, based just
across the Channel from England, in control of the coasts of Holland
and Zeeland and their shipping and supported by the industrial
resources of Flanders and Brabant, would not only threaten the ex-
tinction of English trade but, with the aid of favourable winds
achieve the conquest of England itself.[1] The huge concentration of
Spanish troops on the new northern front aroused the religious fears
of Cecil, the French Huguenot leader Coligny, and the German
Protestants.

Being well aware of these fears, Philip had no desire just now to
incite the northern powers still further by sending an expedition to
Ireland. Besides, the detention of Mary by Elizabeth ended the danger
of a united front of England, France, and Scotland against Spain.
Philip therefore had hopes of renewing the old alliance with England
if Elizabeth could be induced to make restitution for damage from
English privateering.[2] The English traded illicitly in the Caribbean,
for silver and logwood, and in West Africa for slaves; they appealed
to *ius gentium*, the right of nations, against the papal partition of the
New World between Spain and Portugal and sought to make contact with negro and Indian rebels; and they attacked, on the ocean
and off the Spanish coasts, cargoes returning from the Indies to Spain.
The archbishop of Cashel remained in Spain, detained by Philip
'with fair words', while the king waited to see the outcome of his
negotiations with Elizabeth.

The negotiations were fruitless, and Philip was led by the ceaseless
English attacks on his commerce to think of supporting the Catholic
nobles who rebelled against Elizabeth in 1569. But Alba insisted on
peace with England while he was engaged in pacifying the Low
Countries.

Philip was now, in 1569–70, faced with the great crisis of his reign.
Not only were the Netherlands in revolt, but also the Moriscos, or
converted Moors, of Granada who broke out at the end of 1568. They
were believed, and with some reason, to be in sympathy with their

---

1. Cf. Wernham, *Before the Armada*, pp. 19, 292, 320; and in *Elizabethan government and
society*, pp. 340–68; Braudel, *Méditerranée et monde méditerranéen*, pp. 870–6, 882–7.
2. *Cal. S.P. Spain*, 1568–79: Philip II to Alba, 18 Nov. 1569.

co-religionists, the Turks. Philip was convinced that Spain was under attack from two international conspiracies, that of Protestantism and that of Mohammedanism.

But although he still toyed with the idea of intervening in England or, as Archbishop Fitzgibbon suggested, in Ireland, Alba restrained him. Pope Pius V, however, unlike Alba, did not fear provoking Elizabeth. His austere conscience, rather than political expediency, was for Pope Pius the guiding principle of action, and in February 1570 by the Bull *Regnans in excelsis* he excommunicated Elizabeth and deprived her of her rights of sovereignty.

Philip absolutely refused to execute this sentence. Alba seemed to have quelled rebellion in the Netherlands, and Philip, whose reputation for temporizing and for 'prudence' is one of the most curious myths of history, turned back at once to deal with the Turks. Pius and Philip were at one at least on the need to strike at the Ottoman, and a league of the Papacy, Spain, and Venice defeated the Turks in the great sea-battle of Lepanto (7 October 1571).

If Philip had failed him as an instrument for deposing Elizabeth, the pope was comforted to find that there was at least one paladin brave enough to do battle with the English heretics. Or so it seemed to him when Sir Thomas Stukeley, an English soldier of fortune, came to him with a scheme for invading Ireland. Pius, without resources himself, sought to gain Philip's support for Stukeley's plans. But Sir Thomas, although he might deceive the unworldly Pius, was known to the more astute Philip, who had rejected an earlier offer from him to go to conquer Ireland, for the adventurer he was. It was no surprise, therefore, when in January 1572 the king turned down Stukeley's scheme. In any case, with England courting France, Philip was not anxious to antagonize Elizabeth too much. He had shown some favour (although Alba had not) towards the conspirators who, between 1570 and 1572, aimed with Spanish help at dethroning Elizabeth, marrying Mary of Scots to Norfolk and placing her on the throne. But Cecil's vigilance had defeated this plot (the so-called Ridolfi plot), and its only effect was to favour the growth of friendship between England and France, so that the two countries made a defensive pact in 1572 (treaty of Blois).

This was alarming to Philip because of developments in the Nether-lands. In 1572 the Dutch exiles, the 'sea-beggars', returned home and captured Brill and Flushing. William of Orange advanced from

Germany into Brabant and there was open revolt in the Low Countries. The French sent forces in to support the Dutch.

Not only Philip but also Elizabeth viewed these developments with dismay. The queen of England did not desire the total destruction of Spanish hegemony in the Netherlands, since it would only be replaced by French control of the Channel coast from Brest to Brill. England's policy under Elizabeth, as it had been under her father, was to follow a middle course between the Spanish Scylla and the French Charybdis. Elizabeth sought without destroying Spanish sovereignty over the Netherlands to restore to them the securities, political and fiscal, of which Philip had deprived them, and to gain for the Protestants some measure of freedom. To get the Spaniards out altogether would only be to let the French in. For this reason she patched up disputes over the Netherlands in 1575, and sought to negotiate peace between William of Orange and Philip.

Meanwhile, Sir John Perrot had arrived in Cork in 1571 to take over a new office, that of the presidency of Munster. Within two years he had broken resistance, and in 1575 James Fitzmaurice was driven abroad. Rebuffed in France he went to Spain, where he had no better fortune. If either country intervened in Ireland Elizabeth would be driven into the other's camp.

The war in the Low Countries broke out fiercely again, and Elizabeth's attempt to play the role of honest broker was defeated, as was the plan of Don John of Austria for dealing with England. Don John came to the Netherlands as governor in 1576. He hoped to pacify the rebellious provinces and then go on to lead an invasion of England, designed to place Mary of Scots on the throne. He failed in his first objective, and so the second never became a practical possibility. The Dutch renewed the war with vigour, and called on the duke of Anjou, brother of Henry III of France, to be their protector (1578). Elizabeth did not want this, and she re-opened with Anjou marriage negotiations begun in 1572. At the same time she continued to assist the Dutch; she subsidized Duke John Casimir of the Palatinate, who provided mercenaries for the rebel army, and in 1578 she sent Walsingham over to negotiate with William of Orange. Philip, in order to pay her back somewhat in her own coin, allowed James Fitzmaurice to depart for Ireland with a tiny force of not more than fifty or sixty soldiers.

Fitzmaurice came ashore at Dingle in July 1579 to the chant of litanies, and erected the standard of the Holy Cross. He called on the princes and people of Ireland to rally to this standard for the glory of God. The voice of the military counter-reformation, making up in fervour what it lacked in strength, was now for the first time heard in Ireland. The party went on to fortify themselves in Dún an Óir, the Golden Fort, a promontory overlooking Smerwick harbour. Fitzmaurice went out to raise help but was killed in a skirmish by fellow Irishmen. Fray Mateo de Oviedo, a Spanish Franciscan, had been appointed by the papal nuncio in Spain to come with the expedition. He went back to Spain and reported that the majority of the Irish lords would rebel if only a stronger army came. In spite of his enthusiasm Oviedo failed to arouse the interest of the government. But over a year later Bastiano di San Giuseppi came from Santander to Dún an Óir with another six hundred troops (10 September 1580). San Giuseppi, self-styled colonel, had raised these volunteers on his own initiative without mandate from Philip, although he had a papal commission. About two hundred were Spaniards, the rest mainly Italians. Dún an Óir, however, was easily taken by the deputy, Lord Grey of Wilton, who massacred the entire garrison (10 November).[1]

The coming of the foreign aid, small though it was, sparked off risings, not only in Munster, but also in Ulster, Connacht, and even the Pale. These risings were easily suppressed, but they gave evidence of the unifying effect which religion was beginning to have. In the Pale Viscount Baltinglass went into revolt in July 1580. He got little support, but this rebellion marked an important stage in the struggle in Ireland and alarmed the government. Baltinglass, like Fitzmaurice, rebelled solely on religious grounds; he had suffered for his loyalty to the mass, and he could not tolerate Elizabeth's claim to spiritual supremacy. But on the whole James Fitzmaurice's appeal did not touch the consciences of the Catholics of the Pale and the south. Elizabeth's policy of restraint in enforcing the religious laws allowed them to remain firm in maintaining their political loyalty to her.

Philip of Spain had not been officially implicated in the Fitzmaurice–San Giuseppi adventure, and he did not intervene when the government took full reprisal on the Desmond palatinate. The territory was first devastated, 'a most populous and plentiful country', testified Spenser, 'suddenly made void of man and beast', and then planted.

---

1. Documentation for the Smerwick episode in VA, Nunciatures, (*Archiv. Hib.*, vii (1922)). Cf. also AGS, Estado 160, for report by Oviedo to Philip II, Mondoñedo, 13 Nov. 1580.

The lesson of Philip's inaction was not lost on Munster, which refused to respond to Don Juan del Águila's call to arms in 1601.[1]

Philip disengaged himself from the Mediterranean war because his main concern was now to suppress the revolt in the Netherlands. He appointed Alexander Farnese, duke of Parma, who was grandson of Charles V, as governor of the Netherlands in 1578 in succession to Don John. Showing rare military and diplomatic genius Parma began to win back the southern provinces for Spain.

Philip now set his face towards the west. The death of King Sebastian of Portugal provided him with a convenient pretext for annexing that kingdom and its maritime empire. Now Spain took on a new direction in policy, a new vitality in purpose. Foiling the French dream of gaining Portugal and Brazil (1582–3), Philip was engaged in a great northern war: face to face with England, at war with the Dutch, in partial occupation of Brittany. Unfortunately for Spain, Philip failed to exploit his possession of Lisbon, where he should have moved his court permanently to direct the war against England and France.

The Spanish conquest of Portugal threatened the balance of power in the Atlantic. Apart from the territorial gains, Spain took over the Portuguese fleets. In 1585 the Spanish merchant marine rivalled, if it did not outrank, the Dutch, doubled the German, and trebled the English and French.[2] In the same year in which Philip annexed Portugal the Catholic Francophile party, under the earl of Lennox, came into control in Scotland again. Lennox worked in conjunction with the French Catholic League, under the leadership of the duke of Guise, and with Mendoza, the Spanish ambassador in London. They planned an invasion of England, by Lennox from Scotland and by Guise from France, in order to place Mary Stuart on the throne. But Lennox was overthrown by the Scottish Protestants in 1582. A revised plan—that Guise alone, at the head of a detachment of Parma's soldiers, should invade England—was revealed under torture by Mary's agent, Francis Throckmorton, to Walsingham in 1583. As a result diplomatic relations between England and Spain were broken off (January 1584).

Anjou died in June and the Protestant Henry of Navarre and Bourbon was now heir presumptive to Henry III. The Catholic League at once made it its object to exclude Navarre, and Philip II joined the

---

1. O'Rahilly, *The massacre at Smerwick, 1580*; Read, *Walsingham and Elizabeth*, i. 306–422.
2. Hamilton, 'The decline of Spain', in *Econ. Hist. Rev.*, viii (1938), 168.

League in 1585. The Protestant cause in the Low Countries had already received what seemed a mortal blow when on 10 July 1584 William the Silent was assassinated. William, who for a short while had united the Catholics and Protestants in the Low Countries in their struggle for their liberties, had latterly been the inspiration of the northern Union of Utrecht, formed in 1579 with the object of achieving complete independence. William's leadership of the United Provinces devolved on the States-General, a parliament of the representatives of the various provinces; but it was a timid, unwieldy body. With Parma going from success to success south of the Meuse and Philip leagued with the Guises, the counter-reformation gained in momentum.

The Protestant cause looked well-nigh lost. If Brittany and Normandy, as seemed likely, came completely under the control of the Catholic League, and if Flushing and the Scheldt fell to Parma, Spain would have a line of sea bases extending from Lisbon to Flushing, from which, with her superior sea power, she would be able to launch an overwhelming attack on England, the last remaining bastion of Protestantism.

In 1585 Philip seized the English merchant ships in Spanish ports. Elizabeth, now thoroughly alarmed, committed herself by the treaty of Nonsuch (August 1585) to the protection of the United Provinces. Brill, Flushing, and Rammekens, the so-called cautionary towns, were to be security for the money she should spend. In December the earl of Leicester went over to take command of a considerable expeditionary force which had gone to the Netherlands in October.

The acceptance of the title of Governor-General by Leicester was in effect the acceptance for Elizabeth of English sovereignty of the Netherlands.[1] English intervention had one early effect that was ironic, for Sir William Stanley, who had brought over a regiment of Irish to serve under Leicester at the beginning of 1587, went over to Spain with the majority of his troops.[2]

In the growing conflict between England and Spain there were many causes of dispute, both political and economic. The attack by Drake on the Indies in 1585–6 proved the final irritant to Philip. The young James VI of Scotland, already anxious to succeed Elizabeth on the English throne, made a defensive alliance against foreign powers

1. Read, *Walsingham and Elizabeth*, iii. 107–37; Neale, *Essays in Elizabethan history*, p. 171; Handover, *The second Cecil*, p. 47.

2. On Stanley's career cf. *Wild Geese in Spanish Flanders*, ed. Jennings, *passim*; Loomie, *The Spanish Elizabethans*, pp. 130–74.

with the queen in July 1586 (Treaty of Berwick). Feeling confident now of James, Elizabeth consented to the execution of his mother, Mary of Scots, in February 1587 for her complicity in the Babington plot. Mary's death removed the last obstacle to Philip's invasion plans, the 'enterprise of England', for he could not have placed her on the throne without strengthening the French. He therefore launched the 'invincible' armada in 1588, designed not only to conquer England but also to destroy the Dutch.

Medina Sidonia, the armada's commander, adhering rigidly to the strategy worked out for him, failed to attempt a landing at Plymouth or the Isle of Wight, and the armada drove on to defeat. Henry III was encouraged to attack the Catholic League strongly in France. He was however assassinated in August 1589, and France became a battle-ground between the Huguenot Henry of Navarre, claiming the suc-cession as Henry IV, and the League.

If Henry IV were to unite France behind him, both Spanish possession of the Netherlands and Spanish domination in Italy would be en-dangered. Philip determined to prevent this. He himself as son-in-law of Henry II had a claim to the French throne, which he now sought for his daughter, Isabel Clara Eugenia. He sent 3,000 men to Brittany to serve under the duke of Mercouer, general of the League (October 1590). Elizabeth was frightened lest Philip should renew the attack on England from bases in the Netherlands and France. Spain, foiling English attempts to stop her treasure fleets from coming home, was rebuilding her navy. The queen therefore sent expeditionary forces to Normandy and Brittany. Meanwhile Parma, acting on Philip's orders, had to come twice from the Netherlands to France to relieve the Catholic League strongholds of Paris (1590) and Rouen (1592) from siege by Henry. This prevented his dealing the *coup de grâce* to the two remaining dissident provinces, Holland and Zeeland. The Dutch with English help improved their position and the great Parma died, a disappointed man, on 2 December 1592. Maurice of Nassau, William the Silent's son, was a cool and resolute commander. With the best of Philip's Netherlands troops diverted to France after 1589, Maurice was able to begin the campaign which, six years later, was to see the Spaniards cleared from the provinces north of the Lower Rhine and Waal. Maurice even held Ostend, as a base of operations against Flanders, in the south.[1] The northern Netherlands were in effect lost to Spain.

---

1. *Elizabethan government and society*, p. 350.

II · THE NINE YEARS' WAR

> If indeed you remain steadfast for the future in your efforts to
> expel altogether from your territories the enemies of God, you
> may expect all the assistance that Alonso Cobos, in whom you
> are to have full trust, will assure you of.
>
> Philip II to Irish Catholic nobles, 14 August 1596[1]

IN FRANCE TOO, where Henry IV became a Catholic in 1593 and thus began to win the allegiance of the Leaguers, Spain was losing ground. But Philip still fought for possession of Brest, a valuable revictualling stage between Spain and Flanders; while Elizabeth, with her own safety in mind, sought to prevent his getting this port as a base in which his armadas might refit for the invasion of England. The Spaniards with 5,000 men on the Blavet faced the combined opposition of Henry's army and an English force under Sir John Norris.

As if it were not enough for Spain to have armies engaged in both France and the Low Countries, she was now asked to send an expedition to Ireland as well. This request came from the north of Ireland from a confederacy of bishops and chiefs, of which Edmund Magauran, archbishop of Armagh, and Red Hugh O'Donnell, the vigorous young prince of Tyrconnell, were the moving spirits. Magauran had talked with Philip of Spain and had rather rashly formed the conviction that Philip would aid the Irish if they formed a reasonably strong combination and took up arms. The primate found Red Hugh very willing to assist him in forming such a combination, and by May 1593 the two had brought it into being.

To the lords of Ulster, spiritual and lay, it seemed, and with good reason, as if their province, the last stronghold of Gaelic independence and of the free exercise of the old faith, was about to be conquered. To gain the support of Philip II for their fight in defence of their liberty,

---

1. . . . *si vero eodem animo in posterum Dei hostes ex ditionibus vestris omnino expellandos curabitis . . . non est cur minora vobis inde bona promitatis quam ex Alphonso Cobos . . . cognoscetis, cui integram fidem adhibebitis.* AGS, Estado 2604.

25

political and religious, they sent Archbishop James O'Hely to Spain in 1593.

The confederacy of which Archbishop O'Hely was agent was notable for the absence from its leadership of the most important of the Ulster chiefs, the man whose mid-Ulster lordship was the pivot of the whole province. This was Hugh O'Neill, second earl of Tyrone. O'Neill was in an awkward position. Ties of blood united him to both O'Donnell and young Hugh Maguire, the leading chiefs of the confederacy. But while these young men could hope to wrest concessions from the queen by an exhibition of strength, he, more mature, saw much danger to himself if he provoked her. As things stood he was in the good graces of Elizabeth who recognized his title to the earldom of Tyrone. Should he rebel he incurred the risk of unpleasant consequences. The failure of Philip to support Fitzmaurice's rebellion, the devastation wrought in Munster during and after the Desmond wars, and the introduction of the undertakers into the south were all warnings to him not to indulge in treasonable activities, especially as his 'Irish' rivals, O'Neill (Turloch Luineach) and the sons of Shane, could be counted upon to take advantage of any government action against him.

But Maguire took the field in 1593 and O'Donnell a year later, and the septs of Tyrone began to rally behind them. In order to bring in the other provinces the co-operation (for what it was worth) of the exiles living on Spanish pension in Lisbon was sought and gained. These exiles were Edmund Eustace, claimant to the Baltinglass title, Cahil O'Conor, son of Brian O'Conor Faly, and Maurice and Thomas Fitzgerald of the Munster Geraldines.

But O'Donnell waited in vain for the force of five to ten thousand men that he hoped to see piloted into his waters: Philip had his hands full in the Netherlands and Brittany. In April the Spaniards in Brittany, under Don Juan del Águila, moved north from the Blavet and in an attempt to take Brest built for themselves the fort of Crozon, on the northern part of the Roscanvel peninsula, commanding the harbour of Brest. They were besieged by a large English army under Norris. After a month's siege Norris stormed Crozon (10 November 1594) and Águila had to fall back on the Blavet. England need not now fear invasion from Brest.[1]

Notwithstanding therefore the impression that Primate Magauran

1. Lavisse, *Histoire de France*, vi. 405.

had carried away from Spain two years previously, Philip was now little disposed to embark on a fresh and doubtful venture in Ireland. He evidently did not agree with Archbishop O'Hely's claim that an attack on Elizabeth in Ireland would be the most effective means of countering the aid she gave the rebels in the Low Countries and Philip's enemies in France. As the king pointed out to Juan de Idiáquez, his trusted adviser in the sphere of war:

What the Irish ask . . . is much; and I think they will require much more still. Speak to the archbishop of Tuam and make full enquiry, so as to discover what force in the final analysis they really need. If it be such a small one that we can afford to give it, it will be a very good thing to help them.[1]

But no force, great or small, was sent.[2]

Tyrone, in view of the event, had been wise in playing a waiting game. But because of the energy displayed by Maguire and O'Donnell in maintaining the war of the north against the English, the earl's position on the fence was becoming untenable. In September 1595 he assumed the Irish title O'Neill. Still, however, he played for time, and again submitted to the government in October, saying that he had never 'practised with foreign princes to draw strangers into this kingdom' before. Yet he admitted that he had written to Philip in August.[3]

O'Neill (as we shall henceforth call him) was playing a double game. In fact he had then an agent, Edmund MacDonnell, dean of Armagh, at the Spanish court. And as late as 27 September Hugh O'Donnell and he had written letters (which fell into English hands) to Philip II, Cahil O'Conor, claimant to the lordship of Offaly, and Don Juan del Águila. From King Philip they asked for an army of two or three thousand men. The letters mentioned previous appeals which had gone unanswered and made an offer of the kingdom of Ireland to Philip. The bearer, as he confessed under examination, was instructed to say that the two chiefs would carry on the war if Philip undertook to send help by May.[4]

But Philip was hard pressed. Spain, officially at war with France

---

1. *Lo que piden . . . es mucho, y a mi mucho más lo será. Vos le hablad, y os informad del de todo para ver en lo que a lo ultimo habrán menester, que se les pudiese dar, muy bueno sería ayudarlos.* AGS, Estado, 839, f. 51: Philip II to Idiáquez [autumn of 1593].

2. Silke, 'The Irish appeal of 1593 to Spain', in *I.E.R.*, ser. 5, xcii (1959), 279–90, 362–71.

3. *Cal. Carew MSS. 1589–1600*, p. 126.

4. Ibid., pp. 122–3; *Cal. S.P. Ire., 1592–6*, pp. 406–7, 409–10; Walsh, 'Scots Clann Domhnaill in Ireland', in *I.E.R.*, ser. 5, lviii (1936), 23–42; Ó Lochlainn (ed.), *Tobar fíorghlan Gaedhilge*, pp. 55–6.

since March 1595,[1] was fighting all around France's borders. With this
strain on her resources she became bankrupt again, Philip suspending
payment for the third time in 1596; and the war was going against
Spain Clement VIII absolved Henry IV from excommunication in
1595. Already the majority of the members of the Catholic League
had gone over to Henry, who gained Burgundy and Provence in 1596.
But contrary to what might have been expected Henry was unable to
carry the war into the southern Netherlands. In fact, it was the
Spaniards who crossed the border into Artois and Picardy, where
their successes included the taking of Calais (April 1596). However,
their gains drove England and the Dutch to form a triple alliance with
Henry IV against Spain.

With Brittany saved from the Spaniards, Sir John Norris had
brought over his English veterans to Ireland in 1595. In spite of that
the northern allies had recovered Enniskillen, given Bagenal a reverse
at Clontibret, and gained Sligo and Monaghan. O'Donnell exercised
sway over Connacht outside the garrisons, while O'Neill was giving
Norris plenty to do to maintain communications with the garrisons at
Newry and Armagh by way of the Moyry pass. Philip's interest began
to be aroused. O'Neill was obviously providing Elizabeth with formidable opposition, and now with open war between England and Spain
he should clearly be encouraged. Philip therefore gave the Irish to
understand that in their war for the defence of the faith they might
have any assistance they required from Spain.[2]

This offer, brought to them in May 1596 by Alonso Cobos, raised the
hopes of the confederates. O'Neill and O'Donnell replied at once to
Philip that they would now end the truce (in being since the previous
October and renewed in April) with the English and begin the war
again. They asked for some help at once, to be followed by a full-sized
army as soon as it could be got ready. They offered to make Cardinal
Archduke Albert, son of Maximilian II and governor of the Netherlands since 29 January, king of Ireland, with the proviso that he should
live in the country.

In this summer of 1596 Philip sent, besides Cobos, two other military missions to Ireland, to secure information on the basis of which
he might plan his intended invasion. One of these missions reported

1. Dumont, *Corps universel diplomatique*, vol. v, pt. I, pp. 512, 515: reciprocal declaration
of war by Philip II and Henry IV, Brussels, 7 Mar. 1595.
2. *Cal. Carew MSS. 1589–1600*, p. 141: Philip II to Tyrone, Madrid, 22 Jan. 1596.

that there were many difficulties against landing any expedition in the north. Donegal was not to be recommended as a port of disembarkation; Carlingford, Killybegs, Teelin, and Sligo all offered possibilities, but Limerick was to be preferred.

This vital question, where should the expedition land, was the subject of discussion between another mission, that of Captains Cisneros and Medinilla, and the Irish leaders. In this matter various factors had to be taken into account: the suitability of each harbour itself, whether it was defended, whether the surrounding terrain offered opportunities for transport, and so on. On the whole, it was agreed in the discussions, Limerick would make the best landing-place; it could berth a large armada, the 'marquis of Connacht' (probably Tibbot Burke, son of Walter Ciotach, set up by O'Donnell as MacWilliam in 1595) would be at hand to aid the Spaniards, and the other chiefs would keep the enemy occupied until the invaders had established themselves.

The confederate leaders claimed that they commanded 6,000 foot and 1,200 horse. While admitting that the queen had six or seven thousand non-Irish troops in the country, they maintained that the Catholics now subject to her would change allegiance as soon as the Spaniards struck a blow.[1]

In claiming this the chiefs were making free with the truth, as they knew it. In 1590 the first specifically Irish college abroad, Alcalá, was established; and Alcalá was the forerunner of a number of Irish colleges set up in Spain and Portugal, the Low Countries, France, and at Rome. But even by 1590 Irish priests educated on the Continent had already made sure of the allegiance of the old English to Rome in spiritual matters. While devotion to the Holy See was confirmed and grew in strength among the Catholics of the Pale and towns, their loyalty to the crown in political matters remained unshakeable. Thus for the most part they ignored James Fitzmaurice's call to arms, and they were out of sympathy with the aims of the northern rebels. They considered that O'Neill was bent only on establishing his own supremacy in Ireland, and pointed out that the anti-Catholic laws of 1560 (the oath of supremacy and the fine of one shilling for refusal to attend Protestant services) were not being pressed against them. In fact, these

---

1. The foregoing is documented in AGS, Estado 839 (*Cal. S.P. Spain, 1587–1603*, pp. 619–27; O'Clery, *Life of Hugh Roe O'Donnell*, ed. Murphy, introd; *Cal. S.P. Ire., 1592–6*, pp. 517, 519, 522, 526, 542–3).

laws were moderately enforced, except on one or two occasions, after the excommunication of Elizabeth, and after the armada. Their priests supported the old English in their stand, if indeed they did not inspire it. The loyalist Irish argued strongly that O'Neill was not a champion of the faith and that the queen was indifferent to the exercise of their religion.

For this reason O'Neill was making efforts to win over the old English and was seeking through the Holy See to exert pressure on them to support him. In the year 1596 he asked Pope Clement VIII to grant him the patronage of Irish sees and benefices. But the old English were able to take advantage of a changing political climate at Rome, and O'Neill did not secure the granting of this or further requests designed to compel the Catholics of Norman descent to join him. In 1580 a Roman declaration concerning the Bull of excommunication of Elizabeth allowed Catholics in effect to accept the queen as their head in the temporal order. Pope Clement VIII (1592–1605) freed the Papacy from domination by the Habsburgs; he sought, however, to conciliate them as well as the French, and in this he was successful. Henry IV was received back into the Church in 1593 and the pope absolved him from heresy two years later. But so prudent had Clement's handling of this affair been that Spain was not estranged. The Papacy under Clement maintained an influence over the two great Catholic powers. Following the same line of policy Clement refrained from judging between the two Catholic parties in Ireland, rebel old Irish and loyal old English.[1]

Philip II has earned a reputation for 'irresolution' which in view of the facts is not justified. He was already at war in the Netherlands and France. Not content with this, he was now seriously thinking of sending an army to Ireland. It was Elizabeth herself who provided him with the final provocation. After the capture of Calais Elizabeth allowed Essex and the war-party in her council to have their way, and on 20 June the earl of Essex appeared before Cadiz. The English fleet with Dutch help captured or burned fifty-seven ships and left on 16 July, taking a spoil estimated at 20,000 or more ducats and leaving the city in flames. The only resistance met with was from Don Pedro de Zubiaur, leader of a squadron which maintained communications between the Iberian peninsula and Brittany. Don Pedro, in his cruise

1. My article, 'Hugh O'Neill, the Catholic question and the papacy', in *I.E.R.*, ser. 5, civ (1965), enlarges on the subject under discussion here.

of the northern sea, engaged six enemy munition ships, sinking two
and taking four captive.

Philip II sought reprisal for the attack on Cadiz. He fell in with the
plan of Don Diego de Brochero, Zubiaur's fellow commander in the
Atlantic, to support O'Neill with an army against Elizabeth. Preparations were made in Cadiz, Lisbon, and El Ferrol, and the veteran
sailor Don Martín de Padilla, Adelantado Mayor of Castile,[1] was in
1596 made general-in-chief of the Ocean or Atlantic fleet and commander of the expedition.

Philip again sent Cobos as his envoy to the two Hughs to advise
them in advance of the proposed expedition. O'Neill and O'Donnell
wanted the Spaniards to land at Galway (near MacWilliam Burke's
lordship) or, if driven into the North Channel by the wind, at Carlingford in O'Neill's territory. Cobos announced that Philip had approved
in principle the suggestion that Archduke Albert be made king of
Ireland, but wanted clarifying discussion on this proposal.

O'Donnell laid in provisions to be ready on 1 November to victual
the Spanish army, but in vain. Padilla left Lisbon with eighty-one
vessels and was joined by nineteen from Seville. He intended to join
with other ships from Ferrol and Vigo. Seeking to round Finisterre, he
ran into an equinoctial tempest off Viana on 28 October. The fleet was
overwhelmed and thirty-two ships, not counting caravels and lesser
vessels, perished between Corcubión and Cape Finisterre. Two
thousand men at least were lost (estimates vary somewhat) and the
surviving ships got with much difficulty into ports of the Gulf of
Cantabria.[2]

Another expedition, which planned to land at Falmouth and intercept Essex's fleet on its return from the Azores, also failed. On 19
October 1597 Padilla, again captain-general, left Corunna with a fleet

1. The office of *adelantado* was established in the middle ages. The *adelantados mayores*,
whose office was hereditary, were those of highest function and exercised civil and judicial
jurisdiction over the provinces, being responsible only to the king. In wartime they had
command of all the military forces of their district. Cf. *Encic. Espasa-Calpe; Almirante,
Diccionario militar.* Don Martín de Padilla Manrique, conde de Buendía (15 . . ?–1602), had
fought against the French, the Moriscos, and at Lepanto. In 1585 he was appointed captain-
general of the galleys of Spain and Adelantado Mayor of Castile; in 1587 he became first
conde de Santa Gadea and a grandee of Spain. Cf. Fernández Duro, *Armada española,* iii. 130;
D.H.E.

2. AGS, Estado 839 (*Cal. S.P. Spain, 1587–1603,* pp. 637–43): 'Despatches brought by Cobos
to the Pardo'; Museo Naval, Madrid, Col. Sans de Barutell, art. 4, nos. 1262, 1263, 1267
(*Codoin,* lxxxviii, f. 242): Padilla's account to Philip II, 14 Dec. Cf. Fernández Duro, *Armada
española,* iii. 118–26, 129–32; *Epistolario de Zubiaur,* pp. 11–26.

of 136 ships. Don Juan del Águila was land commander, with Conde de Palma in charge of the cavalry. On board were 12,634 men and 300 horses. Again the season was advanced, and in sight of England Padilla's fleet was driven back by storm and several ships were lost.[1]

It was Philip's last offensive. Feeling his end approaching he sought only peace for Spain. The prospects for peace had now increased, for if Philip and, even more so, Archduke Albert were now weary of unprofitable war, the Dutch, English, and French could feel satisfied with the successes they had won against Spain. The Dutch were safe behind the defence barrier formed by the Rhine, with its distributary the Waal, and the Meuse. Their gain was also a gain for England, now freed from the fear of a Spanish attack launched from bases on the Dutch coast. England was also delivered from the danger of an attack from the French coast, for Albert had been forced to retreat from Picardy in 1597 and in March 1598 Mercoeur submitted to Henry. These events also delivered France from the attacks on her unity made by domestic malcontents and foreign enemies, and it was time for her king to set about the task of national reconstruction.

But if, as with our advantage of hindsight we are able to say, Europe was in 1598 moving towards a general disengagement, this was not at all apparent then. Nor, when over the next eleven years peace had been painfully established, was it firm enough to resist for more than a decade afterwards the strains imposed upon it by the jealousies, antagonisms, and fears with which the peoples of Europe regarded each other.

But in 1598 the king of Spain and even the king of France were willing to listen to the archduke's peace overtures. Philip for one thing had gained nothing from his war with France but his third bankruptcy, and for another he wanted before he died to establish his daughter Isabel Clara Eugenia in the rule of the Netherlands. And Henry saw that the aims of his allies were diverging from his. They wished him to continue immobilizing Spain, which was to their advantage but gained him nothing; for him an attack on Savoy or Bresse or the Low Countries would be far more practicable. Besides, his country needed peace for a reconciliation of parties and for economic restoration. And if England and the Dutch need not fear peace, both could yet gain from a continuation of the war. Both countries were growing

1. González Dávila, *Felipe tercero*, pp. 74–5; Fernández Duro, *Armada española*, iii. 166–7; Hume, *Españoles e ingleses*, p. 249; *Elizabethan government and society*, pp. 359–61.

rich on the commercial ruin of the southern Netherlands and were gaining for themselves the trade of the Atlantic, Mediterranean, and East Indies. They were even trading in the Caribbean at a time when the American market for Spanish products was beginning to contract. It was in their interest, therefore, to keep Albert and Philip distracted by the French war while they made further economic gains. The Dutch, moreover, were fully aware that neither Albert nor Philip acquiesced in their hard-won independence.

Both England and the United Provinces accordingly sought to prevent Henry IV from making peace with Philip. The Papacy, however, threw its influence against that of the northern powers. Clement VIII saw clearly that the prolongation of war between the Catholic southern powers benefited only the Protestant north. Rome too, which from 1580 had supported the anti-Protestant war, now under Clement felt that this war had reached its conclusion and wished to turn from it to a renewal of the Holy League against the Turk. The war between the emperor and the Turk in the east had recommenced in 1593, and now there was prospect that the imperial forces might gain Buda, the centre of Turkish power on the Danube. The Papacy was the chief architect of the peace between France, Spain, and Savoy which was concluded at Vervins on 2 May 1598.[1]

There was calm in the Mediterranean between 1597 and 1600 and Spain's chief problem was now the Netherlands. Philip in the month of Vervins tried to solve this problem by making over the country as a quasi-autonomous principality under Spanish protection to Isabel and her husband-to-be, Archduke Albert, upon whom Isabel's actual ruling powers were devolved.[2] The archdukes, as Albert and Isabel were known, were married in November. It was the best that Philip could do.

If Philip was concerned about the future of the Low Countries, he was even more worried about the future of Spain under his son and heir, Prince Philip. 'God,' he lamented, 'who has given me so many kingdoms, has denied me a son capable of ruling them.' It was a worry that added to the vexations of his last painful illness, but his faith did not fail him at the end. As he committed his soul to the divine mercy,

1. Braudel, *Méditerranée et monde méditerranéen*, pp. 1070–3; Lynch, *Spain under the Habsburgs*, i. 335–6; Dumont, *Corps universel diplomatique*, vol. v, pt. I, p. 561.

2. Carter, *Secret diplomacy of the Habsburgs*, pp. 79–80; Dumont, *Corps universel diplomatique*, vol. v, pt. I, p. 573, gives conditons of cession on 6 May 1598 of the Low Countries by Philip II to Isabel Clara Eugenia.

so he committed Spain to the divine guidance, making his testament to his own children that of St. Louis to his son. He breathed his last on 13 September 1598 in the Escorial.

Before he died he had received one last reminder of the war in Ireland, an account brought to him of the victory gained by O'Neill at the Yellow Ford in August. The king dictated a letter congratulating O'Neill and O'Donnell and encouraging them, but in vague terms, for Philip was preoccupied with the unfinished business of peace with England.[1]

1. AGS, Estado 839 (*Cal. S.P. Spain, 1587–1603*, p. 649): Philip to O'Neill and O'Donnell, Madrid, 1598.

III · THE ADMINISTRATION OF PHILIP III

Un rey insipiente y un duque insolente y un confesor absolviente traen perdida toda la gente.

Contemporary *pasquin*[1]

PHILIP II had reason to feel apprehensive about his son's capacity for ruling. Piously inclined, amiable, and colourless, Philip III had little taste for affairs of state, whose direction he was willing to leave to others. At hand to take advantage of this situation was the first of a series of favourites, who in this reign and the next occupied the chief place in Spain after the king. The first *valido*, or *privado*, was Don Francisco Gómez de Sandoval y Rojas, fifth marquis of Denia, created duke of Lerma by Philip in 1599. Lerma continued in favour until 1618 when he fell from power, dragging down with him in his crash a whole retinue of lesser men. His career was so notorious, marked by scandal, bribery, fortune-building, and the picaresque doings of his followers,[2] and his end was so spectacular that it has been hard for historians to approach with dispassion the question whether his ascendancy was beneficial or harmful for Spain. He is variously seen as a mediocrity (Cánovas del Castillo), a debasing influence (Ferrer del Río), and a peacefully inclined statesman, who, whether his motive was to save Spain from bankruptcy (Gardiner) or merely to line his own pockets (Pérez Bustamante), reversed the warlike tendencies of Philip II and gave Spain a new, pacific direction in policy (Ranke).[3]

1. 'A foolish king, an insolent duke, and an absolving confessor are drawing the whole people down to ruin.' Quoted in *Ciudad de Dios*, cxxx (1922), 15.

2. Antonio Ferrer del Río, 'El duque de Lerma', in *R.E.*, xviii (1871), 161–87, gives a vivid picture of the corruption, bribery, and wasteful expenditure of Lerma's ascendancy, as well as of the disorderly and scandalous lives of the duke's pages and gentlemen. Don García de Pareja, Ferrer thinks, was most probably the writer who left the memoirs, which were published in novel form by Le Sage under the title, *Gil Blas de Santillane*.

3. Gardiner, *History of England . . . 1603–42*, i. (1883), 102; Pérez Bustamante, *Felipe III*, p. 112; Ranke, *L'Espagne sous Charles-Quint, Philippe II et Philippe III ou les Osmanlis et la*

After all this it is not surprising to find a modern writer judiciously deciding, after careful argument, that in fact Lerma did not occupy the seat of power at all.[1]

The 'favourite' or 'first minister'—the special quality of this personage derives as much from his political standing in the kingdom as it does from his personal relationship to the monarch[2]—was now an accepted institution in England and France as in Spain. The development of the *privanza* marked a stage in the evolution of the great powers, which sought by means of this institution to deal with the ever-increasing complexity of government. As absolute royal power developed the need arose for some intermediary, some 'first' minister, between the king, now acquiring as 'the anointed temple of the Lord' a semi-divine status, and the representatives, whether of his own estates or of foreign powers.

In the nature of the case it was not to be expected that the Renaissance sovereigns, forced as they were by the lack of development in the bureaucratic machines to choose as first minister a courtier bound to them by personal ties and depending on them for support, would find ministers of real competence to cope with the problems of state.[3]

For the Spanish empire these problems were grave. No longer dominant in arms, faced with the relentless commercial rivalry of the Dutch, English, and French[4] at a time when her own economy was contracting, encumbered by the increasing weakness of her imperial partner, Spain was perhaps inevitably set on the path of decline.

But the decline might not have been so rapid if Philip III had shown a more positive capacity for ruling. Perhaps it is true, as Pérez Bustamante alleged, that the rigorous restraint by which Philip II had sought to control the weakness and frivolity which marred his son's character had indeed been too severe, so much so as to annul his very character and inhibit his power to govern.[5] At any rate the new king took little personal interest in the routine of government; there was no question any more, as there had been with Philip II, of the king's being his own chief clerk. Very occasionally, in matters which affected

1. Carter, op. cit., pp. 71–2.
2. Ibid., p. 70.
3. Mattingly, *Renaissance diplomacy*, pp. 224–5.
4. *New Camb. mod. hist.*, i. 446, 456–69.
5. Pérez Bustamante, *Felipe III*, pp. 26–31.

monarchie espagnole. Translated by J. B. Haiber, pp. 219–23. Quoted, Carter, *Secret diplomacy of the Habsburgs*, pp. 67–8.

his *amour-propre* or devotion, Philip—capriciously and without logic—insisted on his own will. But this was exceptional; the king in the main left the tedious business of ruling to others.

There was no question of a change of direction in the policy of Spain under Philip III; as with Charles V and Philip II the guiding policies continued to be the conservation of the Christian frontiers and their defence against the Turk.[1] The problem is rather whether it was now the favourite or the king's councils (or perhaps the council of state in particular) which exercised the real power in Spain.

For the purposes of the present study the question may be confined to the *privanza* of the duke of Lerma. The duke, in the view of Pérez Bustamante, was the real ruler of Spain until 1618, when the avarice and nepotism which were the characteristic features of his ascendancy brought about his downfall. Lerma himself, as Pérez points out, replaced the royal secretaries on whom Charles V and Philip II had relied; for twenty years he was Philip III's one and universal secretary, enjoying the king's full confidence and alone dispatching business with him orally.

In another view, however, the locus of power is to be sought in the conciliar structure of Spain: in the royal councils in general, as Cánovas del Castillo maintained, or, as C. H. Carter, modifying Cánovas's thesis, suggests, in the council of state in particular.

As in France and England, so also in Spain the king in the exercise of his rule made use of a number of councils. These bodies, whether they were consultative or ministerial in function (a point to be discussed presently), in no way limited the royal prerogative, and their members, chosen (at least under Philip II) from the intellectual aristocracy, were appointed at will by the king.

At the end of the reign of Philip II the councils stood twelve in number. The council of state (*consejo de estado*), analogous to the French *conseil d'en haut*, formed the king's supreme advisory (or ministerial) body, and the king himself nominally presided over it. Its jurisdiction was total and was disseminated through two different types of council, those whose responsibilities were territorial—councils of Castile, Aragon, Italy, Flanders, and Portugal—and those whose functions were departmental—finance, justice, war, military orders, and crusade. Thus, for example, the council of war was simply the

---

1. Chudoba, *Spain and the empire*, pp. 174–5; Carter, *Secret diplomacy of the Habsburgs*, p. 71, who follows Cánovas del Castillo, *Estudios del reinado de Felipe IV*, i. 258.

council of state, with perhaps the addition of a military or naval expert or two, meeting to discharge the functions of high command.

Another way of stressing the importance of the council of state is to say with Carter[1] that it dealt with all large matters, whether pertaining to the peninsula or to Flanders or to Italy. The other councils were subordinate and referred important issues to the council of state, which might and frequently did bypass them.

All this complexity of government moved Philip II in 1592 to form a junta or private council, analogous to a cabinet. This was the famous 'council of night'. It was formed of three members: the old king's loyal Portuguese servant Don Cristóbal de Moura (affairs of Portugal), the efficient Basque secretary Don Juan de Idiáquez (war, state, and foreign affairs), and the count of Chinchón (affairs of Aragon and Italy). Of these three the first, Moura (1538–1613), had since 1573 been the chief adviser to the king in Portuguese matters and had been chiefly instrumental in attaching Portugal to the Spanish throne.[2] For this he was made marquis of Castel-Rodrigo. Idiáquez had succeeded Antonio Pérez as secretary to the council of state in 1579 and in 1584 had been admitted to that council.[3] The conservative Don Diego Fernández de Cabrera y Bobadilla, third count of Chinchón (d. 1608), favourite and majordomo of Philip II, had represented Spain in Rome and Vienna besides holding many other offices. He had come into the council of state in 1573.

Later, Gómez Dávila, marquis of Velada (a creature of Moura), and Cardinal Albert, the future Philip III's brother-in-law, were added.

In the palace revolution engineered by Lerma at the change of reign the more intimate councillors of Philip II were sent away from court. Archbishop Loiasa of Toledo went off, as did also the count of Fuensalida, Don Pedro Portocarrero, who was bishop of Cuenca, and Don Pedro de Guzmán, while Moura was removed a safe distance to the governorship of Portugal. Velada and Idiáquez both remained; they offered no danger to him, and Idiáquez in particular was too efficient a servant to lose.

Philip III, who thus foolishly rid himself of the corps of loyal and experienced servants bequeathed to him by his father, placated the nobility passed over in the previous reign by choosing from their ranks

1. Carter, *Secret diplomacy of the Habsburgs*, pp. 72–3.
2. Biography by Dánvila y Burguero, *Don Cristóbal de Moura* (Madrid, 1900); also a seventeenth-century account in *Codoin*, vi. 23–7.
3. Idiáquez died in 1614. Cf. Pérez-Mínguez, *Don Juan de Idiáquez* (San Sebastian, 1935).

new councillors. Lerma himself came on the council, and most of those newly appointed were his friends and partisans: the count of Miranda, relative of Lerma by marriage, who in May 1598 became president of the council of Castile;[1] the duke of Medina Sidonia; the duke of Nájera; the Adelantado Mayor of Castile; and Don Juan de Borja.[2] The archbishopric of Toledo went to Lerma's uncle, Bernardo de Rojas y Sandoval, who was also now made cardinal. Rojas was already bishop of Ciudad Rodrigo (since 1585), Pamplona (since 1588), and Jaén (since 1595). Soranzo, the Venetian ambassador, had a low opinion of his experience and administrative capability. An important influence on the king was Fray Gaspar de Córdoba, O.P., his confessor since some years before Philip's accession and now a councillor. Fray Gaspar, as Ottaviano Bon, another Venetian ambassador, observed,[3] had a great reputation for having the ear of the king at all times, for being devoted to Lerma, and for being one of those who advised the duke in the most intimate matters of state. However this may be, Lerma in the matter of aiding Ireland at least was not so enthusiastic as Gaspar wished.

In approaching the question whether the reality of power lay with the favourite Lerma or with the councils, one may begin by noting that within the councils themselves power lay with the council of state. To it the other councils were subordinated, and its jurisdiction over them and over the Spanish empire was total. But before the main question can be tackled there is a further issue to be disposed of, namely what was the status of the councils? Opinions among historians range from the view that the councils were merely advisory bodies[4] to the view that they were ministries.[5] An intermediate position is held by a recent historian, J. Lynch, who maintains that the council of state was purely consultative, but that the regional councils, while they were not ministries, 'exercised not only executive functions

1. Don Juan de Zúñiga Avellanada y Cárdenas, sixth conde de Miranda del Castanar, was governor of Catalonia (1585) and then viceroy of Naples (1586–95). Philip III appointed him to the councils of state and war.

2. Conde de Fícalo y de Mayalde, son of S. Francisco de Borja.

3. *Relazioni:Spagna*, eds. Barozzi and Berchet, p. 251. He was chosen, as were all Philip's confessors, by Lerma. Cf. *R.E.*, xviii (1871), 165.

4. 'The council of state . . . was a purely consultative body. Its duty was merely to give an opinion on matters submitted by the king. They (*sic*) had no further competence.' Davies, *Golden Century of Spain*, p. 125.

5. *Los consejos no eran simplemente órganos de asesoramiento pues tenían tambien el carácter de órganos superiores de la administración, y sus miembros el de altos funcionarios o ministros.* Aguado Bleye, *Historia de España*, ii. 692.

but also legislative and judicial ones'.[1] Cordero-Torres, on the other hand, who insists on the executive as well as consultative functions of the councils, argues against Ballesteros y Beretta and Gounon-Loubens that the council of state was an indispensable instrument of government since it was the council of the king and not of the vast number of heterogeneous provinces that it represented with him, whose problems only the councillors out of their special knowledge could lay before him.[2]

This is not to say that the council of state *was* the government, and yet in the final analysis Cordero-Torres agrees with Carter, and for essentially the same reason, in allotting the reality of power to the council of state. For Carter the council of state was made up of those who by birth or ability or experience were the best entitled to conduct the affairs of the Spanish empire. These men formed an élite corps, whose experience and knowledge extended to all the Spanish kingdoms. Any problem of government could be delegated to a small committee of councillors, augmented if needs be by experts from outside, which, when it had resolved the intricacies of the problem, placed it before the council of state for a decision. Thus the effective government of Spain was the council of state in particular rather than the councils in general.

This solution, which has the virtue of neatness, has much to be said in its favour. The various councils had grown so slow-moving and cumbersome as to be unable to transact affairs in any businesslike manner. The council of state found an escape for Spain from this dangerous impasse by reserving to itself all matters of high policy. Adopting the principle of the 'council of night', the council of state referred important matters to small juntas which could be expanded, dissolved, or revived in accordance with the need of the moment. In this way the council of state ensured that there would be a continuity of policy in regard to individual questions—by making each the province of a particular junta—and that (since a junta could be set up to meet each case) no pressing matter would be neglected.

The handling of the expedition to Ireland will serve to illustrate the mode of procedure of the council. When, early in 1601, the decision was taken to send the expedition a junta of three, Fray Gaspar and the

1. Lynch, *Spain under the Habsburgs*, i. 182.
2. Cordero-Torres, *El consejo de estado*, ch. VIII; Ballesteros y Beretta, *Historia de España*, vol. iv, pt. II, ch. I; Gounon-Loubens, *Essais sur l'administration*, ch. V.

secretaries of state and war, was appointed to see to the assembly of men and necessities required. The junta in no way removed the direction of the enterprise from the council of state; nor did it seek to. Its appointment was simply a matter of convenience, a result of the council of state's desire to expedite the preparation of the expedition. The council continued as before to supervise the preparations and the junta, once its specific task was accomplished, simply ceased to exist.

To take another example: in the summer of 1601 Hugh O'Neill's eldest son, resident in Spain, decided to become a Franciscan. This decision embarrassed the Spanish government, who were afraid that if they allowed him to do so his father would regard it as a breach of trust on their part, since the young prince would in due course be expected to succeed to his father's lordship. The matter was referred for advice first to a junta of Salamanca theologians, then to the Valladolid theologians, and finally to a special junta of councillors of state headed by Cardinal Guevara. Other matters as they cropped up were referred to yet other juntas. These were purely *ad hoc* committees and once they had disposed of the problem of the moment they ceased to be.

This analysis of the functioning of the council reveals its indispensability and also the secret of its success as an organ of government. It does not, however, establish beyond dispute that power was located in its hands rather than in those of Lerma. Far from it. In the first place the leading councillors were, as has been stated, the duke's creatures. He thus exercised a considerable, if indirect, control on the workings of the council. Furthermore, Lerma was indolent, his direction of affairs wavering and uncertain; and a number of energetic Spanish diplomats and governors, with no clear guidance from above and concerned with maintaining the greatness of Spain, were led to developing their own policies independently of either Lerma or the councils. The results were spectacular but in the long run disastrous for Spain and for Europe.[1]

Yet Lerma retained the initiative regarding what matters were discussed in council, and when it suited him he also acted independently of the conciliar structure. Whoever, like the Irish leaders and their friends, wished to see Spain embark on a particular policy sought above all to gain the ear of the duke. The documents in the Simancas archives reveal that twice there was a divergence between the king

1. Cf. Mattingly, *Renaisssance diplomacy*, pp. 224-5, 256, 266-8.

and his council over the desirability of sending an expedition to Ireland. First the king was in favour of it, the council against; later, while the council pressed for it, the king shilly-shallied. On both occasions there was an impasse. But when Lerma determined to launch the expedition he acted in complete independence of the council. The decision was his, not theirs. The corollary of this is that without Lerma's decision the expedition would never have sailed.

This is not to deny that in fact the council was concerned from first to last in the direction of the expedition. The invasion at each successive stage, from the first proposals to launch it until the end of the inquiry that resulted from it, was the subject of conciliar debate and advice. Time and again the advice remitted by the council was not acted upon, but each fresh proposal, each new consideration was sent to the council of state (or war) for its opinion, to be given in the light of the councillors' knowledge, both of the Irish problem and of the whole complex of administrative problems of Spain. When decisions were taken they were generally—but not always—arrived at in the light of the considerations presented by the council. The history of the Irish expedition, in short, would tend to reveal the council, in the time of Lerma at least, as an indispensable organ of government, but would also indicate that Lerma and not the council occupied the central seat of power.

If one wishes for a clearer understanding not only of how the government of Spain worked but also of the relations between the council of state, the favourite, and the king, one requires more detailed knowledge of conciliar procedure, already touched upon.

Council meetings might deal with one or several matters of interest. The number of members present at a meeting varied with the number of councillors in attendance at court, the number appointed to a junta, and so on. The record of proceedings, drawn up from minutes made by a secretary, went to the king in the form of a *consulta*, the expression of the council's opinion. For the period under review here the secretary of state who handled northern affairs (including Irish) was Andrés de Prada, while the secretary of war was Esteban de Ibarra. Pedro Franqueza y Esteve, Lerma's protégé, became secretary of state for Italian affairs in 1600, displacing Francisco de Idiáquez, and in 1603 took over the entire secretariat, Prada going to the council of war. Franqueza committed northern affairs to Antonio de Arostegui.[1]

1. Juderías y Loyot, 'Don Pedro Franqueza', in *R.A.B.M.*, 3ª época, vol. xix (1908), II. 319–22; *D.H.E.*, i. 1180.

Consultas were of two kinds, *de oficio*, 'of office', which dealt with matters of state, in this case relations with England, Ireland, Scotland, and other countries, and *de partes*, i.e. decisions on memorials submitted by and about private individuals.

The *consultas* always began with a summary of the document or documents sent for deliberation to the council or junta, perhaps a request for help from O'Neill and O'Donnell, perhaps a memorial on the Irish situation or a problem raised by the king or the favourite. Then the councillors gave their opinion. Often enough a minority view was expressed.

If the council had reached a consensus, and if the king (advised of course by Lerma) approved of it, he signified his agreement in the margin: *está bien* or *como parece*.[1] The formula *no hay que ver*[2] showed that he had decided that no action was required. The secretary then made out a document in the sense indicated by the marginal notation. This was signed by the king *yo el rey*[3] and countersigned by the secretary *refrendaba*.[4] Dispatches were accordingly sent out, letters it might be to the Irish leaders or to Archduke Albert, or instructions to Sessa, the king's ambassador at Rome, Castel-Rodrigo, Caracena (the viceroy of Galicia), or some other servant of the crown.

Policy-making was of course affected by delays in communication. Dispatches might reach Lisbon within a week, Brussels within a fortnight, and Rome within anything from three to six weeks. By the time they had arrived the march of events might have made the dispatches out of date. This was even more true of letters sent to Ireland. Though a fast patache with favourable wind and tide could make the sailing between Galicia and an Irish port in as little as four days, often, owing to delay in securing both licence to depart and shipping, a courier might find weeks or perhaps even months slipping by before he could deliver his documents to the Irish leaders.

In cases where the king did not accept the suggestion of the council or where the council itself advised against action the *consulta* was filed away in the Irish *legajos* or bundles, to await resurrection when the council, inspired by some fresh order, reconsidered the Irish situation. It often proved useful in refreshing the memory of the councillors; sometimes, on the other hand, it merely interfered with the effective-

---

1. 'Very well' or 'As it appears'.   2. 'Action is unnecessary.'
3. 'I the king.'   4. '(He) countersigned.'

ness of their decision, because it referred to conditions that had since changed.

The invasion of Ireland must be viewed in the general context of Spanish policy, which at the time was one of disengagement. Philip III ratified the treaty of Vervins in 1601, made peace with England in 1604, and signed a truce with the Dutch in 1609.[1] He did nothing to upset the truce, in being since 1578, with the Turk in the Mediterranean (appearances in 1601 notwithstanding), and sought alliance with Persia to contain the Ottoman threat to the Empire and to the Portuguese colonies in Asia. The intervention in Ireland was a last attempt to gain an advantage over his English opponent. The king wished by invading Ireland—as also by encouraging Federico Spínola's project to occupy a port in England—to exert pressure on Elizabeth and make her come to a serious discussion of peace terms. Ultimately, he hoped, the invasions of Ireland and England would help him to gain the succession to the English throne for his own candidate.

Peace between England and Spain was not, however, to be achieved until after James I had in 1603 succeeded Elizabeth on the English throne. James took as his motto the text, 'Blessed are the peacemakers'. He was conscious of the futility of war and conscious too of England's need for peace to build herself up. But he was not the only one in high position who for one reason or another sought an easing of international relations.[2] Pope Clement VIII's desire to effect a reconciliation between the Habsburgs and the French and to write *finis* to the anti-Protestant war has already been mentioned. On Clement's initiative negotiations opened in 1601 for a marriage treaty between the prince of Asturias (later Philip IV) and Elizabeth of Bourbon, daughter of Henry IV. In the Netherlands Archduke Albert and his chief advisers,[3] foremost among them the remarkable Ambrosio Spínola who became captain-general of the army of Flanders, all wished to see an end to the war with the Dutch, so that Albert might be enabled to impose his authority, restore the economy, and perhaps win back the Northern Provinces. Lerma himself was the

1. Abreu, *Tratados de paz*, i. 82: oath by Philip III, 27 May 1601, binding himself to keep treaty of Vervins; i. 243: treaty of London, 28 Aug. 1604, between Philip III and the archdukes on the one hand, and James I on the other; i. 458: twelve years' truce, Antwerp, 9 Apr. 1609; i. 484: commercial treaty, Antwerp, 9 Apr. 1609.

2. Carter, *Secret diplomacy of the Habsburgs*, pp. 11–16.

3. Cf. the initiative taken by Richardot, president of the council of state, and other Walloon aristocrats in 1598–9 to end the war with the Estates-General. Loomie, *Spanish Elizabethans*, pp. 77–80.

disciple of Ruy Gomez de Silva, prince of Éboli, who in the time of Philip II had been the advocate of conciliation towards the Netherlands.

There were many considerations urging Spain to seek a disengagement. Spain, in spite of the reverses suffered by her at the hands of the English, Dutch, and French, and in spite of clear evidence of decline, was still regarded as the foremost European power. Her king ruled over the Iberian peninsula and the Americas. He claimed for himself exclusive rights to the trade and navigation of Africa and the Indies, although it was becoming increasingly difficult for him to maintain these claims against English, Dutch, and French interlopers. In Italy he still ruled Milan, Naples, and Sicily, and his control of the Balearics, Corsica, and Sardinia made him lord of the western Mediterranean. He was head of the Habsburg house, whose junior branch ruled the empire and was his faithful ally. His sister and her husband governed the Netherlands, with effective control over the southern provinces and Franche-Comté and with hopes of yet regaining the rebel north.

But with the death of Philip II Spain's great days were over, although the fact was barely recognized as yet. Politically and economically the giant that had been Spain was shrunken in stature. Politically Habsburg Spain had failed in her bid to control the direction of French affairs and in her efforts to make the Dutch return to what she considered their 'proper' allegiance. She had not only failed to conquer England but had been unable to prevent the English from giving aid to the Dutch; she had had to look on, helpless, while the English and Dutch broke into the trade of 'her' Indies. Still the acknowledged leader of the Catholic world, her cherished dream of restoring Catholic unity was shattered. She had no real power even to alleviate the sufferings of persecuted Catholics who appealed to her with tales of intolerable grievances.

Spain had found it impossible to impose her will on Europe, and now her helm of state was taken over by indolent and incapable hands. As Spain grew progressively weaker France, now at peace and engaged in reconstruction, grew stronger, and Henry IV's hostility towards Spain remained undiminished. Henry still pursued the French secular aim of breaking out from Habsburg encirclement; and the eldest daughter of the Church found her natural allies against the Catholic king in the enemies of Catholicism and even of Christendom. There was danger that France might combine with the Turk in an attack upon Spain, or might, allied with some of the west German states, resume the war against Spain on the side of the Dutch and English. Or Henry IV might attack Milan, which was also eyed greedily by Venice and Savoy. Finally, since the treaty of Vervins had left certain matters in dispute between France and Savoy, Henry might attack Savoy. If he did, Spain would be forced to go to the defence of Savoy in order to protect the Milanese. Everywhere she looked Spain saw danger.

If the political situation made it advisable for Spain to make peace with her enemies, the state of the treasury made it imperative for her to do so. The crown was in desperate financial straits, its resources alienated or mortgaged to bankers. From about 1519–20 prices had begun to rise in Spain, partly at least as a result of the increase in bullion, imported from Mexico and Peru, in relation to other goods. The price-rise was maintained throughout the century, so that goods fetched five times in 1600 what they had in 1501.

Charles V had commanded that all traffic with his possessions overseas should flow through Seville. In examining the registers of bullion imports at Seville, Professor Earl J. Hamilton, the American economic historian, observed what seemed to him a significant correlation between the volume of the precious metals, chiefly silver, imported into Spain and the price inflation, and was led to conclude that there was a direct relation between the two. The increase in prices, Hamilton endeavoured to show, coincided with the increase in imports of bullion; while both increases were significant in the first part of the century, both reached their peak in the second part. The increase in silver, it seemed obvious, had a powerful effect on the Spanish economy and was the chief cause of the price revolution.

It is agreed among scholars that there was an expansion in Spanish industrial production in the first half of the sixteenth century but that in the second half this expansion halted and production went into decline. Hamilton argued that since the immediate effect of the increase in treasure imports in the early part of the century was to raise prices, wages began to lag behind prices, thus providing industrialists with an incentive towards increased production. But after the middle of the century wages caught up with prices, whereas in England and France they did not. In fact, whereas the price-rise was now being felt in these and other countries, it was to a much less harmful extent than in Spain. Spanish industry therefore lost its incentive and began to go into decline at the same time that it was faced with the competition, both in the home and American markets, of cheap foreign goods. For Hamilton, then, there was a direct correlation between the influx of treasure and not only price inflation but also the fluctuation first upwards and then downwards of the Spanish economy in the sixteenth century.[1] The Spanish economy suffered from a surfeit of bullion.

More recent studies, however, have suggested that the case was not so simple. Both Hamilton's figures for the quantity of silver entering Spain and his assumption that the bullion entering was all injected into the Spanish economy have been questioned; furthermore, it seems established that the price-rise was proportionately greater in the first rather than (as Hamilton thought) the second half of the century, even if prices continued to rise until they reached their maximum at the end of the century.[2]

The question has thus been raised whether the influx of treasure from the Indies is alone sufficient to account for the inflation in sixteenth-century Spain. Pierre Chaunu, the French scholar, has therefore sought to establish a correlation between the price-rise and the volume of trade between Seville and America.[3] But it seems likely that a convincing explanation for the price-rise and the decline in the economy following upon this inflation will have to take account of a multiplicity of factors, somewhat as follows.

Throughout the sixteenth century Spain, which with its seven and a half million people as compared with France's sixteen million was indeed under-populated, saw a slight increase in population.[4] At the same time that her home market expanded, Spain was faced with an increasing demand for her textiles and agricultural produce in the Low Countries and Italy and found a new market in the Americas. The increase in specie caused prices to mount, while at the same time Spanish production, both agricultural and industrial, was too back-

1. Hamilton, *American treasure and the price revolution in Spain 1501–1650*; 'American treasure and the rise of capitalism 1500–1700', in *Economica*, ix (1929), 338–57; 'The decline of Spain', in *Econ. Hist. Rev.*, viii (1938), 177–9.
2. Elliott, *Imperial Spain 1469–1716*, pp. 184–5; Lynch, *Spain under the Habsburgs*, i. 124.
3. Chaunu, *Séville et l'Atlantique 1504–1650*, viii. II. 18–25.
4. Carande, *Carlos V y sus banqueros*, vol. i, ch. III, placed the apogee of Spanish population between 1530 and 1570, when according to him the figures for Spain were seven and a half million. Chaunu, *Seville et l'Atlantique 1504–1650*, viii. I. 245–6, suggests that the population at the middle of the sixteenth century was somewhat less than seven and a half million rising to that figure or something over at the end of the century. The population of Castile, he suggests, rose during the same period from something under to something over six and a half million.

ward to meet the increased demand, thus aggravating the revolution in prices. By the middle of the century the price inflation and increase in costs were making themselves sharply felt. The Spanish administration, faced with the fact that foreign goods were cheaper than those produced at home, decided that Spain was exporting too much, especially to America.[1] Because of this erroneous diagnosis the government forbade the export of goods from the country. The contraction of markets on top of the high costs of production proved too much for Spanish industry. It became unable to stand up to foreign competition even on the home market, and went into decline.

Other inflationary factors were at work to aggravate the situation. Charles V had issued *juros*, or credit bonds, to finance his borrowings, and he and Philip II mortgaged the American bullion in advance (as they did the European revenues of the Habsburg house) to pay the foreign bankers who financed their wars. The inflationary extent of these two practices cannot be estimated precisely, but at least a great deal of the crown revenues went to pay the bankers. The American bullion was thus eaten up or else was used unproductively by the aristocracy, on the construction of grandiose buildings or on the purchase of luxury goods, clothes, and jewellery, instead of being acquired by industrialists as capital for investment. Thus it came about that from the middle of the sixteenth century, what with the adverse balance of trade, heavy taxation, the unproductive use of wealth, and the expense of foreign wars, the Spanish budget was in a chronic state of imbalance.

The decline in industry, trade, and agriculture was attributable, therefore, among other things to price inflation, the imperialism of Philip II, the extravagance of the court, wasteful expenditure, and the drain in manpower through war, emigration to America, the rise in membership of the religious orders, and the elimination by the Inquisition of many productive subjects. And this decline had caused a great decrease in revenue and had left the crown greatly in debt. The young Philip III succeeded to a throne burdened by his father's debts to the tune of at least 20,000,000 ducats.[2] In 1598, the floating debt apart, the consolidated debt stood at the huge sum of 76,540,000 ducats, while the best revenues of the crown were engaged for years to come to Genoese, Florentine, and native bankers. Income from the plate fleets, owing, it is fair to say, to the vigilance of Lerma, remained

1. *New Camb. mod. hist.* i. 454.   2 Lynch, *Spain under the Habsburgs*, i. 128.

high; after 1601 it was declining, but there was no marked drop before 1630.[1] But this income amounted by 1598 to only a quarter at most of the crown's annual revenues; the rest was borrowed or came from taxes. The traditional taxes were augmented by a new tax of the type called *millones* (sales taxes) in 1590. This latter tax was increased in 1596 and again in 1600, when the Cortes of Castile were forced to vote to the king, for the support of Archduke Albert, the enormous sum of 18,000,000 ducats, to be paid at the rate of 3,000,000 a year for six years. But revenue still fell far below expenditure, which was estimated at 12,000,000 a year by the mid-1590s. While the crown was put to the most extraordinary shifts, such as debasing coinage[2] to raise money, Philip showered immense gifts of money on Lerma and Lerma's friends.

There was no significant inflation in the decade following 1606; but with a debt of 12,000,000 ducats on hand again in 1607 the crown suspended payments to the bankers yet again. Philip II had resorted to this device three times, the last time being in 1596. Just as that last bankruptcy had shattered Philip II's dream of crushing the Protestant powers of the north and had been a major factor in forcing him to make the treaty of Vervins with the French, so that of 1607 ended the Spanish attempt to subdue the Dutch and contributed towards making Philip III conclude the twelve years' truce of 1609.

In a country denuded of men by the war in Flanders and in a state of perpetual financial embarrassment, the decision to send an army of 6,000 troops to Ireland at a cost of 300,000 ducats was not to be lightly taken. The men might be raised at the cost of great efforts, and ships might be found in which to transport them. The money too might be raised; it was of little enough account in comparison with the large amounts squandered on grandiose buildings and displays of pomp by the crown and nobility, or with the sums with which the favourite enriched himself (by 1602 Lerma's annual income stood at 200,000 ducats). But the raising of the expedition placed one more burden on the strained resources of Spain and could only be justified by the expectation of solid political gain.

And in spite of the many considerations that urged Philip towards disengagement there was at least an arguable case for carrying the war into Elizabeth's territory. On the one hand peace would help to restore the credit of the crown and benefit the Spanish economy. It

1. Hamilton, *American treasure and the price revolution*, p. 34.   2. Ibid., pp. 75–9.

4

would, as Albert strongly pleaded, be of economic and political benefit to the Netherlands. On the other hand, it was urged, a strong attack on Elizabeth would force her to give up helping the Dutch and draw off English attacks on the Indies and the plate fleets. In any case, even if Spain did make peace with England, that would not prevent the English from aiding the Dutch secretly. An attack on Ireland would expose Elizabeth's weakness; the war in Ireland had meant a frightful drain on England in men and money, so that England in fact needed peace to draw breath and recuperate. More, England herself would easily be conquered from Ireland. For with Spain in control of Irish harbours it would be an easy matter for her veterans to cross over and land in England. Such an attack on England would prove decisive for making the English politiques, who, Philip was assured, occupied most influential positions in the government, declare themselves openly in favour of the Infanta Isabel as successor to Elizabeth. Thus at one stroke Philip would redeem his father's promise of 1596 to the Irish, demonstrate that Spain was a champion to whose aid hard-pressed Catholics need not resort in vain, impress the king of France and other monarchs with the reality of Spanish might, and prevent any possible alliance between England, France, and the Turk against Spain.

These were strong arguments for making Spain carry the war to England, and when chance provided the nucleus of an invasion army at Lisbon they were to prove irresistible.

IV · O'NEILL

I saw Mark Antony offer him a crown; yet 'twas not a crown
neither, 'twas one of those coronets.
                    Shakespeare, *Julius Caesar*, Act I, Sc. ii

ROBERT DEVEREUX, second earl of Essex, arrived in Dublin on 25
April 1599 to take up office as lord lieutenant. He had left London with
the cheers of the citizens ringing in his ears. His enemies on the council,
led by the second Cecil, had less love than the populace for the haughty
and difficult earl. But the situation in Ireland was desperate, and Essex,
if he exercised the statesmanship and the military quality of which he
was certainly possessed, might be just the man to restore Ireland to
order. His absence would at least relieve the Cecilian faction of his
opposition in the council, and should he fail they might be rid of him.
Elizabeth, however insupportable she might have found his insolence
in the past, had enough confidence in his abilities to agree to the
appointment. And so it was with high hopes of returning, bringing
rebellion 'broached on his sword', that the new Henry V, to whom
Shakespeare in the prologue to his latest play clearly alluded, came to
Ireland.

But the task before him would test the qualities of even the brilliant, arrogant favourite. Hugh O'Neill, after his great victory of the
previous 24 August at the Yellow Ford, the greatest defeat the English
had ever sustained in Ireland, might have been expected to go on to
attack Dublin, the citadel of English rule in Ireland. Yet to the terrified
Dublin council's plea that he spare the remnant of their army, the
last life-line of the English now walled up in the towns, he acceded.
There were various reasons for this restraint, remarkable as it was.
O'Neill knew that Elizabeth would not yield easily, and he would
have difficulty in keeping his allies together for a sustained offensive.
The Irish besides were short of arms, powder, and armour. These war
supplies were obtained from Scotland or from the merchants of the

towns, who bought them in England and sold them to the chieftains at exorbitant prices: six beeves for a sword, a headpiece, or a musket. Again, O'Neill had no siege-cannon. He was also fearful just now lest an English force should land at his rear at Loch Foyle.[1]

Hugh realized that for ultimate victory foreign help was essential. His present military superiority belied very real weaknesses in his position, and his forbearance after the Yellow Ford showed wisdom; it was a card he could play in case he should find himself at some later date brought to sue for pardon from the queen. But scenting victory he now set himself a threefold goal, towards the realization of which he directed all his considerable talent and energy: he attempted in the first place to rally all Ireland to his cause; he tried secondly to build up a modern army capable of meeting an enemy in the field; and he sought finally the outside support, military and political, without which his efforts at home could scarcely hope to succeed.

In O'Neill Gaelic society had found its greatest leader. He had natural gifts for generalship and for diplomacy, and these were allied in him with a flexibility of purpose and a patience that were truly remarkable in an Irishman. The old traditional values of his race appealed to everything that was native in him, the more so as the years went on, and he could give a truly Celtic display of emotion which never at the same time clouded his brain. He had formed a certain detached view of the Irish way of life, although this can hardly, as was once thought, be altogether ascribed to his residence in England, where he had lived between the ages of twelve and eighteen.[2] It was rather his own political sagacity that made him see the weakness of the Gaelic system and its need to change, to adapt itself to meet the challenge from a new order of things. He had a sound understanding of political reality in Europe and was conscious of the effort needed to turn the balance of forces in his own favour. He had the ability to set himself a goal and to work towards its attainment with steady, painstaking purpose. O'Neill was in fact the most formidable adversary that the English crown had ever encountered in Ireland.

By now the conflict known as the 'nine years' war' had hardened into a struggle whose explicit aims were the restoration of the Catholic

---

1. Maxwell, *Irish history 1509–1610*, pp. 42, 191.
2. Cf. J. K. Graham, 'The birth-date of Hugh O'Neill, second earl of Tyrone', in *I.H.S.*, i (1938), 58–9.

religion and the complete liberty of action of the subject,[1] and O'Neill stood out among his confederates as the champion both of national autonomy and Catholicism. Yet that calculating brain of his never allowed him to take a chance without weighing the consequences, and as his aims were never extreme, but modified by circumstances, he always allowed himself a line of retreat.

The basis of confederate strength lay in the north—in the alliance of O'Neill, O'Donnell, and, until his untimely death in March 1600, Maguire. The northern chiefs, however, needed the support of the lords and towns of the south. The southern lords could supply men and the rich lands of the south provision them, and provision too the hoped-for invasion force; the towns could provide arms, ammunition, and money. If O'Neill had command of the ports he could utilize their commercial strength to fill his war-chest and could control entry into Ireland. The south, however, would not accept Hugh's pre-eminence in Ireland, and this he was prepared to sacrifice. He would ask some foreign prince on whom common agreement could be reached to accept the throne of Ireland.

Although unable there and then to press home the advantage gained at the Yellow Ford, O'Neill had achieved much. He had saved Ulster from invasion and driven the enemy to take refuge within the Pale and within the cities. During the following months through his lieutenants he had set Leinster and Munster aflame, and Munster had not stirred since the Desmond wars. James Fitzthomas, nephew of Gerald the 'rebel' earl, who had been disappointed by Elizabeth in his hopes of gaining the earldom, was set up as earl of Desmond by O'Neill. The Geraldines rallied to their new and handsome leader, who cleared the undertakers, including Edmund Spenser, wholesale out of much of Limerick, Cork, and Kerry and was soon master of almost all the territory from Dunquin to the Suir. The English, in impotent rage, spitefully labelled this creation of O'Neill's the 'sugan' or strawrope earl. Sir George Carew fell back on Mallow, Norris on Cork, and the earl of Ormonde retreated to the defence of Kilkenny and Tipperary. A number of Munster gentlemen, the White Knight (Edmund Fitzgibbon), Patrick Condon, Lord Barry's brother John, and Lord Roche's son David joined the Irish, as also did Lords Mountgarret and Cahir.

1. Cf. demands by O'Neill in 1595 and in 1599–1600 in Maxwell, *Irish history 1509–1610* p. 182.

In Leinster the O'Mores took Philipstown and Athy; and on the Shannon Redmond Burke, O'Neill's captain, took one of Ormonde's castles, Druminagh, as a base from which to attack Clanricarde.

Clerics, among whom the Jesuit Father Archer was the most prominent, were at work rallying the southern lords to O'Neill's side. Father Archer wrote for James Fitzthomas to Philip III, advising the king that Fitzthomas had taken the field for the restoration of the Catholic faith and for the maintenance of his right to the Desmond earldom. He asked for cannon and powder to assail the planters who had taken refuge in 'his towns and cities'—while Spenser had escaped with his wife to England other 'undertakers', as the planters were called, had fled to the safety of Youghal and other towns—and for soldiers to lodge in the cities.

Red Hugh O'Donnell, O'Neill's dashing ally, kept up from Tyrconnell a constant attack on English rule in Connacht. He again set up in Mayo Theobald Burke as MacWilliam, took Ballymote castle, and aiming to open a way through Connacht into Munster raided Clanricarde and even Thomond's county of Clare. North of Thomond only the garrisons of Boyle, Tulsk, and Roscommon and the castle of Sligo held out against him.[1]

Up to the present the strategy employed by the two Hughs, O'Neill and O'Donnell, had been purely defensive; they had sought to keep the English out of Ulster, to prevent, by frequent raids southwards, their enemies from massing any attack on them, and to keep the road to Munster open, in case the Spaniards should land in that province. They had avoided pitched battles but had lured the enemy into positions where the odds were altogether in their own favour and where they might always disengage their forces if victory were not falling to them. Generally victory had been theirs.

But until O'Neill could establish his superiority in the field he had no hope of ultimate victory. He therefore created the trappings of a disciplined army with which to oppose the national militia of the queen. He did so by taking over elements of the English system, organizing his forces into separate companies, composed largely of musketeers, calivermen, and pikemen, and by transforming the mercenary *buannachadha*, the service of billeted men. His soldiers were

---

1. *A.F.M., ad an.* 1598; *Cal. S.P. Ire.*, 1598–9, pp. 501–2; Ó Domhnaill, 'Warfare in sixteenth century Ireland', in *I.H.S.*, v (1946), 48–53; Bagwell, *Tudors*, iii. 301–7; Falls, in *The Irish at war*, ed. Hayes-McCoy, pp. 35–46.

trained in the use of firearms and his army combined squares of pike-men, musketeers, and cavalry in the accepted manner of the age.[1]

O'Neill and his allies were able to infuse a certain professional stiffening into the ranks of their enthusiastic but raw levies. A number of Spaniards from the *tercios* of the Armada had remained in their service since 1588, and Irish veterans of the wars in Europe had come home to take service with the northern armies. Amongst these were such as Captain Richard Owen, O'Neill's kinsman, who had twelve years of active campaigning in Flanders behind him and who was now put in command of O'Neill's infantry; Captain Hugh Mostyn or Mostian, an English veteran of the wars in France, Flanders, and Ireland, who had been won over to the Irish cause by Father Archer; and Alexander Walshe, who after four years' service in Brittany came to Ireland with the archbishop of Dublin and Don Martín de la Cerdá, after which he served four years under O'Neill.[2] O'Neill hoped to secure the services of more of these veterans. The confederates were also able out of their scanty resources to hire Scottish 'redshank' mercenaries for periods.

Hugh O'Neill by his 'assumption of the forms designed for open warfare' had created a 'modernized' army. Yet he was hampered by shortage of supplies and by a lack of officers, and the main body of his followers was without the hardening resulting from frequent battle-testing. The Irish cavalry arm in particular was weak, although under Maguire's leadership it had done well at the Yellow Ford. The horses, Don Juan del Águila was to note, were small animals and their riders wore no armour and fought with half-pikes from saddles without stirrups.

O'Neill and O'Donnell had at this time under their command probably 20,000 fighting men in all, but not even half that number, the late Seán Ó Domhnaill (a good authority) estimated, were even moderately well-armed. Red Hugh had after the Yellow Ford sent his dark and indomitable mother to Scotland to hire a thousand Scots from her kinsmen. Hugh Boy MacDavitt and Edmund Birmingham went off to Spain to carry the news of the victory to Philip II and to beg him for the help required to follow up the success.

O'Neill, despite numerous disappointments suffered by him during

1. Hayes-McCoy, 'Strategy and tactics in Irish warfare 1593–1601', in *I.H.S.*, ii (1941); 'The tide of victory and defeat', in *Studies*, xxxviii (1949).
2. AGS, Estado 1745: Memorandum, Walshe to Prada, 17 Feb. 1603.

the reign of Philip II, placed in Spain his main hope of help. A sufficiently strong Spanish army could, united with his own forces, be relied
on to clear the English out of Ireland. Here again, in the international
field as in the national, Hugh had to walk warily to maintain balance
among conflicting interests. In Ireland the Catholics in general would
not accept the northern chief's leadership, while abroad the landing
of a Spanish army in Ireland would be calculated to arouse the fears
of France and the Papacy. O'Neill desperately required papal support
in order that he might be accepted as leader by all the Catholics of
Ireland. But the Papacy, whose main effort under Clement VIII was
directed towards the maintaining of peace between France and the
Habsburgs, would fear that a Spanish invasion of Ireland must make
France uneasy and upset the precarious peace. Hugh sought to man-
œuvre the Papacy into declaring the Irish war a crusade and giving
its blessing to the dispatch of an army by Spain to Ireland. This, as will
appear, was the aim towards which his agents at Madrid, Rome, and
Brussels were working.

Next to Spain O'Neill looked to Scotland for outside help. James VI,
Hugh calculated, would support him in revenge for his mother's
execution by Elizabeth. James was anxious to succeed to the English
throne and (until Cecil became his ally in 1601) sought and welcomed
encouragement from every source, Catholic and Protestant. A yearning
for the throne of England and not revenge for a mother slain was the
passion that inspired this northern ruler's actions, and he was therefore
very careful not to encourage Elizabeth's displeasure by openly traffick-
ing with her enemies. Realizing, however, that O'Neill's friendship
might be invaluable in the event of Elizabeth's death, he secretly
welcomed the Irish leader's offers of service and winked at his hiring
of Scottish mercenaries. But for the queen of England's benefit James
formally forbade his subjects to serve O'Neill or to trade with him.[1]

The two Irish agents MacDavitt and Birmingham, on their arrival
in Spain in October 1598, found Philip II already dead, but they pleaded
with the new government for an army of 6,000 men, with arms and
ammunition, to be sent to Ireland in 1599. MacDavitt was careful to
conceal the intent of his negotiations from the English Catholic exiles,
who wished rather for an attack on England.[2]

1. Willson, *James VI and I*, pp. 138–48; Gardiner, *History of England*, i. 80; Ó Ceallaigh,
Gleanings from Ulster history, pp. 101–2.
2. Loomie, *The Spanish Elizabethans*, p. 146.

This army, it seemed, could come none too soon to be of service to O'Neill. For when Essex arrived in Ireland, he had at his disposal an army of 16,000 foot and 1,300 horse. His aim was the establishment of a base at Loch Foyle to take O'Neill in the rear. But as a result of differences between him and the Cecilian party in the privy council he was left without the necessary carriage-horses and ships to enable him to establish this base.

Left, then, without the required support from England, Essex and the council of Ireland formed a new plan. They decided that the lord lieutenant should march southwards through Leinster to Waterford in order to prevent the complete defection of Munster, so much of which had recently rebelled, and in order to guard against the Spanish landing which they anticipated in the south. Essex therefore went on this campaign, which lasted from May to July.

As recent research has demonstrated, the censorious attitude of the older historians towards Essex's conduct of his lieutenancy is thus seen to be unjustified. It was once the accepted view that the earl squandered time and a great army in Munster and neglected the attack on Ulster to which he had previously been pledged. 'An army and a summer had been wasted', says Bagwell tartly, 'and nothing had been done.' Such strictures take no account either of the fact that Essex was prevented by his enemies on the privy council from setting up his planned base at Loch Foyle or of the fears of a Spanish invasion of Munster entertained by the government. True, the invasion did not materialize (and, as will directly appear, was never intended), but the threat was not one that could have been ignored. Essex did squander an army and a summer, but by showing his strength on the return journey from Limerick through Cork to Waterford he had done the government what could be considered valuable service; there were besides other useful gains to show, in the capture of Cahir (possession of which was necessary for any force operating westwards from the Suir) and in the reduction to obedience of Lords Mountgarret and Cahir.[1]

The English government were convinced that a Spanish invasion of Ireland or England was imminent, but they did not know where the

---

1. Cf. Henry, 'The earl of Essex and Ireland 1599', in *Inst. Hist. Res. Bull.*, xxxii (1959), 1–23; 'Contemporary sources for Essex's lieutenancy in Ireland 1599', in *I.H.S.*, xi (1958), 8–17. Hicks had already ('Sir Robert Cecil Father Persons and the succession 1600–1', in *Archiv. Hist. Soc. Iesu*, xxiv (1955), 100–1) indicated the importance of the denial by the Cecilian party to Essex of the 200 carriage-horses he asked for.

point of attack might be. And so while Essex sought to guard against an invasion of Munster there was also a great mobilization of ships at the Medway to meet a possible attack on England.[1] Since the attack never came, earning for the expected Spanish armada the description 'invisible', it has been suggested that Philip III was deterred from an invasion of Ireland or England by the putting to sea of the queen's ships and chiefly by the presence in Ireland of the man who had sacked Cadiz.[2]

In reality, and in spite of contemporary convictions, which were so strong as to deceive even modern scholars,[3] Philip III was not in 1599 planning any attack on Ireland or any major attack on England. The projected 'invasion' of England amounted to this. At the end of 1598 Philip had agreed in principle to the scheme proposed by the Genoese adventurer Fedérico Spínola that he (Spínola) should with a fleet of six galleys attack and take some port in England, to hold it as a bridge-head for further landings. Fedérico, who was then active in the war in Flanders, had originally made this proposal to Philip II in 1597, namely that at the command of some galleys carrying 5,000 men and a de-tachment of horse,

he would cross over to England and take some place, which when he had fortified it all England would not storm. . . . He would then transport to that stronghold all his army. He would feed and maintain this army by exactions on the country round about, and would support it with his galleys . . . .

Philip II died before deciding upon this proposal. But at the end of 1598 Philip III, when the suggestion was placed before him, accepted it. 'He ordered', said Spínola, 'that an agreement be made with me according to which I should be given the six galleys which were at Santander and had served on the Breton coast, together with 1,000 Italian infantry who were there . . . .' The king agreed that Spínola could as well embargo ships in Dunkirk and raise 1,000 Walloons and 1,000 horse in Flanders, with twenty pieces of artillery and munitions, provided that Archduke Albert agreed. Favouring this plan, Philip therefore rejected the somewhat similar scheme which Sir William Stanley and Father Joseph Creswell, S.J., urged repeatedly from 1597

---

1. Cf. *Elizabethan government and society*, p. 360.
2. Cf. Tenison, *Elizabethan England*, vol. xi: *1599–1601*, p. 161.
3. Henry, in *Inst. Hist. Res. Bull.*, xxxii, 15 n. 3. Cf. the pertinent remarks by Pollard, *History of England 1547–1603*, p. 437.

to 1602. Stanley offered, at the head of an expeditionary force of English exiles, to seize and hold some positions in England.[1]

Fedérico at the beginning of 1599 secured Albert's agreement to the proposal, and in June at the court at Barcelona Philip III made a financial settlement with the Genoese. The latter took ten galleys with him from Santander to Flanders, but then Albert (who had come back to Brussels in September) would not spare him the men and artillery, so that for the time being the project fell through.[2]

Far from contemplating an attack on Ireland or England in 1599, Philip was himself fearful of English aggression against Spain. Given the existing enmity between the two countries, it was to be expected that each should be suspicious and distrustful of the other. In the spring Spain was full of rumours that Elizabeth was preparing a great expedition. This, it was learned, was to be made up of 8,000 foot and 600 horse and was to go to Ireland. Later it was the talk that this army, under cover of going to Ireland, really meant to land in Portugal. Then on 11 June a fleet of an estimated sixty English sail was sighted off Corunna. This fleet went on to attack Great Canary Island on 26 June. The English occupied Las Palmas and demanded tribute before leaving. The Adelantado left Corunna towards the end of July in pursuit, but when he arrived at the Canaries the enemy was gone.[3]

Philip, although more concerned in 1599 to defend himself against attack than to take the offensive himself, did nevertheless encourage O'Neill and O'Donnell to hope for some support from him. MacDavitt was provided with a cargo of 1,000 arquebuses, 1,000 pikes, 150 quintals of powder, and 100 each of lead and match. Don Fernando de Barrionuevo, sergeant-major, was sent with him as special envoy to the Irish leaders from Philip, and the cargo was carried in three zabras commanded by General Marcos de Aramburu. Barrionuevo's instructions were threefold: he was ordered to encourage the Irish chiefs to continue their struggle, to assure them that the king would do what he could to assist them, and to report on their harbours and country from a military viewpoint.

1. Loomie, *The Spanish Elizabethans*, pp. 158–75.

2. AGS, Estado 621 (Rodríguez Villa, *Ambrosio Spínola*, p. 30; summary, *Correspondance*, eds. Lonchay and Cuvelier, i. 97): Memorial by F. Spínola, undated. Lonchay and Cuvelier summarize another document of the same tenor, dated, Vallid., 21 Feb. 1602. The two documents must be about the same date. Cf. Rodríguez Villa, op. cit., pp. 23–5; Cabrera, *Relaciones 1599–1614*, p. 2.

3. Cabrera, *Relaciones*, pp. 17–49, *passim*.

On 29 June Aramburu put in at Killybegs, 'one of the best ports of Ireland', Barrionuevo noted, 'able to take any large armada', and capable of being easily fortified against attack. That same day the sergeant-major went with O'Donnell to Donegal Friary, where the following day O'Neill joined them. Theobald Burke, O'Donnell's MacWilliam, was also there.

Cheered by the hospitality of the friars and with no more warlike sound to disturb them than the midsummer lapping of the waters against the shores of Donegal Bay, the chiefs and their guests sat down to confer. Don Fernando showed himself to be accommodating and subtle.

Don Fernando expressed regret for the failure of Philip II to succour the Irish in spite of the late king's best intentions, which had been foiled most notably when the weather destroyed Padilla's army of 1596, and he assured them of Philip III's resolution to stand by them. Comforted by this reassurance, the two Hughs swore to remain loyal to the king of Spain and not to enter into any treaty or agreement with Essex before the end of November.

Barrionuevo decided that these oaths could readily be accepted, for by November the campaigning season would be over. There would be time for Spain to send some help before the following spring or summer saw pressure mounted on the confederates to submit. Mac-William, to whose independence Barrionuevo testified by referring to him as *señor libre*—'independent lord'—swore without any limitation in time. Don Fernando soon grasped the underlying tensions which the conflicting claims, territorial or jurisdictional, created between the different lords, and was quick to bring home to them the need for presenting a united front, particularly if they looked to Spain for support. The chiefs took the hint and agreed to lay aside disputes about precedence for the duration of the war.[1]

Barrionuevo was a good diplomatist; of that there could be no doubt. Young Brian O'Rourke would not accept O'Donnell's claims to dominion over Brefni O'Rourke, and so stayed away from the conference at Donegal. Barrionuevo hearing of the trouble set out to soothe the prickly young chief, and wrote to him. O'Rourke was easily mollified by the courtesy of the envoy of Spain. O'Donnell in turn was

1. *Trató de confederarlos y lo hizó con que fuessen amigos verdaderos y las causas de su preheminencia se dexassen y suspendiessen por el tiempo que durasse la guerra* (He sought to make them allies and was so far successful that they became real friends, leaving aside and suspending their disputes about pre-eminence for the duration of the war).

persuaded to go to Strabane to meet Brian, and there they made peace, exchanging hostages, and O'Rourke took the same oath as the others.[1] The fruit of Barrionuevo's diplomacy was seen later in the support given by O'Rourke to Red Hugh at the battle of the Curlews in the month of August.

Don Fernando finally divided his cargo of arms equally between the two Hughs and went back to Spain to report.[2]

Whatever then may have been Essex's fears of a Spanish landing in Munster they were unfounded, as Barrionuevo's mission showed. After his return to Dublin the lord lieutenant went into Offaly in the last week of July. Here he relieved Maryborough and Philipstown and went on to confer with Clifford, the governor of Connacht. The latter, by agreement with Essex, took the offensive in the west, moving against O'Donnell. But in an encounter with Red Hugh and O'Rourke on 15 August at the pass of Bellaghboy in the Curlews he was defeated and killed. Thereupon O'Conor Sligo submitted to Red Hugh, surrendering Collooney castle to him. By this victory O'Donnell secured his grip on Connacht and greatly strengthened the Ulster defences.

Essex, although now reduced to 4,000 men, finally set out against O'Neill, but was induced to hold three parleys with the chief near Louth town. The outcome of the parleying was that by verbal agreement Essex and O'Neill agreed on a cessation to last in periods of six weeks until May, either side being free to break it on fourteen days' notice. If any of O'Neill's confederates refused their assent, Essex was at liberty to attack them.[3] From the evidence of Irish sources O'Neill, it can be gathered, made at the first and famous secret parley, when Essex and he met alone for half an hour in midstream, a tentative offer of the kingdom of Ireland to the Englishman. If Philip of Spain or James of Scotland would not take the crown of Ireland, perhaps Essex would; his great name would draw in the Anglo-Irish and he would be acceptable to all the Irish as king. Had Essex agreed, the course of history might have been different; but he did not, either because he feared that Philip would not forgive him for his sack of Cadiz, as Archbishop Oviedo learned, or because he would not trust

1. Ó Clérigh's laudatory biography of Red Hugh has no mention of this dispute.
2. AGS, Guerra Antigua 3143. Barrionuevo died on 17 Oct., but his report later came into the hands of the council of war; cf. Ó Clérigh, *Beatha Aodha Ruaidh*, i. 210.
3. Tenison, *Elizabethan England*, vol. xi: *1599–1601*, p. 196.

himself to the Irish, as Peter Lombard believed; or perhaps because his loyalty would not allow him.[1]

But the truce was quite a victory for O'Neill, as its dating 18 September 'in the new style' underlined. O'Neill, O'Donnell and Maguire had been observing the new Gregorian calendar from 1584; its observance symbolized both their Catholic orthodoxy and their defiance of government. O'Neill might not have gained Essex, but he had won sufficient breathing-space until the army promised by Barrionuevo should come to ensure certain victory. Hugh was left with the hope that this army would come before Christmas,[2] a hope which, the reader will remember, Barrionuevo saw no point in disabusing him of. Meanwhile, there were in the Irish regiment in Flanders veterans in plenty who might be enticed home to add a professional element to the raw native forces. To the Archduke Albert, O'Neill now turned, reminding him that in keeping Essex's army occupied in Ireland he had relieved the Netherlands of English pressure, and asking him to allow all the Irish soldiers resident in the Low Countries to come to Ireland.

But eight months were to pass before a reply came from Albert, and even then it was non-committal. The moment was not indeed favourable for an Irish approach to the archduke. After his resumption of rule in Brussels, in September 1599, the situation had been going from bad to worse. Though the rebels had lost the French alliance after Vervins, Elizabeth continued to support their war with Spain. In March 1599 the archduke had already sent his agent, Jerome de Coemans, to England to prepare the way for peace negotiations. Philip supported this move. If the archdukes were childless, the sovereignty of the Low Countries would in time revert to Spain: Philip therefore was anxious to have Elizabeth withdraw her support from the Dutch so that their revolt might collapse. The king of Spain was also concerned, in view of the now failing state of Elizabeth's health, to ensure that James VI did not secure the succession to the English throne, which he wanted for the Archduchess Isabel, his sister,

---

1. AGS, Estado 840, f. 79; Estado 185 (*Cal. S.P. Spain, 1587–1603*, p. 656): Oviedo to Philip III, Donegal, 24 Apr. 1600; Lombard, *Commentarius*, pp. 174–5. (Mr. Henry is quite wrong in regarding the *Commentarius* as embodying 'the Irish oral tradition of nearly a generation later' than 1599. Cf. *I.H.S.*, xi (1946), 16. It was written in 1600.) For another suggestion that Essex had been in treasonable complicity with O'Neill cf. Hume, *Treason and plot*, p. 416. (For the Fr. Bluet and Dr. Bagshawe mentioned here, cf. *Elizabethan government and society*, pp. 383, 386.)

2. Lombard, *Commentarius*, p. 174.

or for himself.[1] It is in the context of these considerations that Philip's dispatch of Barrionuevo to Ireland must be considered. However much Barrionuevo might stress Spanish interest in Ireland that country was in reality but a pawn on the chessboard. If the pawn must be sacrificed to gain the greater piece of England, then it would be.

Given the situation existing in the Netherlands, it is not to be wondered at that Archduke Albert did little to help Ireland. Albert had much correspondence with the Spanish court and with the duke of Lerma, but the student will search his letters in vain for mention of the Irish struggle.[2]

Undoubtedly some gesture from the archduke would have been of great assistance to O'Neill as he played for time, for he was finding it difficult to persuade his fiery young ally O'Donnell of the wisdom of this policy. It was with much ado that O'Neill got the younger chieftain to agree to the cessation. O'Donnell's recollection of O'Neill's promise not to make peace without licence from Spain was in the circumstances inconvenient.[3]

After the departure of Essex from Ireland in October, and in accordance with his instructions, Sir William Warren went northwards on three occasions to negotiate with O'Neill for an extension of the cessation. The truce, indeed, continued until the end of the year. But it was uneasy. O'Neill's attitude, owing largely to O'Donnell's intransigence, was now hardening, and he was standing strongly on religion, demanding complete freedom for Catholicism in Ireland. In spite of the cessation Father Henry Fitzsimon, S.J., the famous controversialist and kinsman of Ussher, was imprisoned in December. O'Neill demanded his release from Warren.[4] The Jesuit, who had a great influence

1. Cf. Hume, *Treason and plot*, pp. 419–26. The memoranda on the succession question prepared by Fr. Persons, S.J., then rector of the English college, Rome, are dealt with by Hicks in *Archiv. Hist. Soc. Iesu*, xxiv (1955), where he argues the case for Cecil's support of Isabel's claims. This argument is shown to be less than convincing by Hurstfield in *Elizabethan government and society*, pp. 374–9.

2. AGS, Estado 2023 (*Correspondance*, eds. Lonchay and Cuvelier, I. 103): *consulta*, Vallid., 18 May 1602; VA, Borghese III, vol. 98 C, pp. 102–4; AGS, Estado 617 (*Archiv. Hib.*, iii (1914), 235–7, and xxiv (1961), 58–9): O'Neill to Albert, Dungannon, 27 Feb. 1599, and James MacDonnell to same, 'Ndunlibhsi' (Dunluce), 13 Oct. 1599. It seems to have been Albert's letter that Frangipani, internuncio in Brussels, sent to the cardinal secretary of state, 24 June 1600. Frangipani also sent copies of two letters that O'Neill had written to Albert. VA, Borghese III, vol. 98 C, f. 93v (*Archiv. Hib.*, iii. 240 and xxiv. 58).

3. Cf. *Cal Carew MSS. 1589–1600*, p. 269: O'Neill to Philip, July 1597, which letter had contained such a promise.

4. Gilbert, *Facsimiles of national MSS of Ireland*, pt. iv, I, p. 116 (*Cal. S.P. Ire., 1599–1600*, p. 327): O'Neill to Warren, Dungannon, 25 Dec 1599. Cf. *Cal.*, cit., pp. 279–81; *Cal. Carew MSS. 1589–1600*, pp. 348–9; O'Clery, *Life of Hugh Roe*, pp. cvii–cix; Ó Domhnaill, 'History

within the Pale, remained aloof from the rebellion, as did his superior, Father Richard de la Field. Fitzsimon's release, therefore, if O'Neill could secure it, would help to strengthen Hugh's position as the Catholic champion. Still anxious for veterans from Flanders, Hugh in another scarcely veiled hint told Albert at the end of December that he had cancelled the truce, as the English were minded to send their soldiers in Ireland to the Low Countries.[1]

But Albert was in no position to help O'Neill. At the beginning of 1600 mutiny for lack of pay among his troops had led to Maurice's gaining successes in Guelderland. The estates assembled in Brussels refused to support the archdukes with an extraordinary grant, and Albert was forced to negotiate with the rebel states. But a conference at Bergen-op-Zoom proved abortive.[2] In these circumstances Albert was as little inclined to support an expedition to Ireland as he was to provide Spínola with men and artillery for an attack on England.

1. *Cal. S.P. Ire., 1599–1600*, p. 338: O'Neill to Albert, Dungannon, 31 Dec. 1599.
2. Blok, *History of the people of the Netherlands*, pt. III: *The war with Spain*, p. 284.

of Tír Conaill in the sixteenth century', pp. 321–4; *Cal. Carew MSS. 1589–1600*, pp. 349–50: O'Neill to Philip, Dungannon, 31 Dec. 1599.

V · DIPLOMACY

He who would England win
Must with Ireland begin.
Sixteenth-century proverb

O'NEILL HAD SURVIVED the attack on him by Essex, but however he might boast to Archduke Albert he well knew that the queen could not relinquish her effort to conquer Ireland. In the new year he went down to Munster in order (by his presence there) to undo the work of Essex in the south. As in 1599 the nobles again rallied to his side, and only the towns held out against him. To reduce them he sent to Spain for artillery.[1]

Side by side with his use of force at home Hugh waged a diplomatic campaign abroad. The object of this campaign was to secure support for his war against the queen, military support from Spain and moral from the pope.

Father Edmund MacDonnell, dean of Armagh in exile, was Hugh's personal representative in Spain. It was MacDonnell who briefed Fray Mateo de Oviedo with arguments to convince the Spanish government that they should intervene effectively in Ireland. Fray Mateo, ever since his selection twenty years previously by Bishop Sega, then papal nuncio to Spain, to further James Fitzmaurice's cause, had worked tirelessly to promote an invasion of Ireland. In recognition of his usefulness O'Neill gained his appointment to the see of Dublin in May 1599.[2] Dr. Peter Lombard of Waterford, commissary of the university of Louvain at Rome, was from about 1599[3] O'Neill's special agent at the Holy See.[4] Lombard in his efforts to influence Cardinal Mathei, the

---

1. *Cal. S.P. Ire.*, *1599–1600*, p. 416: Thorton to Ormonde, 30 Dec. 1599, old style; *Cal. cit.*, p. 473: Information from Fenton, 14 Feb. 1600, old style. Cf. Kelso, *Die Spanier in Irland 1588–1603*, pp. 53–4.
2. *Archiv. Hib.*, xviii (1955), 84.
3. Cf. Ibid., ii (1913), 283–4.
4. Cf. *Wadding papers 1614–38*, ed. Jennings, p. 2; Reusens, *Éléments de paléographie*, pp. 353–4: University of Louvain to Lombard, 25 July 1601.

5

protector of Ireland, Cardinal Aldobrandini, the secretary of state, the duke of Sessa, the Spanish ambassador at Rome, and above all Clement VIII, was able to recruit the services of Father Persons, S.J., the celebrated rector of the English college at Rome. Besides Oviedo, Lombard, and Persons, O'Neill had other advocates of his cause on the continent, so that he had in fact the elements of a diplomatic service.

But operating against the success of O'Neill's diplomacy was the division among Irish Catholics. Elizabeth, out of motives of policy, allowed a good deal of latitude to Catholics, even in those parts of the country under her control. In Munster, the Pale, and the towns Catholicism had grown in strength in the decade (1583–93) between the Desmond war and the war of the two Hughs. Its increase owed most to the 'Jesuits and seminaries', or priests, secular and regular, who had been trained on the continent and had since about 1570 been returning home in ever-increasing numbers to work in Ireland.

By about 1590 Protestantism was a lost cause among the old English, who were now firmly established in their Catholicism. O'Neill's victories against the government encouraged them to make ever more open profession of their faith. In spite of this, they remained unwavering in their loyalty to the crown. Their priests encouraged this loyalty and maintained that a good Catholic need not meddle in matters of state. The Bull excommunicating Elizabeth was not a problem for these Catholics. Irish loyalists had been quick to point out that Pius V had not deprived Elizabeth of Ireland but only of England. In any case, after 1580 a declaration by Pope Gregory XIII allowed Catholics to accept the queen as their head in the temporal order.[1] In the Desmond wars the corporate towns and the Pale lords had for the most part remained unshakeably loyal, and the Munster lords had learned from the ferocious penalty exacted from them after that war how unwise it was to oppose the crown. The towns, the strongholds and foundation of English rule in Ireland, and the lords of the Pale and of Munster, both old English and old Irish, supplied the government armies with many troops. Of course such troops often deserted, but the supply increased as the nine years' war went on.[2]

The more clear-sighted English officials like Carew admitted the reality of the distinction which the old English themselves made be-

1. Ronan, *Reformation in Ireland*, pp. 313–15; Pollen, *English Catholics in the reign of Elizabeth*, pp. 283–5.
2. Falls, *Elizabeth's Irish wars*, pp. 41, 342–3.

tween their spiritual and temporal allegiances. Lacking sympathy for
O'Neill, whom they considered as bent only on establishing his own
supremacy in Ireland, the old English maintained their loyalty to the
queen, and with Lord Barry claimed that she was indifferent to their
exercise of their religion.

The desire of the Anglo-Irish to dissociate themselves from the
northern rebellion was made plain to the internuncio at Brussels,[1] to
the Jesuit general Aquaviva, and to Pope Clement. Against the voices
of the old English Peter Lombard raised his in an effort to convince
the pope that their loyalty was misplaced and that O'Neill was the
champion of Catholic freedom in Ireland. Instructed by O'Neill,
Lombard sought from Clement an excommunication, such as had
been issued by Gregory XIII during the Geraldine war, against Catholics who favoured the queen; he sought also the crusade indulgence
for O'Neill's supporters, the filling of all ecclesiastical appointments
in Ireland only on O'Neill's nomination, and some temporal help.[2]
Ten days after the truce with Essex O'Neill wrote to Clement directly
to appeal for a subsidy. He had been offered very good terms, he
maintained, but neither he nor his allies would accept them until
their enemies granted the same freedom of religion in the rest of
Ireland as they did in the territories subject to the northern con-
federation. Hugh insisted that he would make no peace that did not
secure the complete freedom of the Catholic religion.[3]

Peter Lombard completed by 1600 a work, *De regno Hiberniae
sanctorum insula commentarius*, in which he sought to convince the
Papacy of the justice of Hugh O'Neill's recourse to arms. He argued
that England had by her misgovernment of Ireland lost her right—
based as it was on papal grant—to dominion over Ireland. The Ulster
chiefs had been forced to take up arms against the queen for the
defence of their religion, and their leader, Hugh O'Neill, was by
birth, education, personal qualities, and zeal the man most fitting
for leadership of that struggle. In delaying to take up arms himself
until he was ready O'Neill had exhibited great foresight and prudence.
For he had long foreseen that the English were determined on the
destruction of all Ireland, and he had with great patience set about
preparing for an effective resistance to this aim.

1. Cf. *Archiv. Hib.*, iii (1914), 242.
2. Ibid., ii (1913), 280–1, 283–4, 286–92; iii. 235–8.
3. VA, Borghese III, vol. 124 C, f. 9 (*Archiv. Hib.*, ii. 286–7): O'Neill to Clement VIII, *Cal. S.P. Ire., 1599–1600*, pp. 337–8: O'Neill to Philip, Dungannon, 31 Dec. 1599.

During the late sixteenth century a succession of English writers, Campion, Camden, Hooker, Derricke, and others, following the earlier model of Giraldus Cambrensis, wrote in uncomplimentary terms of the native Irish. Richard Stanihurst, the Dublin friend of Campion and Hooker, showed in his historical works how he, a Palesman, shared their prejudices. The image of Ireland created by these writers, an image which could indeed receive strength from an unsympathetic reading of the Irish court poets writing in their traditional modes, was one of a society that was barbarous and inflexible, ignorantly superstitious and fickle. Whether the image was a true one is another question. Eoin MacNeill believed that the members of the Irish patrician class, although brave, intelligent, and energetic, were rendered incapable by one radical defect from 'using their intelligence to profit with the times'. This fatal defect, he argued, was pride of caste and it made the chiefs 'conservative, inadaptable, unproviding'. The great Celtic scholar's conclusions find an echo in Seán O'Faolain's strictures on the inflexibility, the inactivity of brain, of the Irish system.[1]

Yet MacNeill himself admitted that we have no real history of the Irish people, based on their own records, from the fifteenth century onwards. The fragmentary remaining Irish records are sufficient to assure us of the grace, emotional appeal, and felicity of Gaelic literature, of the stability of Gaelic society, and of its development and purpose.[2] Until such an history as MacNeill desired comes to be written the historian must reserve judgement.

At all events, the harm done by the creation of this unflattering view of Ireland was apparent to O'Neill. His attempt to lay the ghost of James Fitzmaurice, to whose clarion-call of religion he had been deaf, is apparent now in all his attempts to make himself the Catholic champion, while Lombard's concern to lay the different ghost of Giraldus gives a particular urgency to the classical diction of the *Commentarius*.[3]

O'Neill's diplomacy as exercised at Rome could record some successes. Fray Mateo's appointment to Dublin had been a gain for him; it was another when on 18 April 1600 Clement VIII granted a Bull of indulgence to all who assisted him and appointed him captain-general

---

1. MacNeill, *Phases of Irish history*, pp. 354–5; O'Faolain, *The great O'Neill*, pp. 17–33.
2. Cf. Ó Ceallaigh, *Gleanings from Ulster history*, pp. 93–118.
3. Lombard, *Commentarius*, ed. Moran, pp. 149–78.

of the Catholic army in Ireland.[1] This was a typically Clementine compromise, for O'Neill's greater desires remained unsatisfied.

In Spain Oviedo, acting for O'Neill, sought to induce Philip III to send an expedition to Ireland and to put pressure on the pope to give his official blessing to this expedition and to the war being waged by the two Hughs. But in spite of the urgency of the pleas made to him the only help that Philip was as yet prepared to send was of a minor nature. The war in Flanders, as a correspondent of O'Neill's pointed out,[2] had drained Spain of men. Philip merely consented to Oviedo's accompanying Don Martín de la Cerdá with a shipment of arms to Ireland. The archbishop was refused permission to take Dean Mac-Donnell with him.

Captain Martín de la Cerdá had qualities something out of the ordinary. He was informed, discreet, and capable of intelligent execution of his orders: *que es soldado y tiene noticia de muchas cosas y hombre querdo y inteligente para executar con cuydado lo que se ordenará*. A patriotic Spaniard, he became a wholehearted advocate of the Irish cause and was soon a valued intermediary between Spain and the northern confederates.

As well as sending a shipment of arms to O'Neill Philip agreed to accept Henry, the chief's eldest son, as his father's pledge. The king, lastly, took the Irish Catholics under his protection, but without exacting any oath from them lest that embarrass them.[3] The proposal not to exact an oath is interesting, not for the reason given but because an oath such as that taken in Barrionuevo's presence must prove rather an embarrassment to Spain, should she not be able to send help before O'Neill's time-limit had expired.

Finally, after many delays, early in April 1600 Cerdá sailed with his shipment, two or three small boats in all. Don Martín had with him a sum of one hundred ducats, to provide for the expenses of Henry O'Neill's return journey with him to Spain. He had in his cargo 1,000 arquebuses with their powder-flasks and horns and other equipment,

---

1. Cf. *Cal. Carew MSS. 1589–1600*, p. 523.

2. HMC, MSS. Hatfield, part x, p. 16: Sinnote to O'Neill, 'The Grin' (Corunna), 4 Feb. 1600.

3. AGS, Guerra Antigua 3143 (*Rep. Nov.*, i. 94–5): Martín de Idiáquez to (?) E. de Ibarra, 2 Oct. 1599; Guerra Antigua 3143 (*Rep. Nov.*, i. 96, 98–9): Oviedo to Philip 28 Oct. and *consulta* on Oviedo's proposals; Guerra Antigua 539: *consulta* by council of war, Madrid, 28 Oct.; Estado 839 (O'Clery, *Life of Hugh Roe*, p. cxxi): Philip to O'Neill, Madrid, 24 Dec.; Estado 840, f. 4 (*Cal. S.P. Spain, 1587–1603*, pp. 653, 658): Abp. of Santiago to Philip, 18 May 1600.

100 quintals of powder, 100 of lead, and 100 of fuse. In command of the vessels was Ensign Pedro de Sandoval.[1]

Archbishop-elect Oviedo went as envoy from both Clement VIII and Philip, although, in spite of O'Neill's desires, he had to be content with something less than legatine accreditation from the one and ambassadorial from the other. Clement in a message to O'Neill congratulated him on his victories and exhorted him to persevere in his glorious struggle, so that Ireland might not be subject to heresy. Shortly afterwards, in further token of how successfully O'Neill and Lombard had gained the ear of the pontiff, Clement on 18 April granted a Bull of indulgence to all who assisted O'Neill, whom he appointed captain-general of the Catholic army in Ireland, in the war that the chieftains had undertaken to recover and preserve the liberty of the people of Ireland.[2]

Lombard had found a sympathizer at Rome who was above all things an Englishman. This was Father Robert Persons, S.J., rector of the English college, Rome, between 1588 and 1589 and again from 1598 until his death in 1610. Even better, O'Neill's agent could now avail himself of the support of Don Antonio Fernández de Córdoba, fifth duke of Sessa and Spanish ambassador at Rome.

Persons held the belief that there was a party in the English council in favour of an approach to Philip III, with a view to securing the succession to the English throne of Philip's half-sister, the Infanta Isabel. Persons's authority for this belief was an unnamed English correspondent[3] who maintained that this party of councillors was composed of Cecil, Charles Howard, earl of Nottingham, the lord high admiral, and Lord Buckhurst, the treasurer. The concern of this group of 'politiques', the correspondent maintained, was to prevent James VI from gaining the English crown; James was supported by Cecil's great rival Essex, and Cecil and his friends feared—and this was what really made them take the position that they did—that the king of Scotland would hold them responsible for his mother's death. If Philip would declare the infanta his candidate for the throne, they were ready to

---

1. AGS, Estado 187, Guerra Antigua 3143 (*Rep. Nov.*, i. 355): Royal schedule, Vallid., 31 Dec. 1601.

2. O'Clery, *Life of Hugh Roe*, p. cxvi; Lambeth MS. 608 (*Cal. Carew MSS*, 1589–1600, p. 523).

3. Richard Verstegan kept Persons informed of events in England from Antwerp. Verstegan had correspondents in England, among them Fr. Henry Garnet, S.J., and others who wrote more openly than Garnet. Unfortunately Verstegan's extant dispatches to Persons cover only the period 1591–5. Cf. *Letters and despatches of Verstegan* (CRS., LII), pp. xvii–xviii; Loomie, *The Spanish Elizabethans*, pp. 57–8.

support her claim. But immediate declaration by Philip was essential, for only thus could they be assured of effective military support from Flanders for Isabel's claims when the time came. Besides, the English Catholics, now leaderless, must be given a cause and a champion, otherwise James would succeed without opposition.

The story that Cecil and part of the privy council supported the infanta's claims[1] was apparently without any substance. Yet it is an odd fact that no less a person than the lord treasurer's son was to turn up in Rome early in 1603 to tell Sessa the same story.[2] At any rate, Persons believed it, and he wished to go to Flanders to arouse the infanta's interest, and through her Philip's, in the proposal. Sessa, although prudently refusing Persons leave to go to Flanders, was yet excited enough by the Jesuit's story to urge on the king a Spanish attack on Ireland; he agreed with Lombard that this would now be most opportune, as it would arouse the wavering English politiques to give more practical support to Philip. After listening to Lombard and Persons, Sessa was thoroughly convinced that no expedition directed against Elizabeth could be easier for Philip or of more benefit to him than the one that Lombard sought.[3]

The ambassador's dispatches came more and more to re-echo the arguments of Lombard and Persons for an Irish enterprise. The king should act, urged Sessa, for (according to Father Persons) the death of Elizabeth was imminent. Philip should not desert the Irish Catholics but should aid them in secret as Elizabeth did the Dutch rebels. The parallel between Ireland and the Netherlands was indeed striking, and Hugh O'Neill, as was soon to be made even clearer, was not failing to draw it.

Had Philip, Sessa went on to argue, aided the Irish in the past, Queen Elizabeth would now be very humble indeed. But seeing that he had not and was not even now preparing to do so, the queen was making a mockery of the peace negotiations. The king of France, too, was asserting that he would not allow any attack on Elizabeth while he lived. But the Irish did not care for France, but only for Spain. Ireland was very necessary to Spain for the conservation of the Indies

---

1. Hicks, 'Sir Robert Cecil, Father Persons and the succession 1600-1', in *Archiv. Hist. Soc. Iesu*, xxiv (1953), 111-17. The first letter from Persons's correspondent that Fr. Hicks considers is dated 25 Apr. 1600. But that Persons had heard from his correspondent in the sense in which he later wrote, before 19 Apr. is clear from Sessa's report.

2. Loomie, *The Spanish Elizabethans*, p. 174; cf. *English government and society*, p. 377.

3. AGS, Estado 972: Sessa to Philip III, Rome, 19 Apr. 1600.

—another point to be further developed by O'Neill before long. Philip, Ambassador Sessa ended, if he did not wish to hold Ireland for himself, could appoint O'Neill as its lord; the latter would pay some tribute and recognize his dependence upon the crown of Spain.[1]

O'Neill's arguments—as these substantially were—would, however, have no effect unless they appealed to the duke of Lerma, the real power in Spain. And O'Neill's diplomacy now seemed to be telling at last on the lethargic favourite. What impressed Lerma was firstly that in answering O'Neill's appeals Spain would be relieved at the least possible cost of English attacks, as the major part of England's strength would then be engaged in Ireland; and secondly, that to sustain the war would be to improve the peace conditions for Spain and meantime to encourage the English Catholics to persevere.

Something then would have to be done for O'Neill. The king needed little prompting from his favourite. He wrote to promise O'Neill and his allies the patronage and protection of Spain; even now, he said, a force was being prepared in Spain to go to their aid and to restore them to full liberty.

The king by taking the Irish under his protection had now given such a guarantee as his more politically experienced and circumspect father had never done. But Philip had responded over-enthusiastically to his favourite's suggestions. The duke was not preparing an expedition to go to Ireland; he merely ordered that a sum of 20,000 ducats be raised. This together with 4,000 quintals of biscuit and a quantity of arms and ammunition would be dispatched to Ireland when ready. The decision whether to send the Irishmen O'Neill wanted from Flanders was to be left to the Archduke Albert[2]—which meant that they would not be sent.

The truth was that negotiations for peace were now in train between England and Spain. Elizabeth had at length agreed to a congress to discuss the possibility of a settlement. Boulogne was chosen as the location for the conference and the envoys of Spain, England, and the archdukes arrived there at the end of May. However, neither side was in earnest. Philip wished (the more so as he had reason to believe that certain Walloon nobles, advisers of the archdukes, were

---

1. AGS, Estado 972: Sessa to Philip, 11 May 1600.
2. AGS, Estado 840, f. 104, Estado 2511 (*Cal. S.P. Spain, 1587–1603*, pp. 657–8): council of state to Philip, Madrid, 4 May 1600; VA, Borghese III, vol. 98 C, f. 92 (*Archiv. Hib.*, iii (1914), 237–8; xxiv (1961), 58): Philip to O'Neill, 17 Apr.; AGS, Estado 185: Sec. Prada to Sec. Ibarra, Madrid, 10 May.

offering the queen of England a peace that would exclude Spain) to keep Elizabeth at the conference table and away from meddling in the Netherlands. Cecil, on the other hand, was merely concerned to deter James VI from intriguing with Essex, the pope—the guileful James had since 1599 been giving Clement hopes that he might be converted—and various foreign powers.[1]

Negotiations at Boulogne therefore dragged on between May and July. These negotiations were not concerned with the serious matters at issue—the retention of the security towns by the queen, free trade, and the navigation of the Channel—but on questions of precedence. This was not of course altogether without point, for precedence was a vital matter in the diplomacy of the age. Spain insisted that the Dutch were rebels, without belligerent status, and insisted on her trading monopoly 'beyond the line', a monopoly that included everything westward of the Azores and southward of the Tropic of Cancer. To establish her precedence, therefore, at the conference table would be for her to go half-way towards vindicating these claims. England, which did not grant the Spanish claims, was well aware of this, and therefore refused to admit Spanish precedence. When stalemate was reached the English delegates were recalled by an order dated 26 July.[2]

With peace between England and Spain still too remote a possibility for serious discussion it behoved the Spaniards to keep alive, at the least cost to themselves, the war in Ireland. It was for that reason that Lerma dispatched Cerdá to Ireland.

Don Martín with his companions put into Donegal Bay in April. Again the friars at Donegal made their convent available for a conference, which a large gathering of sixty or more of the confederate leaders, anxious to hear what help they might expect from Spain, attended.

The two Hughs had already waited over six months beyond the time undertaken in their oath to Barrionuevo. O'Neill's presence in Munster had given heart to his allies, notably James Fitzmaurice and Florence MacCarthy (whom he had made MacCarthy More), and he had bound other lords to him by exacting hostages from them. With Munster as loyal as he could make it he had slipped home, leaving a

1. Willson, *King James VI and I*, pp. 142–59; cf. Loomie, *The Spanish Elizabethans*, pp. 77–8.
2. AGS, Estado 2511; Hamy, 'Conférence pour la paix entre l'Angleterre et l'Espagne tenue à Boulogne en 1600', in *Societé Académique de Boulogne-sur-mer Bulletin*, vii (1906), 434–60; *Cal. S.P. Venice, 1592–1603*, pp. xxv–xxvii.

force of up to 2,000 bonnachts behind, under Richard Tyrrell, to hold the province. Now, instead of the Spanish force that would make victory in Ireland certain, there was yet another embassy with its promises! This was maddening when victory at the cost of very little Spanish effort lay so near; and there were clouds on the horizon, for a new lord deputy, Lord Mountjoy, and a new lord president of Munster, Sir George Carew, had arrived in Dublin before O'Neill's return from Munster, and O'Neill waited in daily expectation and dread of a landing by the enemy at his rear on Loch Foyle.

Thus the new embassy found the Irish in more impatient mood than had Barrionuevo. The Irishmen reminded the Spanish envoys that they had been prevented from making an advantageous peace in 1596 only by the clear offer of help which Philip II had then sent by his emissary Alonso Cobos. 'Continue the fight to expel the English', the then king had said, 'and you can be sure of my help'.[1] To this reminder Archbishop Oviedo replied with truth indeed that it was bad luck rather than lack of intention that had prevented Philip II from landing an invasion force in Ireland. Oviedo's patent honesty made O'Neill agree to continue the war for another five months in expectation of an army from Spain; this was the furthest extent to which O'Neill and O'Donnell could guarantee to pay their men and to which they could hope to hold their none-too-firm allies.[2]

Vastly relieved to find that the Irish in spite of their disappointment were agreeing to continue the struggle, Cerdá moved on to a discussion of tactics. O'Neill and O'Donnell assured Cerdá that Limerick was the most suitable port for an army of three or four thousand men to land at, if the intention were to effect a speedy junction with the Irish and to strike a quick blow with the united forces before Elizabeth had time to prepare. If the forces from Spain were of 6,000 men or upwards, Waterford or Cork would be best, but if only of 2,000 or less it should come to Killybegs. This was tactically sound; a weak Spanish force should go where the rebellion was strongest, whereas a strong invading army should aim to gain possession of the southern towns at once. Traces and harness were wanted for the Irish hill horses so that

---

1. . . . si vero . . . eodem animo in posterum Dei hostes ex ditionibus vestris omnino expellandos curabitis . . . non est cur minora vobis inde bona promitatis quam ex Alphonso Cobos qui isthuc a me mit[t]itur cognoscetis, cui integram fidem adhibebitis. AGS, Estado 2604: Philip II to Irish Catholic lords, 14 Aug. 1596. Cf. Estado 840, f. 3 and Estado 839 (Cal. S.P. Spain, 1587–1603, p. 619): testimony by Cobos, Lifford, 15 May 1596.

2. AGS, Estado 840, f. 79 (Cal. S.P. Spain, 1587–1603, p. 656): O'Neill and O'Donnell to Philip III, Donegal, 26 Apr. 1600.

they could transport artillery; there were no carts but plenty of beasts of burden and mounts for cavalrymen.[1]

The meeting finally decided to send Cerdá back to Spain to present the Irish appeal for help to be sent within five months. Archbishop-elect Oviedo remained in Ireland. Cerdá with Henry O'Neill was back in Santiago by mid May and the king received him in Segovia early in June. Henry O'Neill was given a house in Madrid.[2]

Cerdá's new appraisal of the Irish situation was accorded but leisurely attention, for the peace negotiations had just begun at Boulogne. The conference there, however, soon reached stalemate on the point of precedence. On 1 July a junta of councillors, Borja, Idiáquez, Guevara, and the cardinal-archbishop of Toledo, reported to the king on the memorials presented by Cerdá. The latter presented in addition to the other documents a memorial on his own account. It is of interest as giving one of the clearest statements of the motives which induced the court of Philip III finally to send the expedition which came to Kinsale.[3] O'Neill together with Oviedo and Cerdá had gone to great pains to set out the strongest case possible for Spanish help.

At present, said the memorial, the plate fleets were forced to ply out of due season in order to avoid the attention of the enemy. This placed a strain upon the royal navy and exposed the ships to risk from storm. Now an expedition sent to Ireland would set free the coasts of the Spanish empire from attack; the money heretofore spent on the defences of these coasts could be used to attack England from Ireland; commerce would increase, thus, among other benefits, contenting the Portuguese; and Elizabeth could no more indulge in 'piracy'.

Spain was not now in a position, the argument continued, to conduct an offensive war against England; a diversion in Ireland was the safest, as it was the cheapest and most effective, entry into England. If Spain did not answer the Irish pleas, the Irish would be forced to accept

1. AGS, Estado 840, f. 74, Estado 185 (*Cal.*, cit., pp. 656–7): Oviedo to Philip III, 1600; Guerra Antigua 3144, Estado 185 (*Cal.*, cit., p. 663): Answers by O'Neill and O'Donnell to Cerdá's questions (the copy in *Archiv. Hib.*, xvii (1953), 40–1, is rather faulty.)

2. AGS, Estado 840, f. 4: Abp. Sanclemente to Philip, Santiago, 18 May; Estado 840: Lerma to (?) Prada, 8 June.

3. AGS, Estado 2511 (calendared very briefly and indeed inadequately in *Cal. S.P. Spain, 1587–1603*, pp. 680–1, where it is wrongly dated 1601): council of state to Philip, Madrid, 1 July 1600. RAH, Col. Salazar, L 24, ff. 61–5v: P. López de Soto, 'Causas divinas y humanas que obligan a amparar a Yrlanda', is quoted by Fernández Duro, *Armada española*, iii. 218, as stating the arguments which motivated the expedition to Kinsale. But López wrote this *after* the defeat at Kinsale.

terms and would thus be added to Spain's enemies. Elizabeth well knew the value of creating diversions in Philip's territories; thus she sent out a fleet every year to keep Philip's forces occupied and away from her kingdom. Philip by invading Ireland could impose restrictions, impress the northern rulers (Henry IV and James VI), and force the return of Holland and Zeeland to their proper obedience. An army sent to Ireland need consist of only six or seven thousand men: 20,000 Irishmen, most of them armed, said the memorial optimistically, would be ready to join the Spaniards; no resistance would be offered. Finally, the sea off the Irish coast was free from rocky shoals.

An old proverb ran current in England, *Qui Angliam vincere vellet ab Ybernia incipere debet*:

> He who would England win
> Must with Ireland begin.[1]

This proverb had acquired a profound significance, since the Irish war had cost Elizabeth the loss of 40,000 of her men and her best captains. The same reasons of state counselled the sending by Spain of men to Ireland as to Brittany; indeed, they applied in greater force, since the enemy there was greater and the queen and the world would have to know that those who attacked Spain must pay.

The queen, in spite of holding all the chief towns and strongholds of Ireland, made such great efforts to gain the inferior parts of the country held by the Catholics as to demonstrate how valuable possession of these parts would be to her. Philip in holding Ireland would have a strong bargaining counter in the peace negotiations. It was a like motive that had decided Elizabeth against the advice of many in her council to take the Dutch (in the treaty of Nonsuch) under her protection.

If France broke the peace, as she was like to do, Cerdá's discourse went on, she would make an expedition to Ireland very difficult. Now was the time to act before England came to agreement with France. If France did break the peace and the Turks descended on the coasts of the Spanish empire, England would be prevented from joining forces with Frenchman and Turk, provided that Spain already held her engaged in Ireland. English interference in Flanders, the king should remember, had enabled Philip's rebellious vassals to thwart the greatest expeditions.

---

1 This couplet was much in vogue at the time in England. Cf. Froude, *England: Wolsey to Elizabeth*, x. 480; Ronan, *Reformation in Ireland*, pp. 487, 501.

The Irish Catholics were constant to Spain and in Ireland the king would gain friends, soldiers, sailors, and timber for his navy and deprive the queen of all these. But if Philip did not decide on the Irish enterprise, Cerdá (faithful beyond doubt to O'Neill's briefing) concluded, he must on no account pay the Irish soldiery, but rather pay their leaders very well and let them pay their troops.[1] So O'Neill and O'Donnell sought to guarantee their independence of the Spaniards, should they indeed invade Ireland.

This memorial, presented by Cerdá and inspired, if not dictated, by O'Neill, was a shrewd compound of reasons of state, commercial motives, and prospective military gains, all urging the profit to be derived by Spain from an attack on Ireland. Not the least important consideration in the case presented was the benefit to be gained by Philip from an increase in Hispano-Irish commerce.

The Gaelic resurgence of the fifteenth century had brought with it a development in Irish commerce, and trade had continued to flourish throughout the first part of the sixteenth century. The trade with the continent was more important than that with England. Ireland's exports were mainly of raw materials: fish, hides and leather, woollen and linen cloth, tallow, salt beef, grain, pipestaves, and boards for shipbuilding. Spain, England, and other countries were in eager competition for these products, in return for which Ireland imported salt, wine, iron, and in increasing degree various luxuries.

Ireland's main trading partner was Spain; with that country and with France, Portugal, and Flanders she conducted trade through the ports of the west and southwest: O'Donnell's ports and Galway, Limerick, Dingle, and Kinsale among others. In 1569 it was reported that two hundred sail came annually to the south-west coast, fished there, and carried away (besides fish) two thousand beeves, hides, and tallow.[2] The ports of the south and east traded mainly with the English west country, exporting fish, hides, and cloth, although they traded with the continent as well.

In the second part of the sixteenth century the Tudors, for commercial reasons, sought to transfer the profits of the Irish trade to Anglo-Irish and English hands, and for political reasons sought to divert the Irish trade with Spain to England. The effect of this interference, however, an effect that was aided by the devastation of war, by the

1. AGS, Estado 185 and Estado 840, f. 80 (abbreviated version): Discourse by Cerdá (1600).
2. Longfield, *Anglo-Irish trade in the sixteenth century*, p. 105.

devaluation of the currency, and the attraction of European fisher-
men to the richer fisheries of the Newfoundland banks, was rather to
injure the trade: industry (linen cloth and friezes) and exports
both declined. An Irish carrying trade with the colonies began and
new towns, which exported raw linen yarn and wool-fells to Liverpool
and Chester, arose north of Dublin. At the same time the smuggling
trade in meat, butter, and corn became significant. But none of these
developments compensated for the decline in the fishing trade, in
finished products, and in provisions.[1]

As Cerdá reported to the council of state, an Hispano-Irish victory
in Ireland would bring with it among other things important commercial advantages to Spain and would seriously injure Elizabeth, by
diverting the produce of the south and east of Ireland from England
to Spain. Spain would once again receive from Ireland abundant
supplies of fish, provisions, and corn, and from the vast Irish forests—
now at the beginning of their exploitation by Sir Richard Boyle,
Raleigh, Petty, and others[2]—pipestaves and timber for her galleys;
for these naval supplies Spain was now dangerously dependent upon
the Baltic trade.[3] She would win back again the valuable export of
wines to Ireland, which because of Elizabeth's imposts she was now
losing to France,[4] and would find in Ireland a ready market for iron,
salt, spices, and luxury goods. Finally, as Cerdá said, Spain would have
in Ireland a recruiting ground for soldiers and sailors.

1. The foregoing paragraphs have for basis Miss Longfield's invaluable work.
2. McCracken, 'The woodlands of Ireland circa 1600', in *I.H.S.*, xi (1959), 280–1.
3. *New Camb. mod. hist.*, i. 456.
4. Kearney, 'The Irish wine-trade 1614–15', in *I.H.S.*, ix (1955), 400–42.

VI · CHANCE

> This expedition and enterprise is so important for the peace of
> Spain and the preservation of the Indies and the reduction of
> the States.
>
> Oviedo to Lerma, 26 January 1602[1]

CERDÁ'S ELOQUENT PLEA for an invasion of Ireland was given a
hearing, but without effect. Lerma would not go beyond the order
given in May to send money, food, and arms to the Irish to encourage
them to continue the war. The council, taking into consideration that
an armada could not now sail before mid September, which would
expose it to risk of storm, that the money required to finance it (estimated at 150,000 ducats) could not be raised in time, and that an effort
was already being made to mobilize four thousand men for service in
Flanders, agreed with the duke in disregarding Cerdá's appeal.

King Philip, however, did not; he wanted to send an armada to
Ireland, and in 1600. The king, rarely concerned about affairs of state,
grew quite obstinate in this, and he and the council found themselves
at variance. Philip showed himself obdurate, and the council had to
yield and agree to try to raise the Irish expedition in 1600. The king's
final argument was that he would pay the expedition's cost out of his
own pocket:

This enterprise [he wrote] must so further God's service, and the earnestness
and zeal shown by the council for it must so animate those entrusted with its
execution as to overcome all the difficulties foreseen. I myself will see that the
money is provided, even at the expense of what is necessary for my personal
state—*aunque sea quitándole de lo necessario para mi persona*. The expedition must
go this year; to that end the council will put all in order with the utmost
speed . . . .[2]

1. *Si esta jornada y impresa importa tanto a la quietud de España y conservación de las Indias y
redución de los Estados.* AGS, Guerra Antigua 3145.

2. AGS, Estado 840, f. 107 (*Cal. S.P. Spain, 1587–1603*, p. 663), Estado 840, f. 4, Estado 2511:
consulta by council of state, 1 July 1600; Estado 187: Philip to Adelantado, Madrid, 10 July;
Estado 2511 and 840, f. 105 (*Cal.*, cit., pp. 666–7): *consulta*, 13 July; Estado 2511 and 840, f. 106
(*Cal.* cit., pp. 666–7): *consulta* 23 July; Estado 2511: *consulta*, 29 July; Estado 2023: *consulta*,
5 Aug.

But although Philip might wish to invade Ireland, he was not yet
prepared to name the Archduchess Isabel as his candidate to succeed
Elizabeth on the English throne. This was what Lombard, Persons,
and Sessa now wished him to do. They warned him that James VI was
mobilizing the support of the English and other Catholics for his succession to Elizabeth. They wished Philip to try to win the pope's
support for the infanta. They urged him to spend what was needed on
the army in the Netherlands and the fleet in Spain and to send an
army of 6,000 men to Ireland, so that the day Elizabeth died Isabel's
succession might be backed up without delay both from the Low
Countries and from Ireland. On the other hand, they suggested,
should Philip decide to make peace with England, Ireland should be
exempted from the treaty terms so that she might be covertly aided
to continue the war against Elizabeth.[1]

These schemes won the council of state's approval more readily
than Philip's. It was true that if the infanta became queen of England,
that would not necessarily make England a Spanish dependency.
Indeed, it was no part of Father Persons's intention to make England
subject to Spain. He simply wanted a Catholic successor to Elizabeth
and his support of the archduchess was motivated by his realization
that without Spanish backing no candidate could hope to succeed
against James.[2] But of course any threat to disturb the balance of
power by placing Philip's half-sister, the sovereign of the Netherlands,
on the English throne must alarm France and the pope. Clement VIII,
the Aldobrandini pope, who had in 1595 absolved Henry IV despite
the best efforts of Sessa to prevent him, was in reality more affected
towards France than Spain; and during Archbishop Gennasio's tenure
of office as nuncio in Madrid (February 1600–June 1605) there was continuous friction between the Holy See and the court of Philip III.

In regard to the English succession the pope was undecided. He was
in two minds whether to support Cardinal Farnese—whose claim was
derived through his mother, the Infanta Maria of Portugal, from
Edward III—or to be satisfied with any Catholic who might be likely
to make his claim succeed.[3]

1. AGS, Estado 840, f. 82 (*Cal. S.P. Spain, 1587–1603*, pp. 663–5): *consulta* of 11 July; Estado
972: letters from Sessa, 19 Apr. and 11 May. Cf. Hume, *Treason and plot*, pp. 411–14.
    2. Cf. *Cal. S.P. Spain, 1587–1603*, p. 665, no. 686; AGS, Estado 840, f. 81 (*Cal.*, cit., pp. 682–3):
council of state to Philip, Madrid, 1 Feb. 1601. Cf. Meyer, *England and the Catholic church
under Elizabeth*, p. 382.
    3. Cf. Pollen, 'The accession of James I', in *Month*, ci (1903), 573–5.

To attempt then to secure the English throne, as Lombard, Persons, and Sessa suggested, would be a serious step for Spain to take in view of the international implications. There was time enough yet, Philip realized, to name the infanta as his candidate.

While Philip was insisting that a major expedition go to Ireland in 1600, and while the council of state pressed him to make public his support of the archduchess's claims, the sending to O'Neill of the help agreed on in May was delayed. Neither army nor guns had come from Spain; and the pope still withheld plenipotentiary powers from Oviedo.

Denied help from Spain, O'Neill was in straits. In May 1600 Sir Henry Docwra had landed at Culmore on Loch Foyle behind O'Donnell's back; he won over Sir Arthur MacHenry O'Neill and later Sir Arthur's son, Turloch, Niall Garbh O'Donnell, who felt, and with some justice, that he had a better right to the chieftaincy of Tyrconnell than Red Hugh and Rory O'Cahan. 'Woe to the country and fair land', wrote a chronicler of these events in the stereotyped, academic style, 'woe to the territory and district in which ill-luck permitted relatives and kinsmen to hew and destroy each other . . .'[1] Docwra set up three garrisons along Loch Foyle, obliging O'Donnell to maintain three encampments opposite them. And in September O'Neill was obliged to go to the Moyry to meet an attack by the lord deputy, who commanded three thousand men. Of course, for Philip's benefit O'Neill made the number of the opposing forces much larger, all of seven thousand men. But he could hardly be blamed for painting a black picture. He had neither food for his own men nor money for payment, and his allies were deserting him for Elizabeth. Mountjoy's strategy in attacking O'Neill front and rear was having results.[2]

Hugh might have felt less overwhelmed with troubles had he known that at last the king of Spain and his council had agreed to send an army to his aid. To ensure secrecy the men were to be levied on the pretext that they were going to Italy (whither it had already been decided to send infantry), and the ships to carry them, with the munitions and arms necessary, were to be got ready on the excuse that they were bound for the Indies. The council planned that a total force of

1. Ó Clérigh, *Beatha Aodha Ruaidh*, i. 272.
2. O'Clery, *Life of Hugh Roe*, p. cxvii: O'Neill to Philip, the Catholic camp, 3 Aug. 1600; pp. cxix–x: same to same, 17 Sept.; pp. cxx–xxi: Oviedo to (?) Lerma and to Philip, 18 Sept. Cf. Bagwell, *Tudors*, iii. 372, and *infra*, pp. 88–9; Falls, 'España e Irlanda', in *Segundo curso de metodología y crítica históras*, p. 335.

10,000 men was to be embarked for Ireland: 6,000 infantry to land,
1,500 to guard the ships, and 2,500 seamen. Philip accepted these plans
and agreed to give Don Antonio de Zúñiga command of the army and
Brochero, admiral-general of the Atlantic fleet, command at sea. The
ships must return as soon as they had disembarked the men; if they
remained in Ireland, the council believed, nothing would be gained
beyond the consumption of victuals by the seamen. Besides, the Irish
had defended themselves so well against England without anyone's
help that they would need only the Spanish infantry to support them;
it would be unnecessary for the fleet to remain. This line of argu-
mentation was unfortunate, as events were to show. Shipping to a
grand total of 14,780 tons was to be prepared to carry the expedition,
the total cost of which was estimated at 601,700 ducats.[1]

O'Neill had sent his son to Spain as a pledge of his placing his person, territories, and state at Philip's command. The king now, in view
of Cerdá's imminent return to Ireland, wrote to O'Neill to express his
joy at Henry's arrival. At O'Neill's request he agreed in principle that
only those Irish ships which carried passports from O'Neill and the archbishop of Dublin would be allowed into Spanish ports. This move was
designed to bring pressure to bear on the towns through the merchant
class to come over to Hugh's side. Counting the smuggling trade there
was, as has been seen, still a considerable commerce between Ireland
and Spain. It was not, however, before the following spring that
Philip gave final orders to embargo Irish vessels which did not carry
the required passport, and the embargo had little effect on the war.
O'Neill also wished Maurice, son of John Og Fitzgerald,[2] to come from
Lisbon with the expedition to Ireland. Though a rival of James Fitzthomas for the Desmond earldom, Hugh hoped that he would not
press his claims and that his coming with the expedition would
strengthen the confederate side by encouraging Maurice's kinsmen
to come over.

As the war went on, there were signs that the English of the Pale
were coming to have more belief in O'Neill. Fathers de la Field and
Fitzsimon were by the end of 1599 coming round to the view that
victory by Hugh would mean the re-establishment of Catholicism,
and at Douay at the same time the young gentlemen of the Pale, who
formed the majority of the student body in the college, were (at least

---

1. AGS, Estado 2053 (two copies): council of state on help to Flanders and Ireland,
Madrid, 5 Aug. 1601, with Philip's autograph reply.   2. Cf. I.E.R., ser. 5, xcii (1959), 289.

by report) coming to identify themselves with the national struggle now being carried on at home.[1] At the same time, however, Nuncio Frangipani, who at his sounding-post in the Netherlands heard the views of many Catholic exiles, was coming to distrust the purity of O'Neill's motives.[2]

From Rome, Sessa, urged on by Dr. Lombard, continued to plead the Irish cause with Philip. Through Lombard, O'Neill sought to get Pope Clement to order public prayers in Rome for a happy outcome of the struggle, to send an excommunication against all who carried arms against the Catholic belligerents, and to restore to O'Neill the *juspatronatus*, the patronage of benefices, held by his ancestors. Hugh also asked that to subsidize the war there might be given all the ecclesiastical income from places vacant; and he sought Oviedo's appointment, with wide faculties, as papal nuncio. His grand design was that the pope would grant investiture of Ireland in Philip, who would then send a force from Spain to liberate the country.[3]

While Lombard won Sessa's support for these aims, he made little progress with the pope. O'Neill therefore sent Father Archer off to plead with Clement. The Jesuit went by way of France to Rome, where he arrived in November, after a six-week journey from Ireland. He was armed with credentials not only from O'Neill but also from Florence MacCarthy, Edmund Fitzgibbon (the White Knight), Cormac MacDermot of Muskerry, and the O'Sullivans.[4]

Father Archer insisted in Rome that all the Irish Catholics either openly or secretly opposed Elizabeth; all that was required to make her secret opponents publicly declare themselves was the express announcement by the pope of a religious war and the support of a Spanish army sufficiently strong to free Ireland. Following his instructions, Archer went on to say that although the Irish recognized the pope as their lord they saw the need for Philip's help for their release from servitude. The forces of the pope, he pointed out, were far away and besides were too weak at sea. He asked Clement therefore to use his authority with Philip to send a Spanish army and to agree with

1. Cf. Hogan, *Ibernia Ignatiana*, pp. 50–1, 68; *Distinguished Irishmen*, pp. 167–71; J. Brady, in *Measgra Mhichíl Uí Chléirigh*, ed. O'Brien, p. 101. There is an interesting statement made by Richard Stanihurst in 1601 that he was then acting as O'Neill's agent at Brussels. Cf. Loomie, 'Richard Stanyhurst in Spain', in *Huntingdon Library Quarterly*, xxviii (1965), 147.

2. Edwards, *Church and state*, p. 290.

3. Cf. VA, Borghese III, vol. 124 C, f. 57 (*Archiv. Hib.*, ii (1913), 297–300, xxiv (1916), 79): memorial to the pope; *Archiv. Hib.*, ii. 287–97: letters of date 1600; AGS, Estado 972: Sessa to Philip, Rome, 2 Aug. and 12 Sept. 1600.   4. Cf. *Cal. S.P. Ire.*, 1601–3, p. 160.

Philip on a king whom the Irish would all obey, or else to give Ireland as a fief to Spain.[1]

Unfortunately for the success of Archer's mission he was the bearer of a message of a very different tenor to Rome. This was a letter from his superior, Father de la Field, to the General Aquaviva. De la Field, even if his sympathy for O'Neill might be growing, was yet mindful of his general's monition not to let his spiritual mission be damaged by his becoming too involved in political matters. He therefore wrote to assure Aquaviva of the existence of Irish Catholics who did not support O'Neill. He advised the general that a re-issue of the Bull of excommunication—as O'Neill desired—would have no other effect than to create difficulties for these Catholics. If they heeded such a Bull, de la Field argued, they would have their property confiscated and their persons condemned for high treason; if they did not, they would incur the Church's censures and be deprived of the sacraments and the mass.[2]

Because of the division between old Irish and old English in Irish Catholicism, therefore, Father Archer's mission was not successful. Relations in any case between the Papacy and Spain continued to be glacial. Outstanding were the papal grievances against the viceroy of Naples, Lemos. Clement claimed that Lemos was seeking to damage the trade of Benevento, which belonged to the papal states. This matter and other disputes which had resulted from infringement of ecclesiastical jurisdiction were not settled until 1601.[3]

While O'Neill's diplomacy gained little in Rome, the preparation in Spain of the proposed expedition hung fire. Lack of money was the main cause; there was no reserve to draw on. So little had been done by November 1600 that king and council agreed to postpone the expedition for the current year and to concentrate on sending help to Flanders. In vain did Richard Owen, infantry commander in his cousin O'Neill's army, warn that unless Spain shortly sent help O'Neill would do as he was urged by James of Scotland and accept the generous terms being offered by the queen.[4] Philip had lapsed into indifference about the fate of Ireland. Ironically, the council of state

1. AGS, Estado 972: Sessa to Philip, 27 Nov. 1600.
2. Hogan, *Ibernia Ignatiana*, p. 68; *Distinguished Irishmen*, pp. 170–1.
3. Pastor, *History of the popes*, xxiii. 217–18.
4. AGS, Estado 840, f. 89 (*Cal. S.P. Spain, 1587–1603*, pp. 673–4); memorial by Owen, Madrid, 20 Nov. 1600; Estado 840, f. 90, Estado 2511 (*Cal.*, cit., p. 673): council of state to Philip, 28 Nov. 1600. For James's letter and O'Neill's answer cf. Gardiner, *England from the accession of James I*, i. 80.

was now pleading with him to take the Irish expedition in hand. Heretofore the king's determination to aid Ireland had contrasted with the council's lukewarm reception of his plans. Now that the expedition had been agreed on the council sought to go forward with it, while Philip's interest began to fail. In this the capriciousness of Philip III appeared. The men who were now being levied, said the council, must go to Italy; the council of war should then be ordered to choose more captains, with a view to raising men for Ireland. Philip, though pressed further, now showed himself rather in favour of following up the peace negotiations and seeking a suspension of arms. Nor would the king yet commit himself to the proposal of the English Catholics and Jesuits that he should have an invasion force ready to back up the claims of the Infanta Isabel (or some other candidate) to the English throne when Elizabeth died.[1]

Like O'Neill, Federico Spínola was called upon to exercise a good deal of patience. Federico, when in 1599 Archduke Albert had refused him the artillery he needed for his proposed expedition to England, had had perforce to remain in Flanders, where with his galleys he caused havoc to Dutch shipping. Now in August 1600 when the peace negotiations broke off Philip again showed interest in Federico's project. It was decided to give Spínola six new galleys, so that if peace were not made he would then have twelve for his expedition. Philip wrote to Albert in October saying that Spínola—saving the peace negotiations, which were the primary thing—should get the help that he wanted.[2] But after that months were to go by before anything more was done.

At last Philip took the step of proclaiming the infanta as successor to Elizabeth and wrote to secure the pope's approval and aid. It was not until later that Philip advised the archdukes of his decision. When he did so Albert showed no enthusiasm for pressing his wife's claim. For the safety of the States, Albert desired nothing better than peace with England.[3] And even the council of state in time came to see the hopelessness of trying to establish Isabel on the English throne.

1. AGS, Estado 2023 and 840, f. 101: council of state to Philip, 12 Dec.; Estado 2023: same to same, 19 Dec.; Estado 840 (*Cal. S.P. Spain, 1587–1603*, pp. 674–6. Cf. Estado 840, ff. 95 and 135 and Hume, *Treason and plot*, pp. 415–17): memorandum from Fr. Creswell, S.J., 2 Dec., and report thereon by council of state.

2. AGS, Estado 617: *consulta*, 5 Oct. 1600; Estado 2224: Philip to Albert, 13 Oct. 1600; Estado 621 (Rodríguez Villa, *Ambrosio Spínola*, p. 25): undated memorial by Federico Spínola.

3. AGS, Estado 187: Philip to Sessa, 24 Jan. 1601. Cf. *Cal. S.P. Spain, 1587–1603*, pp. 649, 660, 663–5, 669, 675, 650–3, 668; Pollen, articles in *Month*, c (1902), ci (1903); *Dodd's church history of England*, ed. Tierney, iii. 30 n., lxx–lxxii.

But that was in the future, and at this juncture, as Father Persons warned that James of Scotland was intriguing with the pope, the council urged Philip to declare publicly his support of Isabel's candidature. This would forestall James, whom the council thought to be playing a double game in order to gain the English councillors (Nottingham, Buckhurst, and Cecil) whom Persons reported to be favourable towards choice of the infanta. Sessa, while seeking to win over the pope in the matter, should, the council recommended, keep continually before Clement the question of investiture of Ireland in Philip. Every effort should be made to persevere in the Irish business until the decision taken to send an army of 6,000 men to Ireland had been carried out.[1]

While the king and his council argued over the question of aid to Ireland, Cerdá, who was eager to return to O'Neill with definite assurance of an army to follow, had to kick his heels in Spain. Eventually, early in December, he was allowed to leave Corunna, in command of two pataches and bound for Killybegs. But although he did not come empty-handed, he bore with him no news of an intended expedition. Storm drove him into Broadhaven, on the Mayo coast, but finally he made Teelin and unloaded his cargo of 2,000 arquebuses and 150 quintals each of powder, lead, and fuse. He had also brought a sum of 20,000 ducats for division between the Irish leaders. O'Neill and O'Donnell arrived and divided the munitions between them, each apportioning his share among his sub-chiefs, who were also present. Dean Edmund MacDonnell divided the money according to the terms of the royal schedule.[2]

The chiefs, after their long wait, were bitterly disappointed at receiving only such inconsiderable help, and their disappointment was not alleviated by letters from Philip which only urged them to continue the struggle and gave no definite promise of major support. O'Neill pointed out to the Spaniards that he had not the munitions or infantry with which to oppose the superior English forces. At length Cerdá prevailed on the Irish to wait until the feast of St. James, 25 July

1. AGS, Estado 840, f. 81 (Cal. S.P. Spain, 1587–1603, pp. 682–3): consulta by council of state, 1 Feb. 1601.

2. AGS, Estado 186: statement by Ensigns Cuenca and Trigo and Sergeant Niebla to Governor Caracena, sent with dispatch, Caracena to Philip III, Corunna, 28 Jan. 1601; Ó Clérigh, Beatha Aodha Ruaidh, i. 280–4; A.F.M.; Docwra, 'Narration', in Celtic Soc. Misc., ed. O'Donovan, p. 247; AGS, Estado 1743: 'Ermundo Donaldino's' testimony, Donegal, 5 Jan. 1600 (recte 1601). Ó Clérigh says the Spaniards unloaded cargo at Killybegs, but Teelin is more likely. Cf. Silke, 'Where was "Obemdub"?', in Ir. Sword, vi (1964), 276–81.

1601; if an expedition had not come by then, O'Neill would be free to follow his best interest, even if that entailed making peace. Archbishop Oviedo, for his part, pledged his word that in May, if Spain were not going to support the chiefs, he himself would come to inform them. And so Cerdá, accompanied by the archbishop and Father Chamberlain, O'Neill's confessor, returned again to Spain at the end of January to beg Philip once more to send the Irish the help they needed.[1]

It says not a little for O'Neill's constancy, a year and a half after the original undertaking given by Barrionuevo, that he was still prepared to yield to the Spanish envoys' request that he continue the war. For he had already abandoned hope; with France and Savoy at war, he thought (as Cerdá's discourse made clear) that Philip's armies would be engaged on the side of Savoy and that therefore the Spanish king would have no men to spare that year. Hugh was a great realist, but his fidelity to his country's cause was just now surviving a great test.

Still exercised about the port of disembarkation of the expedition, Hugh advised the archbishop that if it were small, it should go where the ships carrying messages (de aviso) went; if it consisted of 6,000 men or more, it should go to Munster. What O'Neill meant by the place where the ships de aviso went is without doubt Donegal Bay, and more particularly the port of Teelin or Killybegs. What he had in mind was this: Munster offered more prizes to an invading army and was easier to operate in and live off than Connacht or Ulster; but only a large army could maintain itself and hold the initiative there until O'Neill had come south to effect a junction with it. A small force then, if only such arrived, should come to Donegal Bay, where O'Donnell had all the ports at his command now, from Teelin to Broadhaven, and where the Spaniards could easily unite with the Irish armies.

Besides the north and south there was a third choice, the east, and of all Irish ports Drogheda was in O'Neill's opinion the best for the landing. Disembarking there would bring the Spaniards right away into contact with the enemy, while O'Neill himself could be there inside a day and a half. Artillery could easily be moved in the level country round about. But the way to Drogheda by Connacht round Loch Foyle meant a long journey, exposing the fleet to the peril of storms, while entry by St. George's Channel was dangerous too. And

1. AGS, Estado 619: Zúñiga to Philip, 12 July 1601; Estado 186: Caracena to Philip, 28 Jan. 1601; Estado 187: royal schedule, Vallid., 31 Jan.

also the queen held two adjacent ports—Dundalk and Carlingford—
with garrisons of foot and horse.

While O'Neill preferred the southern ports, all things considered, to
the northern, he preferred Cork to all of them. To one side of Cork
lay Clancarty, which, in so far as the setting up of Florence MacCarthy
as MacCarthy More, could effect it, was loyal to O'Neill; to the other
lay the lands of the earl of Desmond and of the Barrys. Although the
Barrys were now subject to the queen, it was, O'Neill claimed without
much regard to truth, perforce. MacCarthy and Desmond would be
at Cork to join the Spaniards within two days and O'Neill himself
within ten. There was plenty of food available in the vicinity.[1]

The Irish confederates begged Spain for an army of 5,000 men. They
told of most severe damage inflicted on them by Elizabeth the preceding summer, by land and sea, with 16,000 foot and 2,000 horse.[2]

O'Neill was indeed very much on the defensive. He was shut in on
all sides, was short of cattle, and lacking in corn, bread, and butter.
The English force on Loch Foyle held Inishowen and established Niall
Garbh at Lifford. Meanwhile, Mountjoy had during 1600 forced the
submission of Conor Roe Maguire—one of the rival claimants to the
Fermanagh chieftainship—ravaged Laois and Offaly, killed Owen
MacRory O'More, and in February dispersed Tyrrell's troops. Be-
tween October and November 1600 he had hemmed in O'Neill north
of the Moyry, razed the defences there, and established the fort of
Mountnorris, eight miles north of the Newry.

Bad as was all this, there was worse to come. Keeping up the campaign throughout the winter, a departure that came as a shock to the
Irish, accustomed heretofore to a breathing-space when their enemies
had retired to winter quarters, Mountjoy early in January 1601 des-
poiled Wicklow, and in March Felim MacFeagh submitted. The lord
deputy placed garrisons in Tullagh and Wicklow; in March he received
the submission of Ever MacCooley, lord of Farney, in Monaghan.
O'Neill's communications with Munster were cut off, and he was
rendered unable to go to the assistance of James Fitzthomas.

Dermot O'Conor Don, Desmond's captain of bonnachts, had been
driven back into Connacht, and there on 3 November 1600 he was
murdered by Tibbot na Long. Carew drove James Fitzthomas into

---

1. AGS, Guerra Antigua 3144: Archbishop of Dublin on choice of port, 1600.
2. AGS, Estado 840, f. 38: *consulta* by junta of councillors, Simancas, 9 Feb. 1601. Elizabeth
had by July consented to raise the establishment to 16,000 men. Cf. Falls, *Mountjoy*, p. 136.

the woods and intimidated Florence MacCarthy. By the end of the
year 1600 not a castle in Munster remained in rebel hands.

But while in Ireland O'Neill's cause declined, at last there seemed
promise of real help from Spain. By the treaty of Lyons in January
1601 France made peace with Savoy. The peace was favourable to
Savoy, so that Spain was relieved from the likelihood of being called
to go to the aid of the Savoyards. For once fortune smiled on the Irish,
for it was at this juncture that Oviedo and Cerdá arrived at the court
to remind King Philip of his father's and his own promises to the Irish,
and to lay before the king the memoranda with which O'Neill and his
fellow leaders had supplied them.[1] The council of state was not at the
time with the king, who therefore appointed a junta of court councillors, the marquis of Velada, Don Juan de Idiáquez, Fray Gaspar,
Franqueza, and Esteban de Ibarra, to hear the archbishop and Cerdá.

The peace between France and Savoy altered the international
situation in favour of Ireland. The shrewd O'Neill had grasped the
fact that as long as Savoy was threatened by attack from France Spain
would not be in a position to send an army to Ireland. Savoy and the
Netherlands were of more importance to Spain than was Ireland.
Encouraged by the failure of Archduke Albert to make headway at
the conference table, either at Bergen-op-Zoom or Boulogne, the
States had sent Maurice with an army into Flanders. Near Nieuport
Maurice found himself cut off by Albert from his base at Ostend. He
therefore stood to fight on the sands of the Dunes. In the battle of the
Dunes (2 July 1600), in which the Irish regiment fought in Albert's
rearguard, Maurice inflicted a very serious defeat on the archduke.
Albert lost over a hundred infantry companies, 6,000 men, and appealed to Spain for troops. Philip did not let the archduke's appeal go
unheard, and 2,000 men were levied in Spain. In the state of relations
between France and Savoy it was not considered safe to send this army
by the landward route through Milan to Flanders; consequently they
were embarked in ships at Lisbon, with a view to sending them by sea.

But with the treaty of Lyons, it became unnecessary to send them.
The treaty of Vervins, embracing in its terms France, Spain, and Savoy,
had left unsettled the claims of Duke Charles Emmanuel of Savoy or
Piedmont to the marquisate of Saluzzo. At Lyons the duke was allowed to keep Saluzzo, while he ceded to France the less important
territories of Bresse, Bugey, Valromey, and Gex. The treaty really

1. Cf. *supra*, p. 75.

showed diplomatic wisdom on the part of Henry IV; Savoy controlled
the passage of troops from the Rhône valley into Milan, or vice versa.
A friendly Savoy was a real asset to France, as it was to Spain.[1]

The danger to Piedmont had now receded, and Spain could afford
to send to Flanders some of the men the count of Fuentes had taken
to the Milanese. Besides, the winter was now advanced, and an expedition from Lisbon at this time of the year would run a grave risk at sea.
The 2,000 infantry were therefore held in reserve at Lisbon for further
calls; meanwhile they were set to guard the Portuguese coast.[2]

With this nucleus of men and ships at the ready Spain was at last in
a position to prepare an army for Ireland. Lerma decided to send an
army of 6,000 men, and Philip gave orders for the raising of this force;
to the 2,000 infantry at Lisbon were to be added 4,000 other soldiers,
made up of recruits then being raised in Spain, 1,200 veterans from
Terceira, in the Azores, and other veterans from Galicia.

Orders were given for the making of biscuit in the ovens at Corunna
and Lisbon; 10,000 quintals would be embarked, 4,500 as food for the
two month's voyage provided for, and 5,500 to be disembarked in
Ireland; while 10,000 must remain in Lisbon as food for the men in
the ships there, in Andalusia, and elsewhere.[3]

Plans were formed for providing storehouses in Corunna, which was
the most convenient place from which to provision the men in Ireland
as well as the ships continually coming and going with news and reconnoitring in the English Channel, and for providing artillery and arms.

A summary of the estimates was as follows. The 2,000 infantry in
Lisbon, together with the crews of the transport ships, had already
been provided with everything necessary for a stay of two months in
Lisbon. Next, there were the costs of raising and sending to Ireland a
further 4,000 soldiers and 500 seamen:

	Ducats
Embarkation and maintenance of 4,500 men for two months	40,000
One wage for the 4,000 new recruits	20,000
Two wages for the veterans for the garrisons in Galicia and Portugal	12,000
Shipping for and maintenance of the men from Terceira	17,000
Two wages for the infantry from Terceira	16,000
Money to be taken to Ireland for payment of the men and other needs	200,000
Total	305,000

1. Petrie, *Earlier diplomatic history 1492–1713*, p. 104.   2. AGS, Estado 840, f. 276; Estado
961 (*Cal. S.P. Spain, 1587–1603*, p. 676): *consulta* by council of state, Vallid., 4 Aug. 1601.
   3. The quintal was the equivalent of four arrobas, each of twenty-five libras. The libra
was somewhat heavier than the avoirdupois pound, or 1·014 lb. avoirdupois. The quintal
therefore weighed 101·4 lb. avoirdupois.

The 'wage' mentioned in the estimates was a subsistence. Soldiers in Spanish as in English armies knew to their cost that it was not always forthcoming.[1] Out of the grand total of 305,000 ducats the council expected a sum of 200,000 that the king had lent for the maintenance of the Indies' fleet, to be already available at Lisbon.[2]

1. Cf. the system of payment in the English army, described by Neale, *Essays in Elizabethan history*, p. 181.

2. AGS, Estado 840. ff. 41–6 (*Cal. S.P. Spain, 1587–1603*, p. 685): estimates of expenses of Irish expedition.

VII · PREPARATION

Señor, conozca V.M. a un hombre que nació sin miedo (Don
Fernando de Toledo introduces Águila to Philip II).
                                    González Dávila, *Felipe tercero*

THE COUNCIL OF STATE's hope that the expedition would be ready
to sail by the feast of St. James (25 July) was not realized. Speed and
secrecy in preparation would give the expedition the advantage of
surprise over the enemy. In April 1601 an embargo was imposed by
Philip on Irish ships entering Spanish ports without a passport from
O'Neill and O'Donnell. This was a year after the chiefs had first recommended the step. It failed either to ensure secrecy, since Elizabeth's
spies were already reporting to her (in wildly exaggerated terms it is
true) on Spanish preparations for an invasion of England, or to provide
sailors and pilots for the expedition, since the few poor little craft
embargoed had not many to offer.[1]

Don Diego de Brochero y Añaya was appointed naval commander
of the expedition and about the beginning of March presented himself
for orders at Lisbon. By mid April there was some progress to report
in the raising of the expedition. Twenty-five companies of recruits
were being raised in Castile and would soon be on their way to Lisbon,
while nine companies whose numbers had gone down had left that
capital to return on being re-formed into a lesser number of companies. There were in the sixteenth-century company nine officer
ranks or 'places': captain, ensign, sergeant (to keep accounts), cor-
porals, quarter-master, drummers and fifers, colour-sergeant, and (a

1. AGS, Guerra Antigua, 3143 (*Rep. Nov.*, i. 352): Oviedo to Lerma, Madrid, 4 Apr.; Estado
188: letters from Thomas Charli to Elizabeth, Cecil, and others, Feb. 1601 (intercepted and
sent to Philip, 3 Apr.; Estado 2511: O'Neill and O'Donnell to Philip, Donegal, 24 Apr. 1600;
Estado 186: Adelantado to Philip, 7 Jan. 1601; junta to Philip, 9 Feb.; Estado 187: Philip to
Adelantado, Vallid., 31 Jan. and to Adelantado and others, 8 Apr.; Estado 186: Cerdá to
Philip, undated, with covering note by Lerma. Five craft were embargoed in Cadiz and
Puerto de Santa María. Estado 186: Adelantado to Philip, Cadiz, 2 May; abstracts by Notary
Molina of the processes heard in Cadiz, Pto. de Sta. María, 7 and 15 July.

tribute to his importance) baker. This re-forming therefore would mean some saving in expenses. Three companies of veterans as well, comprising four hundred men, were due to leave the garrisons of Galicia for Portugal. Castel-Rodrigo, the viceroy of Portugal, was sent some money, and promised more, to provide for the needs of these soldiers. But the money arrived in driblets only and the promises were slow in honouring, and in the garrisons, in Galicia as in Lisbon, there was great distress.[1]

A levy of seamen was ordered in the ports of Guipúzcoa, Biscay, and Quatro Villas. The incidence of plague and the bad treatment of the men in earlier levies made it difficult, however, to raise sailors. But by degrees and with many injunctions from the king to speedy action and many complaints from his ministers of insufficient funds, with ever-recurring delays and not a little rancorous exchange among those charged with the mobilization, the little force began to assemble at Lisbon.[2] Don Antonio de Zúñiga de Gimiel de Mercado, who at the end of April had been appointed land commander, made such difficulties, however, that it was decided to replace him by a new captain-general.[3]

Brochero, who came to Lisbon on 31 May, this time to take up his command, devoted himself with the energy he always displayed to the securing of everything that was necessary to making the expedition a success: money, an embargo of foreign ships, equipment, pilots, and hospital facilities. But he was at loggerheads with the viceroy, who resented having anyone to share with him the direction of the preparations. Differences such as these were to affect the success of the expedition greatly.[4]

With the preparations for the Irish expedition in train, Philip sought again to give impetus to the Spínola scheme, which appealed to him so much. At his order Fedérico came to Spain in April 1601, while

1. AGS, Guerra Antigua 3145 (*Rep. Nov.*, i, 352): Oviedo to Lerma, Madrid, 10 Apr.; Guerra Antigua 3144: estimate of troops, 18 Apr.; junta to Castel-Rodrigo, Vallid., 18 Apr.; Lerma to same, 18 Apr.; Guerra Antigua 587: Castel-Rodrigo to Philip and to E. de Ibarra, 29 Mar.; Caracena to Philip, 23 Apr.

2. AGS, Guerra Antigua 3144: junta to president of Casa de Contratación and to Adelantado, 29 May; Philip to Castel-Rodrigo, 4 Apr.; estimate by Ibarra; Guerra Antigua 587: Carlos de Amezola to Philip, Bilbao, 12 May; F. de la Riva Herrera to same, Santander, 13 May; Francisco de Fuica to same, Bilbao, 12 May; Verastegui and others to same, Portualgalete, 17 May.

3. AGS, Guerra Antigua 3144: Castel-Rodrigo to Philip, 26 May.

4. AGS, Guerra Antigua 3144: Castel-Rodrigo to Philip, Lisbon, 4 June; Guerra Antigua 3145: Brochero to Philip, 4 June.

Philip secured the council of war's agreement to an attack on England. Difficulty with the archduke, the council suggested, would be avoided if the army were raised not in Flanders but in Italy. Philip therefore ordered Fuentes to give Federico Spanish and Italian veterans and to allow him to levy other men up to a total of 6,000; these 6,000 would be taken to Flanders, where 2,000 of them would be mounted. Ambrosio Spínola would be *maestre de campo*. Federico would take four hundred Turks for the galleys from Hungary by way of Genoa, Barcelona, and Santander to Flanders, while Albert would help with the mounting of the men and their equipment in Flanders and would send twenty pieces of artillery to Sluys. Of this great undertaking Federico would provide the costs.[1]

Such was the plan. Philip was now bent on carrying the war to Elizabeth; he would attack her on two fronts, in Ireland and in England. If his plans succeeded, England would soon be faced with the grim threat of conquest.

But if O'Neill had at last gained one of his objectives, namely an army—or at least the promise of one—from Spain, he had been less successful in gaining the other, the co-operation of Pope Clement in the enterprise of Ireland. The pope, after consultation with Cardinals Bellarmine and Mathei and the Jesuit general Aquaviva, appointed by brief of 17 May 1601 Father Ludovico Mansoni, S.J., as his legate *a latere* to Ireland. While Clement did not choose Oviedo, or even a Spaniard, as O'Neill desired, Mansoni had for many years been provincial of his order in Sicily, which was, of course, under Spanish domination, and had acted in a confidential capacity to Philip II. The pope was thus going some of the way towards satisfying the Spanish king in the choice of a legate.[2]

He did not, however, satisfy the two Hughs. O'Neill and O'Donnell were disappointed that Clement had listened to the representations of the old English at Rome and had appointed not Oviedo but Mansoni as his legate. Although the appointment of a papal representative was a gain for their cause, Oviedo would have identified himself much more clearly with their interests. The Irish leaders sought to play on Spanish antagonism for Italians in order to make Philip inter-

1. Rodríguez Villa, *Ambrosio Spínola*, pp. 25–7, 29–30; Cerrolaza, *Spínola*, pp. 36–7.
2. Cf. *Archiv. Hib.*, xvii (1953), i. 18, 52–60; HMC, *rep.* 10, app. v, p. 346: Bellarmine to Aquaviva, 3 Nov. 1600; AGS, Estado 972; Sessa to Philip, 14 Nov. 1600. The first part of this dispatch (dealing with the succession to England) is translated in *Archiv. Hist. Soc. Iesu*, xxiv. 126–8.

vene to have Mansoni replaced by Fray Mateo. Philip, however, afraid of offending the pope, contented himself with seeking to persuade Clement not to send any nuncio until Ireland was reduced to a better state and in the interim to commit to the archbishop of Dublin the dispatch of necessary business. In this he was unsuccessful.[1]

Suddenly there was a new problem. Henry O'Neill, surety for the good faith of his father and uncle (Henry's mother was Siobhán O'Donnell, Red Hugh's sister), took the dramatic but unwelcome step of entering the Franciscan noviciate at Salamanca. This decision of O'Neill's eldest son to renounce the world posed an awkward problem for his protectors, in whom O'Neill was likely to feel his trust misplaced. Oviedo, who in fulfilment of his promise to the Irish chief was trying anxiously to get Lerma to send news of the intended invasion to Ireland, had in May to go to Salamanca at the duke's request to try to get the troublesome affair put to rights.

At the beginning of June Archbishop Mateo was back, armed with a theological opinion from the university of Salamanca, which was to the effect that in becoming a friar Henry would sin mortally and that the best course for Philip to follow was to secure an order from the nuncio for the boy to give up the habit. The worried Lerma did not accept this opinion until it was confirmed by the Valladolid theologians and then by a special junta headed by Cardinal Guevara and appointed by the favourite to decide the matter. Still the patache to warn O'Neill was not sent, and with the feast of St. James, the deadline set by O'Neill for the arrival of the Spanish army, only twenty days away Oviedo fretted that Hugh would retire from the war and that the armada would consequently suffer the common fate of Spanish expeditions, failure.[2]

But now infantry and sailors were coming steadily into Lisbon, and there was embarkation for 8,000 men there, many more ships than were needed. Eight hundred effectives from Terceira landed at Lisbon on 6 June.[3] A total of nine Irish ships had been embargoed on the

1. AGS, Estado 840, ff. 285–6 (*Cal. S.P. Spain, 1587–1603*, p. 683 n., where the proper date does not appear) and Estado 2511: *consulta* by council of state, 19 May; Estado 187: Philip to Sessa, 21 June; Estado 972: *consulta*, 19 June.

2. AGS, Guerra Antigua 3144 (*Rep. Nov.*, i. 352): Oviedo to Lerma, Madrid, 4 Apr.; Guerra Antigua 387: Oviedo to Philip, Vallid., 3 May; Guerra Antigua 3143 (*Rep. Nov.*, i. 353–8): Oviedo to Ibarra 7 May, 5 and 12 June; Oviedo to Lerma, 12 June; Estado 2511: Guevara to Philip, 19 June. Cf. Walsh, *The O'Neills in Spain*, pp. 5–7; Walsh, *The will and family of Hugh O'Neill*, p. 30.

3. AGS, Guerra Antigua 3144: Castel-Rodrigo to Philip, 6 June; Brochero to Philip, 6 and 10 June.

Andalusian coast, and three at Bilbao. They were all small vessels, and hopes that they might provide seamen and pilots were disappointed; these little craft carried no skilled seamen and their sailors showed no desire to serve with the expedition.[1]

General Pedro de Zubiaur arrived on 11 July with eleven ships sent by the Adelantado from Andalusia. These ships carried a total personnel of 415, nine or ten of whom were down with plague. Twelve out of the twenty-five companies of recruits from Castile had arrived from Alcántara by that day, and the three companies of veterans, led by Captain Juan de Albornoz, had come from Galicia. Sailors were coming from Bilbao and San Sebastian—unwillingly enough, for past experience taught them to expect poor treatment. In order to keep the men who had arrived from running away they were being fed on the food set apart for the voyage. Unfortunate as this might be it was a necessity, because there was no money to buy other provisions. By 2 August the twenty-five companies from Castile were all in Lisbon and embarked in their ships. But so far only 2,000 men had been found in the garrisons of Portugal.[2]

The *maestre de campo* Don Juan del Águila was the man chosen to replace Zúñiga as captain-general. With the appointment, announced by royal schedule of 2 July, went a delimitation of the commands of Águila and Brochero. The latter was supreme in all that belonged to the navigation, ships, sailors, and seamen, and the former was made land commander in Ireland. Each was forbidden to interfere in the other's sphere. This was a clumsy arrangement and an appeal by the king for the two commanders to work in harmony went largely unheeded; it soon became clear that co-operation between them was sadly lacking.

Águila was born in Barraco in the province of Avila and had his military formation first under Sancho Dávila in Flanders and then under Don García de Toledo against the Turk in the Mediterranean theatre. He returned to Flanders under Alexander Farnese, duke of Parma, and had distinguished service, rising from the rank of infantry

1. AGS, Guerra Antigua 587: Lic. Verastegui, corregidor of Biscay, to junta of war, 25 June; Irabién, purveyor of Biscay, to Philip, 6 July; Guerra Antigua 3144: junta to Verastegui, to Irabién and to Padilla, 28 June.

2. AGS, Guerra Antigua 3144 (cf. *Epistolario de Zubiaur*, p. 140): Report on Zubiaur's ships, forwarded by Ibarra to Castel-Rodrigo, 25 May; Castel-Rodrigo to Philip, 5 and 11 July; Guerra Antigua 3145: Brochero to Philip, 5 and 10 July; Guerra Antigua 587: Irabién to junta and Verastegui to same, 2 July; Castel-Rodrigo to Philip and to Ibarra, 2 Aug.

captain to that of *maestre de campo*, commander or colonel of a regiment.

Águila returned to Spain after twenty-four years' soldiering and after some home service was in 1590 sent as captain-general by land and sea to Brittany to help the French Catholics, who were led by the duke of Mercouer. In France, where he was supported by Admiral Brochero, by dint of hard fighting he gained for a time mastery of Brittany. But, owing to dissensions between the Spanish commanders and Mercoeur and the bad state of the Catholic troops, the advantage gained was lost even before Vervins. Already in June 1597 the forces in Brittany, whose lot was most miserable, had taken their captain-general and his captains prisoner and informed Philip II that they could no longer bear Águila's extreme harshness. They had had seven years of misery, they said, without food or clothes. Other grave charges were soon laid against Don Juan, and on 27 May 1600 he, his wife, and the paymaster of his army were lodged in prison on information that they had benefited over-much from the royal treasury. When the decision was taken to appoint him to the Irish command he was released from gaol.[1]

This was the man chosen to lead the Spanish troops in Ireland, a very seasoned campaigner in different theatres of war and a commander with considerable success to his credit, even though he might not have earned the eulogium of his fellow Avilan González that he was one of the greatest luminaries that war gave birth to in his age. But although some of the charges against him must be considered in the light of the circumstances in which Spanish armies of the time fought, without sufficient equipment or money, with their supply-lines often cut and with an administration ill-organized, his was without doubt a difficult temperament, stern and bleak as the landscape of his native province. But even if Águila had been of one mind with the others responsible for the conduct of the war in Ireland, the task before him was indeed formidable: forced to fight in a theatre of war so far removed from Spain, with not enough troops, with inadequate supplies, he was asked to embark on an undertaking whose success would almost have demanded a miracle. There was every possibility,

---

1. González Dávila, *Felipe tercero*, p. 246; A[bilio] B[Arbero], in *D.H.E.*; Fernández Duro, *Armada española*, iii. 67–77, 83–93, 168–70, 218; Lavisse, *Histoire de France*, vi. 405; Hauser, *La prépondérance espagnole, 1559–1600*, p. 159. The Venetian ambassador reports on Aguila's command in Brittany in *Cal. S.P. Venice, 1592–1603*, pp. 149, 164, 227. Cf. also Cabrera, *Relaciones*, p. 70.

7

indeed that the armada might not even make a landfall in Ireland.[1]

Águila arrived in Lisbon on 18 or 19 July. Orders now issued from Valladolid said that the viceroy was to bring up the number of effectives sailing to 6,000 and that Archbishop Oviedo was to be in charge of the hospital with the army. Águila was ordered to avail himself of his and Cerdá's mediation with the two Hughs and of their experience of Ireland, and to take with him also Bishop Thady Farrell, O.P., of Clonfert. Father Archer, S.J., was also appointed to go as adviser with Águila, and Bishop O'Mulrian of Killaloe was to go as well. The expedition must be off by the beginning of August.[2]

Brochero had this order from Philip on 26 July and finding nothing in it about the port of disembarkation consulted with Águila. In doing so he started off a great controversy. At the conference in Donegal friary, in 1600, it will be recalled, O'Neill had laid down the principle that the port of landing must be determined by the size of the army sent. If it were of 6,000 men or larger, it should land at Waterford or Cork; if between 3,000 and 4,000 at Limerick; but if only 2,000 or under it should come to Killybegs or Teelin. To Cerdá at the turn of the year he reiterated the principle; an army 6,000 or more in size should go to Munster, preferably to Cork, but a small force must come to a port in Tyrconnell or perhaps in Connacht.

Such was O'Neill's thinking on the port of disembarkation. An invading army of 6,000 men would be strong enough to take the initiative without immediate help from the confederate Irish. Strategy then demanded that it should aim to take the key Munster towns. The army could move its siege-cannon readily in the level country of Munster and it would have abundant supply of food in that fertile province. Florence MacCarthy and the sugan earl would rally west Munster to the Spaniards at once, and the northern armies would come to join it in good time. For reasons of both strategy and logistics, therefore, an army of 6,000 men should come to Cork, or else Waterford.

If the Spaniards numbered only 4,000 men and were therefore too weak to take the offensive in Munster, they should come to Limerick.

1. Olagüe, La decadencia española, i. 355.

2. AGS, Guerra Antigua 3144 (cf. Rep. Nov., i. 368): Royal schedules to Girón, Padilla and Castel-Rodrigo, Vallid., 7 June; to Oviedo, Águila, and Castel-Rodrigo, 20 July; to Aguila, 31 July; Guerra Antigua 3145: Royal schedule to Brochero, 12 July; Brochero to Philip, 23 July; Guerra Antigua 3143 (Rep. Nov., i. 359–60); Oviedo to (?) Ibarra, Vallid., 10 July and Tordesillas, 16 July; Guerra Antigua 3144: junta to Castel-Rodrigo, to Aguila, and to Brochero, Vallid., 20 July; to Águila, to Bp. O'Mulrian, and to Castel-Rodrigo, Vallid., 31 July.

O'Neill and O'Donnell could join them more quickly at Limerick than at Cork and until the northern chiefs came they would be seconded by O'Donnell's western client, Theobald Burke. From Limerick the united armies would be well enough placed to strike hard at Elizabeth before the English had time to concentrate their forces.

Only if the Spaniards were too weak to take the initiative or even to defend themselves, O'Neill contended, should they land in or near the northern stronghold of rebellion. The north was inhospitable country, unable to provide food for the invaders and unsuitable for the transport of artillery. The voyage there was, besides, long and inconvenient for both the square-rigged ships and high-sided galleons,[1] and the north was too far removed from strategic objectives. Drogheda was central; it lay between O'Neill and the seat of government power, Dublin, and therefore had great strategic advantages, but a landing there would run too many risks. The queen held Dundalk and Carlingford and, while a voyage by way of Loch Foyle was perilous because of storm, entry by way of the shallow St. George's Channel was dangerous too. Once they had entered the ships too could easily be prevented from leaving the Channel again by the enemy, who could also prevent supplies and reinforcements from reaching the men. For these reasons O'Neill rejected Drogheda and also Carlingford, Richard Owen's choice. Owen favoured Carlingford because he believed that Dublin, not Munster, was the key to Ireland.[2]

These principles were noted and understood by the royal council at Valladolid. Since the army was to be 6,000 strong, Cork therefore should have been designated as the port of disembarkation. But at Lisbon, between Águila on the one hand and Oviedo, Cerdá, and Brochero on the other, a bitter argument developed which lasted for over a month. The argument really was between Oviedo and Águila, two men of strong personality. But whereas the friar was more passionately committed to what he regarded as best for Ireland, the general took a calmer, more objective view of the military issues involved.

In the discussion of 26 July, Águila wanted the landing to be in St. George's Channel, where he might occupy the ports facing England

1. AGS, Estado 840, f. 276; also Estado 961 (cf. *Ir. Sword*, ii (1954), 29): council of state on expedition to Ireland, Vallid., 4 Aug. 1601.
2. AGS, Estado 840, f. 89 (*Cal. S.P. Spain, 1587–1603*, pp. 673–4): memorial by R. Owen, Madrid, 20 Nov. 1600.

in preparation for an attack on that country. Brochero, on the other hand, felt that the Channel was too dangerous (it was shallow and had treacherous currents, the ports were in enemy hands, and English ships could prevent the Spaniards from either retiring or being reinforced). Don Diego therefore wanted to go to the north, to 'Obemdub' (a code-word for Donegal Bay), so as to join forces with the Irish at once. Agreement between the two commanders proving impossible, Marcos Hernández, Brochero's admiral in 1600, was sent off to Valladolid to inform King Philip of the divergence in view and secure his decision.[1]

The following day Ensign Pedro de Sandoval sailed from Corunna for Ireland. He carried news of the impending invasion to O'Neill and O'Donnell and was commissioned to find out their views on where the fleet should land.[2] A few days later, and before Hernández had arrived at court, the council of war sent instructions to Castel-Rodrigo, Águila, and Brochero to agree on a choice of port. The council laid down four conditions which the port should satisfy: it must be abundant in food, the terrain round about must be level for carriage-transport, it must be the port to which O'Neill and O'Donnell could come most swiftly, and it must be situated most advantageously for seeking out the enemy and fighting with him:

Siempre que se ha platicado donde será bien que se desembarque el socorro para Yrlanda se ha tenido por la parte más conveniente aquella que fuese más abundante y más tratable para el carruaje y donde con más breuedad puedan venir las fuerças de los condes Onel y Odonel y la más acomodada para buscar al enemigo y pelear con el.

Águila, the council said, should bear two things in mind, what was best from the viewpoint first of receiving support from his Irish allies and second of carrying the offensive to the enemy:

... que el sitio de la desenbarcación sea aquel que más se ajustará con su [Águila's] intención y con la comodidad de la gente y para que quede en la parte que más a la mano estuvyere para ser favorescida de los amygos y hazer ofensivo a los enemygos ...[3]

On 4 August the council of state learned from Captain Hernández of the divergence of views at Lisbon. The council advised the king that no precise order on the disembarkation could be given from Valla-

1. AGS, Guerra Antigua 3145: Brochero to Philip; Moura to same; Guerra Antigua 3144: same to Ibarra; all 26 July. Cf. Silke, 'Where was "Obemdub"?', in *Ir. Sword*, vi (1964), 281.

2. AGS, Guerra Antigua 3144: junta of war's commission, 14 July.

3. AGS, Guerra Antigua 3145: Schedules to Moura, to Águila, and to Brochero, Vallid., 31 July.

dolid. Águila and Brochero must decide between them, Águila to have the final choice. Lerma accepted this opinion and urged Águila to come to an agreement with the Irish on the matter.[1] To aid the captain-general's choice the council of war issued an *aide-memoire* on the risks of landing in the north (which, the council said, could not victual the Spaniards and from which the march to meet the enemy must encounter many rivers and other natural obstacles) or in the Channel.[2]

As soon as Castel-Rodrigo received the junta's instructions of 31 July he called together Águila and Brochero, the fleet's pilots, and Richard Owen to a meeting. 'Obemduff' (Donegal Bay) was the choice of this meeting.

At this point, however, Archbishop Oviedo and Don Martín de la Cerdá arrived in Lisbon. Learning of the discussion they, relying on the advice that they had received from O'Neill and O'Donnell, pressed the claims of Cork or Limerick. They persuaded Brochero that the choice lay between these two ports, but Águila maintained his preference for Donegal Bay. The order that Águila must make the final decision failed to satisfy the opposition, now led by Oviedo, and each side again presented its case by means of memoranda to Valladolid. Águila's objections to the south were stronger than ever. If he landed at Donegal Bay, he declared, he would be joined within ten days by O'Neill and O'Donnell and would have time to train his raw men and take some of the eastern ports before reinforcements came from Spain. Help would come from Spain, said Águila, more easily to Donegal Bay than to the south. If he landed on the east coast, the Irish would find it difficult to join him. But if he landed in the south, they would, he reasoned, find it impossible to get through an enemy deploying 8,000 foot and 1,500 horse to bar his way. Even if they did break through it must take them a month and they would arrive without food. The south, contrary to Oviedo's opinion, would never rally to him. There was news, said Águila, that the lords of the south had made peace with the queen. O'Neill too, he declared, had lately been unable to get his forces together to go to the aid of the south. Águila believed that if he were to land in Munster, the southern lords would flee with their cattle and wagons to their fastnesses, and he would be forced to dig himself in, to his great disadvantage.

1. AGS, Estado 840, f. 276; also Estado 961 and 2511 (cf. *Ir. Sword*, ii (1954), 29–30): *consulta* by council of state, Vallid., 4 Aug.; Estado 187: Lerma to Ibarra, Vallid., 8 Aug.
2. AGS, Guerra Antigua 3144: junta of war to Castel-Rodrigo, 14 Aug.

These arguments were not admitted by Oviedo. He claimed to be spokesman for O'Neill and O'Donnell, and, maintaining that the choice was reduced to one of the three ports Limerick, Waterford, or Cork, he insisted that the southern Irish would declare for the Spaniards once they had landed in Munster.[1]

The memoranda embodying these different opinions came to the war council on 26 August, and that very night the council dispatched an answer to say that if Sandoval had not returned before the armada sailed, bringing directions from the two Hughs, then the armada must go wherever directed by Oviedo and Cerdá, who spoke for the two chiefs.[2]

While the dispute over the port of disembarkation raged, Zubiaur was trying to get the order revised which said that the transports must return immediately after disembarking the soldiers. Don Pedro felt strongly that the ships should remain in Ireland throughout the winter until Águila was seen to be well placed. But neither the king nor Águila would listen to him, and Zubiaur was excluded from the conferences among the high command at Lisbon.[3]

Sandoval landed at Sligo apparently, for O'Donnell came to meet him there on 10 August. O'Neill was unable to get through Mountjoy's garrisons, which now ringed his territory. But from Dungannon he sent a message giving Sandoval his opinion on where the Spaniards should land. Since Florence MacCarthy and James Fitzthomas, as O'Donnell and O'Neill now advised, were prisoners in English hands and the English had fortified Waterford and Cork, the Spaniards ought to make for Limerick; in the event of mishap they could come to any port between Limerick and Loch Foyle.[4]

The northern leaders therefore no longer thought, as they had given Oviedo to understand, that Cork and Waterford were the most suitable ports to land at. Unfortunately Sandoval did not return with

1. AGS, Guerra Antigua 3144, 3145 (*Rep. Nov.*, i., 360–1, 366–7): memorials by Águila, Brochero, and Oviedo, forwarded 18 Aug. by Castel-Rodrigo to Philip; Guerra Antigua 3145 (*Rep. Nov.*, i. 361–2): Oviedo to Philip, 17 Aug.; Guerra Antigua 3144, 3145: Oviedo to Castel-Rodrigo, 16 Aug., Brochero to Philip, 16 Aug; Castel-Rodrigo to Philip, 18 Aug., with copies of three preceding letters; Guerra Antigua 3144: Castel-Rodrigo to Ibarra, 18 Aug.

2. AGS, Guerra Antigua 3144: junta to Moura, 26 Aug.

3. AGS, Guerra Antigua 3145: Zubiaur to Philip, Luarca, 15 Jan. 1602.

4. AGS, Guerra Antigua 3144: junta to Caracena, Vallid., 17 July; Guerra Antigua 587: O'Neill and O'Donnell to Philip, Sligo, 17 Aug.; Guerra Antigua 3144: junta's commission, approved and corrected by Philip, to Sandoval, 14 July; Guerra Antigua 587: Sandoval to junta, Corunna, 27 July; Caracena to Philip, Santiago, 7 July, and Corunna, 1 Oct.; O'Donnell to Philip, Sligo, 17 and 26 Aug.; O'Neill to Philip, Dungannon, 17 Aug.

this message until after the fleet had sailed. Detained by contrary winds, he did not reach Corunna until 1 October.[1]

On receiving the order of 26 August from Valladolid, the viceroy on 1 September communicated its contents to Águila, Brochero, and Oviedo. Águila protested strongly against going to the south, and in particular objected to Cork, since it was fortified. The sole concession he could win from Oviedo was that the armada might go to Kinsale (although that port had not been mentioned by O'Neill and O'Donnell) rather than to Cork. And so in this conference of 1 September the decision to land at Kinsale or Cork was arrived at, although the archbishop maintained his preference for Cork. Afterwards Oviedo gave Castel-Rodrigo, at the latter's insistence, official confirmation of this decision, for which he thus accepted responsibility.

To sum up. The position now in regard to the port of disembarkation was that Oviedo had decided that it should be Kinsale or, failing that, Cork (which port he himself would prefer). When Moura later heard from Brochero of the landing at Kinsale he expressed satisfaction that it had been made at one of the ports determined on, and the one which had been most considered.[2]

Sandoval's main mission to Ireland was to inform O'Neill and his allies of the imminence of the invasion. He also reported to O'Neill the matter of Henry's taking the Franciscan habit and of the king's command that he leave the order again. Despite what had been feared in Spain, Henry's father made no complaint about this. O'Neill was much more concerned about the appointment of Mansoni as nuncio; he maintained that this appointment had been at the instance of an Irish Jesuit who falsely represented that Mansoni was the choice of O'Neill and O'Donnell. By this Jesuit he probably meant Fr. de la Field, or possibly Fr. William Bathe.[3] Nothing could be further from the truth, said the two chiefs; their choice had always been Oviedo, who had worked so hard on behalf of Ireland and knew and loved them so well. O'Neill again asked Philip to request Oviedo's appointment as nuncio. The nuncio must be a Spaniard in order to secure that in their spiritual and temporal affairs O'Neill and O'Donnell got fair and impartial treatment.[4]

1. AGS, Guerra Antigua 587: Caracena to Philip, 1 Oct.
2. AGS, Guerra Antigua 3144: Castel-Rodrigo to Philip, 6 Nov. 1601.
3. See p. 107, *infra.*
4. AGS, Guerra Antigua 587: letters from O'Neill, Dungannon, and O'Donnell, Sligo, to Philip, 17 Aug.

On 28 August the armada for Ireland was brought down to the bar
of Lisbon at Belém. Pedro López de Soto arrived that day to take up
his duties as *veedor* (inspector) and paymaster to the troops. His post
was more or less equivalent to that of quartermaster-general. López
during twenty-five years' service in Spain, Italy, and Flanders had acted
as secretary to four captains-general. Energetic and assertive in the
discharge of his duties, López showed himself of a meddlesome, not to
say fractious, disposition and became much involved in controversy
over the conduct of the expedition.[1]

The armada set sail from Belém on Monday, 3 September 1601,
between 6 and 7 a.m., and crossed the bar at 10 a.m.[2] The number of
ships was thirty-three, of which twenty belonged to the king and
thirteen were privately owned. The number of effectives, 4,432, fell
considerably below the stipulated 6,000. They were distributed in
forty-three companies, Spanish and Italian. Besides the infantrymen
there were 1,383 others, made up of sailors, ship-boys, cabin-boys, and
artillerymen.[3] Brochero was ordered, as soon as the infantry were
landed in Ireland, to dismiss the private vessels, whether hired or embargoed, and to return with the king's ships, these latter manned
with armed sailors. The special guard of infantry he had repeatedly
requested for this return voyage could not be spared; the sailors would
have to do, and he was reminded that the enemy trusted in his
artillery and fearing to come to close quarters with the Spaniards
refused to board their ships.[4]

Fortunately Brochero was not called on to put this belief to the test.
For lack of seamen he was using all the English prisoners he could.
He had also taken men from German hookers and French ships in
Lisbon. The Frenchmen and Germans had shown a reluctance that
was likely to be shared by their princes. It was bad, felt Don Diego, to

1. AGS, Guerra Antigua 3144: Castel-Rodrigo to Esteban de Ibarra, Lisbon, 28 Aug., and
to Philip, 5 Sept.; schedules appointing López de Soto, 13 Aug.; Guerra Antigua 591: five
memorials by López, with covering letter from Don Rodrigo de Calderón to Ibarra,
Vallid., 4 Mar. Cf. *Cal. S.P. Spain, 1587–1603*, p. 646 n. 1.

2. AGS, Guerra Antigua 3144: Castel-Rodrigo to Philip, 5 Sept.: Guerra Antigua 587:
Caracena to Philip, 14 Sept.

3. Muster by Juan de la Peña Zorilla, 30 Aug. AGS, Guerra Antigua, 587: inventory by
Peña Zorilla, 1 Sept.; Peña Zorilla to Philip, 4 Sept. Juan de Pedrosso's account gave 4,464
infantry and 1,052 sailors, with some others. Guerra Antigua 3144: inventory by Pedrosso,
with letter, Castel-Rodrigo to Philip, 8 Nov. But the difference seems to be one of classifica-
tion only, and is negligible (Castel-Rodrigo gave 45 companies). Seventy men remained
behind in the hospital.

4. AGS, Guerra Antigua 3145: Brochero to junta, 18 July; Guerra Antigua 3144: junta to
Brochero, Vallid., 31 July.

have to be more wary of one's own seamen than of the enemy. But Brochero had nothing but praise for the service given by the Germans.[1]

Velasco, the constable of Castile,[2] had thought that an army of 6,000 men was only half the size required for the invasion of Ireland, since too many troops would be needed to garrison whatever places were taken so that the others could be operational. The king had to agree with him, but accepted the view of the rest of the council that the overriding consideration was to make the Irish retain confidence in Spain; and so he agreed to the departure of the armada as it stood. He promised the constable that reinforcements would be sent in fast vessels to supplement these. But since the number of effectives fell so far below the expected 6,000, where were the reinforcements to come from?[3]

Centeno commanded one of the two *tercios* into which the infantry were divided; the other went without its *maestre de campo*, for Don Francisco de Padilla lay ill at Estremoz. The thirty companies of recruits had been re-formed into sixteen, to save money on 'dead' places. Diego Ruiz de Salazar, paymaster of the expedition, carried with him a sum of 164,681 escudos, in contemporary values some £45,000. This was the famous 'treasure' carried by Águila, which increased so much in the telling. Reports put it anywhere between 500,000 and 8,000,000 ducats.[4] Juan de Pedrosso had put on board 13,000 quintals of biscuits, so he said, 7,000 for 7,000 men for the journey, and 6,000 for 6,000 men disembarking in Ireland.[5] Of the food López complained that there had been such deception in the provisioning of the armada with victuals for its two months in Lisbon that only the biscuit lasted for that time, and not in all the ships either.

1. AGS, Guerra Antigua 3145: Brochero to Philip, 7 and 17 Nov.

2. The constable of Castile was captain-general of the land armies, the equivalent of the admiral-general at sea. Under Ferdinand and Isabella the title became honorary. Juan Fernández de Velasco was constable from 1585, was a grandee of Spain, and was governor of Milan at different periods. He was made president of the council of Italy and belonged to the councils of state and war.

3. AGS, Estado 840, f. 276; Estado 961 and 2511: council of state on expedition, 4 Aug. 1601, with Philip's holograph. Estado 187: Lerma to Esteban de Ibarra, Vallid., 8 Aug.

4. AGS, Guerra Antigua 3144: Peña Zorilla to Philip, 4 Sept.; Castel-Rodrigo to Philip, 5 Sept. In contemporary values the escudo stood at 5s. 6d. (Loomie, *Spanish Elizabethans*, p. 240 n. 1), the ducat at about 6s. 3d. In a report that 2,000 marks had been set (by Mountjoy; cf. Bagwell, *Tudors*, iii. 372) on O'Neill's head dead and £2,000 alive, a marginal note gives the value of 2,000 marks as 5,333 ducats and some pesetas over (AGS, Estado 620: news from London, 29 Feb. 1602, old style).

5. AGS, Guerra Antigua 3144: account by Pedrosso, sent with letter, Castel-Rodrigo to Philip, 8 Nov.

The meat had ended at the first month or before, the cheese also; the wine had been put on half-ration and even that had been cut after a month. Águila had had only one pipe of wine from Pedrosso to take with him.

While Brochero complained of the shortage of seamen (many had fled) and of food, Águila wrote as his galleon the San Andrés was already leaving the gulf to complain that he was short in everything, money, clothes, munitions, men, and food. Practically all his men were naked and barefoot too.[1] The 600 suits made in Lisbon, added López, were little good for 4,500 men. (By Pedrosso's account, the most naked of the men from Terceira had 1,100 suits divided among them and 300 other suits were taken for the most needy men in Ireland.)[2]

Supplies on board for the army included six battery pieces, 600 quintals of powder, 600 of match, and 300 of lead, with spare armour, saddles, bridles, and a large number of swords and lances for the Irish, picks, shovels, spades, and so on. That the army went short-supplied there can be no doubt, but López perhaps exaggerates short-comings. For instance, he declared that Águila had with him only a hundred pine boards from Flanders for building fortifications; whereas the official account gave 1,500.[3]

Aboard the flagship San Andrés were Brochero and Águila, with Archbishop Oviedo and the bishop of Clonfert. The bishop of Killaloe did not arrive in time to sail, and Cerdá in the moist Portuguese air had contracted malaria, a 'double tertian', a few days before and so was unable to travel on the expedition he had worked so long to foster.[4] The admiral vessel San Felipe, a galleon of 960 tons, carried Zubiaur, López de Soto, Centeno, and Sebastián de Oleaga, paymaster and inspector-general of the fleet. Father Archer went as Águila's chaplain. The Jesuit had selected Brother Dominic Collins, S.J., as a companion. There were also a Dominican friar and many other Spanish friars and priests, as well as nuns and other women. Richard Owen was with the expedition, as were Captains Raymond Lavin,

1. AGS, Guerra Antigua 3145: Brochero to Philip, 2 Sept.; Guerra Antigua 587: Águila to Philip, 3 Sept. Cf. Guerra Antigua 3144: junta to corregidores and officials of Guipúzcoa, Biscay, and Quatro Villas on the seamen who had run away.
2. AGS, Guerra Antigua 3144: López to Philip, El Ferrol, 26 Oct., and Corunna, 11 Nov.
3. AGS, Estado 840, f. 157 (Cal. S.P. Spain, 1587–1603, p. 692).
4. Cerdá was able to write after about ten days, after he had been blooded six times. He had been advised to take the Castile air, and sought leave to go there. He also sought back pay and office somewhere. AGS, Guerra Antigua 587: Cerdá to Philip and to E. de Ibarra, 14 Sept.

Andrew Butler, Darby or Dermot MacCarthy, Cormac MacFinnin MacCarthy, Maurice Fitzgerald, Walter Lea of Waterford, married in Spain, and a number of other Irishmen and Englishmen. Lambert Gould, said English reports, was chief pilot and among the other pilots was Captain Upton.[1]

Father Mansoni was not with the expedition. He did not leave Rome until the autumn, and reached Valladolid only in December; Father William Bathe, S.J., who belonged to the county Dublin gentry, travelled with him. The nuncio was still in Valladolid, having failed to get shipping for Ireland, in August 1603. He was then preparing to return to Rome. O'Neill did not want him in Ireland, and the rout at Kinsale and return of the Spaniards put paid to any last hopes he had of going there.[2]

One who was glad to see the expedition leave was the viceroy, the marquis of Castel-Rodrigo. Don Cristóbal unburdened his feelings on Águila and Brochero in a frank letter to Secretary Ibarra. What an amount of work it had been, he said, to send off that armada under two different heads, two men besides so opposite in their humours. One wanted to go to the north, the other to the south, while both, alleged Moura, rested as much as they could. And yet there was no end to the demands they made.

Never, the viceroy urged Ibarra, never advise the king to divide a command so equally between two leaders, neither of whom had any respect for the other. Castel-Rodrigo hoped that a certain soldier's gloomy prognostication would not be realized. This soldier had said that four 'good' things lay in front of his comrades and himself— *buenas quatro cosas llevamos*—winter, Ireland, Centeno, and Pedro López de Soto.[3]

1. AGS, Guerra Antigua 587: Caracena to Philip, with memorial by López, 24 Apr. 1601; Hogan, *Distinguished Irishmen*, pp. 91, 339, *Pac. Hib.*, ii. 67; *Cal. S.P. Ire.*, 1601-3, pp. 85, 87, 129; MacCarthy (Glas), *Florence MacCarthy*, p. 347.
2. *Archiv. Hib.*, xvii. 36-9; Hogan, *Distinguished Irishmen*, p. 379.
3. AGS, Guerra Antigua 3144: Castel-Rodrigo to Ibarra, 5 Sept. He had originally written Don Juan del Águila's name before that of Centeno, but stroked it out, substituting López's name.

VIII · LANDFALL

El invierno, que haze largas y mal siguras las cossas de la mar . . .
Secretary Ibarra, 22 December 1601

WITH WHATEVER FOREBODING the rank and file might regard their
future, at first all seemed to go well. The little armada went off with
a fair wind, and a week out from Lisbon stood thirty leagues from
Ireland. Now a further and final consultation took place on where it
should land. It was on Brochero's initiative that this staff-meeting
took place, and taking part in it on board the flagship *San Andrés* were
Brochero himself, Águila, Archbishop Oviedo, General Zubiaur, and
López de Soto. The conference got off to a bad start, the regimental
commander Centeno refusing to attend. Águila and he were on bad
terms, for Centeno, spurning recruits, had against Don Juan's wishes
taken with him only veterans in his galleon, the *San Felipe*.

Brochero had excuse for calling the conference. The chance of en-
countering Sandoval had enabled Águila to maintain a stubborn
opposition to Kinsale or Cork, but now that chance was certainly gone.
An added reason for Brochero's wishing to have the thorny question
of disembarkation settled once and for all was most likely the fact that
the fleet was running into foul weather; for it took another three
weeks for it to reach the Irish coast. 'The winds', says *Pacata Hibernia*
at 27 September, 'were *still* contrary (to ships coming from Spain) and
the weather very stormy and tempestuous.' Oviedo spoke of the storms,
malos temporales y tempestas, which kept the armada so long at sea on
the way.[1]

Some master pilots and men familiar with the Irish coast were
called to attend the meeting. Águila again voiced his preference for

---

1. *Pac. Hib.*, i. 275. Italics present writer's; cf. *Rep. Nov.*, i (1956), 365. Dermot MacCarthy
gave as a reason for the conference that the Spaniards had heard of the apprehension
of the sugan earl and Florence MacCarthy. But they did not apparently learn of this until
after arrival in Kinsale. Cf. *Cal. S.P. Ire., 1601–3*, pp. 160, 84; *Pac. Hib.*, i. 290.

sailing to the north, but Oviedo, although none too clear-headed from sickness, insisted that the landing must be in the south, and gained the majority decision in his favour. By agreement of the meeting Brochero therefore gave an order in writing to each ship's captain that the vessels if separated should rendezvous at Kinsale, or if that were impossible at Castlehaven.

Another issue which apparently came up at this meeting was the desire expressed by some that Brochero should remain with his ships to support the land army. Don Diego, however, pleaded that he was ordered, once he had disembarked the army, to send the embargoed vessels away and return home with the king's ships. The order could not be gainsaid, but Oviedo could see that it satisfied nobody. He therefore offered his plate and all that he had or might be possessed of to pay the sailors. Zubiaur, not to be outdone, supported him with an offer of his salary; but Brochero would not disobey orders—publicly at any rate. In private he said in Oviedo's hearing that he wished that Águila would force him to stay. The archbishop during the voyage sought the captains' opinion on the question. Some of them suggested that Águila could easily prevent Brochero from returning so soon by not disembarking the men and munitions.[1]

The belief is persistent that Brochero's real intention was to land at Limerick or Galway. But this belief rests merely on reports received by Sir Geoffrey Fenton and corroborated by one Andrew Lynch, a Galway merchant, that such was the intention of the armada. Lynch had had his information, he said, from one of Brochero's pilots. Very likely the Spanish command allowed this story to circulate among the fleet in order to throw possible spies off the scent. This counter-intelligence device, reminiscent of Operation Overlord of 1944, was a common ruse then as now.[2]

Still Águila would not accept defeat. He talked to Brochero and got him to accompany him to Oviedo's sick-bed to try to persuade the archbishop to go to the north. In spite of his sickness the archbishop would not give way, and his only answer was that he had nothing to add to what he had said in Belém. Much nettled, Don Juan rose to his feet and, saying that that would be the last dispute, left him alone.[3]

1. AGS, Guerra Antigua 3144: Oviedo's answers to D. de Ibarra, 6 Aug. 1602.
2. Oviedo's answers, cit.; AGS, Guerra Antigua 590: Brochero to E. de Ibarra, Lisbon, 14 Apr. 1602; *Cal. S.P. Ire.*, 1601–3, p. 122: Fenton to Cecil, Dublin, 12 Oct. 1601, old style, and p. 129: testimony of Lynch. Cf. Dulles, *Craft of intelligence*, p. 146.
3. Oviedo's answers, cit.

The fleet sailed on until on the evening of 27 September it reached the Irish coast. Between the Blaskets and Dursey Island it took on pilots preparatory to landing in the morning. That night, however, a storm struck, driving away two galleons and six accompanying craft from the main fleet and upsetting Águila's plans. The mistake of sending great galleons, especially without Irish pilots, on such an expedition, rather than small vessels, was now all too apparent. Brochero asked Águila what was to be done. Don Juan replied that if they could make one of the ports they had determined on with even one ship, he would disembark. Brochero then managed to make Kinsale, where Águila disembarked on 2 October. With his much-diminished force of 1,700 men in twenty-five companies he took possession of the town, allowing the garrison to depart to Cork. Don Juan, still against Oviedo's judgement, had deliberately avoided Cork.

Of the ships driven away by the storm Zubiaur's galleon *San Felipe* with three hookers spent the next five days in a vain attempt to renew contact with the other ships or alternatively to make Kinsale or Castlehaven. A south wind was now blowing, and Zubiaur resolved to make for Teelin. On his first attempt he reached lat. 53°N. before the wind turned him back. When the wind shifted to the south again he tried a second time for Teelin, only eventually to be driven far to the south. He therefore sailed for home and came in to El Ferrol. With Zubiaur were López de Soto, Centeno, and Oleaga, as well as the infantry captains Castellanos, Arbe, and Barragán. The four ships carried between them eight infantry companies, 674 men in all. To add to the misfortune they carried most of the munitions and match for the arquebuses, which left Águila very short.

With the men from the galleon *San Pedro* and the hooker *León Dorado*, both of which also had been separated from the main fleet by the storm but managed eventually to make Kinsale, Águila had by 9 October a force of 3,300 or 3,400 men at his command.[1]

Little as it was, here was a Spanish army in Ireland. Would Munster rise? Surprisingly it was Águila himself whose action prevented this from happening, when he rejected an offer made on behalf of his

1. AGS, Guerra Antigua 3145: Brochero to Philip, Cascaes, 6 Nov.; Guerra Antigua 3144: Águila to Philip, Kinsale, 8 Oct.; López to same, from *San Felipe*, Ferrol, 22 Oct.; and to Caracena, 22 Oct.; account (by López) of adventures of *San Felipe* (22 Oct.); Guerra Antigua 3143 and 3145 (*Epistolario de Zubiaur*, pp. 70–2): Zubiaur to Caracena, three letters, from *San Felipe*, 22 and 23 Oct.; Guerra Antigua 3145 (*Rep. Nov.*, i. 362–3): Oviedo to Philip, Kinsale, 6 Oct.; Guerra Antigua 589: Oviedo to Philip, 1 Aug.; Guerra Antigua 3144: report by Albornoz. Cf. *Pac. Hib.*, i. 274–85; O'Sullivan, *Kinsale*, pp. 193–6.

fellow chiefs and himself by Daniel O'Sullivan Beare, who ruled the
peninsula between the Kenmare river and Bantry Bay. O'Sullivan
offered to provide two thousand men, a thousand armed and another
thousand to be armed by Águila, in order to block Mountjoy's road
and prevent a siege until the arrival of the northern armies. In excuse
for Águila it can be said that he was extremely disappointed to learn[1]
that Florence MacCarthy and James Fitzthomas had been committed
to the Tower. One of the chief reasons for landing in Munster had been
the expectation that these two would second the Spaniards. Once
Águila had secured his base, he would, reinforced by the troops of
Florence and Desmond, have taken the field with both infantry and
cavalry, the latter on mounts supplied by his Irish allies. His hopes
were shattered; these allies and any others who were well-affected to
Spain had been taken prisoner, and he had excuse for suspecting of
proven loyalty to the government those who now came to offer
service. He would wait until he had assurance from O'Neill and
O'Donnell before trusting them. It was a fateful decision, for as later
events were to show there were still, in spite of O'Sullivan's record of
loyalty hitherto and in spite of Carew's precautionary ruthlessness,
the embers of revolt left in Munster.[2]

Out of the province then 'nobody worth a garron'[3] but only a few
followers of Florence MacCarthy came in to Águila. Ruling the local
Irish out of his reckoning and commanding such a small, poorly
armed, and poorly provisioned force, without *maestres de campo*, Don
Juan dismissed the notion of taking the field and decided to fortify
himself as best he could until he was reinforced by the armies of
Ulster and by Spain.

The harbour of Kinsale runs straight from the entrance in a nor-
therly direction for about a mile and a half before turning sharply
westwards to where the river Bandon meets the sea. The town, built
on the northern side of this bend, lay almost on an island, as its whole
eastern side was bounded by the sea, which was almost connected
with Ballinacurra Creek; this creek in turn ran from the Bandon
along the town's west and north sides.

Parallel to Kinsale harbour on the east, separated from it by a

1. *Cal. S.P. Ire.*, 1601–3, p. 84.
2. AGS, Guerra Antigua 3144: memorial by López de Soto, 22 Dec.; O'Sullivan Beare,
Hist. Cath. Ibern. comp., p. 224; Butler, *Gleanings from Irish history*, pp. 31–8.
3. *Cal. S.P. Ire.*, 1601–3, p. 119.

promontory a mile or more wide, and extending to cut off the approach further to the north runs Oyster Haven. North again from Oyster Haven but less than a mile from the town is Knockrobin Hill (268 ft.); south-west of Knockrobin and due north of the town is Camphill or Spital Hill (also 268 ft.). West again of these are two other hills, Ballinacubby and Kippagh. The terrain to the eyes of the Spaniards was very rough, uninhabited land, with great marches and rivers, most of them without bridges, so that (they saw) to besiege any place ordnance must be brought by sea.[1]

Rincorran Castle stood on the east bank of the harbour, about a mile from the entrance. It commanded the harbour in two directions, both southwards towards the entrance and westwards towards the town. This castle Águila garrisoned. On a little promontory half a mile across the bay from the town and just where the harbour turned from northward to westward stood another castle, Castle-ny-Parke or Castle Park, which commanded the town and its anchorage. Águila put another garrison here.

Don Juan lost no time in advising O'Neill and O'Donnell of his arrival, but by 10 October he had had as yet no answer to several appeals sent to them to come and join him. He already feared that they would not get through the barrier of fortresses erected to the south of their mountain fastnesses. The news of the Spaniard's coming spread quickly, and Hugh O'Neill soon knew of it, but he shared Águila's fear. He could not understand why Águila, seeing he had not sufficient forces to take the field, would not remove to Killybegs, Sligo, or even Galway, where he himself might join him.[2]

But as Águila looked northwards to the four hills that dominated the town, he felt himself trapped in a pit, *un hoyo*. Mountjoy told the council that Kinsale had 'a good wall, and many strong castles in it', but to Don Juan it was merely a slate wall, a bare two and a half feet wide, without moat or traverse, and he felt his situation to be more vulnerable than in the open field. Mountjoy later conceded that the town was weak against cannon, but maintained that it was impossible to place artillery anywhere but that the Spaniards commanded it. This invites the comment that if they did, it was with shot from the

---

1. AGS, Guerra Antigua 3144: report by Sandoval, Mar. 1602.
2. AGS, Estado 620: news from London, 20 Dec. 1601, old style; Guerra Antigua 3143: O'Neill to Águila, 12 Oct.: copy sent by Águila to Philip, with letter of 31 Oct.

castles more than with guns; Águila made good use of what artillery he had retained, but it was light.[1]

Don Juan rejected the notion of removing to a better port. Cork he had ruled out, and he feared that if he set about removing, the enemy would have time to prepare for his disembarking elsewhere, for example, at Castlehaven. He was afraid too to take the risk of having the ships scattered once more by putting to sea along this gale-tossed coast. He had had to send pilots to Baltimore to bring to Kinsale the *León Dorado*, which carried the companies of Captains Pedro Henríquez de Tejada and Francisco de Piños.[2]

On 9 October Brochero, accompanied apparently by Captain Albornoz, who was sent by Águila to report to Philip, left Kinsale with the royal ships. The admiral left behind 5,000 quintals of biscuit, still being unloaded from the hookers, while the *León Dorado* had brought another 600. This was deficient provisioning in Águila's reckoning. Brochero's withdrawal, as Águila complained, exposed the disembarkation to fire from the enemy, who were able to come into the mouth of the harbour and gain control there. The Spaniards had lost access to Kinsale by sea, and would therefore find the defence of the town so much more difficult.

But in view of the antipathy between them, Águila refused to take the responsibility of countermanding Don Diego's orders to sail, and the latter was adamant that he must go. He had now food aboard for his sailors for only twenty-one days, which would certainly not see him through winter and was dangerously little for the return voyage in the weather at this time of year. He mistrusted his foreign sailors pressed for service from ships in Lisbon. Don Juan charged that Brochero had thrown the food so carelessly on the shore that most of it was broken in pieces and was damp. The munitions too disembarked by Brochero on the shore or even in the sea were not, he complained, nearly enough.

To all this Don Diego retorted that the foreign sailors were fleeing and that he had had to put a Spanish guard over each to stop them. His ships were anchored half a league from the town, but he had taken everything to the town in boats. Águila, he pointed out, was in

1. AGS, Guerra Antigua 3144: Águila's report to Philip, 8 Oct. and (*Pac. Hib.*, i. 280–5) report by Albornoz; Moryson, *Itinerary*, iii. 25, 35: Mountjoy to English Council, 17 Nov. and to Cecil, 23 Nov.

2. AGS, Guerra Antigua 3144: Águila to Philip, Kinsale, 31 Oct.; *consulta*, 12 July 1603; Guerra Antigua 3145: Brochero to Philip, Lisbon, 17 Nov.

8

Kinsale with all his men, with control over the town and its citizens. Why then did he not take the food from the boats and put it under cover and take the artillery and other stores to their proper place?

As to control of the harbour, Brochero maintained that Don Juan could secure control by taking artillery off the ships to fortify Castle Park. Don Diego offered him as much artillery as he wanted for fortifying it. Águila agreed that by fortifying Castle Park he could keep the entrance open for ships from Spain and make himself secure in the town. He knew that Castle Park was the key to Kinsale. But the castle was too weak as it stood, and he would need to build a proper fort there, enclosed within a strong four-walled stockade, where he could mount artillery. For that he needed lime, and to man the fort he needed more men than he could spare from the defence of Kinsale and of his uncovered munitions. For the want of men and materials too he was unable to throw up fortifications on the landward side of Kinsale. Besides, he had no horse for moving heavy artillery about, and he needed in any case to spare his meagre supply of powder for the muskets and arquebuses. So although Brochero made repeated offers of artillery to him, and was joined in his pleas by Oviedo and the other ecclesiastics, Águila yielded to their importunities sufficiently to disembark only two field-pieces and two demi-cannon; the rest of the artillery he returned with Brochero. The two leaders could not agree on anything and Brochero made all haste to depart. The next day, 10 October, the hookers (all but the *León Dorado*, which left Kinsale on 30 October) sailed too, and Águila was left to cope as best he might with the Irish winter and the English enemy.[1]

He still had hopes of help from Spain and asked for men and materials to fortify Castle Park. He wanted also (he wrote) to build a fort at the entrance to Cork harbour, so as to starve Cork into surrender. Kinsale and Cork, he reckoned, would be bases for an invasion of England when large reinforcements came from Spain.

Cavalry were perhaps Águila's greatest lack. The enemy were collecting all the cattle and corn round about and breaking the mills, and with their cavalry were coming daily up to the walls of Kinsale. Don Juan had his men sally out time and time again against them, but to little effect. He was worried by the fear of cavalry reinforce-

---

1. AGS, Guerra Antigua 590: Brochero to E. de Ibarra, Lisbon, 14 Apr. 1602; Guerra Antigua 3145: Brochero to Philip, Lisbon, 17 Nov. 1601; Guerra Antigua 3144: Águila to Philip, 8 and 31 Oct.

ments coming to the enemy from England. He soon found that Irish cavalry were of poor quality and would be of no use to him. Irish cavalrymen, who rode without stirrups, held their spears by the centre over the shoulder—fought, as Águila said, 'with half-pikes'; their hobbies were very light and they could not meet the English in equal combat. But Don Juan's experienced eye soon saw what in fact O'Neill had already demonstrated in combat, that the native Irish with training would make good infantrymen. Husbanding his treasure rather too well (he was preoccupied with the need to supplement his men's rations of dry tack with meat bought from the Irish), he sought more money from home in order to buy Irish soldiers over from the queen. But he needed reinforcements from Spain too, and they should come, he desired, in ships able to do battle with those that Elizabeth was preparing.[1]

The Spanish force was, in fact, too small unless reinforced and it had come none too early if the rebellion were to be saved from collapse. It had taken Mountjoy and Carew less than two years to break the rebellion in Munster, where Carew's campaign had been especially efficient, and in Leinster. Mountjoy hoped by a third expedition into Ulster before the end of 1601 finally to stamp out the revolt in its last stronghold.

By March 1601 Carew was master of Munster and was able to send troops into Connacht. The 'sugan' earl and Florence MacCarthy were both taken and were sent to England on 24 August 1601 to be committed to the Tower. Just as the lord deputy established garrisons in Leinster to keep the O'Mores, O'Conors, and O'Byrnes subdued, so did Carew maintain his grip on Munster by putting garrisons in a number of castles south of the Shannon. Sir George concentrated his forces at the towns of Cork and Limerick, since he expected the Spaniards to land at one or other of these ports. Here too he gathered in provisions and tools for siege-work. If the Spaniards had landed anywhere else Carew did not know how the English army could have been provided until the following summer 'with victuals and carriage to lodge by them'.[2]

In Ulster the way was prepared for the final onslaught. From Lifford, Niall Garbh, Docwra's ally, had gone to seize Donegal abbey and

1. AGS, Guerra Antigua 3144: Águila to Philip, 8 and 13 Oct.; Guerra Antigua 3145: Brochero to Philip, Cascaes, 6 Nov.; Guerra Antigua 589: Águila to Philip, Avila, 25 July 1602; Guerra Antigua 587: Bertendona to Philip, 6 Nov.
2. Cal. S.P. Ire., 1601–3, pp. 118–19, 120.

maintained it against Red Hugh's siege. South of the Ulster line of defences, which ran from the river Erne to Loch Neagh, Mountjoy had a chain of garrisons running all the way from Boyle abbey in north Connacht, through Brefni and south Monaghan, where he had conquered the barony of Farney, to Lecale. Docwra's total of effectives was reduced to 1,675, but at Carrickfergus Chichester commanded a force of 850 foot and 150 horse; while in the garrisons between Dundalk and the Blackwater Mountjoy had 800 foot and 100 horse. In Lecale he had 150 foot, in the Pale and adjoining parts 3,150 infantry and 175 horse, and in Connacht 1,150 foot and 62 horse.[1]

With these bases in Connacht, the north midlands, the Pale, and Ulster ready for concerted action, the lord deputy was now prepared to launch a final offensive on Ulster. But as rumours of the intended Spanish invasion gathered force Mountjoy, in September, went south to Kilkenny, leaving the garrisons behind. He was thus prepared for the alternatives of combining with Carew against the Spaniards, should they come, or of fighting another winter campaign against the enemy.[2]

At news of the Spaniards' arrival Mountjoy gave orders for the bringing of troops from the Pale, the northern garrisons, and Connacht to Cork and went there himself, arriving on 7 October. Carew could guarantee him supplies of victuals for two or three months and had also a good supply of munitions in stock. The lord president had arrested all the lords he mistrusted and taken pledges from the others; thus the leading men of the province remained loyal from the coming of Águila until those of the south-west defected with the arrival of Zubiaur at Castlehaven in December.[3]

Mountjoy sought by burning and proclamation to deprive the Spaniards of corn and cattle. Lack of ordnance and rainy conditions delayed his taking the field, but on 10 October he sent out from Cork a strong force, reckoned by the Spaniards at 1,000 foot and 500 horse, to test the Spaniards' strength. Águila, with loss to himself of fifteen or twenty men, beat them off.[4] By 26 October the lord deputy was able to leave Cork, and that night he encamped at a point five miles from Kinsale. He now had under his command a force of about 6,800

1. *Cal. S.P. Ire.*, 1601–3, p. 27; *Pac. Hib.*, i. 231–2; Moryson, *Itinerary*, iii. 11–13; Falls, *Mountjoy*, pp. 160, 162; E. M. Jones, 'The Spaniards and Kinsale 1601', in *Galway Arch. Soc. Jn.*, xxi (1944).

2. Hayes-McCoy, 'Strategy and tactics', in *I.H.S.*, iii. 269; Moryson, *Itinerary*, ii. 445.

3. *Cal. Carew MSS.* 1601–3, p. 179; *Pac. Hib.*, i. 286–9; Moryson, *Itinerary*, ii. 451–3, 464; iii. 13.

4. AGS, Guerra Antigua 3144: Águila to Philip, Kinsale, 31 Oct.; Guerra Antigua 3145: Brochero to same, Lisbon, 2 Nov. (*recte* Dec.).

foot and 611 horse in list; these included[1] the men he intended for dispatch to the Limerick border in order to hold that country. Of the 4,000 men Cecil had earlier earmarked for Ireland, 2,000 had already arrived there; the other 2,000 would follow, together with ten ships of war. Yet a further 2,000 men would be sent at the end of October.[2]

In Spain meanwhile, the king, on receiving news of Águila's departure, made arrangements to send him 5,000 quintals of biscuit and to raise ten companies of infantry as reinforcements—measures which did not nearly approach in scale those being taken by Cecil.[3]

Before he left Cork the lord deputy issued a proclamation in which he maintained that the Irish had no cause to take up arms against their lawful sovereign and that the war was unjustly maintained by the pope and the king of Spain. This drew a quick response from Águila, a counter-proclamation which bore the stamp of Oviedo's authorship and in which Don Juan justified his invasion altogether on grounds of religion. These grounds were the excommunication of Elizabeth and the appeal by the Catholic Irish to the pope and the king of Spain for help against the English, who were treating them cruelly. Águila then called on the Irish Catholics, telling them that the pope ordered them to take up arms for the defence of the faith: *summusque pontifex . . . vobis imperat ut arma in defensionem fidei vestrae sumatis.*[4]

Águila's claim answered the demands of propaganda rather than of truth. Pope Clement VIII, who had removed the Papacy from dependence on Spanish might, had given Águila no order for the Irish Catholics to rise. The fruit of Clement's diplomacy was the reconciliation with the Church of Henry IV in 1593 (he was solemnly absolved on 17 September 1595), a reconciliation that paved the way towards the effecting of peace between the two Catholic powers in 1598. Relations now between Rome and Madrid might be somewhat strained,[5] but this was an inconvenience that Clement's well-directed policy could afford.

1. Falls, *Elizabeth's Irish wars*, p. 295, appears to be inaccurate here.
2. *Pac. Hib.*, i. 290–1, 293, 294; *Cal. Carew MSS. 1601–3*, pp. 179, 180; Moryson, *Itinerary*, ii. 464–6, 457–8; ii. 1–15, 41; O'Sullivan, *Kinsale*, pp. 42–3; Falls, *Mountjoy*, pp. 166–7.
3. AGS, Guerra Antigua 3144: junta to Águila, to Moura, and to Juan de Pedrosso, Vallid., 3 Oct.; Águila to Philip, 13 Oct. (The answer to this letter, dated 4 Dec., was never received by Águila. Cf. *Pac. Hib.*, ii. 103.)
4. AGS, Estado 1570; VA, Borghese, ser. III, vol. 65C, f. 12 (*Archiv. Hib.*, iii (1914), 244–5). There are other copies in BM Add. MS 5847 (Cole Papers), pp. 316–17, and elsewhere (cf. NLI, *Report of the council of trustees, 1951–2*, pp. 48, 83, 94). The proclamation is dated 31 Oct. (Cole Papers).
5. Cf. Ranke, *History of the popes*, ii. 44, 104–14; Hinojosa, *Los despachos*, pp. 348, 355–6.

The pope therefore appointed Father Mansoni, an Italian Jesuit, as his legate *a latere* to Ireland, instead of the Spanish Franciscan desired by O'Neill. Clement refused to proclaim a religious war in Ireland, to enfeoff Ireland under the Spanish crown, or to excommunicate the Catholics who refused to support Hugh. When Águila sailed Mansoni was not even with him.[1] Small wonder then that the nuncios, Buffalo in Paris and Frangipani (whose distrust of O'Neill's motives has already been noted), were horrified at Águila's indiscretion. Frangipani forecast serious danger to Catholic interests in England and Flanders, while Buffalo recorded the displeasure of the king of France, who was 'grieved that his holiness has placed more confidence in the king of Spain than in him'.[2]

But there is another side to the picture. Although it is true that the pope did not make support for Águila a matter of conscience for Irish Catholics, Clement did not deny all support to O'Neill and to the invasion. He did recognize O'Neill as captain-general of the Catholic army in Ireland and did grant the chief's supporters the crusade indulgence. Clement had gone as far as he could to meet O'Neill's and Philip's wishes in the appointment of a nuncio. The pope could not and would not decide against the loyalist Catholics, but he had appointed a legate to Ireland. The appointments of Oviedo to Dublin and Lombard to Armagh (he was provided on 9 July 1601) must also be considered in the general reckoning. The truth is simply that Clement VIII, in line with his general policy did not wish to pronounce between conflicting Catholic interests; he sought to reconcile them as far as possible and to maintain his influence over both.

Águila's proclamation, the Bulls of indulgence, and even a threat of excommunication against recalcitrants from the bishop of Cork, all broadcast wholesale in Munster, failed to arouse the province.[3] One reason was that the priests of Munster were preaching, as Oviedo found to his distress, that the Irish should take up arms against the Spaniards and their Irish allies. Oviedo had some discussions with these priests on the matter, but they refused to give up their position until

1. F. M. Jones, 'The Spaniards and Kinsale 1601', in *Galway Arch. Soc. Jn.*, xxi (1944), 20; 'Pope Clement VIII (1592–1605) and Hugh O'Neill', in *I.C.H.S. Bull.*, no. 73 (1953); *Mountjoy*, p. 122.

2. VA, Borghese, ser. III, vol. 65C, p. 11 (*Archiv. Hib.*, iii (1914), 246 and xxiv (1961), 63): Buffalo to cardinal secretary of state, 25 Jan. 1602.

3. *Cal. Carew MSS, 1589–1600*, p. 523: Bull of indulgence, 18 Apr. 1600; *Archiv. Hib.*, iii. 244; *Pac. Hib.*, i. 295–8; AGS, Guerra Antigua 3145 (*Epistolario de Zubiaur*, p. 94): Zubiaur to Philip, 29 (? 22) Dec.

the Holy See deprived loyal Catholics of the sacraments and excommunicated them.[1]

Don Juan was therefore left to his own resources, which were poor. Unable to erect proper fortifications to guard sea or land approaches, he garrisoned Rincorran and Castle Park so as to impede as far as possible the approach of English shipping to Kinsale, and entrenched his outposts at Camphill, so as to command to some extent land access to the town. The lord deputy's tactical answer to both measures was swift and effective. Without as yet tools for entrenching, so that his men had to lie in the open, he encamped on 27 October at the foot of Knockrobin Hill, near the present village of Brownsmills and at the head of Oyster Haven. This useful inlet, as well as protecting Mountjoy's left flank and rear, gave him a waterway up which supplies landed by ship could be ferried to the very camp at high tide and thus bypass Kinsale. At the same time he could to some extent prevent the approach by land of victuals to the Spaniards. Don Juan saw the danger, but in ten days' skirmishing failed to drive the English back from Knockrobin.

He saw little to comfort him as at the end of a month in Ireland he took stock of his position. He was badly outnumbered, with only 2,500 effectives now, who were pitifully inexperienced and shivered in their thin clothes in the raw late-autumn Irish weather. Don Juan wished that money and reinforcements would come; if only they did, many of the Irish would join him. Yet knowing this he continued to spare his own money. When he came back to Spain he still had 59,000 ducats with him. His niggardly policy is as hard to justify as it is to explain.

For food Águila's men had only a little rotten biscuit and water. Every day more of the poor wretches were falling ill because of so little to eat and so much to do; the remainder were harried by the enemy's continuous attacks and were called to guard duty so much that the arms never left their hands. No wonder some deserted. Don Juan had another worry, for supplies of fuse for the arquebuses were running critically short.[2]

His main problem however was that he was separated from O'Neill by the length of Ireland. Six or seven weeks previously O'Neill had been warning Ensign Sandoval that on no account must the Spanish army land south of Limerick. With Florence MacCarthy and James

1. AGS, Guerra Antigua 591: memorandum by Oviedo, with letter to Ibarra, 31 Mar.
2. AGS, Guerra Antigua 3144: Águila to Philip, Kinsale, 31 Oct.

Fitzthomas both in the Tower, and with Carew's grip on Munster firm, the invaders would have no support in the south. O'Neill had indirect news of the Spanish landing within a week or so of Águila's coming. By the time, a few days later, that Danvers began to draw off the northern garrisons Hugh was well aware that Águila's army was too small to take the field in Munster. He waited for Don Juan to take to sea again and come north to Sligo or Killybegs. He did not know of Águila's objections to removing from Kinsale. Don Juan at the end of October received Hugh's message asking him to come to the north. This merely confirmed him in his belief that he should have gone to Donegal Bay in the first place. He became even more embittered against Archbishop Oviedo and Cerdá, and took out his spite on them by accusing them of following their own ends in insisting that the armada should go to the south.[1]

The rancour between Oviedo and Águila was unfortunate, as was the lack of confidence between Don Juan and his captains. These officers were aggrieved that Águila did not appoint colonels or majors from among them, or appoint a council of captains to advise him. The archbishop became a centre of disaffection, around whom formed a group of disgruntled captains, who blamed Águila for not fortifying himself properly to landward or seaward, for not purchasing mounts from the Irish, and for not buying the services of the Irish themselves.

Away in the north, with the garrisons from Armagh, Blackwater, and the Newry out of the way, O'Neill was engaged from 10 October in daily incursions into Monaghan, the Fews, Brefni, and the Pale. He had two objects in this: he wanted, firstly, to win back the border lords who had submitted, Ever MacCooley MacMahon of the Farney, Tirlagh MacHenry of the Fews, MacMahon, Maginess, Sir Oghy O'Hanlon, and O'Reilly; and secondly, he wished by devastating Louth to force Mountjoy to draw back to the defence of the Pale.

To O'Neill's consternation, however, it gradually began to appear that Águila was tamely allowing himself to be besieged in Kinsale and that Mountjoy was not going to give up the siege. The privy council in Dublin called in vain upon the lord deputy to come to the aid of the harassed Pale gentry like Sir Edward Moore and the bishop of Meath; the lord deputy was not to be turned aside from the real task of the moment, which was to eject the Spaniards from Ireland.

1. AGS, Guerra Antigua 3144: O'Neill to Águila, 12 Oct.; copy sent with letter, Águila to Philip, 31 Oct.

O'Neill was thus in a dilemma. O'Donnell was summoning his Tyrconnell and Connacht levies to rendezvous at Ballymote. But O'Neill's newly won border allies pointed out with considerable trepidation that their departure would leave their countries open to attack from the garrisons, should they be augmented, or even from an army of Scots if, as the council were suggesting, such an army should descend on Ulster. King James VI, at news of the Spanish landing, had offered Elizabeth aid of troops. That 'wisest fool' in Christendom, as the shrewd Henry IV called him, showed his astuteness in this crisis by allowing Sir Robert Cecil to guide him in taking proper steps to secure the succession.[1]

O'Neill's hesitation at this moment indicated, as Seán O'Faolain's excellent analysis has shown, neither incompetence nor cowardice. The Spaniards, in spite of their pleas for his assistance, could surely stand siege in a walled town indefinitely against much superior numbers. The hardship of winter weather would tell more on besiegers than besieged. The expected reinforcements from Spain, especially if they landed at a better-chosen port, must restore the advantage to the Irish and Spaniards. It was entirely foreign to O'Neill's character and completely out of keeping with the tactics which had brought him such considerable successes to leave the security of his fastnesses and march his main force at this season of the year, lightly equipped as they must be if they were not to be bogged down, through an unfriendly country the long distance to Cork. Both Chichester and Fenton doubted that O'Neill would, as Fenton said, 'go up now when he will have to strive against rivers and waters and will have to meet the extremities of winters'.[2]

And even arrived in the south, what could O'Neill achieve? He must be confronted with Mountjoy's and Carew's armies on open ground where he would no longer have the advantages of cover and mobility. And must his men lie in the open, with only beef to eat after what slender supplies of meal and butter they could carry were exhausted, to engage in the wholly unaccustomed work of besieging an enemy?

Yet within three weeks of his first hearing of the Spaniards' arrival, he had decided to go to Kinsale. Given the weighty considerations urging him to remain at home, the proven ability of the Spaniards to stand siege and his real doubts about the wisdom of his going to the

1. *Cal. S.P. Ire.*, 1601–3, pp. 81–165; *Cal. Carew MSS*, 1601–3, p. 154.
2. Cf. *Cal. S.P. Ire.*, 1601–3, pp.152–3, 163, 187; O'Faolain, *The great O'Neill*, pp. 247–51.

south, it was not such a long delay. But although O'Donnell, who for his matchless speed of movement went first to draw off pursuit, left Ballymote on 2 November and O'Neill followed a week later, it was a fortnight after that again before anyone on the government side realized Hugh's real intention of going to Munster. Though closely watched, still 'closer in his resolutions' was O'Neill.

Red Hugh reached Ikerrin in north-west Tipperary and halted. And O'Neill held off, waiting to see what the besiegers would do in view of O'Donnell's proximity.

IX · SIEGE

Ciúnas, ná cómhnaidhe, tathamh, nó tionnabradh . . .
A.F.M., ad. an. 1601[1]

THE ACCOUNT of the early skirmishes at Kinsale is all from the English side and some of it strains credulity.[2] But of the English gain when on the night of 4 November Sir John Barkley drove the Spaniards out of their trenches, enabling Mountjoy to advance camp there can be no doubt. It was a further victory when Captain Taaffe forced the Spaniards to slaughter some cattle and sheep that Águila had grazing on the Castle Park peninsula. Taaffe's objective had been the capture of the animals, and in this he had failed. But the English could be satisfied: Águila had lost much valuable food. More than that, he had given occasion to the critics in his own camp to declare that he could have killed and salted these animals beforehand.

From his new encampment on Spital Hill Mountjoy began a damaging bombardment, to prevent which Águila had not strong enough forces to mount an effective sortie though time and again he tried. And out of range of Águila's musket-fire Mountjoy's cavalry still ran the country at night, burning the corn.[3]

Ships arrived at Oyster Haven from Dublin, bearing provisions and artillery for Mountjoy. Soon the lord deputy had a battery firing on Rincorran; this battery was aided by fire from the pinnace *Moon* stationed in Kinsale Harbour. The *Moon* also prevented Águila from sending reinforcements to Rincorran. On 11 November Mountjoy forced the surrender of the fort. The garrison yielded on condition that they be allowed back to Spain. The lord deputy agreed to this

1. 'Nor quiet, rest, sleep, nor repose . . .'
2. The journals kept by Stafford (Carew's secretary) and Moryson (Mountjoy's secretary) are evidently the common source for the accounts of the siege in Moryson's *Itinerary*, *Pac. Hib.*, *Cal. Carew MSS.*, and *Cal. S. P. Ire.*
3. AGS, Guerra Antigua 3144; Águila to Philip, 31 Oct.; *Pac. Hib.*, i. 298–302; cf. *Ir. Sword*, ii (1954), 72.

condition because he wished to avoid delay and to impress the Spaniards with his clemency; he in turn was impressed with the stubborn resistance set up by the commander of the castle, Ensign Paez de Clavijo. The town, Charles saw, would be stoutly defended, and he wished for more artillery to bombard it.[1]

But at least there was heartening news of reinforcement of troops coming: Elizabeth promised him a further 5,000 levies, 4,000 for Kinsale and 1,000 for Loch Foyle. The Spanish council of state were ignorant of the scale of the help being prepared in England to help Mountjoy and were deaf to the appeals of López de Soto to send strong reinforcements of men and material to Águila and to pile up supplies at Corunna. Preferring to listen to Castel-Rodrigo when he said that Águila's fleet had sailed properly supplied, the council were making wholly inadequate plans for reinforcing Don Juan. These plans, completed on 25 November, were that nine ships under Zubiaur's command would sail from Corunna, carrying 900 men and 2,000 quintals of biscuit and flour, wheat, and rye; while Cerdá, now recovered from his bout of malaria, would sail from Lisbon with four ships carrying 150 or 250 men, together with 4,500 quintals of biscuit. These two small squadrons would carry as well powder, fuse, and lead, with pick-axes, shovels, and other materials and implements required for fortifications and artillery-trains. Galleons could not go to Ireland in the wintry weather, and so Águila would not get his cavalry; but an effort must be made to send a company of lances, or heavy cavalrymen. Águila was encouraged to try to raise two companies of arquebusiers in Ireland.[2] Ibarra, the secretary of the council of war, learned on 12 December that England was planning to send six to seven thousand men, with artillery, aboard thirty ships, to destroy Águila before Spanish reinforcements arrived, and had sent four large galleons, well-armed, to patrol the Straits of Dover. This report contained enough of the truth to show the scale of the English

1. *Pac. Hib.*, ii. 1–17; Ó Clérigh, *Beatha Aodha Ruaidh*, i. 312–14.
2. AGS, Guerra Antigua 3144: dispatches from council of war to Castel-Rodrigo and others, Vallid., 31 Oct. (*Epistolario de Zubiaur*, pp. 73, 74–5), and La Serreta, 16 Nov.; Guerra Antigua 3144, 3145 (*Epistolario*, cit., pp. 75–6): dispatches to Águila and others. 25 Nov. (*Rep. Nov.*, i. 363–4), and to Águila and to Zubiaur, Vallid., 27 Nov.; Guerra Antigua 3144; Castel-Rodrigo to Philip, Lisbon, 6, 7, 8, and 16 Nov., and to Ibarra 5 Nov.; López to Philip, 15 Nov., twice, 21, and 28 Nov.; Brochero to Castel-Rodrigo, Cascaes, 5 Nov.; Zubiaur to Caracena, 23 and 24 Oct. (*Epistolario*, cit., pp. 71–2); Guerra Antigua 3145: Brochero to Philip, 6, 7, and 17 Nov., and to junta, 2 Dec.; Guerra Antigua 587: Caracena to Philip, 6, 14 and 22 Nov.; López to Philip, Corunna, 6 Nov.; Moryson, *Itinerary*, iii. 20–3.

counter-attack, but alarming as it was it did not galvanize Spain into action.[1]

The fact that Águila's bases were a thousand miles away in Lisbon and Corunna was now all too apparent, while Mountjoy's were much more convenient in Chester, Bristol, and Barnstaple. How much further away again from Kinsale was Madrid, the capital whose selection by Philip II in preference to Lisbon—or Brussels—has been so justly censured as a grand political and strategic error. And as if Madrid was not remote enough the business of state was now regularly conducted from Philip's hunting-lodges in the mountains around Madrid, Valladolid, or Zamora![2]

When news was brought to the besiegers of Kinsale that O'Donnell was approaching Munster and that O'Neill as it was wrongly thought was but a few days behind, Mountjoy on 16 November fortified his camp on its northern side; and next day Carew led off two regiments on what he suspected would be a vain attempt to intercept the elusive Red Hugh. Sir George marched to the Suir, where he lay on the east side of the river in the vicinity of Golden across the path that he thought O'Donnell must take.[3]

O'Donnell burned his boats by coming south, for his departure meant the fall at last of Ballyshannon (the key to the western passage from Munster to Ulster) to the English. It was a desperate throw, which only victory in the south could justify. The Erne was Red Hugh's Rubicon. He eluded Carew by a famous night march of thirty-two Irish (forty English) miles over an opportunely frozen defile of the Slieve Felim range on 2 December. He then rested for a week in Connelloe in Limerick while he sought to constrain the lords of that part of Munster to his side.

The lord president was back at Kinsale on 6 December. He had been joined on the way by the young Lord Clanricarde, with a regiment of foot, and by Donough O'Brien, the third earl of Thomond, who had brought 1,000 foot and 100 horse from Bristol. All these troops were now quartered in a new camp under Thomond on the slopes of Ballincubby Hill, on the west side of the town. This camp was set up with the double objective of preventing a junction between the Spaniards and O'Donnell and of investing the town more closely.

1. Guerra Antigua 587: F. de la Riva Herrera to Ibarra, 17 Nov.
2. *Cal. S.P. Ire., 1601–3*, pp. x–xi; Braudel, *Méditerranée et monde méditerranéen*, pp. 773–4, 883; Gounon-Loubens, *Administration de Castille au xvie siècle*, pp. 43–4.
3. *Pac. Hib.*, ii. 9–10.

Carew and Clanricarde remained with Mountjoy in the great camp on Camphill.[1]

From Connelloe O'Donnell came on to Bandon. He now had the allegiance of Thomas Fitzmaurice, Lord Kerry, of Clanmaurice, who had come with him from the north; John O'Conor Kerry, of Carriga-foyle; and many other leading men of west Munster; but notably not Donal MacCarthy Reagh, who commanded the territory extending from Bantry Bay to the Bandon river, or Cormac MacDermot Mac-Carthy, lord of Muskerry, who ruled over the watershed of the River Lee from Ballincollig westwards. Fear of MacCarthy More domina-tion kept Cormac still loyal, and he came to the aid of Mountjoy during the siege of Kinsale. With Florence now in the Tower, his rival Donal, base son of the dead Clancarty, was again recognized by O'Neill as MacCarthy More. Florence's brother, Dermot Maol, also joined the northern leaders.[2]

O'Donnell arrived at Bandon on or before 12 December, and estab-lished communications with Águila.[3] O'Neill, in turn, leaving his son in charge behind him, left his territory a week after All Saints. He chose the eastern exit, over the northern Blackwater and Boyne. The companies from his own territory of Tyrone attending him were estimated in number at 4,060 horse and foot, while Red Hugh's re-ported muster was 4,000 foot and 3,000 horse. These estimates must be received with a certain reserve. If Sir Geoffrey Fenton may be taken as an authority, the effective rising-out at O'Neill's command, even making allowance for 'cowkeepers and horseboys', would fall far below this estimate. O'Neill was accompanied by many other Ulster lords and their contingents and by John, son of Thomas Roe, earl of Desmond. In Leinster he was joined by Captain Richard Tyrrell, of Brenockton, Co. Westmeath, who had pledged himself to O'Neill in return for a colonelcy, when the Spaniards came, and the lordship of Westmeath. Tyrrell led between four and six hundred men. 'Many other Leinster rebels' also joined Hugh.[4]

1. Ó Clérigh, *Beatha Aodha Ruaidh*, i. 298–310, 318–20; *Cal. Carew MSS., 1601–3*, p. 187; Docwra, 'Narration', in *Celtic Soc. Misc.* (Dublin, 1849), pp. 255, 257, 258–9; *Pac. Hib.*, ii. 10–17; O'Sullivan Beare, *Hist. cath. Ibern. comp.*, pp. 226–7.

2. *Epistolario de Zubiaur*, p. 80; Ó Clérigh, *Beatha Aodha Ruaidh*, i. 332–3; Butler, *Gleanings from Irish history*, pp. 13, 106–37; S. T. MacCarthy, *The MacCarthys of Munster*, pp. 64–85; *D.N.B.*, entry Florence MacCarthy.

3. AGS, Guerra Antigua 3144: Águila to O'Donnell, Kinsale, 14 Dec. 1601.

4. *Cal. S.P. Ire.*, 1601–3, pp. 187, 141; AGS, Guerra Antigua 592: agreement between O'Neill and Tyrrell, Dungannon, 2 Jan. 1598; *A.F.M., ad. an.* 1601; *I.H.S.*, ii. 264–5.

Hugh, purposely going slowly, spent some time pillaging and burning in the Pale and came on by way of west Meath and east Munster to join his ally at Bandon River. The traditional site of O'Donnell's encampment is somewhere to the west of Inishannon, along the north bank of the river in the barony of Kinalmeaky. O'Neill had joined O'Donnell here it seems by the evening of 15 December. The two chiefs had done well in transporting their armies three hundred miles in the depth of winter. They had crossed fifty swollen rivers by flinging wooden bridges across them, as well as many others that took them up to the belt or breast. The gamble taken, it seemed, had been worthwhile. Not only had O'Neill and O'Donnell overcome all obstacles on their march southwards but, they were reassured, a relieving force of 3,000 Spaniards had landed at Castlehaven and would provide all the stiffening that O'Neill could demand for his unproven levies. Their delight was to be short-lived.[1]

Now began a war of nerves, but it was not Mountjoy's which broke. Forced by the grim opposition of the Spaniards and the news of the arrival of the Irish to change tactics, the lord deputy gave up his present attempt to carry Kinsale by assault following an intensive bombardment, and instead set about drawing his investment of the town tighter.

With Rincorran taken, Mountjoy had next sought possession of Castle Park in preparation for the assault on Kinsale. Águila, learning of Carew's departure, had sent out a sortie, but the Spaniards met with such hot resistance that they retreated and remained unaware of the reduced state of Mountjoy's numbers. With only 2,500 effectives, many raw men among them, to command, Don Juan was afraid to leave the town defenceless and risk a general engagement.

At this critical point large reinforcements came to the English. Thomond's men had to be sent to Cork to rest, but an equal number of men came into Waterford and a day later (24 November) Sir Richard Levison, admiral of the queen's Irish fleet, came into Kinsale with the warships and the remaining 2,000 reinforcements.

Subjected to gunfire from the camp and from the warships now in control of the harbour, Castle Park capitulated after four days.[2]

Archbishop Oviedo was furious, and blamed Aguila for the loss of

1. Moryson, *Itinerary*, iii. 27–8; *Epistolario de Zubiaur*, p. 126: report of Zubiaur's adventures, Luarca, 14 Jan. 1602.
2. Moryson, *Itinerary*, iii. 38–44.

Rincorran and Castle Park. He dwelt bitterly on the fact that Águila had rejected the advice proffered by Brochero and himself to fortify Castle Park. Oviedo believed that Águila had shown great irresolution. He had not only not fortified the castles but he had thrown up no other defences and had shamefully let the forts be taken. Womanlike he had let himself be invested by land and sea and had repelled the Irish who wished to come in, so that not only did they not come in but some of his own soldiers deserted.[1] A story was later carried back to Spain by Deacon Pedro de Colmenares (no friend of the archbishop's, it is true), to the effect that Oviedo had had certain of the captains to visit him in his house. Colmenares could name most of these officers: Muñeza, Cuellar, Cardenosa, Jaén, Navarra, Jara Millo, Don Pedro Morejón, Henríquez de Tejada, and perhaps one or two others. At their secret meetings Colmenares alleged that criticisms of Águila's courage were freely exchanged, Oviedo going so far as to say that Águila wished to hand them over to the enemy and enter the service of the queen.[2] Whatever the truth of this tale, it is certain that relations between the archbishop and Águila were marked by mutual distrust.

Mountjoy now had men, artillery, and victuals in plenty. With the reinforcements he had under him a list total of 11,500 foot and 857 horse. This included Carew's detachment of 2,100 foot and 320 horse, which had not yet returned. A flying squadron of 1,050 infantry relieved of watch duty was detached from the total to answer alarms.[3]

Strangely enough Mountjoy and his council chose not now to attempt to breach the town but to continue the siege, bombarding at the same time the Spaniards' houses. Thus, they thought, hunger and exposure would decimate the Spaniards. Exposure was killing Mountjoy's own men at the rate of forty a day (6,000 of the besiegers—Stafford, López, and Oviedo all agree—were actually to be lost during the siege), but remembering how desperately men of Águila's command had fought in a similar situation in Brittany, when three hundred of them under siege at the Pointe Espagnole had sold their lives

---

1. AGS, Guerra Antigua 3145: memorandum by Oviedo, 27 Jan. 1602.
2. AGS, Guerra Antigua 3144: declaration by Colmenares.
3. Moryson, *Itinerary*, iii. 40–3: *Cal. S.P. Ire.,1601–3*, p. 200, errs by defect in stating that the list in Munster stood on 4 December at 9,650 foot and 675 horse. Reinforcements had landed at Loch Foyle on 24 November, bringing the number of effectives there and in Donegal up to 1,685 men (in list 3,000), apart from officers; a force of 295 foot and 13 horse landed at Carrickfergus on 25 Nov. (*Cal.*, cit., pp. 174, 176, 178–80 189).

dearly, Mountjoy did not relish a hand-to-hand encounter at a breach with the Spaniards.[1]

The lord deputy now set up two batteries, one near the camp on the north-east side and the other on the Castle Park peninsula. The former had a cannon, demi-cannon, and four other pieces; three culverins from the latter played on the old town on the north-east side. On the night of 3 December the English in the face of frost, enemy fire, and Spanish sortie worked furiously to dig parallels nearer the town on the north-east side on commanding ground and two nights later raised another battery at this point. Levison also bombarded the old town from the admiral and vice-admiral, which were now moored in a little pool between Castle Park and the town and near the blockhouse or fort defending the old or 'base' town.

The combined effect of Carew's return with Thomond and Clan-ricarde and of the news that O'Donnell maintained his advance made Mountjoy change his plans and try what a breach might do. The three culverins for their precision firing were removed to the east battery, and the bombardment was continued until 8 December, when Águila contemptuously rejected a call to surrender. But two days later the east gate and a great part of the wall next to it were broken down.

Mountjoy, still cautious, launched a 'bravado' by 2,000 infantrymen led by Sir John Barkley on this breach, not as an actual assault but rather to discover whether an assault were possible. At least, so said the English, in spite of their numbers. After an hour's sharp fighting, with the Spaniards lodged in a trench outside the breach, the English found their answer and withdrew. The Spanish troops, inspired by the careless contempt for the English displayed by one of their cap-tains, Morejón, the similarity of whose name to his own intrigued Fynes Moryson, had again proved themselves stout defenders.[2]

That night and the next day, 12 December, the English established a fort closer to the town than Thomond's camp, on the west side. When night had fallen on 12 December the lord deputy manned this fort with seven companies, leaving some divisions of Thomond's men on guard without. Mountjoy designed these troops to second the artillery that was to be planted nearby; the trenches besides the gun-emplacements on the east side he also manned with seven companies.

Águila's outposts on Compass Hill south of the town noted all this;

1. Cf. Falls, *Mountjoy*, pp. 33–4.
2. Moryson, *Itinerary*, iii. 38–40, 44–50.

the Spaniard saw the lines of investment being drawn tighter around him both to west and east, cutting off the entry of even the limited supplies he was getting and eliminating any hope of communication with the approaching Irish; he foresaw that his men and defences were to be subjected to an even heavier bombardment and that the general assault must now be imminent. He determined to do what he could to remove or at least lessen the danger.

The day was very wet and the rain increased as darkness fell. An hour after dark, at eight o'clock, Águila's men, in number about 1,500, made their sortie. They attacked the trenches on the east and spiked two guns before they were made to give ground, then fell on the new fort on the west side and took it, broke down the platform prepared for the ordnance that was to be placed there on the next day, and filled the trenches before they were made to retire by Clanricarde. The captains leading the sortie insisted that they would not have retired but for Águila's repeated orders to them to do so.[1] Accounts of the sally are conflicting, the English claiming that they had killed two hundred Spaniards with little loss and that only one cannon was spiked and that but temporarily, while Zubiaur heard that the Spaniards had slaughtered 1,500 English. Águila made a more conservative claim, four hundred enemy dead for the loss of only a few Spaniards, among whom were Captains Bernardino de Soto, son of Pedro López, and Charles MacCarthy ('Zarate'). But Mountjoy, who admitted that it was a 'strong salley', now gave up the idea of an assault, towards the preparation of which he had been working and fighting night and day for over a week, and more particularly for the last two days. The approach of the northern Irish and the arrival of the Spaniards at Castlehaven with, it was said at first, 3,000 men, increased, whatever he might say, Charles's anxiety to take the town. But Águila's demonstration of mettle under attack and the strength of his counter-attack deterred him. Equally they impressed the hitherto cautious lords of the south-west, who now flocked to Castelhaven in numbers.[2]

The folly of sending out expeditions that were so small that they resulted, as Don Martín de Padilla, Adelantado of Castile, complained, 'more in annoying than in punishing the enemy', was now being

1. AGS, Guerra Antigua 3145: paper from Philip for the information of the council, 1 Apr. 1603.
2. Pac. Hib., ii, 32–42; Epistolario de Zubiaur, pp. 80, 127; A.F.M., ad. an. 1601.

borne in upon the Spanish administration. In December Spain decided to reinforce Águila with three cavalry companies, to be sent before the end of the month, and with a Portuguese *tercio* of 2,000 infantry, to be sent later. These orders increased the viceroy of Portugal's testiness. In view of the levy in Portugal of a regiment already ordered for the Indies, where, he asked, could the men be found? And where in Portugal was there suitable embarkation for cavalry?[1]

Given this situation, it was some sort of achievement when Spain was able to send General Pedro de Zubiaur back to Ireland. Zubiaur, it is true, suffered ill-luck on this voyage too; setting out from Corunna on 6 December with ten ships, he landed at Castlehaven five days afterwards with only six, the others being driven back to Spain. Kinsale had been Zubiaur's goal, as he was bringing supplies to Águila, but luckily for him a contrary wind had kept him out of it, so that he escaped destruction or capture by the English warships there.

Zubiaur had with him food, arms, and artillery for Águila's use and a total of 621 infantry under the command of the veteran Captain Alonso de Ocampo. López de Soto described the men as being of very poor quality, even the Gallegos who had served two years in the Azores; some of them, he said, were jail-birds, including one whole company of Portuguese, and they were naked as well. That they could also fight and die like true Spanish infantry these men so unflatteringly described would soon show.[2]

Don Pedro, who would have earned marks from Machiavelli for *virtù*, displayed an intrepidity and a gift for improvisation which belied his sixty years. He set about making the best of his misfortune in not gaining Kinsale, if misfortune it was. Ocampo wanted to go home again, but López sided with Zubiaur. The latter gave out an exaggerated account of his numbers, a stratagem which boomeranged when O'Neill refused to believe that the Spanish reinforcements were less than 3,000 men. But for the moment the stratagem achieved its purpose in inducing the lords of Castlehaven, Baltimore, and Bantry to put him in possession of their harbours. Sir Finnin O'Driscoll More

1. AGS, Estado 840, f. 166 (*Cal. S.P. Spain, 1587–1603*, pp. 690–1; cf. pp. 688–9): Padilla to Philip, Pto. de S. María, 10 Dec.; Estado 840, ff. 273–4 (*Cal.*, cit. pp. 681–2): council of state to Philip, 11 Dec.; Guerra Antigua 3144: Castel-Rodrigo to Philip, twice, 11 Dec.

2. AGS, Guerra Antigua 3144: Ocampo to Philip, Castlehaven, 21 Dec.; López to Philip, Baltimore, 6 Mar. 1602; Moryson, *Itinerary*, iii. 60. Cf. Guerra Antigua 3143 (*Epistolario de Zubiaur*, p. 122), and summary in Estado 840, f. 157 (*Cal. S.P. Spain, 1587–1603*, pp. 683–4): inventory by Juan de la Concha, Corunna, 7 Dec.; *Cal. S.P. Venice, 1592–1603*, p. 492: Cavalli to doge and senate, Paris, 5 Feb. 1602.

held Baltimore, with its castles of Donnelong on Inisherkin island and Donneshed on the mainland. Sir Finnin, as Carew's secretary said, 'never in the course of his whole life had been tainted with the least spot of disloyalty', but Zubiaur was able to take advantage of discord between him and his eldest son Cornelius to secure control of the castles. Sir Finnin's cousins of Glen Barrahane Castle on Castlehaven Bay gave it over to the Spaniards, who also received Daniel O'Sullivan's castle of Dunboy or Berehaven on Bantry Bay. In each case Zubiaur made a formal treaty with the Irish lords, taking the strongholds in the name of the king of Spain.

Don Pedro decided to hold Baltimore harbour as a place for future Spanish landings. Glen Barrahane was only a tower with a little ravelin before it and was indefensible landwards, but Zubiaur, who did not need Águila's warning that Admiral Levison would come to attack him, placed six artillery-pieces on the barbican at the foot of the tower, to cover the entrance to the harbour. He strengthened the tower, repaired the ravelin, and made an esplanade, setting up the six pieces. In Donnelong he placed Captain Andrés de Arbe with eighty soldiers and nine guns.

Dermot O'Sullivan, Daniel's brother, brought young Captain Saavedra to Dunboy on 20 December and there Saavedra installed himself with sixty soldiers and eight pieces. Zubiaur's coming brought a general rally of the lords of south-west Munster to Castlehaven, where they took oaths of homage to Philip before López de Soto. Zubiaur armed 1,000 men with 350 arquebuses and 650 pikes; the other 2,000 soldiers commanded by these gentlemen must await the arrival of further arms from Spain. Daniel O'Sullivan Beare set about assembling his force of a thousand men, while Cornelius O'Driscoll, who claimed that his father now adhered to the Spanish cause, raised a company of horse.[1]

Of the other leaders who now declared for Philip, López was most impressed by the MacCarthys who, he declared, were greater than the Mendozas in Spain.[2] The brothers Donough Moyle and Finnin,

1. AGS, Guerra Antigua 3144: Ocampo to Philip, Castlehaven 21 and 25 Dec.; Guerra Antigua 3145: López to Philip, 20 and 25 Dec.; Estado 188: López to Franqueza, 1 Feb. 1602; to Philip, 12 Feb.; to Zubiaur, 13 Feb.; and to Franqueza and to Caracena, 15 Feb.; Guerra Antigua 3145 (*Epistolario de Zubiaur*, p. 68): Zubiaur to Philip, 19 Dec.; O'Sullivan Beare, *Hist. Cath. Ibern. comp.*, pp. 225, 226; *Pac. Hib.*, ii. 41.

2. Nicholas Browne wrote in 1596: 'At this tyme these Irishe septs [i.e. the MacCarthys] are of greater force and strength than they weare these 300 years.' Quoted, Butler, *Gleanings from Irish history*, p. 10 n. 11.

the sons of Sir Owen ('of the parliament') MacCarthy Reagh with almost all the Clan Carty of Carbery swore allegiance to Philip. So did Donal, O'Neill's MacCarthy More, and the imprisoned Florence MacCarthy's brother, Dermot Maol. Among others doing homage were Daniel O'Donovan, Felim MacCormac, and his brother, and among the Geraldines John O'Connor Kerry, the Knight of Kerry, and Thomas Fitzmaurice, the baron of Lixnaw. The captains Richard Tyrrell and his elder brother, Walter, and William Burke came to join Daniel O'Sullivan; between them they commanded 600 men.

By his display of verve Zubiaur had secured the adherence of the gentlemen of west Munster, who had already noted Águila's success in defending Kinsale and spoke very enthusiastically of his repulse of the English assault of 11 December, in which they believed 1,500 English had been killed. As O'Neill approached their borders they realized too from past experience the wisdom of joining him. It was no doubt in order to stiffen their resolution that O'Neill sent the Tyrrells to join them. Yet, as noted by López, not a single hamlet in Cork or elsewhere, apart from this south-western corner, declared for Philip.[1]

Mountjoy in turn now strengthened his defences in preparation for a siege, and at the same time set about investing the town completely so as to starve it out. All the horse were drawn into the lord deputy's camp, and Thomond's camp, strengthened by the posting to it of Wilmot's regiment, was moved nearer Kinsale, towards the south gate. The ordnance from both eastern and western platforms was hauled into Mountjoy's camp. Two small forts were erected between Thomond's camp and the water to the south so as completely to debar access to the town. Parallels linked up these forts with Thomond's camp, and then with Mountjoy's. The town was now completely surrounded. The English fleet held the harbour, and the investment was continuous from Scilly Point north-eastward to Camphill and thence westward to the Bandon river.[2]

It took Mountjoy a fortnight of very stormy weather thus to prepare, but now he was invested in turn. O'Neill had a total force of

1. AGS, Guerra Antigua 3145 (*Epistolario de Zubiaur*, p. 85): Zubiaur to Philip, 20 Dec.; Guerra Antigua 587 (*Pac. Hib.*, ii. 47–9): Daniel O'Sullivan to Philip, Camp near Kinsale, 29 Dec. (original Irish, with Spanish trans.); Guerra Antigua 3144: López to Philip, Corunna, 20 Mar. 1602; *Relación*, in *Epistolario de Zubiaur*, p. 124.
2. Cf. O'Sullivan, *Kinsale*, pp. 60–1.

perhaps 6,000 infantry and 800 horse under his command.[1] This was besides the Munster Irish who now came in. The Irish besiegers prevented supplies of grass and water, corn and grain, straw and fuel from entering the English camps. Many men and horses began to die of hunger and cold within the camps and the English did not even dare emerge to bury their dead. O'Neill and O'Donnell hoped that plague and illness would soon do their work for them by destroying the enemy army.

Sickness and desertion played havoc with the English; the severe winter weather was causing sentinels to drop dead at their posts, killing men in dozens each night and causing hundreds to run off. Deprived of forage the horses were starving. On the other hand, Águila's position had materially improved. O'Neill was able to send him in cows and other supplies between the two camps, as the English knew, and, unknown to the English, by way of the Castle Park peninsula in spite of the battery there. The meat came as a welcome addition to the hard tack which had been the sole food of the Spaniards up to this. The spirit shown by Águila kept Mountjoy, as he himself admitted, 'at bay'. He could not carry his approaches any nearer or put his battery into effect. Levison's fleet also now had to perform the double duty of guarding the entrance to Kinsale and the storeships there (for the English had no magazines ashore) and of patrolling the coast so as to prevent another Spanish landing at Baltimore or Bantry. Mountjoy urged London to send him reinforcements of four thousand men as well as reinforcements for Levison.[2]

In spite of his threatening situation, however, Mountjoy continued the work of extending his approaches and erected new platforms from which to bombard the west wall, where he now hoped to make a new breach. Águila opposed these preparations with shot from the castles in the walls and with sallies; in a sortie on 27 December the Spaniards broke down one of the platforms.[3]

Both Águila and the Irish leaders urged Zubiaur to send men to join O'Neill. But Don Pedro himself was attacked by Levison, on

1. There are discrepancies in the accounts, but cf. AGS, Guerra Antigua 3144: dispatch by Cerdá with letter, Castel-Rodrigo to Philip, 24 Jan. 1602, and Estado 620: news from London, 26 Dec. 1601, old style. Estado 620: another estimate from England, of 5,000 men altogether, 5 Jan. 1601, old style, is too low.

2. AGS, Estado 620: news from London, 5 Jan. 1601, old style; Guerra Antigua 3145: Philip to council, 1 Apr. 1603; Ó Clérigh, *Beatha Aodha Ruaidh*, i. 326; Moryson, *Itinerary*, iii. 62–80.

3. *Pac. Hib.*, ii. 44–5.

Sunday, 16 December, when the admiral with four galleons and three lesser craft sailed into Castlehaven harbour. The arrival of Daniel O'Sullivan with five hundred foot and some horse prevented Levison from landing his men, and Zubiaur because of contrary winds could not come to close quarters; so the battle was fought with artillery, Zubiaur replying from the land to Levison's fire.

The English squadron anchored closer than Zubiaur, had he had better soldiers, would have allowed, and on the Sunday the English fire drove one Spanish ship, the *María Francesa*, aground. But that night Zubiaur landed more artillery from the grounded ship. He personally directed the fire on Monday and Tuesday, and Levison felt it so hotly that he would gladly have retired but that the wind was against him. At last on Wednesday he managed to have himself towed or warped out but had to leave behind his mooring anchors and cables. The honours lay about even; one Spanish ship had been sunk and seemingly two of the English squadron never made it back to Kinsale. But Levison had failed to dislodge the doughty Zubiaur.[1]

That general in his enthusiasm for his schemes to conquer Ireland, Scotland, and England sent urgent pleas home for the necessary aid in men, ships, equipment, and food; but these appeals could not shake the lethargic administration. O'Neill's intention was, once Don Pedro's contingent of Spaniards had joined him, to force a breakthrough to Águila. But Zubiaur and López, heartened by beating off Levison's attack, meant to hold the three ports for Spain and dismayed O'Neill and disgusted Águila by retaining the bulk of their Spaniards in the castles that they had received. Zubiaur sent to join the Irish in the week before Christmas only two hundred Spaniards under four captains and Daniel O'Sullivan Beare with 700 Irish, followed by O'Sullivan's brother with 500 more Irish. In Donneshed Zubiaur placed nine cannon and planned to install himself there; Christmas over, he loaded boats with ten pieces and sent them off to Dunboy. He kept six pieces, which he meant for Águila, on two ships at Castelhaven.[2]

1. AGS, Guerra Antigua 3145: López to Águila, Castlehaven, 15 (?) Dec. 1601; Guerra Antigua 3144: Sandoval's account; Ocampo to Philip, 25 Dec.; Águila to Philip, Cork, 19 Jan. 1602; Guerra Antigua 3145: Zubiaur to Philip, 19 Dec.; López to Philip, 26 Dec. Cf. *Epistolario de Zubiaur*, pp. 87, 125–7, 136–7; *Pac. Hib.*, ii. 43–4; O'Sullivan Beare, *Hist. cath. Ibern. comp.*, pp. 225–6.

2. *Epistolario de Zubiaur*, pp. 68–70, 84–91: Zubiaur to Philip, 19, 20, 22, 24, 25, 27, and 30 Dec.; AGS, Guerra Antigua 3145 (*Epistolario de Zubiaur*, p. 127): Zubiaur to Caracena, 22 Dec., and summary of adventures; Guerra Antigua 3144: memoranda of 22 Dec.; Tyrell to

The two hundred Spaniards, even if they carried six standards and eight drums, were hardly enough to transform the Irish army from an amateur into a professional force which could be relied on to stand the test of battle. O'Neill was bitterly disappointed. His men, good guerrillas although they were, were wanting in experience of pitched encounters where troops needed discipline to press home a charge against an unyielding foe or to receive in turn a charge and not panic. Even Hugh's greatest victory at the Yellow Ford was won against an army on the move and with its divisions strung out too much.

The Irish had even less experience of fighting against an entrenched enemy. It would be difficult for O'Neill, as Carew said, 'to force trenches or fight upon hard ground'.[1] Águila wanted the Irish to come up and occupy some point to which he would sally out to join them. The two Hughs accompanied by one of the Spanish captains, Francisco Ruiz de Velasco, went on Sunday 23 December to within a musket shot of Kinsale to make reconnaissance. They had a plain view of the enemy's position, with Kinsale at his back, the sea with his warships on his left flank, and on his right the Bandon, on which Thomond's right wing rested.

The Irishmen pointed out to Ruiz that Mountjoy's men were lodged in trenches a lance-length in height, and emphasized that they were better armed and had artillery. This Ruiz saw; the trenches in fact were so high that they could only be climbed with ladders. Moreover, O'Neill's army numbered only 6,000 infantry and 800 horse effectives, in opposition to Mountjoy's 10,000 foot and 1,000 horse. Ruiz, however, urged him to go up; the Spaniards, he maintained, cared nothing for trenches and would open a way through for the Irish. O'Neill therefore agreed to stake all on an attempt to break through to Águila, but he delayed fulfilling his promise. For another ten days he remained where he was, some five miles from Kinsale, and did not move camp.

There was reason in this; the winds continued westerly and no help therefore could be expected to reach Mountjoy, whose food supplies were failing. In the continued stormy weather the English army, in

1. *Cal. S.P. Ire.*, 1601–3, p. 241: Carew to Cecil, 26 Dec., old style.

López, Berehaven, 3 Mar. 1602; Águila's answers to Diego de Ibarra, 29 Mar. 1602; Águila to O'Neill and O'Donnell, 28 Dec. (Moryson, *Itinerary*, iii. 23), and to López; Guerra Antigua 591: López to Philip, 27 Mar 1602; Guerra Antigua 3145: López to Philip, 20 and 25 Dec. 1601.

mud to its knees, was losing great numbers through exposure: on
Carew's testimony the 6,000 English levies were practically all consumed by death, sickness, and desertion.[1] O'Neill's own men were
dying of hunger; he was without biscuit and had only meat to offer
them. But he could endure that, as the sufferings of the enemy were
greater. Unfortunately Águila's troops too were in great extremities,
and Don Juan kept urging the Irish to move up to the attack. He sent
Ensign Bustamante with guides to conduct O'Neill to a rendezvous,
promising that he himself would sally out there as soon as he heard
the Irish giving battle.[2] Prompted by this encouragement, the Irish
leader decided to accede to Águila's pleas and on Friday, 28 December,
gave orders to move up.[3]

The consequences of the delay in communication between Águila
and his government now became apparent. At the time when O'Neill
was deciding in response to Don Juan's pleas to move up to Kinsale
the council of state were considering the Irish situation on the basis of
reports that were a month or in some cases two months old. The
council then had to rely on information from Águila that was no more
recent than the end of October, on news of Zubiaur's return to Corunna,
and on rather more recent news, which was quite correct, that Elizabeth had dispatched thirteen warships with 4,000 men to Ireland.
Águila's situation as it had been at the end of October, besieged by
Mountjoy, short of provisions, and in particular need of cavalry, was
known to the council; but of Zubiaur's return to Ireland and of the
arrival in Munster of the northern Irish they did not know.

Unaware of the speed with which Águila was urging matters to a
decision in Ireland, the council believed that the war there would be
prolonged until the summer. Then, they agreed with the Adelantado
of Castile, Elizabeth would be in a position to assemble a force in
Ireland large enough to gain the country.

To counter that threat Spain must take effective measures in the
spring. This was all the more necessary as there was reason to suspect
that Elizabeth would persuade France to break off relations with

---

1. *Cal. S.P. Ire.*, *1601–3*, pp. 216, 234.
2. AGS, Guerra Antigua 3144: Ruiz de Velasco to López, 22 Dec.; O'Neill and O'Donnell
to López, Irish camp, 22 Dec.; Ruiz to same, 23 (? 24) Dec.; account by Sandoval; Guerra
Antigua 3145: López to Philip, 25 Dec.; (*Rep. Nov.*, i (1955), 115–6): memorandum by Oviedo,
27 Jan. 1602.
3. AGS, Guerra Antigua 3145 (*Epistolario de Zubiaur*, p. 94): Zubiaur to Philip, Castlehaven, 29 Dec. 1601; *Pac. Hib.*, ii. 49.

Spain and unite with England in expelling the Spaniards from Ireland and in raising the siege of Ostend. Victory in Ireland for Spain would impress France and Scotland and put a curb on English support of the Dutch. Thus Philip II's Atlantic ambitions were revived by his son.

The council therefore approved once more its decision of a fortnight or so earlier to dispatch three companies of light cavalry as soon as might be and to levy and send off as quickly as possible afterwards a Portuguese *tercio* of two thousand men. The cavalry, under the command of Captain Duarte Núñez, would comprise two hundred and twenty effective lances, made up of the companies of the count of Puñoenrostro, Don Pedro Pacheco, and Don Sancho Bravo, and would embark at Lisbon. The council added to these earlier orders a fresh measure authorizing the raising of regiments of Walloons and Germans in Flanders, under the direction of the archduke. These troops should land at Kinsale or at whatever port in Catholic hands O'Neill and O'Donnell might designate.

Meanwhile Águila would be supplied with meat, wine, and vegetables. Orders were sent to him and the northern Irish to join forces, but not to risk battle if the enemy were too great.

Juan de Contreras Gamarra, late commissary-general of light cavalry in Flanders, wanted an army of 14,000 infantry and 1,200 horse sent from Dunkirk to Ireland. This was to forestall any move by France; but the idea was rejected by the council because of lack of money and because such an army, to be raised in Flanders, Italy, and Spain, would not be ready by the spring.

The council in fact were apprehensive of more immediate threats to Spanish safety from both France and England than from Ireland, however events might develop there. Elizabeth was preparing, so intelligence reported, a fleet of twenty armed galleons to attack Ceuta and Tangier, in retaliation for the Spanish invasion of Ireland. Thoroughly alarmed by this report, the council as well anticipated attacks on the Indies by English warships and on the Spanish kingdoms by France. A series of orders reflecting the gravity of the concern felt by the administration was issued at the beginning of January to put Ceuta, Tangier, and the Caribbean ports on the alert and the militia and cavalry of the Spanish kingdoms at the ready to meet attack. Greatest emphasis was placed on the preparation of the galleys of Spain and Italy. New galleys were ordered, and all were to be armed and manned with the Spanish infantry in Italy. These manned warships were to be used not, as the Adelantado wanted, to reinforce Águila, but to deal with any possible attack from France. In effect, the larger considerations of Spanish policy meant the denial to Águila of vital support.[1]

1. AGS, Estado 840, ff. 158, 160–7 (*Cal. S.P. Spain, 1587–1603*, pp. 695–9): reports, letters, and *consulta* of 22 Dec.; Estado 840, f. 157 (*Cal.*, cit., pp. 692–5): Castel-Rodrigo to Philip, 11 Dec. (not Sept.); Guerra Antigua 3144: Philip to Castel-Rodrigo, Vallid., 20 Dec.; council of war to F. de la Riva Herrera, 20 Dec. and to Castel-Rodrigo, Vallid., 31 Dec.; Guerra Antigua 591: council of war to Águila, Castel-Rodrigo, Caracena, Duarte Núñez, etc., Vallid., 4 Jan. 1602.

X · ROUT

> When, without stratagem,
> But in plain shock, and even play of battle,
> Was ever known so great and little loss,
> On one part, and on the other?
> Shakespeare, *Henry V*, Act iv, Sc. viii

THE STORM CLEARED on Sunday, 30 December, and Mountjoy renewed his bombardment of Kinsale, breaking down 'a good part' of the wall of the town. He made another trench beneath the remaining platform and completed it that night in spite of thunder and lightning.[1]

Reports now began to come in from his scouts of the approach of the Irish army. Eventually, towards the night of Monday 31 December, the Irish appeared in view on a hill, Coolcarron, between the English and Cork, and bivouacked that night on the other side, at Belgooly.

O'Neill had brought up his whole army; O'Donnell, Tyrrell, and the Munstermen who had come in were there, while Ocampo had joined them,[2] leaving Captain Barragán behind in Castelhaven as his deputy, and had taken over command of the two hundred Spanish infantry. Mountjoy was reduced to 7,000 men and was planning to send his horses, which lacked fodder, to Cork. When he saw the Irish force come into view the lord deputy exclaimed, report goes, 'This kingdom is lost to-day.'[3] Although the English were not deceived by the show of Spanish standards, O'Neill had now cut Mountjoy's land supply-line from Cork, though the sea-route remained open; and to the west, over the Carrigaline river, the whole country was declared for O'Neill and Spain.

1. *Pac. Hib.*, ii. 45–7, 49; AGS, Guerra Antigua 3145 (*Epistolario de Zubiaur*, pp. 94–6): Zubiaur to Philip, 29 and 30 Dec.
2. AGS, Estado 188: Águila to López, Kinsale, 17 Jan.
3. AGS, Guerra Antigua 3144: report by Cerdá, with letter, Castel-Rodrigo to Philip, Lisbon, 24 Jan.

That night and the following night the Spaniards launched strong attacks on the new English trenches beneath the platform on the west, while during the intervening day they harassed the English with shot from the walls and turrets. O'Neill's horse and foot too kept appearing that same day on the crest of Coolcarron. Thus Spaniards and Irish sought to keep Mountjoy's army always at the ready and so expose it to fatigue and the rigours of the cold, stormy weather. The English artillery returned the Spanish fire, but now with no intention of making a breach. O'Neill was too close at their backs, and Mountjoy, put on his guard by intercepted letters from Águila to O'Neill, awaited the Irish attack.[1]

A line of hills runs from Coolcarron on the north-east to Horsehill on the south-west. A rather wide valley lies between this line and the other line of ridges on which the English emplacements were situated, the ground sloping upwards from the valley in gentle, undulating fashion towards the English position. At the south-western end of the valley, near where White Castle creek flows towards the Bandon river, was fought the battle, of inglorious memory for Irish arms, of Kinsale.[2]

Early in the morning of 3 January the Irish moved up 6,000 foot and 800 horse from Belgooly.[3] Tyrrell commanded in the van his men of Meath and Leinster and the Munster Irish, perhaps a thousand men, together with Ocampo's two hundred Spaniards. The main Irish force, the battle, was led by O'Neill himself and was formed mainly of his own Cenél Eoghain levies, while O'Donnell commanded the rear of Tyrconnell and Connacht men.

The Irish planned, as Águila had proposed to them, that at about daybreak Tyrrell's vanguard should have placed itself at an agreed position between Thomond's camp and the west fort. Here, Águila had insisted, they would be quite safe. When Tyrrell had made known his presence there by musket-fire or some other predetermined signal Águila should sally out to join him. Then together they should at once, or perhaps after they had all retired to the town and re-formed, attack Thomond's camp. At the same time the combined Irish battle and rear should fall on Mountjoy's, the main camp.

Such is the substance of what we know from the available evidence.[4]

1. *Cal. S.P. Ire., 1601–3*, p. 239; Moryson, *Itinerary*, iii. 74–5.
2. Cf. O'Sullivan, *Kinsale*, pp. 67–8.
3. AGS, Guerra Antigua 3144: Ruiz de Velasco's estimate of 22 Dec. to López agrees nearly with that of Ocampo. Cf. Moryson, *Itinerary*, iii. 81.
4. Cf. Appendix I.

That the plan was betrayed to Carew for a bottle of whiskey by one of the inner council of Irish lords, Brian MacHugh Oge MacMahon, is a story in which the classical daemons of Irish tragedy, drink and treachery, appear and one, moreover, which receives authority from Carew himself. Nevertheless, the story is a fabrication, composed later with perhaps the intention of damaging MacMahon's name.[1] The letters that he had intercepted and the information brought by his spies were enough to put Mountjoy on his guard. He saw that an attack that night was extremely probable, but its precise design was unknown to him.

An hour before midnight he was warned that the attack would come before dawn. He therefore ordered his troops to be in readiness and positioned Power's squadron volant, with Sir Richard Graeme's scouts in front, beyond the west of the main camp and close to the main guard of cavalry.[2]

An army of the time moving into battle went with the horse in the lead, then the foot in order: van, battle, and rear. But the rivalry between Cenél Eoghain and Cenél Conaill, that was as old as the eighth century and that with the formation of the alliance between the two Hughs seemed to have died, was in fact only dormant and now awoke again. O'Donnell had favoured attack, while the wiser O'Neill had not; the latter's preferred course had been to harry the lord deputy and subject his army to exposure and famine, while avoiding a direct encounter. But O'Donnell's view had prevailed in council, and now out of the argument grew bitter animosity. The younger chief would not yield precedence to the older, and so the divisions marched out shoulder to shoulder instead of in order. 'Their chiefs were at variance,' say the Four Masters, 'each of them contending that he himself should go foremost in the night's attack; so that the manner in which they set out from the borders of their camp was in three strong battalions, three extensive and numerous hosts, shoulder to shoulder, and elbow to elbow.' They soon lost contact with one another and went astray as well. It was close to daybreak when O'Neill came in view of the English scouts. By now Tyrrell should have been in position for Águila to come out of the town, but the plan had misfired. Tyrrell was not in position and Águila stayed in.

1. *Pac. Hib.*, ii. 53–5; AGS, Estado 620: news from London, 17 Jan., old style. Cf. P. Moore, in *Clogher Record*, i (1956), 100–105.
2. *Cal. S.P. Ire.*, 1601–3, pp. 241–2; *Pac. Hib.*, ii. 55–6.

Warning came from Graeme to Mountjoy of the enemy's presence, and the lord deputy ordered a general stand-to. While the men were arming he sent his marshal, Wingfield, ahead. The marshal returned with confirmation of Graeme's report. Mountjoy's immediate concern was to guard against attack from Águila, if the latter should become aware of O'Neill's presence, and he ordered the main part of his army, under Carew, to stay within the encampments, five regiments within his own camp and four within Thomond's, to defend them against possible assault by Don Juan. He sent all the horse with the support of two regiments of foot, those of Sir Henry Ffolliott and Sir Oliver St. John, forward to join Power. These three regiments made a force of some 1,500 to 2,000 men and the horse numbered four or five hundred. Expecting O'Neill to attack in front, Mountjoy chose a battleground before and in front of Thomond's camp and the west fort that was joined by trench to this camp. This ground, which was open, suited the English and besides offered them the advantage of flanking fire from Thomond's camp.[1]

O'Neill, however, did not advance. From the crest of the ridge in front of Millwater Ford, to which after recognizing the English scouts he had gone forward, he saw the three regiments and the cavalry confronting him. The Spaniards had not come out of the town, and with the English prepared for him he would have to fight on ground of their choosing, which he was not willing to do. He therefore went back and ordered his men to withdraw over the ford. The retreat led over boggy ground, and he hoped to prevent the English from crossing or at least to renew contact with his other divisions and face the enemy on firmer ground. The Spanish captains with him at once questioned his orders and he told them that he feared the enemy would sally out and cut off his passage. Ocampo advised him to draw up his men in battle order and cut his way through to Águila. It was impossible, the Spanish captains urged, that the enemy would leave his trenches having Águila in his rear. If indeed he did so, all the better, for Don Juan would at once leave Kinsale to attack him.[2] The Irish leader, however, refused to take the risk, and continued his withdrawal, while the English cavalry under Sir Henry Danvers followed him up to Millwater.

1. *Cal S.P. Ire.*, 1601–3, p. 240: Carew to Cecil, 26 Dec., old style; AGS, Estado 620: news from London, 10 and 17 Jan., old style (300 horse and 1,600 foot on the queen's forces); *Pac. Hib.*, ii. 57; Hayes-McCoy, 'The tide of victory and defeat', in *Studies*, xxxviii. 314.

2. AGS, Guerra Antigua 3144: report brought by Sandoval on 9 Feb. from Castlehaven; *Pac. Hib.*, ii. 57.

The lord deputy, seeing his opportunity, at once decided to pursue. This, in view of the Irish numerical superiority, was taking a great risk; but the danger was outweighed in Mountjoy's mind by the fact that the further he followed the greater must be the chance that any engagement would take place out of earshot of Kinsale; and in the country beyond the ford, a 'fair champion' as he was told, he could hope to avoid an Irish ambush.

The Irish now, followed by Danvers's cavalry, which were accompanied by Wingfield, had crossed the boggy ground to firm land beyond, near White Castle. About half an hour had gone by since first contact had been made with the enemy and O'Neill's supporting divisions were coming up. He therefore began to embattle his army, with Tyrrell in the centre, his own battle forming the right, and O'Donnell coming up with the rear to form the left wing. Marshal Wingfield saw an opportunity in this confusion, and he and the dashing Clanricarde obtained permission from Mountjoy, who was following up with the regiments of foot, to attempt a charge.

Power's infantry had come up to support the cavalry; from this infantry the eager Wingfield took a hundred shot and sent them in, together with a hundred horse, to drive back the Irish loose shot whom O'Neill had appointed to hold the crossing. A sharp musketry engagement followed, which it seems was heard in Kinsale. Águila, however, suspected that this firing was an English ruse to draw him out and rejected Oviedo's appeal to lead out his men. Repulsed at first, the queen's shot after being reinforced drove back the Irish, and the marshal, Clanricarde, Graeme, and Captains Taaffe and Fleming, all hot for a fight, crossed over with their horse.

These English cavalry contingents, finding themselves confronted by O'Neill's own division, the Irish main battle, immediately charged. Finding the Irish horse stand firm, they did not press home the attack but wheeled off to their flank. The Irish cavalry raised a great shout, but their exultation was short-lived. By now two other cornets of horse, Mountjoy's own and Carew's, had come up, together with the remaining two regiments of infantry. Again the English horse charged and this time the Irish cavalry broke and fell in upon the ranks of their own foot. Wingfield now with his cavalry took the Irish foot in the rear while his infantry attacked them in front. The sharp fighting in 'plain ground' was too much for the Irish, who were further dismayed by the flight of their horse, composed as it was of their leading men, and they in turn broke and fled, a disordered mob. They were too demoralized to retreat on their van and rear, which were in any case too far removed from them. The English cavalry pursued them as they ran, butchering them mercilessly.

Only at this late stage did Tyrrell in the centre go to O'Neill's support; with the object of putting himself between the pursuers and the main body of English foot he began a flank movement. But St. John's regiment, sent in by Mountjoy, attacked Tyrrell's men as they were wheeling. Tyrrell's division after a short resistance gave ground and retreated to a hilltop behind. Ocampo's Spaniards, who were with the Irish van, were not so fleet of foot and stood up to the attack of Mountjoy's troop of horse, under Godolphin, until many of them were killed. Ocampo with forty-nine others surrendered, while about sixty escaped to Castlehaven. Tyrrell's foot, although they had removed in good order and although the main English attack was concentrated on the Irish battle, now followed the example of the battle in taking to their heels.

O'Donnell's men had given no support, probably because they were stationed too far off. Now in turn they became demoralized; they were not attacked, but the sight of the two other battalions being routed and the example of the fugitives who ignored Red Hugh's exhortations to turn and fight was too much for them and they too fled.[1]

Such was the rout—*derrota*, as the Spaniards truly called it—of the Irish chiefs at Kinsale. The English cavalry had won the day and the lord deputy in knighting young Clanricarde on the field (his second knighthood) acknowledged that his fiery zeal had played a major if not decisive part in the victory. The Irish horse, on the other hand, had offered only token resistance to the English cavalry and O'Neill had not been seconded by O'Donnell. The English claimed capture of 2,000 arms which O'Neill's men in their precipitate flight threw away, and O'Neill lost all his baggage and cows. The English pursuers, some companies of horse and infantry, followed, doing great execution for about a mile and a half, which was as far as the half-starved horses could go. Estimates of the Irish losses vary, O'Neill admitting to 500 dead, Águila putting the number at 1,000, and the English claiming to have accounted for fourteen captains and up to 1,200 men dead. The most acceptable figure seems to be somewhere between 500 and 1,000 Irish dead, chiefly from the battle; the English horse were too

1. *Pac. Hib.*, ii. 58–61; *Trevelyan Papers*, pt. ii, p. 105; *Cal. S.P. Ire., 1601–3*, p. 242.

exhausted to do more execution. The English losses were few: by their own account, which is probably true, fewer than a dozen men were killed, although many of the horses lay dead or wounded.[1]

Meantime what of Águila? His men were all ready in arms waiting to go out as soon as the Irish gave their signal. When the firing of musketry and arquebuses was heard they displayed, at least Archbishop Oviedo so reports, great eagerness to join the battle. But as they prepared to take the field Águila ordered them back, and when they showed impatience at being restrained he issued an edict declaring that the Irish were not engaging the enemy but that the firing was an English stratagem designed to draw them out. This edict duly quietened them.[2]

Then at the end of the battle the English fired a volley in token of victory. This at last Don Juan decided was the Irish signal to him that they had engaged the enemy, and he sallied out to help. But the real nature of the situation became apparent to him at once when he saw the Spanish colours being carried by the English and he beat a hasty retreat. The English drove some forty or sixty badly wounded soldiers into the town to let Águila know the disaster that had befallen his allies. The relentless Mountjoy spared no Irish prisoners and hanged many, some two or three hundred it was said, within sight of the town.[3]

The brief fight at Kinsale was of disastrous consequence for native Ireland. The Irish armies were now dispersed and their Spanish allies were again encircled in Kinsale, with the enemy in control of all land and sea approaches. While the Spaniards at Castlehaven deplored the opportunity that had been missed they were unaware that the Irish had been faced with a task really beyond their powers. A half-hour's resistance by the chiefs would, as López said, have ensured victory.

1. *Pac. Hib.*, ii. 60–1; AGS, Estado 620: news from London, 17 Jan., old style; Guerra Antigua 3144: Castel-Rodrigo to Philip, 24 Jan., with report by Cerdá (estimate of 300–1,500 dead); account by Sandoval (500 Irish and 90 Spanish casualties, between dead and captured); Guerra Antigua 3145: Águila to Philip, Cork, 26 Feb.

2. AGS, Guerra Antigua 3145 (*Rep. Nov.*, i (1955), 115–116; *Epistolario de Zubiaur*, p. 138): memorandum by Oviedo for king and royal council, 27 Jan.

3. *Pac. Hib.*, ii. 62; Moryson, *Itinerary*, iii. 81–2; AGS, Estado 620: news from London, 10 and 17 Jan., old style. López's story that Don Juan sallied out and killed four hundred of the enemy and gained seven standards and some English pieces receives no other confirmation, and in spite of its circumstantial detail cannot be accepted. Oviedo, if it were true, could hardly accuse Águila of cravenness or worse. Oleaga, who carried this story with him from Castlehaven on 6 January, left before there was time properly to sift the truth of the rumours about what had happened at Kinsale.

For the combined Irish and Spanish forces had had a considerable local superiority in numbers to the enemy and (as Ensign Sandoval pointed out) ought, considering Don Juan's successes in his sallies, to have had easy victory. Yet, López decided, to maintain this was to forget that in the ability to conduct an engagement the Irish were altogether without experience. They were without military discipline and up to the time of the battle of Kinsale they had conducted the war by means of ambuscades in rough country, with each man acting individually. They had no idea of any other method of fighting or of battle-formation. So they had carried on the fight for over eight years, and their success had given such hope of conclusive victory that the relief of Águila was taken for granted when the chiefs arrived. This belief was supported, as Oleaga suggested, by two factors: the fear shown by the lord deputy who began to entrench himself very strongly on all sides, and the declaration of the Munster Irish for Águila. The chiefs came a great distance, overcame a thousand difficulties and upsets, gamely endured hunger and fear, only to fail at the important hurdle.[1]

O'Neill's forces, hotly pursued by St. Laurence, fled in disorder from the battlefield, the infantry throwing away their arms to lighten themselves. About 140 were drowned crossing the Blackwater; others going by way of Connelloe lost 200 of their number in the river Moy and at Owen Abbey; carriages were abandoned; and the wounded were cut down in north-west Munster. It would seem that O'Donnell retired his men, who had been only very lightly engaged, in better order and came to rest on a hill eight miles away. O'Neill, who had lost all but a fraction of his army, was with him. Next day, 4 January, O'Neill wrote to Águila that he could no longer help him since enemy devastation in his own territories called him home. He then set out for the north again. A report said that he led home only 600 troops out of the 6,000 that he had brought to the south. The latter figure was exaggerated by at least one-third, but the former may be near the truth.

Soon Richard Owen was seeking on O'Neill's behalf to negotiate a pardon for the chief. But O'Neill's feelers produced such unacceptable terms from Mountjoy, including agreement to the shiring of his country, that he gave up the negotiations.[2]

1. *Epistolario de Zubiaur*, p. 133.
2. *Pac. Hib.*, ii. 93, 95–100; AGS, Guerra Antigua 3144: Águila to Philip, Cork, 11 Feb.; Guerra Antigua 3145: same to same, 26 Feb.

O'Donnell gave command of the army of Tyrconnell to his brother Rory, who led it home by way of Connacht. Red Hugh himself went to join Zubiaur. O'Neill's intention was that O'Donnell would remain with Zubiaur and his Spaniards until further reinforcements should come from Spain. Only if such help came would the native cause now survive. Captain Richard Tyrrell escaped westwards and eventually installed himself with some of his men in the castle on Cape Clear; the rest of his companies were dispersed in west Cork, Kerry, and Limerick.[1]

On Saturday, 5 January, Hugh O'Donnell arrived at Castlehaven to tell the astonished Spaniards of the rout of the Irish army, seven or eight thousand men in number, by an enemy force of only 500 men. The young chief, as he confessed, was still at a loss to explain the defeat. Next day Zubiaur, accompanied by Sebastián de Oleaga, took ship for Spain. Red Hugh insisted on accompanying them, although Zubiaur and López insisted that King Philip would be displeased at his leaving when his men so badly needed encouragement. O'Donnell felt strongly that only by appealing in person to Philip could he secure the help that Ireland needed. He took with him his confessor, the Franciscan Father Florence Conry, and some captains.[2]

Prospects of adequate help from Spain were now, however, poor in the extreme. The duke of Medina Sidonia, the luckless sea commander of the 'invincible' armada, reported that shipping was in a poorer state in his command of Andalusia than it had been for forty years. The native Spaniards were rapidly giving up seamanship. The duke's well-known pessimistic outlook had not improved with the years, but in fact he could find no-one in Cádiz or San Lucar to take the risk of bringing food or clothes to Ireland.[3]

But from Lisbon the five ships that Moura had been preparing since October sailed out for Ireland on 1 January, with Captain Martín de Ballecilla in command. Ballecilla was captain of the *San Pablo*, flagship of the Atlantic fleet, and had already been in Kinsale with Brochero. They carried two infantry companies, together with a supply of

1. AGS, Guerra Antigua 3144: account by Sandoval; Estado 620: news from London, 10 Jan., old style; *Pac. Hib.*, ii. 69–70, 116; Guerra Antigua 3144: O'Neill to Philip, from his camp, 16 Jan., with covering letter, Zúñiga to Philip, Ostend, 14 May; Águila to Philip, 17 Jan.
2. *Pac. Hib.*, ii. 64; AGS, Guerra Antigua 3145: Zubiaur to Philip, Luarca, 15 Jan.; (*Epistolario de Zubiaur*, p. 99): López to Philip, two letters, Castlehaven, 6 Jan.; Estado 1745: memorandum by 'Mac Dermud', 2 Apr. 1603.
3. AGS, Guerra Antigua 592: Medina Sidonia to Philip, San Lucar, 5 Jan.

biscuit. Three were driven back to Spain by contrary winds and Balle-cilla arrived off Kinsale with the other two on 14 January only to learn that Águila had surrendered; whereupon he returned to Lisbon.[1]

The same day that Ballecilla arrived off Kinsale Zubiaur was making port at Luarca in Asturias. From Luarca Oleaga brought the news of the rout at Kinsale to the king on Saturday, 20 January. Zubiaur repeated Águila's complaint that Don Juan had been placed in an impossible position in an indefensible hollow in unfriendly country. Castlehaven, Baltimore, and Berehaven were, Don Pedro maintained, more easily defensible than Kinsale, and Philip should strengthen their land and sea defences. Philip ought also, he proposed, send an armada to Limerick, to take Limerick or Galway and effect a junction with O'Neill and O'Donnell at Galway.[2]

Águila had already surrendered to Mountjoy on 12 January. His men were now down to 1,800 effectives, and of the 800 or so others who were ill some ten to twelve were dying every day. He was with-out two great advantages which commonly enabled a besieged place in that age to hold out indefinitely against attack: control of the water approaches, enabling reinforcements or supplies to land, and strong fortifications. It was knowledge of these weaknesses, coupled with his belief that the Irish had failed him, first in refusing to give battle and then in withdrawing, that prompted him to seek honourable terms when he was not without certain advantages over Mountjoy. For the wind still favoured ships from Spain and Águila had six weeks' food—though only bread and wine—against the lord deputy's six days' provisions. Mountjoy's fleet was almost without food. In spite of the three breaches he had made in the walls and in spite of the three forts at the western side designed to prevent Águila from sallying out, he had no hope of taking the town by storm, his men were so weakened and discontented.[3] Águila had made three vigorous sorties from his western gate since the battle, two on 4 January, which by their own

1. AGS, Guerra Antigua 591: memorandum by Ballecilla, Corunna, 18/20 Jan. 1602; Guerra Antigua 592: statements by A. Carreno y Baldés, 13 Jan.; Guerra Antigua 3144: Castel-Rodrigo to Philip 9 Jan. and (with report by Cerdá) 24 Jan.; Águila to Ibarra, Kinsale, 18 Jan.; Guerra Antigua 3145: Riva Herrera to Philip, Santander, 13 Jan.; statement by Aguilar, 13 Jan.; Iguizcuiza to Caracena, Vivero, 14 Jan.; Mexía to same, Ribadeo, 14 Jan.; Guerra Antigua 592: Caracena to Philip, 27 Jan.

2. *Epistolario de Zubiaur*, p. 138; AGS, Guerra Antigua 3145: Zubiaur to Philip, Luarca, 15 Jan., and Corunna, 21 Jan.

3. *Pac. Hib.*, ii. 85; AGS, Guerra Antigua 3145: Oviedo to Philip and his royal council, 27 Jan.

admission 'crased' five English pieces, and one the following night, and had been repulsed only after difficult fighting. Mountjoy feared from conversations with his Spanish prisoners that a relieving force must soon come from Spain and overcome his own fleet. His main strength lay in his cavalry, but he had no oats for his horses. He was anxious to strengthen his grip on the country again and acutely aware of the fact that the Spaniards held three other strongholds in Munster. The lord deputy, therefore, was glad to accept Águila's terms.[1]

In the articles of composition signed by the rival commanders on 12 January Don Juan agreed to surrender Kinsale and the forts of Castlehaven, Baltimore, and Berehaven. He undertook that his men would not bear arms against Elizabeth, no matter what reinforcements might come from Spain, before their return home. In guarantee of good faith Águila agreed to remain behind until the second embarkment, should two echelons of shipping be necessary to take his troops back to Spain. Three captains, Pedro Morejón, Pedro Zuazo, and Diego González Sigler, would remain behind as pledges when all the others had gone.

Mountjoy agreed for his part to give Águila enough shipping and victuals (to be paid for by Don Juan) to transport his men, whether Spaniards or others, back to Spain with all he had, his arms, artillery, money, ensigns, and so on. Archbishop Oviedo is alone in saying that the ships were to be provided within a month, for none of the various versions of the articles of capitulation contains such a clause. Finally it was agreed that there would be a cessation of arms and a truce at sea until the Spaniards were shipped home.[2] Fr. Archer, S.J., understanding that Águila during the three days' discussions which it took to conclude the peace was consenting to hand him over to the English, escaped to join the Spaniards at Dunboy. There he found his fellow Jesuit, Brother Dominic Collins.[3]

On 19 January the lord deputy, taking with him Águila and many of his captains, removed to Cork. From there he intended to conduct a campaign to extinguish the revolt in Munster. Águila agreed to hand

1. AGS, Guerra Antigua 3144: report by Sandoval, Mar. 1602; Águila to Philip, Cork, 19 Jan.; Guerra Antigua 591: Águila to Ibarra, Kinsale, 18 Jan.; Estado 620: news from London, 2 Feb., old style; *Epistolario de Zubiaur*, p. 319: account of Zubiaur's experiences, 25 Jan.; *Pac. Hib.*, ii. 71–7.

2. AGS, Guerra Antigua 3145: Oviedo to Lerma, Kinsale, 26 Jan.; *Pac. Hib.*, ii. 78–81; *Cal. S.P. Venice, 1592–1603*, p. 496; VA, Borghese III, 65 C, f. 41 (*Archiv. Hib.*, iii (1914), 247–8): articles of capitulation.

3. *Archiv. Hib.*, xvii (1953), 11.

over the castles of Castlehaven, Donneshed (or Baltimore), Donnelong, and Dunboy, and so informed López de Soto.[1] But the return home of the Spaniards from Kinsale and the handing-over of the castles was held up for a month because of bad weather.[2]

In the period of waiting neither Don Juan nor Oviedo, who had remained in Kinsale, was idle. Each set down for Philip's benefit his own opinion of what had been amiss with the handling of affairs and of what was now to be done. Oviedo blamed Don Juan for not keeping open the entrance by sea to Kinsale or a passage for O'Neill and O'Donnell to enter by land. He blamed him also for turning away the Irish who had offered service and for not keeping his word to join O'Neill on the morning of the battle.[3]

While the archbishop wanted Spain to disregard the treaty, Don Juan had given up the fight. He credited Mountjoy with having 10,000 veterans of the wars in 'Flanders, France and Brittany' in Ireland now, with four to five thousand levies to come. In fact Mountjoy had just cashiered 2,000 men in list, and the new English levies existed yet only in intention. The truth was that Don Juan had turned against the Irish and now lent a ready ear to everything the astute lord deputy told him. Águila accused the Munster Irish, some of whom were now eagerly seeking pardon from Mountjoy, of double-dealing, as he did O'Neill for now negotiating through Richard Owen with the queen. Águila had fault to find with Brochero and the ecclesiastics who had supported him for insisting on the landing in the south. He had fault too to find with Pedro López: if López had sent the bulk of his men to O'Neill, said Don Juan, the Irish would not have failed to take the position he himself had assigned them. In regard to the castles, what López and Zubiaur should have done, Don Juan contended (and it is impossible not to agree with him), was make the Irish keep secret their declaration for Philip and let them remain in possession of all the castles but one.

Don Juan found three causes for the Spanish failure in Ireland. In the first place, he said, it was possible to take any port in Ireland; a Spanish expedition might yet take Cork. But to defend a port was the trouble. If Águila had been sent to join the chiefs in the beginning, he

---

1. *Pac. Hib.*, ii. 85–9, 110; AGS, Guerra Antigua 3144, Estado 188: Águila to López, Kinsale, 17 Jan.

2. AGS, Estado 188: López to Philip, Castlehaven, 22 Feb.

3. AGS, Guerra Antigua 3145 (*Rep. Nov.*, i. 115–16): Oviedo to Lerma, 26 Jan., and to king and council, 27 Jan.

would have had time to fortify some places, to which reinforcements could have been sent. Secondly, Zubiaur had not heeded Águila's order to send his men to join O'Neill. Thirdly, Brochero when he returned from Kinsale should have gone directly to Corunna (for report said he had had time) and come back with reinforcements to Águila.[1] He might have added, but did not, another cause: Spain's failure to heed Zubiaur's advice to keep Brochero's ships at Kinsale throughout the winter.

1. AGS, Guerra Antigua 3144: Águila to López, Kinsale, 17 Jan., with note added by López; Guerra Antigua 3145: Águila to Philip, 11 Feb.; same to same, 26 Feb.

XI · WITHDRAWAL

Thus was Tyrone made the tennis-ball of fortune, and abandoned by Spain's over-prized greatness.

Thomas Gainsford, *The true exemplary and remarkable
history of the earl of Tyrone* (1619)

I cannot believe that Your Majesty is planning to send an army
to Ireland, for that I hold would be the course of least value and
most risk, with failure almost certain.

Don Diego Brochero to Philip, 4 June 1602[1]

THE SURRENDER OF ÁGUILA was cruel luck for the lords of the south-
west, whose long record of loyalty prior to the coming of Zubiaur
would not now preserve them from the vengeance of the lord deputy.
Their decision to throw in their lot with the Spaniards and O'Neill had
been a mistake, and now they must pay the penalty. But they could
not believe that Spain would abandon them. Daniel O'Sullivan Beare
and the O'Driscolls therefore renewed again their oaths of fidelity
before López, and vowing to maintain themselves against the English
until the end of May, even if they did lose their castles, retreated with
two or three thousand men to a mountain pass five leagues from
Castlehaven.

López de Soto, although he agreed with these lords that they had
been unjustly treated, handed over the castles to the English when
they came to take delivery. Captain Harvey took over Castlehaven
Castle on 22 February and Donneshed and Donnelong Castles on 7
March. López was interested to see that the English soldiers were even
more dispirited and miserable than the poor wretches of Gallegos who
had come to Castlehaven; until now he had thought that no soldiers
could be inferior in quality to these. On 12 March, Pedro López,
Barragán, and the garrisons set sail for Spain, taking with them the
seven cannon from Donnelong. On board the three ships were four

---

1. *No me persuado que V. Md. trate de meter gente en Yrlanda, porque lo tengo por cossa de
menos substancia, mas arriscada, y casi cierto el ruin subcesso.*

hundred and thirty men from Castlehaven, Donneshed, Donnelong, and Dunboy in eight companies.[1] They were in Corunna by 20 March. Richard Tyrrell vacated the castle at Cape Clear, in which Harvey placed a guard; but Captain George Flower was prevented by the harsh weather from reaching Dunboy from Berehaven.[2]

The news of the defeat at Kinsale caused great alarm in Spain. The government feared that England would now be free to send more troops to Flanders and to dispatch her sea forces to help the Dutch and prey on the Spanish treasure fleets. Ironically, the English also expected a fresh attack by Spain on Ireland, to retrieve the situation there. But Lerma, for want of 'ships, soldiers, sailors, arms and munitions', could not consider strong reinforcements at short notice. With Velada, Idiáquez, and Fray Gaspar he devised a plan to send a small flotilla at once, either to remove Águila to a better position or to retire his army to Spain.[3] The council of war planned to follow up this force with an army of 6,000 men, 3,000 Portuguese and 3,000 levies, to be sent as soon as possible.

But that these plans would ever materialize was doubtful in the extreme. There was a dearth of men in Portugal. Moreover, the men returned from Ireland told such tales of the harsh and poverty-stricken conditions there as to frighten others from going. In any case transports could not be found to take an army to Ireland. Finally, even if such a large army as was planned could be raised, it was very unlikely, as the council well knew, that it could be withdrawn from Spain.[4]

While the council were in fact still debating what ought to be done for Ireland Ensign Retés landed at Corunna on 25 February with news of Águila's surrender. Retés was followed within a fortnight by the

1. *Pac. Hib.*, ii. 115–16; AGS, Guerra Antigua 3144: López to Philip, Baltimore, 3 and 6 Mar., and Corunna, 21 Mar.; memorandum by López 28 Feb.; Guerra Antigua 591: Barragán to (Philip), Vivero, 22 Mar.

2. AGS, Guerra Antigua 3144: López to Philip, Corunna, 20 and 21 Mar. and 2 Apr.; Águila to López, 17 Jan. with note by López; Guerra Antigua 591: López to Philip, 27 Mar.

3. AGS, Estado 840, f. 48 (*Cal. S.P. Spain, 1587–1603,* pp. 699–703): *consulta* by junta of four, Valdavida, 29 Jan.; f. 34 (*Cal.*, cit., p. 703): Philip to Águila, Mansilla, 30 Jan.; f. 35: Philip to López, 31 Jan.; Estado 188: López to Zubiaur, 13 Feb.; Guerra Antigua 591: Philip to Caracena and to Caracena (*recte* Zubiaur), Zamora, 13 Feb.

4. AGS, Guerra Antigua 589: *consultas* by council of war, 25 Jan. and 8 Feb.; Estado 840, f. 47 (*Cal. S.P. Spain, 1587–1603,* pp. 703–4): Franqueza to Lerma, 13 Feb. 1602; Estado 840, f. 159 (*Cal.*, cit., pp. 705–7): *consulta* by council of state, Vallid., 21 Feb.; Guerra Antigua 591: royal schedules to Águila and others, Zamora, 13 Feb.; Guerra Antigua 3144: Castel-Rodrigo to Philip, twice, Lisbon, 11 Dec. 1601; Guerra Antigua 590: memorandum by council of state, Vallid., 13 Feb. (?).

ships carrying Legoretta's *tercio*, 1,374 men in all, led by Ocampo. As a result the Spanish administration called off all preparations and decided merely to send 20,000 ducats to the lords of Berehaven, Castlehaven, and Baltimore.[1]

There in south-west Munster things had taken a dramatic turn. Daniel O'Sullivan, with Tyrrell and Father Archer, had been refused pardon by Mountjoy. When Castlehaven was handed over the news was brought straightaway to O'Sullivan, who was also told that his own castle of Dunboy was next to be delivered up. This was more than the proud chieftain would stand. Stationing a thousand men near Dunboy, he, Father Archer, and another priest sought and gained admission from Saavedra. That night Daniel admitted two hundred of his followers through the cellars, and the next day after a short struggle he wrested possession of Dunboy from Saavedra. This was on Saturday, 23 February.[2]

Associated with O'Sullivan in his coup were many of the lords of the south-west, and others rallied to his side. Supporting him now he had Denis O'Driscoll of Castlehaven, Daniel MacCarthy More, Sir Finnin O'Driscoll's son Cornelius, and O'Sullivan More's son Daniel. Sir Finnin himself had already returned to the queen's allegiance, but all his followers were with Cornelius. With O'Sullivan also were Captain Richard Tyrrell and his brother Walter; Richard came, although he realized full well the futility of O'Sullivan's action.[3] The Tyrrells and William Burke, brother of Redmond the baron of Leitrim, brought between them a thousand men. A number of the principal men of the Desmond connection, among them Thomas Fitzmaurice, baron of Lixnaw, the Knight of the Valley, and the Knight of Kerry, came too. In all these lords commanded 3,000 men, armed according to the Irish fashion, except for the 350 who had received arquebuses from Zubiaur and the 650 who had received pikes. Many others waited to see the outcome of O'Sullivan's stand before declaring themselves.

O'Sullivan made as brave a show as he could. He put 150 men to

1. AGS, Guerra Antigua 591: Caracena to Philip, Corunna 9 Mar. Cf. Estado 188: same to same, 27 May; Guerra Antigua 589: *consulta* by council of war, Vallid., 14 Mar.; Guerra Antigua 591: Philip to Caracena, Vallid., 19 Mar.; Guerra Antigua 3144: Ocampo to Philip, Corunna, 8 Mar.

2. AGS, Guerra Antigua 591: Águila to Philip, Corunna, 2 Apr. 1602; Guerra Antigua 3144: Saavedra to López, 23 Feb.

3. AGS, Guerra Antigua 3144: Tyrrell to López, Berehaven, 3 Mar.

guard Dunboy and stationed 1,200 outside to skirmish. He sent the Spaniards to be embarked with López at Baltimore, but retained their artillery and three of their gunners.[1] He held the castle for the king of Spain, he declared, and would render it up only at Philip's order. López, far from displeased at O'Sullivan's coup, urged the king to send help to Dunboy before April.[2]

Águila, on the other hand, was annoyed at Daniel's impulsiveness. He suspected that Carew and others were urging on Mountjoy that the seizure of Dunboy excused him from being any longer obliged by the treaty. Yet, although it has been alleged that he offered to win back Dunboy for Mountjoy, the fact is that Don Juan stoutly maintained that the treaty was in no way affected by O'Sullivan's action and that the lord deputy was still bound to return to him the artillery in Dunboy. The latter, to his credit, agreed with Don Juan and promised when he had regained the castle to embark the artillery for Spain, provided that O'Sullivan received no voluntary Spanish help to enable him to defend the castle.[3] Mountjoy foresaw little difficulty in taking an Irish castle when the time came.

O'Sullivan too was aware that Dunboy would be difficult to defend against English bombardment. He planned to make a last stand, should it come to that, on Dursey Island and placed Cornelius O'Driscoll with sixty men there. Cornelius with three pieces fortified the island to the best of his ability.[4]

As for Mountjoy, he was more concerned with O'Neill than with O'Sullivan. Taking Carew with him, he set out on 19 March for Dublin; from there the lord deputy planned to attack O'Neill in Ulster. Águila meanwhile, taking advantage of the first fair wind for Spain, set sail and landed at Corunna on the evening of Palm Sunday, 31 March. With him came Archbishop Oviedo. The army was now all returned: some 2,200 men from Kinsale and some 440 from the other ports. Don Juan had brought back besides his munitions a treasure of 59,000 ducats. Before he left he heard that Richard Owen had gone to England to treat of pardon for O'Neill. All in all his experience in

---

1. AGS, Guerra Antigua 3144: Saavedra to López, Berehaven, 23 Feb.; López to Philip, Baltimore, 6 and 21 Mar.; O'Sullivan to López, Berehaven, 23 Feb.; Guerra Antigua 591: López to Philip, Corunna, 27 Mar.; Guerra Antigua 590: O'Sullivan's replies to López, Ardea, 17 June; *Pac. Hib.*, ii. 118–20; P. O'Sullivan Beare, *Hist. cath. Ibern. comp.*, pp. 234–5.

2. AGS, Estado 188: O'Sullivan to Caracena, 25 Feb.

3. AGS, Guerra Antigua 3144: López to Philip, Baltimore, 6 Mar.; Águila to López, Cork, 28 Feb.; Guerra Antigua 3145: Mountjoy to Águila, Cork, 23 Feb., old style.

4. *Pac. Hib.*, ii. 127–9.

Ireland had left him with a thorough distaste for all things Irish and an equal regard for the English and their greatness.[1]

There in effect the matter rested. López continued to plead for support for O'Sullivan in Dunboy and for a force to re-take Castlehaven and Baltimore.[2] But Spain would do no more, and the troops being levied were already being redirected to the Indies. The efforts still being made by the archduke to raise private Irish soldiers in Flanders to go to O'Neill's aid could then be of little avail.[3] O'Donnell was entertained with fair words by the governor at Corunna and this encouraged him in his pathetic belief that an armada would yet go to Ireland this summer and fortified him against abuse flung at him by the Spaniards returned from Ireland, who maintained that the Irish had betrayed them at Kinsale. Supported by the ever-faithful archbishop of Dublin, he kept up his pleas for an auxiliary force to keep the war going until summer had brought the armada.[4]

In Oviedo's mind there was no question but that Philip would come to Ireland's rescue. His concern was rather with the problem of winning over the loyalist Irish, on whom the queen's strength depended. His association with Ireland went back over a quarter of a century, during which period he had visited the country seven times in all. Heart and soul committed to O'Neill's cause, he was convinced that the great need was to get from Rome a clear order forbidding Catholics to oppose O'Neill and the Spaniards. In Munster he had found the priests urging their flocks to take arms against the Spaniards and their Irish allies; these clergy had thus effectively prejudiced the success of the expedition. Until such a definite order as he wanted came from Rome, Oviedo knew from discussions with these priests, they would continue to preach political obedience to the crown. Philip, he decided, must renew at Rome the attempt, defeated by the Anglo-Irish in the previous year, to secure from the pope a *motu proprio* forbidding

1. AGS, Guerra Antigua 591: Águila to Philip, 2 Apr.; López to same, 31 Mar.; Oviedo to Ibarra, 31 Mar. All Corunna; Guerra Antigua 590: attestation by López, 2 Apr.; Guerra Antigua 3144: Caracena to Philip, 23 May, with musters of 14 Apr. and 15 May; *Pac. Hib.*, ii. 136.

2. AGS, Guerra Antigua 3144: López to Philip, Castlehaven, 3 Mar; Guerra Antigua 591: same to same, Corunna, 27 Mar.

3. AGS, Guerra Antigua 592: Philip to Medina Sidonia and to the commissioners going to Lisbon, Vallid., 30 Mar.; Estado 620: Zúñiga to Philip, Nieuport, 23 Apr., and Ostend 14 May.

4. AGS, Estado 188: O'Donnell to Philip, Corunna, 21 and 22 Mar.; Caracena to same, 21 Mar.; *consulta* on these letters; Estado 840, f. 5: Philip to Caracena, 3 Apr.

all the Irish under severe censures to take arms against the Spaniards
and O'Neill in their fight for the Catholic faith.

The archbishop, did he but know it, was wasting his breath. Lerma
saw himself well out of the Irish war and had no desire to enter that
arena again. After all, he had shown England that the queen was not
immune from attack in her own sphere of interests, and as the main
strength of the expedition had returned home, the demonstration had
been worth the cost.

But even the indolent Lerma agreed that the Irish account could not
be written off just like that. Charges and counter-charges were being
hurled about. Wearisome though they were, some effort must be
made to deal with them. While López de Soto refused to agree with
Águila that Spain must withdraw from the Irish theatre, Oviedo
accused the general of both ineptitude and cowardice. López, who was
undoubtedly a meddler, again quarrelled with the archbishop over
the conduct of the hospital and complained that Oviedo had been
ready on the slightest occasion—*por quítame essa paja*—to impede him
at Kinsale.[1] Don Juan, while he agreed with López in accusing Oviedo
of interference, charged that López himself had refused to obey his
orders. He himself, of course, had done his best at Kinsale. Had not
Mountjoy come under censure from his own side for not holding
Águila to ransom? The lord deputy, said Águila, would not have made
peace had he not mistakenly believed that Águila had had food for
three months; and had Don Juan not by continuous sallies deceived
him into thinking that the Spaniards were greater in number than
was the case? Mountjoy had not realized that so many of the Spaniards
were ill.

Lerma, in face of these and other reproaches cast so freely by the
leaders of the expedition against one another, had no option but
to refer the matter to the council of war, which reported back on 6
April that a full investigation was necessary. Lerma, on the advice
of the council, appointed Castel-Rodrigo at Lisbon, Caracena at
Corunna, and Diego de Ibarra of the council of war at court to collect
evidence.[2]

Philip, also on the council's advice, rejected López's proposal to send
a force of 3,000 men before the end of April to Berehaven, but agreed

---

1. AGS, Guerra Antigua 591: López to Philip, Corunna, 23 Apr.
2. AGS, Guerra Antigua 3144: note on folder enclosing López's papers: Guerra Antigua
589: *consulta* by council of war, Vallid., 6 Apr.

to send a cargo of arms and munitions with money to O'Sullivan, to show that the king was not deserting him.[1]

The commission of inquiry soon had in its hands the testimony of Diego de Brochero. Don Diego gave his account of the disputes over the port of disembarkation and of his quarrel with Águila over the landing of the provisions and munitions at Kinsale and over his departure from Kinsale. With the substance of his account the reader is already familiar.[2] Brochero was now a member of the council of war, and the council on his advice ordered a halt to the levy of infantry in Portugal. Brochero also advised Lerma against sending another expedition to its doom in Ireland. Spain, he suggested, should rather keep the war alive by sending a subsidy of 100,000 ducats to the chiefs.[3]

Knowing that the king was in receipt of such advice, and denied permission to go to court to counter it, Hugh O'Donnell ate out his heart in Corunna. He begged first for a force of 2,000 men and then even a smaller force to take with him to Ireland, and finally at least to be himself allowed to go to fall fighting besides his friends in the north. But his appeals were in vain; Brochero had convinced the council of state, which now endorsed the council of war's decision against sending 3,000 men, as being too small a force, to Berehaven.[4]

The Adelantado stood alone in the council for attack, and strong attack on Elizabeth. He proposed to lead an army of 25,000 men against England, 14,000 of his own and the rest to be raised in Flanders by Fedérico Spínola. The stout-hearted old warrior had in his enthusiasm forgotten what his shrewder brother-councillors saw, that if such a force as Spínola offered to raise materialized in Flanders it would get no further, for the archduke would appropriate it. But not to discourage Don Martín altogether, the council suggested that he might be provided with a sum of 1,000,000 ducats in order to finance an expedition by Fedérico Spínola, not to England now, but to Ireland.[5]

1. AGS, Guerra Antigua 3144: dispatches from López, Baltimore, 6 Mar, and Corunna, 21 Mar.; Guerra Antigua 589: *consulta* by council of war, Vallid., 10 Apr.

2. Cf. pp. 109, 113–14, *supra*.

3. AGS, Guerra Antigua 587: *consulta* by council of war, Vallid., 20 Apr.; Estado 188: Brochero to Philip, Lisbon, 4 June.

4. AGS, Estado 840, ff. 76–7, 73 (*Cal. S.P. Spain, 1587–1603*, pp. 709–12): O'Donnell to Philip, Corunna, 15 and 25 Apr.; Estado 840, f. 68: Caracena to Philip, 25 Apr.; Estado 840, ff. 32–3 (*Cal.*, cit., p. 713. Hume's summary is inaccurate): *consulta* by council of state 1 May.

5. AGS, Estado 840, f. 36 (*Cal.*, cit., pp. 713–15): *consulta* by council of state, Aranjuez, 13 May.

For the English invasion Ambrosio, Fedérico's brother, had raised 9,000 Italians. With these he left Italy on 2 May 1602 and marched through Burgundy to Luxembourg. At Puerto de Santa María Fedérico made ready eight galleys and left on 14 April, but in a sea-fight with Richard Levison and William Monson off the coast of Portugal he lost two and so reached Lisbon with only six.[1]

This was the position when in May the Adelantado put forward his plan. It was, however, now clear, if not to the Irish, that Lerma would send no further aid of any substance to Ireland. Red Hugh O'Donnell throughout April and May continued to cherish hopes of being sent back to his country with a force of 2,000 men, the forerunner of a full-sized army to be sent to Ireland before winter. But his repeated calls for this force went unanswered.

Instead on 24 May Ensign Diego de Cuenca sailed from Corunna in the *Santiaguillo*, carrying 20,000 ducats in money and some supplies for distribution to O'Sullivan, the O'Driscolls and other southern leaders. Governor Caracena advised these lords by letter that they could expect an abundance of similar supplies in the near future.

Pedro López de Soto strongly supported the sending of aid to O'Sullivan, and sought to convince the administration of its obligation, on both spiritual and material grounds, to maintain the Irish Catholics in their struggle. Pedro López appealed to his king in the latter's role of defender of the faith; not only the Irish, he said, but the English Catholics put their trust in the king of Spain. So far, said López, the help sent to Ireland had been too small, and both time and landing-place had been wrong.

Besides supernatural there were human motives which must, López believed, inspire Spain in this matter. Spanish aid to Ireland, he said, would leave England with her hands full in Ireland and prevent her from embarrassing the sea-lanes which the plate fleets took or from aiding the rebels in Flanders. This was shown, Pedro pointed out, when the Spaniards landed at Kinsale, for the queen then withdrew her galleons and men from Ostend. Even were Ostend to capitulate, Maurice would still maintain the struggle in the Low Countries, and a diversion in Ireland would yet be useful for preventing England from giving him anything but weak support.

López went on to suggest that Spain use Ireland as a base for launching an attack, with ten to twelve thousand men, on England,

1. Rodríguez Villa, *Ambrosio Spínola*, pp. 32–5, 51.

as soon as that country divided on the succession question. He made proposals for sending immediate help, perhaps in May, to Ireland, and especially to Daniel O'Sullivan Beare, before Dunboy was forced to surrender.[1]

But although George Kerr, the Scottish exile, who had long been working for a Spanish invasion of Scotland, now put the interests of Ireland first and supported López in his demand for an invasion of Ireland, he did so in vain. Father Florence Conry attended the court at the Escorial from June onwards, trying to get a licence for Red Hugh to come to court; but without result. Meanwhile O'Neill had turned to Archduke Albert for help. But his request for four shiploads of munitions and other war-stores was merely referred by Albert to Philip, who on the advice of the council of state ignored this request too.[2]

Ireland was in fact written off; but in spite of the council of state's lukewarm attitude towards the Adelantado's proposals, Lerma and Philip were still attracted towards the idea of an attack on England. The king consulted Brochero, who advised that an attack by ships of high freeboard on England was bound to fail. With galleys, on the other hand, Don Diego thought it would be very easy to conquer England, but difficult thereafter to hold the country. His own suggestion was to send ten to twelve galleys, which he himself offered to command, well-manned with good, seasoned troops, to burn and pillage around the English coast and make Elizabeth come to terms.

But Philip had another idea. Without taking Albert (or Brochero) into his confidence the king instructed his ambassador Zúñiga that Ambrosio Spínola and his Italians (6,000 thought Philip, going on the Adelantado's figures, but in reality 9,000), with 5,000 Germans and Walloons, must go to Lisbon, there to embark on Federico's galleys. Federico would be given eight of the galleys of Spain to bring his total up to eighteen. A thousand Spaniards at Lisbon, as Castel-Rodrigo was instructed, would also be embarked. Philip wrote asking Albert not to impede Ambrosio:

... I ask you to allow Marquis Spínola ... to go with his 6,000 Italians where he wishes, and not to detain him a single hour. Where he is going Your

1. RAH, Colección Salazar, L, t. 24, ff. 61–8v: P. López de Soto, 'Causas divinas y humanas, que obligan a amparar a Yrlanda', May 1602 (?).
2. AGS, Estado 840, f. 201 (*Cal. S.P. Spain, 1587–1603*, p. 718): *consulta* by council of state, 13 Feb. 1603; Estado 620: Albert to Philip, Camp at Ostei d, 23 May 1602; Estado 2023: *consulta* by council of state, 15 June.

Excellency will still have him very near you, and he will keep the enemy so occupied that it will be as good as if you had them by your side. These men form the basis of his whole design, which you would wreck if you were to detain them.

Fedérico, engaged at Lisbon in repairing and fitting his galleys, was ordered by Lerma to the Escorial for final instructions. The Genoese then embarked a regiment of infantry at Santander, and on 9 September set out on his voyage. On 3 October he reached the English Channel. Here after running the gauntlet of some enemy ships he had his fleet broken up by storm. Two of his ships were lost, two made Nieuport, and he himself with the remaining two limped into Sluys on 16 October.[1]

Meanwhile Albert's siege of Ostend was proving ineffectual and he was being hard pressed by Maurice. Philip was then forced to divert Ambrosio from the proposed English expedition, and to send him in July to assist Don Francisco de Mendoza, the admiral of Aragón, who was besieging Diste. There for the rest of the summer Ambrosio served.[2]

At the same time the inquiry into the conduct of the Irish expedition proceeded. A total of fifty-three men, it was estimated, had deserted the Spanish ranks to join the English side during the siege of Kinsale, between 10 October 1601 and 12 January 1602, and Philip had arrests made among the troops returned to Corunna. Others were arrested because of seventeen barrels of powder not accounted for. Captain Basco de Saavedra was also placed under arrest, but Caracena after investigation satisfied himself that Saavedra was innocent of the charge against him, namely that it was through his negligence that O'Sullivan Beare had recovered his castle. Caracena's heart was not in the inquiry, for the idea of apportioning blame where everyone could be censured appeared to him to be pointless: 'siendo culpas tan generales que por lo menos se escapan muy pocos de cargarlos unos a otros.'[3]

While the inquiry took its snail-like pace, Ireland was left to its fate.

---

1. AGS, Estado 2224 (*Correspondance*, eds. Lonchay and Cuvelier, i. 105): Philip to Albert, San Lorenzo, 11 June 1602); Estado 2224: Philip to Zúñiga, 11 June, and to F. Spínola, San Lorenzo, 16 June; Rodríguez Villa, *Ambrosio Spínola*, pp. 36–7, 51–2.

2. Rodríguez Villa, op. cit., pp. 52–8.

3. AGS, Guerra Antigua, 3144: list sent by Juan Ochoa de Vaztorra, Corunna, 19 May; RAH, Col. Salazar, L, t. 24, f. 73: López to Caracena, 29 May; AGS, Guerra Antigua 591 Philip to Caracena, Aranjuez, 2 May; Guerra Antigua 3144: Caracena to Philip, Corunna, 25 May; Guerra Antigua 592: same to same, 20 May.

Mountjoy and Carew were reducing the country to subjection, Carew with savagery in south-west Munster and Mountjoy, though far from well, with determined ruthlessness in Ulster and the west. The lord deputy was anxious for a quick conclusion of the Irish business. For one reason, the results of his campaign against O'Neill were such as to sicken even an Elizabethan general in Ireland. With sword and famine he attacked O'Neill, and the famine brought cannibalism in its wake.[1] For another reason, Mountjoy could best win the gratitude of his queen by bringing the long costly war to a speedy close.[2] Docwra gained Ballyshannon castle on 4 April, while Mountjoy in June and July laid the foundations of Charlemont Fort on the river Blackwater and of Mountjoy Fort on the shores of Loch Neagh, caused O'Neill to flee from Dungannon to the shelter of Glenconkein Forest, devastated Monaghan, and established Conor Roe, the 'queen's Maguire', in Fermanagh.

Carew had Thomond ravage the country around Bantry Bay, while he himself proceeded westwards by way of Dunnemark to Dunboy. Meanwhile Sir Charles Wilmot had been laying Dingle and Iveragh waste and had driven the Lord of Lixnaw and the Knight of Kerry into Desmond. Carew left Cork on 3 May and arrived at Berehaven on 16 June. O'Sullivan Beare and his confederates were still awaiting with a strong trust the coming of the Spaniards.[3] But Sir George sent a force to take Dursey Island, which fell easily, and he took Dunboy after only one day's siege (27–8 June). After that it was only a matter of stamping out the embers of revolt in south-west Munster; and this was done with grim efficiency. Tyrrell fled to King's County in December and on 13 January O'Sullivan set out on his famous march to Leitrim, which he and the remnant of his following reached after fourteen days.[4]

With grand indifference to the spectacle of Gaelic Ireland writhing in her death-agony, the Spaniards pursued their investigation into the causes of the failure of Águila's expedition. Archbishop Oviedo's evidence to the commission of inquiry covered familiar ground; he had nothing new to add to his earlier strictures on Águila's conduct

1. '... finally [O'Neill and Rory O'Donnell], hoping for help from Spain, never surrendered until innumerable numbers of their people died from pure hunger and until some of them were eating one another ...'; AGS, Estado 840, f. 56: paper presented by O'Neill to Castro, Spanish ambassador at Rome, with *consulta* by council of state, 24 Mar. 1610.

2. Falls, *Mountjoy*, pp. 194–5.

3. AGS, Guerra Antigua 590: dispatches and letters forwarded by Caracena to Philip, Corunna, 28 July.

4. A.F.M.; *Pac. Hib.*, ii. 148–315; O'Sullivan Beare, *Hist. cath. Ibern. comp.*, pp. 234–54.

except on one point. Águila, he said, had entered Kinsale harbour not of his own choice; his ships were there before Don Juan knew where he was. When he discovered his position he was disgusted, but found himself unable to sail to Castlehaven: 'pero que por hallarse ensenados en el Quinzal, antes de acavalle [=acabarle] de reconocer, no pudieron entonces yr a Castelaven.' Afterwards, though, Oviedo maintained, it was quite possible for Águila to go to Castlehaven; why he did not the archbishop could not say.[1]

If Oviedo made charges against Águila, the latter had an advocate who was able to reply to the archbishop in kind. Deacon Pedro de Colmenares had gone to Kinsale with Águila and was there all the time until the treaty. He made allegations about secret meetings between the archbishop and some captains at Oviedo's house, where extraordinary things were said.[2]

The archbishop, said Colmenares, had sent without Águila's order or knowledge certain dispatches to the chiefs. These dispatches were carried by Oviedo's servant, Pedro Ibáñez, who had gone with the consent of Captain Zarate over the wall with them. The day that the chiefs were routed, said the deacon, no fighting was seen, but the musket-fire was heard most plainly. Colmenares spoke of the 'great fear' then displayed by the archbishop and his friends and of their desire to surrender themselves. But his charges of intrigue are vague and were prompted most likely by sheer pique or malice, his own or Águila's.[3] Oviedo's charges had more influence on the minds of the commission, which now in view of the testimony so far collected reduced the matters to be answered by Águila to five heads: 1. The number of men on the expedition being what it was, its destination (as O'Neill and O'Donnell had laid down) should have been Cork or Limerick. But a week out from Lisbon the order was given, in case the fleet should be scattered, to rendezvous at Kinsale or Castlehaven. Where was this change made, why, and on whose advice? 2. Did Águila ask Brochero to stay until another order came from the king? If he did ask, when was it, and where? Were there any witnesses? 3. On realizing the difficulty of defending Kinsale and its harbour, why did not Águila go to Cork? Did he ask Brochero to take the armada to Castlehaven, or elsewhere? If so, when and how? and were there any

1. AGS, Guerra Antigua 3144: Oviedo's answers to D. de Ibarra, 6 Aug. 1602.
2. Cf. p. 120, *supra*.
3. AGS, Guerra Antigua 3144: declaration by Colmenares.

witnesses? 4. On deciding to stay in Kinsale, why did Águila not fortify the place by sea, since reinforcements from Spain would have to land at the port, and by land? Why did he not make use of the houses in Kinsale, erect a fort, and collect all the cattle possible, burning everything else on the enemy? 5. When the chiefs arrived at the place that Águila had, through Bustamante, indicated to them and were, as some said, heard to be fighting, why did not Águila go out, as he had promised, to their aid?[1]

To sift truth from error was not an easy task for the commission in view of the many stories about the expedition that were circulating among the troops at Corunna. For example, it was asserted that the pilot of the *San Pedro* on the voyage to Ireland had bored the galleon, so that it might ship water and be forced to return to Spain. His action, so it was said, had won general approval from the crew, who hated having to go to Ireland. There were suggestions too that Zubiaur could have made Ireland on the first voyage, had he so desired. Such suggestions, reflecting as they did on the redoubtable Zubiaur's bravery and honour, could hardly be taken seriously.

An allegation that was, however, taken seriously by the commission of inquiry was that Don Pedro (or Diego) de Heredia, a sergeant of Captain Zuazo's company, together with twenty or thirty of his men went over to the enemy from Rincorran. Their arrest was ordered.

On the basis of the evidence by now collected the council of war issued some findings. As to why the landing took place at Kinsale the council found that none of the three, Águila, Brochero, or Archbishop Oviedo, was at fault here:

> ... que no hay causa para poner culpa a ninguno de los que llevavan cargo de la armada y de la gente de guerra ny al arçobispo de Dublin, porque no hay cargo que les hazer sobre ello.

In regard to Brochero's returning from Kinsale the council absolved him from blame, since he had borne an order to return with the ships. The manner in which Don Diego had disembarked the victuals and munitions the council did not find worth pursuing. Investigation was to proceed on the other heads of inquiry.[2]

1. AGS, Guerra Antigua 3144: heads of questions to Águila and others (D. de Ibarra's hand).
2. AGS, Guerra Antigua 3143: *consulta* by council of war, Vallid., 21 Oct.; Guerra Antigua 591: Philip to Castel-Rodrigo, Tordesillas, and orders from Philip to Zubiaur and others, Tordesillas, 4 Dec.; Guerra Antigua 3144: D. de Ibarra (?) to Caracena and others, 12 Apr. 1603; resolution by full council, 12 Apr.

Red Hugh O'Donnell wanted not an investigation into the failures of the past but rather action in the present. Still hopeful of Spanish aid, he managed to get a hearing for another proposal. Father Conry suggested it to Fray Gaspar, who put it to the council. The new proposal was that a force of 3,000 men be sent to Ireland; they could easily take Galway, and by keeping 14,000 of Elizabeth's troops busy in Ireland they would relieve the archduke of great pressure. But the marquis of Poza voiced the feelings of the majority in the council when he said that since Flanders made the first call on Spanish resources and since there was not enough aid for both Flanders and Ireland, all the available aid should be sent to the Low Countries, without any diversion allowed.[1] And Philip was forced to agree that this was basic arithmetic.

But at least some money could be found to aid O'Neill and keep the spark of rebellion alive. The premature death of Hugh O'Donnell, on 9 September 1602, further grievous blow as it was to the Irish cause, made Spain hasten the sending of the sum of 50,000 ducats that Philip had decided on in March. It was agreed to send 30,000 ducats immediately to O'Neill, together with a quantity of arms, and the remainder afterwards in two further instalments. Father Conry was indignant at this; it was, he protested, paltry aid. Philip's conscience made him agree sufficiently to decide to send Conry at once with 30,000 ducats to O'Neill, with promise of 10,000 a month to follow, to pay his Irish soldiers and men to be raised in Scotland to carry on the war. Later, it was decided, Cerdá should also go and take the chains and swords previously destined for distribution among the Irish; these were still in Corunna.[2]

But Ireland wanted more substantial help than this. A French ship left Berehaven on 18 July and arrived at a port near Ribadeo, in Asturias, within ten days. On board were the O'Driscolls, Denis, lord of Castlehaven, and Cornelius, son of Sir Finnin. These two came as envoys from the Irish lords, holding out in the south-west still after the fall of Dunboy. With them was Ellen O'Donoghue, widow of Dermot MacCarthy, the brother of Florence. Dermot, after six years' service against the English, had been killed by a musket shot at Dun-

1. AGS, Estado 621: *consulta* by council of state, 22 Oct.

2. AGS, Estado 840, f. 37 (*Cal. S.P. Spain, 1587–1603*, pp. 715–16): Philip's holograph to *consulta* by council of state, 1 Oct. 1602; Estado 840, f. 203: Prada to E. de Ibarra, Vallid., 1 Feb. 1603; Estado 840, f. 202 (*Cal.*, cit., p. 729): *consulta* by council of state, 17 Feb. 1603. Cf. *supra*, p. 69. Oviedo had thought to take these presents with him in 1600.

boy. The Lady Ellen had one daughter with her, her eldest son, a boy of ten years, remaining a prisoner in Cork. Father Archer and Alférez Cornelio Maris, an Irishman who had gone with Zubiaur to Ireland, were also on board to ask for further aid. These together with many other Irish refugees, such as Hugh Mostian, Redmond Burke, baron of Leitrim, and Matthew Tully, O'Donnell's secretary, were given pensions and in many cases places in the Spanish service.[1] But their mission was for all that a failure; the help they asked for Ireland was not given.

By February 1603 no money had been sent to O'Neill, in spite of Philip's decision of the previous October; and Father Conry had given up hope that this decision would ever be honoured. Another palliative measure was now proposed by the council to Philip: Cornelius O'Driscoll, they advised, should be sent to Ireland with a boat-load of provisions for his friends.[2] It was painfully clear that Spain would send no more real help; for her the Irish adventure was over.

The leisurely inquiry was now nearly at an end too. Don Juan del Águila had taken his time to reply to the charges laid against him. Contrary to the common opinion of historians he had not been imprisoned, but had retired to his native Avila. From there he sent his secretary, Gerónimo de la Torre, with a letter to Philip in March. In this letter Águila claimed to have acted throughout the Irish campaign with conspicuous valour. Don Juan forwarded a letter which Pedro López had sent him from Castlehaven, after López's arrival there; in this López had written that he would sent five hundred Spaniards—'one figure five and two zeros more of good soldiers'[3]— to join O'Neill and O'Donnell, together with a thousand Irish. López however, said Águila, had written later to the chiefs to say that he could not send them any men and that they should give battle. Both O'Neill and Don Juan had sought to induce López to send more men to join the Irish, but without effect.[4]

Águila's evidence was considered by the councils of state and war in

1. AGS, Guerra Antigua 591: Caracena to Philip, Corunna, 28 July; schedule for Caracena of list of pensions for Irishmen, 4 Dec., and schedules of various dates for others; Guerra Antigua 589: memorials by Cornelius and Denis O'Driscoll and Ellen O'Donoghue, with covering letter from Caracena, 8 Aug.

2. AGS, Estado 840, ff. 200–1 (*Cal. S.P. Spain, 1587–1603*, pp. 718–19): *consulta* by council of state, 13 Feb. (not Jan.) 1603; Estado 840, f. 206 (*Cal.*, cit., p. 739): *consulta*, 13 Mar. 1603.

3. 'Un cinco de guarismo y dos zeros mas de buenos soldados.' AGS, Guerra Antigua 3145: López to Águila, 15 (?) Dec. 1601.

4. AGS, Guerra Antigua 3145: Águila to Philip, Avila, 29 Mar. 1603. Cf. *supra*, pp. 134–6.

full session on 12 April. The council, of course, were unaware that O'Neill, 'prostrated grovelling to the earth', as one eye-witness said, had three days previously submitted to Mountjoy. Esteban de Ibarra had prepared for the council a list of charges against Don Juan. This indictment began by reciting that on the day of the battle Águila had defaulted in his agreement to sally out and meet O'Neill; that instead of Cork or Limerick he had gone to Kinsale and thereafter had refused to remove himself from there; and that he had failed to fortify himself properly. He could, the allegation went on, have secured command of the sea approaches and prevented any enemy ship from entering by making a cavalier on the seaward side and placing there four pieces. The land at the foot of Rincorran was very suitable for fortifying in this manner, and there was a wood very near, from which the enemy had drawn timber to fortify his quarters. There was an island[1] at the front, on the left, with a very strong tower (the reference is to Castle Park), which he might suitably have fortified with another four pieces. It was by way of this island that the Irish Catholics communicated with the Spaniards in Kinsale, sending in news and many provisions, and that O'Neill and O'Donnell sent in help. As soon as peace was made the enemy made a fort at the foot of the tower with four cavaliers and placed at the sea-side four pieces, with which he now guarded the whole port.[2]

Águila, the charge continued, had a month during which no enemy appeared. He could have availed of this opportunity to fortify himself, using the services of five or six hundred of the poor people as pioneers at very little cost, but he refused. He could have victualled himself with many cattle, young and mature, and could have used two storehouses of salt belonging to the queen to cook all the meat he wanted; and he could have baked flour from wheat and barley available within sight of the walls to provide rations for many days. If he did not want to barter, he could have bought the flesh very cheaply at four *maravedís* a pound. Thus there was no cause for over nine hundred persons to die of hunger and for the others to live miserably on a ration of twelve ounces of biscuit and water.

Águila, the recitation continued, could have mounted two hundred men, for he had saddles and bridles, and there were many horses to be

---

1. *Pac. Hib.* also describes the promontory on which Castle Park stood as an 'island'.
2. The English on 25 January 1602 began the erection of the great fort at Castle Park. O'Sullivan, *Kinsale*, p. 99.

bought at from fifty to eighty *reals*. This would have prevented the enemy from taking away the cattle before the eyes of the garrison and coming up to the walls of the castle and town.

Águila was guilty of negligence, ran the next charge, for he had no *maestres de campo*, did not make sergeants major of experienced veterans, did not set up an advisory council of his captains, and treated those who offered advice as ruffians. He allowed the enemy to level the town without placing artillery there to reply, something he could have done in four hours. There was a trench on the landward side which he had occupied from the beginning with one company by day and another by night. Many captains had wanted him to erect a fort there to shelter the town, but Águila would not. The enemy had come and taken it, and had built a fort in which they placed 2,000 men. They had done much damage to the walls, so that if a man halted in the town even his feet were visible to them. A sally had been made on the vespers of St. Lucy,[1] in which the Spaniards had taken the fort and killed many of the men there, making the others flee. Águila had sent three times to make the captains retire and they finally had done so, allowing the enemy to return. This had been the reason why the chiefs had been unable to make the junction, because that was the route they must have followed when coming.

When, in fact, the indictment went on, the northern chiefs came to encamp four leagues away, the captain-general had not resolved on a junction, but had kept them waiting a fortnight, dispiriting them and strengthening the enemy.[2] One day, the final charge read, he had told the chiefs to attack from their last (transit) camp, a league from Kinsale, saying that as soon as the attack had begun he would sally out. He had not done so, and they and the Spanish companies had been lost as a result.[3]

The plenary session of 12 April heard the evidence presented to date, and ordered fuller inquiry on various points. The session advised that Captains Saavedra, Díaz de Navarra, Caja de Cuellar, Jara Millo, and Don Gómez de Vargas should be absolutely discharged and that Captains Cardenosa and Jaén should be acquitted on the charges

1. Cf. pp. 129–30, for an account of this sortie.
2. But as has been seen it was the effort to get López to send his Spaniards to join the chiefs that caused the delay here. Águila was very eager that the Irish should hasten to the attack; of that there can be no doubt.
3. AGS, Guerra Antigua 3145: paper from Philip for the information of the council, 1 Apr. 1603.

against them; if further charges were laid, the door would thus be left open for their punishment.[1] Lerma, it now came to light, had given orders that Brochero, since he had followed his orders very well, was not to be discussed in the inquiry. No doubt his fellow councillors were relieved to be rid of the embarrassment of subjecting Don Diego's record to critical scrutiny. To be in favour is, it must be admitted, often a convenience. Those who are not especially favoured can always, as Águila did (at least, so we are told), console themselves with the thought that in justice they have merited favours.[2]

Águila was diverted from the contemplation of his unrewarded meritoriousness by the need to give some further testimony, this time on the behaviour of two of his officers. Don Juan laid charges of indiscipline against Captain Francisco de Muñeza. In regard to Paez de Clavijo it was true, Don Juan agreed, that Rincorran was weak, but Paez could have held out longer. Águila could not corroborate Paez's excuse that his soldiers left him since Mountjoy had given them passage before the treaty, but he would accept the excuse.[3]

Another plenary session of the council was held exactly three months after the previous one. O'Neill had meantime gone to England, to make his submission to King James. And already Philip had on James's accession sent Juan de Tassis Peralba, now created conde de Villamediana, to congratulate him. Villamediana had left Valladolid in May for the English court. Such a diplomatic gesture meant that peace was in the air. In only three months' time, in fact, on 31 October 1603, Philip's peace commissioners would be leaving Valladolid on a journey that would take them by way of Paris and Brussels eventually to London. Archduke Albert had at the end of 1602 yielded, though with very bad grace, to Philip's insistence that the Spínolas attack England. But when Fedérico was killed off Sluys on 25 May 1603 the final obstacle to peace was overcome. Ambrosio, who had been raising men in Germany and Italy, was in September put in charge of the siege of Ostend. He won great fame in taking that city, but there was to be no Spínola invasion of England.

Lerma's intent was as pacific as James's, and the Irish diversion would not be without its uses to Spain in the peace negotiations.

---

1. AGS, Guerra Antigua 3144: resolutions by council of state and war, 12 Apr. 1603.
2. González Dávila, *Felipe tercero*, p. 247.
3. AGS, Guerra Antigua 3144: Águila to Philip's secretary (Bartolomé de Aguilar y Añaya), Avila, 16 Apr. 1603.

Besides, the succession (which the attack on Ireland had unfortunately not decided) was now settled. Stern judgements, therefore, were not in order and the councillors found for Águila (and incidentally Brochero, who, while escaping the peril of censure, did not have to forgo praise) on each of the five charges against him. The findings may be summarized as follows:

Firstly, on the matter of the port of disembarkation the finding was that Águila before leaving Lisbon used all proper diligence to select the place most suitable for quick junction with O'Neill and O'Donnell and least open to the English fleets, but he was deprived of choice in everything.

Secondly, in regard to Brochero's return the council found that Brochero did try to stay, but could not because of his order to return as soon as the men were disembarked. Besides, he had left Lisbon with food for but seventy days, and when setting out to return from Kinsale he had food for only twenty.

In the third place, the council inquired why did not Brochero take the army from Kinsale to a better port? He did not do so, it was found, because of lack of food, the fatigue felt by his men, and the possibility that he might have been driven back to Spain by adverse weather. Moreover, Águila did not propose such a removal to him. If they had set about it the enemy would have had time to prepare for their disembarkation elsewhere. The effect of cross-winds on that coast was proved by the fact that the ship carrying Captains Pedro Henríquez de Tejada and Don Francisco de Piños was driven eight or ten leagues from Kinsale and arrived there more than twenty days late, after Águila had sent pilots.

The fourth question to be decided was did Águila fortify himself? Here the council vindicated Águila completely. He fortified Kinsale, the council concluded, within and without as much as was possible. He had to cover up the food from weather and waves, and had not the time, men, or materials to make a real fort. As soon as Brochero was gone he had to spend some days in gathering the victuals, partly from the hulks in which they remained and partly from the sand. The enemy were molesting him before he had the food covered. He did occupy a little castle with a tower in front of it, which in a manner guarded the port, to occupy the enemy until the help of which he was certain came. These places (the council are evidently not very clear on the distinction between Rincorran and Castle Park) were defended, but not as well as they might have been, for from one of them some of the men went over to the enemy. In a place defenceless against attack from above, and with very little food, he had made a heroic stand for three months. Though there was no hope of help from Spain after the rout of the Irish Águila gained very favourable conditions in the treaty.

Finally, as to the battle, the council decided that the chiefs did not arrive at the place appointed them by Bustamante. Thinking that they would, Águila had given orders to go out to help them, although this would have endangered the safety of Kinsale. The men were ready, sentinels were posted, and Águila himself was at the gate, but no-one heard or saw the chiefs fighting. O'Neill and O'Donnell were beaten by a few of the enemy because of their bad order of fighting and their poor resolution. This lack of resolution was shown by their having sent baggage back three leagues that morning, an indication that they did not mean to advance. When a large part of the day had gone by without anything having been heard Águila, leading about a hundred men, sallied out. So many English came to their posts that none seemed to be missing. This proved that they had not been heavily engaged with the Irish.

The council, finding thus for Águila on all points, expressed their opinion that he had done his duty very well, prudently, and bravely, and deserved no blame but rather equal or greater commands. Don Juan, however, did not survive the verdict long, dying as González Dávila complains before he had received any return for his services. He was interred in Barraco, a town which, his pious biographer remarks, thus earned fame for its association with Águila's ashes and his triumphs.

The verdict of the council, though it left certain questions unanswered, was all things considered just. The count of Puñoenrostro, however, gave a dissenting opinion in which he held Águila to blame for not securing the port at the beginning and for not effecting a junction with the Irish. Águila, Puñoenrostro held, failed in his first duty when he entered Kinsale, which was to see if the port could be held and, if it could, to fortify it without an hour's delay, to dig a trench for defence, and then and only then to disembark the artillery and munitions. What he did, however, was to disembark these first and, without fortifying the port, place himself in a pit surrounded by heights. He did not occupy these or any place that would protect his position. If, as Águila and others said, Kinsale was impossible to fortify in this manner, the first day would have made that clear. Brochero remained nine days there, but Águila (who had too few men to be master in a campaign) failed in his first duty, that of reconnoitring. He would have done better, said Puñoenrostro flatly, to return to Spain.

The count's criticism is well made; yet it ignores the fact that Águila did not allow Kinsale to be carried by storm but capitulated only when he saw no hope of further aid from Spain in time and could at the same time negotiate from strength. Most of the criticism that can be made against his conduct of the campaign loses in weight if it is remembered how badly provisioned and equipped the expedition was; how few men he commanded (and that lack of men was certainly the greatest single factor in limiting the operation's success); how he was prevented from sailing to the north as he wished to do and should have done; and how he was left without ships. On the one outstanding point where there was flat contradiction between Águila and his most severe critic, Archbishop Oviedo, namely whether Don Juan knew that the Irish were engaged with the enemy, the council found that he did not know. That this was a reasonable decision cannot be gainsaid; the Irish unfortunately had been unable to make the appointed rendezvous and, whatever appearances might suggest, Águila had to be wary of a stratagem. He is perhaps to blame for urging against O'Neill's better judgement a premature engagement, as O'Donnell is to blame for supporting him in this.

But so could Zubiaur be blamed for not sending all his force to strengthen the unseasoned Irish armies. All in turn could be excused, however: Águila, because the Irish failed to keep the rendezvous; O'Donnell, because (as indeed the Four Masters suggest) he was weary of half a year's sieges, at Derry, Lifford, Donegal, and now against the English besiegers at Kinsale, and all to no effect; and Zubiaur, because the alternative he decided on offered an excellent selection of harbours for the hoped-for reinforcements to choose between. If Archduke Albert and Aragón had been able to conduct a more successful campaign against the Dutch rebels, Spínola might have been freed to create a diversion in England or reinforcements might have been released for Ireland that would have made all the difference to the outcome of Águila's invasion. Águila might, finally, have done better, but he had created a diversion at England's back door, many hundred miles away from Spain, and had brought the bulk of his army home intact. Worse results there might have been.

The council gave Brochero full acquittal; they found that there had been neither lack of care nor fault in his handling of the navigation to Ireland, disembarkation, or return to Spain. King Philip accepted these findings in full and ordered further investigation in the case of others who did appear guilty.[1]

But with Águila and Brochero cleared of all charges, it was not to be expected that very stern action would be taken against the men of lesser rank. Indeed, Spanish interest in Ireland had now diminished, and it was almost two years before judgement was given in the cases of López de Soto and Zubiaur. The former was then deprived of his office of *veedor* for four years and was forbidden to appear within five leagues distance of the court for two years. The council found for Zubiaur on three counts and against him on one unstated in the minute, but presumably the matter of not sending all his men to join the Irish. For punishment, especially in view of the fact that he had been for a long time imprisoned at court, a reprimand was deemed sufficient. So under something of a cloud a notable career closed, for Don Pedro died a few months later.[2]

The archbishop of Dublin lived on for five years, dying on 10 January 1610 in his order's convent of Valladolid, to which he had retired.[3] Strange in his final years must have seemed to him the designs of providence as he worried about his beloved Ireland, now given over to the heretics, or knelt to pray and mourn at the grave of the prince, Red Hugh, whom he had known in all his vigour, or listened to the news about Ireland brought to him by the many Irish refugees who thronged the court:[4] Hugh Mostian, Redmond Burke, Edmund Eustace of Baltinglass, or Alexander Walshe,[5] who would remind him of that voyage that they two and Cerdá had made to far away Donegal. To these and most of all perhaps to Father Florence Conry he would speak of his hopes that Ireland must yet be freed. These hopes he must have thought, when in 1607 the startling news of O'Neill's coming to

1. AGS, Guerra Antigua 3144: *consulta* of 12 July, with Philip's holograph thereon.
2. AGS, Guerra Antigua 640 (*Epistolario de Zubiaur*, pp. 109–10, cf. p. 23): *consulta* by full council on cases of López and Zubiaur, Vallid., 12 May 1605.
3. Colmenares, *Historia de Segovia*, iv. 182.
4. Captain Eduardo Geraldino, in an undated memorial (? 1603), said that there were more than 600 Irish and Scots at the court and in other parts of the Spanish kingdoms.
5. The names of these and others at court in 1603 will be found in AGS, Estado 1745.

Europe to raise another expedition was brought to him, would now surely be realized. Were his illusions finally shattered when O'Neill, at English insistence, was refused entry to Spain; or did he cherish until his death the belief that Hugh would prevail on the pope to arouse on behalf of Ireland the conscience of Catholic Europe? One can but conjecture.

France and Spain, under English pressure, both refused to assist O'Neill's plans to return to Ireland with an army, and he was driven to accept asylum in Rome. With the passing of O'Neill, Oviedo, and Águila from the scene there faded the hope of Irish independence won by Spanish aid. A new era was beginning for Europe and for Ireland, and from his vantage-point in Rome (where O'Neill was hospitably treated but not encouraged to hope for papal backing for his restoration) Archbishop Lombard read the signs. The appeal to arms had failed and wisdom for Ireland, Lombard felt, now lay in accepting the bitter fact of her political conquest and concentrating on the preservation of her religious liberty. It was time to explore the possibilities of the text, 'Render unto Caesar', to which de la Field had already appealed. And so as primate of Ireland Lombard set out to promote Catholic acceptance of Caesar, James I, as lawful sovereign of Ireland and to convince the king of the reality of Catholic loyalty. In the new international climate, with religion 'beginning to lose its position as the keystone'[1] of politics, Henry IV was willing to make compromises in France, as was Philip III on both the Atlantic and Mediterranean seaboards. James too, besides accommodation with Spain, was ready to seek compromise with the pope on the religious question. Lombard felt this was a situation to be exploited.[2]

Before the council's findings of 12 July 1603, Cerdá, sent off at last with the money together with munitions for O'Neill, had learned of the latter's submission to Mountjoy, and was already back in Spain accompanied by MacWilliam Burke. A final voyage was made by Denis O'Driscoll on a Spanish ship to take away O'Sullivan Beare and O'Rourke, and the Irish adventure was over.[3]

1. Edwards, in *Measgra Mhichíl Uí Chléirigh*, p. 2.
2. Silke, in *Ir. Theol. Quart.*, xxii (1955), 15–30, 124–50.
3. AGS, Estado 840, ff. 219, 232: *consultas* by council of state, 22 July and 23 Aug.; Cabrera, *Relaciones*, p. 184. On the later history of the O'Sullivans in Spain cf. Hume, *Españoles e ingleses*, p. 268.

APPENDIX I

A NOTE ON THE BATTLE

CHAPTER ELEVEN gives what from the available evidence seems to be the best reconstruction of the intentions of the Irish and their ally Águila on the morning of the battle. Certain evidence from Spanish sources has mistakenly been taken as suggesting that not only would Tyrrell place his force within the town that morning but that the attack on the English, by Águila and Tyrrell against Thomond, and by O'Neill and O'Donnell against Mountjoy, would take place only on the following night.[1] Whether or not Tyrrell's force was to enter the town, the attack was to take place that morning.

The two Spanish authorities in question here are Alonso de Ocampo, who was taken prisoner by the English during the engagement, and Zubiaur. Ocampo's evidence, as given to his captors, does not indicate that the attack was to be delayed until the night of 3 January.[2] What Zubiaur, or rather López for him, quite clearly states is that O'Neill on that morning would occupy a position assigned to him by Águila, whereupon the latter would there and then sally out and join him in a combined attack on the enemy:

Que quedaron de acuerdo con . . . Águila que aquel día [3 January] se pondría con toda su gente en un recuesto donde . . . don Juan le señaló que haziendo cierta señal *que* pudiese salir y dar por su parte en los enemigos.[3]

Zubiaur's account is, of course, at second-hand. On 25 January 1602 Sebastián de Oleaga presented to the council of war a report of events in Ireland from the coming of Zubiaur until the time that he (Oleaga) had left on 6 January. This memorial, made from López's dispatches, is in the hand of Secretary Ibarra, and is printed *Epistolario de Zubiaur*, pp. 134–9.

Whether even the intention was to throw Tyrrell's van into the

---

1. Cf. Hayes-McCoy, in *Studies*, xxxviii (1949), 312–13, and evidence there quoted.
2. Cf. *Cal. S.P. Ire., 1601–3*, p. 240: Carew to Cecil, 26 Dec., old style; p. 241: Power to Cecil, 27 Dec., old style (*Cal.*, cit., p. 241). But cf. *Cal. Carew MSS, 1601–3*, p. 192.
3. *Epistolario de Zubiaur*, p. 128; this statement is repeated almost word for word on p. 137.

town is a moot point. Reports that Tyrrell did design so to place his force, made up of the Irish, estimated at 1,000, and Ocampo's Spaniards, have no confirmation from Spanish or Irish sources. Cavalli, the Venetian ambassador at Paris, who confirms Power's report,[1] learned that Mountjoy intercepted some letters written by O'Neill to Águila, in which Hugh said that on Christmas eve (old style) he would attack with his army the English from one side, and that Águila ought to sortie out with 1,500 of his men from the other, so as to allow the placing in Kinsale of 1,000 Irish and 500 Spanish.[2] This is clearly derived from the English sources. Mountjoy's later dispatches say nothing about an intention to throw Tyrrell's men into the town or to attack the English the following night, but say rather that when Tyrrell had occupied his position Águila would sally out and the attack on the two camps would immediately take place.[3] Later argument among the Spaniards was concerned with whether Águila should have gone out to join the Irish; nothing was said about Tyrrell's going into Kinsale.

1. *Cal. S.P. Ire.*, 1601–3, p. 241.
2. *Relazioni degli stati Europei*, ser. II: *Francia*, i. 41 n. 1: Cavalli to doge and senate, 22 Jan. 1602.
3. *Studies*, xxxviii. 313 n. 1; *Cal. S.P. Ire.*, 1601–3, p. 261.

APPENDIX II

A. MUSTER TAKEN AT BELÉM
30 August 1601[1]

THE MUSTER, taken by Juan de la Peña Zorilla, states that there are forty-three companies of Spanish and Italian infantry under the command of the *maestre de campo* Don Juan de el Águila at Belém.

Tercio *of the* maestre de campo *Don Francisco de Padilla* (*not counting companies of recruits*)

	By Poll
Padilla's own company	155
Company of Don Christóbal de Ayala	146
„ „ Diego de Vega	149
„ „ Juan Bautista Castellanos	135
„ „ Jusepe de Escobar	149
„ „ Hernando Barragán	92
Companies which came from Andalusia (the others which came were re-formed, as containing few men)	
Company of Gaspar de Molina	129
„ „ Pedro Enríquez de Tejada	55
Companies which came from Galicia	
Company of Pedro Muñiz de Jaén	106
„ „ Juan de Albornoz	102
„ „ Don Francisco de Piños	102
Italian company of Orlando Tesauro	130
Total in *tercio*	1,450

Tercio *of the* maestre de campo *Antonio Centeno*

Centeno's own company	73
Company of Andrés Leal	54
„ „ Francisco Vanegas	54
„ „ Gerónimo de Guevara	64
„ „ Don Bartolomé de Biamonte	44
„ „ Alonso de Ocampo	60
„ „ Francisco Maldonado	66
„ „ Don Sancho de Biedma	61

1. AGS, Guerra Antigua 3144.

	By Poll
Company of Diego de Salaçar	65
„ „ Diego de San Briente	61
„ „ Don Gaspar de Castel Blanco[1]	62
„ „ Don Pedro Xarava del Castillo	66
Italian company of Antonio del Tuffo	132
Total in *tercio*	862

Companies of recruits, to be distributed among both tercios

Company of Francisco Ruiz de Velasco	116
„ „ Francisco Muñeza	110
„ „ Diego González Sigler	113
„ „ Luis Díaz de Navarra	119
„ „ Pedro de Çuaço	107
„ „ Juan Yñíguez de Çarate	107
„ „ Marcos de Porres	113
„ „ Francisco de Heredia	112
„ „ Bernardino de Soto	116
„ „ Christóbal de Cardenosa	113
„ „ Andrés de Arbe	114
„ „ Pedro de Pereda	112
„ „ Miguel Caja de Cuellar	114
„ „ Diego Cascarro	111
„ „ Alonso Xara Millo	113
„ „ Sebastián Graneros	109
Total of recruits	1,799

Men taken from the castles of Lisbon and San Gián

174 men formed into a company under Don Luis Vela Núñez, and not yet added to a *tercio*	174
Portuguese: 147 soldiers, including certain persons sentenced to serve in Portuguese India, whose banishment was commuted to service with the armada to Ireland. Formed into a company under Roque Pereyra	147

Summary

Tercio of the *maestre de campo* Padilla	1,450
„ „ „ „ „ „ Centeno	862
Companies of recruits	1,799
Men taken from the castles of San Gián and Lisbon	174
Portuguese	147
Total, in 43 companies	4,432

1. Águila allowed him to go home with Brochero, and gave his company to Don Pedro Morejón. AGS, Guerra Antigua 3144: Águila to Philip, 13 Oct. 1601.

B. MUSTER OF ARMY OF IRELAND
1602[1]

This account, by Pedro López de Soto, accompanied a letter from Caracena, 2 April 1602, to the court.

Companies of tercio of Esteban de Legorreta, which came under command of Ocampo

	By Poll
Company of the *maestre de campo* himself	55
,, ,, Captain Andrés Leal	34
,, ,, ,, Juan de Albornoz	64
,, ,, ,, Pedro López de Jaén	74
,, ,, ,, Gaspar de Molina	72
,, ,, ,, Francisco de Eredia	55
,, ,, ,, Luis Díaz de Navarra	32
,, ,, ,, Juan Iñíguez de Çarate	67
,, ,, ,, Francisco Maldonado	42
,, ,, ,, Diego de San Vicente	42
,, ,, ,, Don Pedro Morejón	71
,, ,, ,, Miguel Caxa de Cuellar	61
,, ,, ,, Don Pedro Jarava del Castillo	52
,, ,, ,, Pedro de Echaves	45
,, ,, ,, Don Diego de Biedma	42
Italian company of Captain Orlando Thesauro	110

Companies of tercio of Don Pedro Sarmiento, which came with Águila

Company of the *maestre de campo*	114
,, ,, Captain Pedro de Suazo	64
,, ,, ,, Marcos de Porral	64
,, ,, ,, Christóbal de Cardenosa	42
,, ,, ,, Diego de Vega	116
,, ,, ,, Don Luis Núñez Vela	84
,, ,, ,, Don Christoval de Ayala	92
,, ,, ,, Alonso de Xara Millo	49
,, ,, ,, Diego Cascarro	64
,, ,, ,, Diego Palomeque	70
,, ,, ,, Diego González Sigler	53
,, ,, ,, Jusepe Descovar	105
Italian company of Captain Antonio del Tuffo	108

1. AGS Guerra Antigua 590.

Three companies from Kinsale, which landed at Bayonne

	By Poll
Company of Don Felipe de Beautmonte	129
„ „ Don Gómez de Bargas	51
„ „ Pedro Enríquez	66

Company which landed at Asturias, and is now here

Company of Don Francisco de Piños, with added men	140

The eight companies of Castlehaven, Baltimore, and Berehaven

Company of Captain Hernando Cabeza de Vaca Barragán	65
„ „ „ Francisco Ruiz de Velasco	48
„ „ „ Sebastián Granero	37
„ „ „ Roque Pereyra	41
„ „ „ Alonso de Ocampo	37
„ „ „ Vasco de Saavedra	93
„ „ „ Andrés de Arbe	61
„ „ „ Juan Bautista Castellanos	50

Portuguese companies which came from Lisbon in the hookers and with Ballecilla

Company of Captain Martín Alonso Valiente	95
„ „ „ Chirinos	70
„ „ „ Diego de Aguilar y Castro	62

New companies now come from Castile

Company of Captain Diego de Medina	101
„ „ „ Bernabé de Buitrán	74
„ „ „ Gerónimo de Herradas	77
Total in 47 companies	3,250

Summary

41 companies come from Ireland	2,771
3 „ „ „ Portugal	227
3 new companies	252
Total	3,250

A note by Pedro López says that this muster includes officials and sick, and that between the muster and 2 April over 130 men died. The sick, he adds, are now getting better, and there ought to be over 2,000 effectives.

BIBLIOGRAPHY

I. SPANISH SOURCES

A. *Guides to sources*

The most complete and useful bibliography of Spanish studies is R. Foulché-Delbosc and L. Barrau-Dihigo, *Manuel de l'hispanisant* (Hispanic Soc. of America, 2 vols., N.Y., 1920, 1925), which contains catalogues and inventories of and detailed guides to archival and other sources. The most important bibliography of Spanish history is Benito Sánchez Alonso, *Fuentes de la historia española e hispano-americana: ensayo de bibliografía sistemática de impresos y manuscritos que ilustran la historia política de España y sus antiguas provincias de ultramar* (3rd ed., CSIC, 3 vols., Madrid, 1952). Guillermo Bauer, *Introducción al estudio de la historia*, ed. Luis G. de Valdeavellano (2nd ed., Barcelona, 1952), embodies useful bibliographies. Guides to sources of more particular interest will be found in Pedro Aguado Bleye, *Manual de historia de España*, vol. II: *Reyes católicos—casa de Austria* (8th ed., Madrid, 1959), chap. XIII: 'Casa de Austria 1517–1700: las fuentes', and in Huguette et Pierre Chaunu, *Séville et l'Atlantique 1504–1650* (8 vols., Paris, 1955–9), viii. I, pp. xxi–cxxv. A guide to modern publications during the years indicated is D. Gómez Molleda, *Bibliografía histórica española 1950–4* (CSIC, Madrid, 1955); while the *Índice histórico español: bibliografía histórica de España e Hispanoamerica . . ., 1953–4*, etc. (Centro de Ests. Hists. Internacs., Barcelona, 1955–) is a critical index, listing current works, Spanish and foreign. A. Ballesteros y Beretta, *Historia de España y su influencia en la historia universal*, vol. IV, pt. i (2nd ed., Barcelona, 1950), covers the period from Philip II to Charles II and has extensive bibliographies.

A comprehensive guide to Spanish archives is F. Rodríguez Marín (ed.), *Guía histórica y descripción de los archivos, bibliotecas y museos arqueológicos de España que están a cargo del Cuerpo Facultativo del Ramo* (Secc. de Archivos, Madrid, 1921). The Archivo General de Simancas is treated, pp. 129–371. Francisco Sintes y Obrador is author of *Guía de los archivos de Madrid* (Dir. Gen. de Archs. y Bibls., Madrid, 1952). Finally, there is the *Inventario general de manuscritos de la Biblioteca Nacional* (Min. de Educ. Nac., Madrid, 1953–).

B. *Archival*

I. ARCHIVO GENERAL DE SIMANCAS

This is the chief source of documentation for the Spanish landings in Munster. *The letters and state papers relating to English affairs, preserved principally in the archives of Simancas*, ed. M. A. S. Hume, vol. IV: *Elizabeth I, 1587–1603* (1889) (*Cal. S.P. Spain, 1587–1603*), must be used with care, and checked at all stages against the originals. There are transcripts of documents in *Epistolario del General Zubiaur, 1568–1605*, ed. Conde de Polentinos (CSIC, Madrid, 1946), and 'Some unpublished letters of Mateo de Oviedo', ed. P. MacBride, in *Reportorium Novum*, i (1955–6), and (faithfully enough translated) in *Pacata Hibernia*.

a. Guides

Guia del archivo de Simancas (Dir. Gen. de Archivos y Bibliotecas, Madrid, 1958) refers to the different printed catalogues that had appeared by 1958. The work of cataloguing is continuing and the most complete list of catalogues will be found in the current hand-list, 'Catálogos del Archivo General de Simancas', available at the archives. As yet cataloguing is far from being completed; besides, the printed 'catalogues' are really only inventories and give for the most part but a very brief indication of the contents of each *legajo* (or bundle of documents).

Of much assistance to the Irish investigator in locating documents are the 'Reports on documents of Irish interest in the Spanish archives', by Fr. Canice Mooney, O.F.M. (1945), in NLI, and by J. G. Healy (1939), in the files of IMC.

These 'Reports' cover the microfilms of Simancas material made for the National Library of Ireland. The 1950–1 *Report of the Council of Trustees* lists these microfilms on pp. 119–21. Fr. Mooney has also reported on the Simancas Archives to the Irish Catholic Historical Committee (*Proc.*, 1955, pp. 18–21).

b. Citation

The two groups (*fondos*) embodying the deliberations of the councils of state and war, respectively Estado (section *Secretaría de Estado*) and Guerra y Marina (section *Guerra Antigua*), were found to be of most value for a study of the invasion. Reference in the present work is given to the section, the number of the *legajo*, and, where, exceptionally, it is indicated, the number of the folio or page. Thus 'AGS, Estado 840, f. 80' refers to Archivo General de Simancas, *fondo* Estado, *sección* Secretaría de Estado, *serie* Negociaciones de Nápoles, *legajo* 840, folio 80. Similarly, 'AGS, Guerra Antigua 3145' refers to the group Guerra y Marina, section Guerra Antigua, series [III], Parte de Mar [=Marina], file 3145. (The group Guerra y Marina is divided into the sections Guerra Antigua, Guerra Moderna and Marina. Guerra Antigua is subdivided into the series Tierra y Mar, Tierra and Parte de Mar.)

2. OTHER ARCHIVES

a. Collections

Real Academia de Historia, Madrid

MS. Colección Salazar, L, tomo xxiv (Papeles Varios, t. i), ff. 61–76, contains memorials by Pedro López de Soto, written after the defeat at Kinsale and urging further Spanish help.

Museo Naval, Madrid

Colección Sans (or Sanz) de Barutell, in two series, of 27 and 23 vols. respectively, contains information collected by Barutell in Simancas on shipping used in the expedition. Barutell, who died 1819, has left two inventories in the museum to his collection.

British Museum

Bergenroth's and Froude's transcripts from Simancas (Add. MSS., vols. 28595–7, 26056 A–C) were already on microfilm in NLI. They have now been largely superseded, as far as the Irish student is concerned, by the microfilms from Simancas in NLI treated above. A number of extracts that are relevant, from the Sloane MSS., collections of Cole, Fane, etc., have been microfilmed for NLI. References to them will be found in the 1950–1 *Report of the Council of Trustees*, pp. 35, 43, 44, 48, 50, 51, 71, and 1951–2 *Report*, pp. 51, 83, 94.

b. Printed and calendared material

Relations des Pays-Bas et de l'Angleterre sous le règne de Philippe II, ed. Kervyn de Lettenhove (10 vols., Brussels, 1882–91), has material of Irish interest. Concerning the war in Flanders, *Correspondance de la cour d'Espagne sur les affaires des Pays-Bas au xviie siècle*, eds. H. Lonchay and J. Cuvelier, vol. I: *Précis de la correspondance de Philippe III 1598–1621* (Brussels, 1923), embodies research done chiefly in Simancas and in the Archives Générales du Royaume in Brussels. Correspondence between Archduke Albert and Lerma and others has been edited in the series *Colección de documentos inéditos para la historia de España*, vols. XLII–III. The index vols., CI and CII, of this great series of 112 vols. (Madrid, 1842–95. Cf. *Manuel de l'hispanisant*, ii. 113–79, for contents) should be consulted. A. Rodríguez Villa is editor of *Correspondencia de la infanta Archiduquesa Isabel Clara Eugenia con el duque de Lerma y otras personalidades* (Madrid, 1916).

AGS, Estado 2511, has much documentation on the Boulogne peace conference; transactions and correspondence in Ralph Winwood, *Memorials 1597–1603*, ed. E. Sawyer (3 vols., 1725), i. bk. III.

Two works which illustrate Spanish relations with the Papacy are Ricardo de Hinojosa, *Los despatchos de la diplomacia pontificia en España: memoria de una misión oficial en el archivo secreto de la santa sede*, vol. I (Madrid, 1896), a report on twenty months' research in the Vatican and other Roman and Italian archives; and *Archivo de la embajada de España cerca de la santa sede*, vol. I, ed. Luciano Serrano, *Índice analítico de los documentos del siglo xvi*; vol. II, ed. José M. Pou y Martí, *Siglo xvii* (Rome, 1917). *Archivium Hibernicum* gives transcripts of documents bearing on relations between Spain, Ireland, and Rome during the period from the Vatican Archives, especially vols. II (1913), III (1914), XXIII (1960), and XXIV (1961), for documents from the Borghese collection, and XVII (1953), containing the correspondence of Father Mansoni, S.J. (ed. Rev. F. M. Jones, C.SS.R.). R. A. Breathnach has edited a letter from Donal O'Sullivan Beare to Philip III, in *Éigse*, vi (1952), 314–25, while vol. I of *Spanish knights of Irish origin*, ed. Micheline Walsh (IMC, Dublin, 1960), is relevant.

c. Secondary works

I. GENERAL

Altamira y Crevea, Rafael, *Historia de España y de la civilización española* (3rd ed., 5 vols. in 6, 1913–30; vol. 5 by Don Pío Zabala y Lera).

2. THE ADMINISTRATION

C. Pérez Bustamante, *Felipe III: semblanza de un monarca y perfiles de un privanza* (Madrid, 1950), provides an introduction to the person and court of Philip III. In this connection, F. Tommy Perrens, 'Le duc de Lerme et la cour d'Espagne sous la règne de Philippe III', *Compte-rendu de l'Acad. des Scs. Mors. et Pols.*, xxi–xxii (Paris, 1870); Edouard Rott, 'Philippe III et le duc de Lerme', in *Rév. d'Hist. Diplomatique*, i (1887), 201–16, 363–84; and A. Ferrer del Río, 'El duque de Lerma', in *R.E.*, xviii (1871), 161–87; may also be consulted with profit. Detailed studies on the administration of the reign are lacking. Among works found useful were J. M. Cordero Torres, *El consejo de estado: su trayectoria y perspectivas en España* (Inst. de Ests. Pols., Madrid, 1944); M. J. Gounon-Loubens, *Essais sur l'administration de la Castille au xvi*[e] *siècle* (Paris, 1860); A. Ballesteros y Beretta, *Historia de España*, cit., vol. IV, pt. ii, chap. I; F. X. Garma y Durán, *Theatro universal de España: descripción ecclesiastica y secular de todos sus reynos y provincias* (Barcelona, 1751), and the court chronicle by Luis Cabrera de Córdoba, *Relaciones de las cosas sucedidas en la corte de España desde 1599 hasta 1614* (Madrid, 1857). Cf. also Ignacio Olagüe, *La decadencia española* (4 vols., Madrid, 1950–1), and Ramón Carande, *Carlos V y sus banqueros*, vol. I: *La vida económica de España en un fase de su hegemonía 1516–56* (Madrid, 1943); vol. II: *La hacienda real de Castilla* (Madrid, 1949). The author has not been able to consult Francisco Tomás Valiente, *Los validos en la monarquía española del siglo xvii: estudo institucional* (Inst. de Ests. Políticos: Coll. Historia Politica, Madrid, 1963).

3. BIOGRAPHY

A particular difficulty that confronts the student of Spanish history is that Spain has no equivalent of the *D.N.B.* The *Diccionario de historia de España* (2 vols., Madrid, 1952) to some extent supplies this lack, as also do *Enciclopedia universal ilustrada europeoamericana*, in course of publication by Espasa-Calpe (Barcelona, 1907–   ), and Louis G. Michaud, *Nouvelle biographie universelle ancienne et moderne* (2nd ed., 65 vols., 1843–65). An incomplete Spanish edition of this work by J. de Burgos, *Biografía universal antigua y moderna* (3 vols., Madrid, 1822) gives additions and corrections for Spain. The *Diccionario biográfico español e hispanoamericana*, ed. Gaspar Sabater (Instituto Español de Estudios Biográficos: vol. I, Palma de Mallorca, 1950), is also useful.

Works which give biographical data on military and naval officers and are besides useful for giving an appreciation of military and naval affairs are José Almirante, *Bosquejo de historia militar de España hasta fin del siglo xviii* (3 vols., Madrid, 1923); Conde de Clonard, *Historia orgánica de las armas de infantería y caballería españolas* (16 vols., Madrid, 1851–9); Cesareo Fernández Duro, *Armada española desde la unión de los reinos de Castilla y León* (9 vols., Madrid, 1895–1903); C. Ibáñez de Ibero, *Historia de la marina de guerra española desde el siglo xiii hasta nuestros días* (Madrid, 2nd ed., 1943); Manuel Juan Diana, *Capitanes ilustres y revista de libros militares* (Madrid, 1851); and Abbot Payson Usher, 'Spanish ships and shipping in the sixteenth and seventeenth centuries', in *Facts and factors in economic history: articles by former students of Edwin Francis Gay* (Harvard, 1932), pp. 189–213.

Other useful works in this connection are Gil González Dávila, *Monarquía de España: historia de la vida y hechos del ínclito monarca, amado y santo D. Felipe tercero . . .* (Madrid, 1771); Garma y Durán, *Theatro universal*, cit.; *Relazioni degli stati Europei lette al Senato degli ambasciatori Veneti nel secolo decimosettimo*, ed. N. Barozzi and G. Berchet. Ser. I: *Spagna* (this work gives the opinions of Soranzo, Venetian ambassador, 1597–1602, on various counsellors); Mariano Alcocer y Martínez, *Archivo histórico español: colección de documentos . . .* (Valladolid, 1930), vol. III, *passim*; R. Hinojosa, *Los despachos de la diplomacia pontificia en España: memoria de una misión oficial en el archivo secreto de la santa sede*, vol. I (Madrid, 1896). There are biographies by J. Juderías y Loyot, *Don Pedro Franqueza, conde de Villalonga* (Madrid, 1909); A. Dávila y Burguero, *Don Christóbal de Moura* (Madrid, 1900); Fidel Pérez-Mínguez, *Don Juan de Idiáquez* (San Sebastian, 1935); and Atanasio López, O.F.M., 'Fr. Mateo de Oviedo', in *El Eco Franciscano*, xxvi (1919).

4. FOREIGN RELATIONS

Fernand Braudel, *La méditerranée et le monde méditerranéen à l'époque de Philippe II* (Paris, 1949) (*El Mediterraneo y el mundo mediterraneo en la época de Felippe II*, trans. M. Monteforte Toledo and W. Roces (2 vols., Mexico, 1953)), is a basic work, which does not neglect Philip's interest and involvement in the Atlantic. A. Rodríguez Villa, *Ambrosio Spínola, primer marqués de los Balbases: ensayo biográfico* (Madrid, 1904), includes a number of documents from Simancas relative to the proposed expedition of the Spínolas. Other useful works are Antonio Cerrolaza, *Spínola: un genovés en Flandes* (Madrid, 1946), and J. M. García Rodríguez, *Ambrosio Spínola y su tiempo* (Barcelona, 1942).

Relations with England form the subject-matter of M. A. S. Hume, *Españoles e ingleses en el siglo xvi: estudios históricos* (Madrid, Biblioteca de Derechos y de Ciencias Sociales, 1903); cf. Cyril Falls, 'España e irlanda durante el reinado de Isabel de Inglaterra (1558 a 1603)', in *Segundo curso de metodología y crítica histéries* (Estado Mayor Central del Ejercito: Servicio Histórico Militar, Madrid, 1950), pp. 325–54.

The question of a successor to Elizabeth, as it presented itself to Philip III, has been considered by L. Hicks, S.J., 'Sir Robert Cecil, Father Persons and the succession, 1600–1', in *Archiv. Hist. Soc. Iesu*, xxiv (1955). On the Boulogne peace conference of 1600 cf. *Cal. S.P. Venice, 1592–1603*, pp. xxv–vii; cf. also L. Hamy, 'Conférence pour la paix entre l'Angleterre et l' Espagne tenue a Boulogne en 1600: étude historique', in *Soc. Acad. de Boulogne-sur-Mer Bull.*, vii (1906), 434–60.

II. OTHER SOURCES

A. *Guides to sources*

The indispensable guide is *Bibliography of British History: Tudor period 1485–1603*, ed. Conyers Read (Amer. Hist. Assn. and RHS, 2nd ed., New York; 1st ed., Oxford, 1959); this comprehensive work contains a chapter on sources and secondary works relating to Ireland, classified according to subject. R. D. Edwards, *Church and state in Tudor Ireland* (Dublin, 1935), pp. 313–32, provides an exhaustive guide to sources, archival as well as printed and calendared, chronicle material, and modern works. Current writings on Irish history are listed in *Irish historical studies* (Dublin, 1938–).

B. *Archival*

1. MANUSCRIPT

PROL. State papers, Ireland, Elizabeth I–George III.

2. PRINTED

Annála Ríoghachta Éireann: Annals of the kingdom of Ireland by the Four Masters, ed. J. O'Donovan (7 vols., Dublin, 1848–51).
BREATHNACH, R. A. (ed.), 'Elegy on Donal O'Sullivan Beare (†1618)', in *Éigse*, vii (1954), 168–21.
Calendar of Carew papers in the Lambeth library (6 vols., 1867–73).
Calendar of state papers relating to Ireland, Henry VIII–Elizabeth I (11 vols., 1860–1912).
Calendar of state papers and manuscripts relating to English affairs . . . in . . . Venice . . . , 1202–1674 (38 vols., 1864–1947).
Cox, Sir Richard, *Hibernia Anglicana* (2 vols., 1689).

Docwra, Sir Henry, 'A narration of the services done by the army employed to Lough Foyle . . .', in *Celtic Soc. Misc.*, ed. J. O'Donovan (Dublin, 1849), pp. 247–61.

Gilbert, J. T., *Account of facsimiles of national manuscripts of Ireland*, iv. I (HMSO, 1882).

[Haynes, S. ?] *Description of Ireland . . . in anno 1598*, ed. Rev. Edmund Hogan, S.J. (Dublin, 1878).

Historical Manuscripts Commission:
Hatfield MSS, pt. x (1904).
Ninth report, appendix, pt. i (1883).
Tenth report, appendix, pt. v (1885).

Hogan, Edmund, S.J., *Ibernia Ignatiana* (1880).

Irish historical documents 1172–1922, eds. E. Curtis and R. B. MacDowell (1943).

Lombard, Rev. Peter, *De regno Hiberniae sanctorum insula commentarius*, ed. Cardl. P. F. Moran (Dublin, 1868).

MacCarthy, D., *Life and letters of the MacCarthy Mor* (1867).

Mooney, Rev. Donagh, 'De provincia Hiberniae S. Francisci', ed. Rev. B. Jennings, O.F.M., in *Anal. Hib.*, vi (1934), 15–131.

Maps of the escheated counties of Ireland: Ulster 1609 (facsimile, Ordnance Survey Office, Southampton, 1860).

Maxwell, Constantia, *Irish history from contemporary sources 1509–1610* (1923).

Moryson, Fynes, *An itinerary: containing his ten yeeres travell through the twelve dominions of Germany, . . . Scotland and Ireland* (4 vols., Glasgow, 1907–8).

Ó Clérigh, Lughaidh, *Beatha Aodha Ruaidh Uí Dhomhnaill*, ed. Rev. P. Walsh (Ir. Texts Soc., 2 vols., Dublin, 1948 and 1957). Another ed., with English trans.: O'Clery, L., *The life of Hugh Roe O'Donnell, prince of Tirconnell 1586–1602*, ed. Rev. D. Murphy, S.J. (Dublin, 1893).

Ó Huiginn, *The bardic poems*, ed. E. Knott (Ir. Texts Soc., 2 vols., Dublin, 1922–3).

O Lochlainn, C., *Tobar fíorghlan Gaedhilge: deismireacht na teangadh 1450–1835* (Dublin, 1939).

O'Sullivan Beare, Philip, *Historiae catholicae Iberniae compendium*, ed. Rev. M. Kelly (Dublin, 1850).

—— *Selections from the Zoilomastix*, ed. Rev. T. J. O'Donnell, S.J. (IMC, Dublin, 1960).

Persons, Rev. Robert, S.J., *Letters and Memorials*, ed. Rev. Leo Hicks, S.J. (CRS, XXXIX 1942).

Reusens, Chanoine, *Éléments de paléographie* (Louvain, 1899).

[Stafford, Thomas], *Pacata Hibernia*, ed. Standish [J.] O'Grady (2 vols., 1896).

Trevelyan papers, pt. ii: *1446–1643*, ed. J. Payne Collier (Camden Soc., 1893).

Verstegan, Richard, *Letters and dispatches*, ed. A. G. Petti (CRS, LII, 1959).

Wadding papers 1614–38, ed. Rev. B. Jennings, O.F.M. (IMC, Dublin, 1953).

c. *Secondary works*

I. GENERAL HISTORIES

Bagwell, Richard, *Ireland under the Tudors* (3 vols., 1885–90).

Blok, P. J., *History of the people of the Netherlands*, pt. iii: *The war with Spain* (N.Y., 1900).

Cambridge modern history, iii: *The wars of religion* (Cambridge, 1904); *New Cambridge modern history*, i: *The renaissance* (1957), ii: *The reformation* (1958), and iii: *The counter-reformation and price revolution 1559–1610* (1968).

Davies, R. Trevor, *The golden century of Spain 1501–1621* (1937; repr. 1958).

Elizabethan government and society: essays presented to Sir John Neale, eds. S. T. Bindoff, J. Hurstfield and C. H. Williams (1961).

ELLIOTT, J. H., *Imperial Spain 1469–1716* (1963).

ELTON, G. R., *England under the Tudors* (1955).

—— *Reformation Europe 1517–59* (Fontana Hist. of Europe, 1963).

FROUDE, J. A., *History of England from the fall of Wolsey to the defeat of the Spanish Armada* (12 vols., 1856–70; rev. ed., 1862–70).

GARDINER, S. R., *History of England 1603–42* (10 vols., 1883–4).

GEYL, P., *The revolt of the Netherlands 1559–1609* (2nd ed., 1958).

HAUSER, Henri, *La prépondérance espagnole 1559–1660* (Collection Halphen-Sagnac, 2nd ed., Paris, 1940).

HOGAN, James, *Ireland in the European system: 1500–57* (1920).

HUME, M. A. S., *Spain: its greatness and decay* (Cambridge, 1898).

HURSTFIELD, Joel, *Elizabeth I and the unity of England* (Teach Yourself History, 1960).

—— *The Elizabethan nation* (BBC, 1964).

LAVISSE, E., *Histoire de France*, vol. vi (Paris, 1904).

LYNCH, John, *Spain under the Habsburgs*, vol. I: *Empire and absolutism* (O.U.P., 1964).

MATHEW, Abp Davis, *The celtic peoples and renaissance Europe: a study of the Celtic and Spanish influences on European history* (1933).

MACNEILL, Eoin, *Phases of Irish history* (Dublin, 1937).

MERRIMAN, Roger, B., *The rise of the Spanish empire in the old world and in the new* (4 vols., N.Y., 1918–39).

PETRIE, Sir Charles, *Earlier diplomatic history 1492–1713* (1949).

POLLARD, A. F., *History of England 1547–1603* (1910).

PASTOR, Ludwig Freiherr von, *History of the popes from the close of the middle ages*, eds. F. I. Antrobus and others (40 vols., 1891–1935).

RANKE, Leopold von, *History of the popes during the last four centuries*, trans. Mrs. Foster and G. R. Dennis (3 vols., 1913).

TENISON, E. M., (ed.), *Elizabethan England: being the history of this country 'in relation to all foreign princes'* (12 vols., Royal Leamington Spa, 1932–58).

WERNHAM, R. B., *Before the armada: the growth of English foreign policy 1485–1588* (1966).

WILLIAMSON, J. A., *The Tudor age* (1953).

2. SPECIAL STUDIES

a. Unprinted

Ó DOMHNAILL, Séan, 'History of Tír Conaill in the sixteenth century'. NUI Thesis, 1946.

b. Printed

BINCHY, D., 'An Irish Ambassador at the Spanish court 1569–74', in *Studies*, x–xiv (1921–5).

BRADY, Rev. J., 'Father Christopher Cusack and the Irish college at Douay 1594–1624', in *Measgra i gcuimhne Mhichíl Uí Chléirigh*, ed. S. O'Brien, pp. 98–107.

Britain and the Netherlands: papers delivered to the Oxford-Netherlands Conference, 1959, eds. J. S. Bromley and E. H. Kossmann, introd. P. Geyl (1960).

BUTLER, W. F. T., *Gleanings from Irish history* (1925).

DODD, Charles (Hugh Tootel), *The church history of England from 1500 to the year 1688, chiefly with regard to Catholics* (3 vols., Brussels (prob. London), 1737–42; new rev. ed. M. A. Tierney, 5 vols., 1839–43).

DULLES, Allen, *The craft of intelligence* (1963).

EDWARDS, R. D., *Church and state in Tudor Ireland* (Dublin, [1935]).

—— 'Church and state in the Ireland of Michel O'Cleirigh 1626–41', in *Measgra gcuimhne Mhichíl Uí Chléirigh*, ed. S. O'Brien, pp. 1–20.

FALLS, Cyril, *Elizabeth's Irish wars* (1950).

—— 'Mountjoy as a soldier', in *Ir. Sword*, ii (1954), 1–5.

—— 'The growth of Irish military strength in the second half of the sixteenth century', ibid., ii (1955), 103–8.

—— 'Hugh O'Neill the great', ibid., vi (1963), 94–102.

GWYNN, Rev. Aubrey, S.J., *The medieval province of Armagh 1470–1555* (Dundalk, 1946).

HAMILTON, E. J., *American trade and the price revolution in Spain 1501–1650* (Harvard, 1934).

—— *Monetary inflation in Castile 1598–1600* (1931).

HAYES-McCOY, G. A., 'Ballyshannon: its strategic importance in the wars in Connacht 1530–1602', in *Galway Arch. Soc. Jn.* xv (1931–3), 141–59.

—— ed., *The Irish at war* (Cork, 1964).

—— 'Strategy and tactics in Irish warfare 1593–1601', in *I.H.S.*, ii (1941), 255–79.

—— 'The tide of victory and defeat', in *Studies*, xxxviii (1949), 158–68, 307–17.

—— 'The army of Ulster 1593–1601', in *Ir. Sword*, i (1951), 105–17.

—— 'Irish cavalry, i: the sixteenth century', ibid., i (1953), 316–17.

HENRY, L. W., 'Contemporary sources for Essex's lieutenancy in Ireland', in *I.H.S.*, xi (1958), 8–17.

—— 'The earl of Essex and Ireland 1599' in *Inst. Hist. Res. Bull.*, xxxii (1959), 1–23.

—— 'Essex as a strategist and military organiser, 1596–7', in *E.H.R.*, lxviii (1953), 363–93.

HOGAN, James, 'Shane O'Neill comes to the court of Elizabeth', in *Féilscríbhinn Torna: essays and studies presented to Professor Tadhg Ua Donnchadha (Torna)*, ed. S. Pender (Cork U.P., 1947).

HUME, M. A. S., *Treason and plot: struggles for Catholic supremacy in the last years of Queen Elizabeth* (1901).

JENNINGS, Rev. Brendan, O.F.M., 'Irish swordsmen in Flanders 1586–1610, i: Stanley's regiment', in *Studies*, xxxvi (1947), 402–10.

JONES, Rev. F. M., C.SS.R., 'The Spaniards and Kinsale 1601' in *Galway Arch. Soc. Jn.*, xxi (1944), 1–43.

—— 'Pope Clement VIII (1592–1603) and Hugh O'Neill', in *ICHS Bull.*, new series, ii. no. 73 (1953), 5–6.

—— 'The destination of Don Juan del Águila in 1601', in *Ir. Sword*, ii (1954), 29–32.

—— 'An indictment of Don Juan del Águila, ibid., ii (1955), 218–20.

—— 'The counter-reformation'. Vol. iii. III of *A History of Irish Catholicism*, ed. P. J. Corish (Dublin, 1967).

KEARNEY, H. F., 'The Irish wine-trade 1614–15', in *I.H.S.*, ix (1955).

KELSO, J. B., *Die Spanier in Irland 1588–1603* (Leipzig, 1902).

LONGFIELD, A. K., *Anglo-Irish trade in the sixteenth century* (1929).

LOOMIE, Rev. Albert J., S.J., *The Spanish Elizabethans: the English exiles at the court of Philip II* (Fordham U.P., N.Y., 1963).

LYNCH, J., 'Philip II and the papacy', in *Trans. RHS*, 5 ser., ii (1961), 23–42.

MANGAN, Henry, 'Del Águila's defence of Kinsale 1601–2', in *Ir. Sword*, i (1952), 218–24.

—— 'Comments on "An indictment of . . . Águila"', ibid., ii (1955), 220–3.

—— 'A vindication of Don Juan del Águila', ibid., ii (1956), 343–51.

MEYER, A. O., *England and the Catholic church under Queen Elizabeth* (1916).

MOONEY, Rev. Canice, O.F.M., 'The Irish sword and the Franciscan cowl', in *Ir. Sword*, i (1951), 80–7.

NEALE, J. E., *Essays in Elizabethan history* (1958).

O'BRIEN, Rev. Sylvester, O.F.M., *Measgra i gcuimhne Mhichíl Uí Chléirigh* (Dublin, 1944).

Ó CEALLAIGH, Séamus, *Gleanings from Ulster history; punann ó Chois Bhanna* (Cork U.P., 1951).

Ó DOMHNAILL, Séan, 'Warfare in sixteenth-century Ireland', in *I.H.S.*, v (1946), 48–53.

O'RAHILLY, Alfred, *The massacre at Smerwick 1580* (Hist. and Arch. Papers, ed. S. P. O'Riordain, i. Cork, 1938).

O'SULLIVAN, Florence, *The history of Kinsale* (Dublin, 1916).

POLLEN, J. H., *The English Catholics in the reign of Elizabeth: a study of their politics, civil life and government* (1920).

—— 'The politics of English Catholics during the reign of Queen Elizabeth', in *Month*, c (1902).

—— 'The question of Queen Elizabeth's successor', ibid., ci (1903), 511–32.

—— 'The accession of James I', ibid., ci (1903), 572–85.

PORTER, Whitworth, *A history of the knights of Malta or the order of St. John of Jerusalem* (1883).

QUINN, D. B., 'Ireland and sixteenth-century European expansion', in *Historical studies* (i): *papers read before the second conference of Irish historians*, ed. T. D. Williams (1958).

—— 'Henry VIII and Ireland 1509–34', in *I.H.S.*, xii (1961), 318–44.

READ, Conyers, *Mr. Secretary Walsingham and the policy of Queen Elizabeth* (3 vols., Oxford, 1925).

—— *Mr. Secretary Cecil and Queen Elizabeth* (1955).

—— *Lord Burghley and Queen Elizabeth* (1960).

RONAN, Rev. Myles V., *The reformation in Ireland under Elizabeth 1558–80* (1930).

SILKE, Rev. J. J., 'The Irish appeal of 1593 to Spain: some light on the genesis of the nine years war', in *I.E.R.*, ser. 5, xcii (1959), 279–90, 362–71.

—— 'Later relations between Primate Peter Lombard and Hugh O'Neill', in *Ir. Theol. Quart.* xxii (1955), 15–30.

—— 'Primate Lombard and James I', ibid., xxii (1955), 124–50.

—— 'Why Águila landed at Kinsale', in *I.H.S.*, xiii (1963), 236–45.

—— 'Spain and the invasion of Ireland 1601–2', ibid., xiv (1965), 295–312.

—— 'Where was "Obemdub"?', in *Ir. Sword*, vi (1964), 276–82.

—— 'Hugh O'Neill, the Catholic question and the papacy', in *I.E.R.*, ser. 5, civ (1965).

WALSH, Rev. Paul, *Irish chiefs and leaders*, ed. Colm O'Lochlainn (Dublin, 1960).

3. BIOGRAPHIES AND BIOGRAPHICAL AIDS

ASTRAIN, A., S.J., *Historia de la Compañía de Jesús en la asistencia de España*, iii: *Mercurian-Aquaviva*, i: *1515–73* (Madrid, 1909).

CLEARY, Rev. G., O.F.M., *Father Luke Wadding and St. Isidore's college, Rome* (Rome 1925).

C[OKAYNE], G. E., *Complete peerage of England, Scotland, Ireland, Great Britain and the United Kingdom . . .*, eds. Vicary Gibbs and others (13 vols., 1910–59).

CORBOY, Rev. James, S.J., 'Father James Archer 1550–1625 (?)', in *Studies*, xxxiii (1944), 99–107.

Dictionary of national biography, eds. Sir Leslie Stephen and Sir Sidney Lee (22 vols., London, 1908–9). First published in 66 vols., 1885–1901.

ESSEN, Leon van der, *Alexandre Farnese, prince de Parme, gouverneur général des Pays-Bas 1545–92*, préface de Henri Pirenne (5 vols., Brussels, 1933–9).

EUBEL, C., O.F.M. Conv. (ed.), *Hierarchia catholica medii aevi, 1198–1503* (2 vols., Munich-Ratisbon, 2nd ed., 1913–14; vol., iii: 1503–92, eds. C. Eubel, G. van Gulik, L. Schmitz-Kallenberg, Munster, 2nd ed., 1923; vol. iv: 1592–1667, ed. P. Gauchat, Munster, 1935).

FALLS, Cyril, *Mountjoy: Elizabethan general* (1955).

FITZGERALD, Brian, *The Geraldines: an experiment in Irish government 1169–1601* (1961).

FOLEY, Rev. Henry, *Records of the English province, S.J.* (7 vols., 1877–84).

GILLOW, Joseph, *Biographical dictionary of the English Catholics* (5 vols., 1885–1903).

HANDOVER, P. M., *The second Cecil: the rise to power 1563–1604 of Sir Robert Cecil, later first earl of Salisbury* (1959).

HAWKES, Rev. William, 'Matthew de Oviedo: birthplace, parentage, place of burial', in *Rep. Nov.*, i (1955), 236–7.

HOGAN, Rev. Edmund, S.J., *Distinguished Irishmen of the sixteenth century: first series* (1894).

JENNINGS, Rev. B., O.F.M., 'Florence Conry, archbishop of Tuam', in *Galway Arch. Soc. Jn.*, xxiii (1948–9), 83–93.

JONES, Rev. F. M., C.SS.R., *Mountjoy 1563–1603: the last Elizabethan deputy* (Dublin, 1958).

Leabhar Chlainne Suibhne, ed. Rev. Paul Walsh (Dublin, 1920).

LODGE, J., *The peerage of Ireland* (7 vols., Dublin, 1789).

LOOMIE, Albert J., S.J., 'Richard Stanyhurst in Spain: two unknown letters of August 1593', in *Huntingdon Library Quarterly*, xxviii (1965), 145–55.

MACCARTHY, S. Trant, *The MacCarthys of Munster: the story of a great Irish sept* (Dundalk, 1922).

MOORE, Philip, 'The MacMahons of Monaghan 1593–1603', in *Clogher Record*, i (1956), 85–107.

NEALE, J. E., *Queen Elizabeth I* (1934; Pelican Books, 1960).

O'FAOLAIN, Sean, *The great O'Neill: a biography of Hugh O'Neill, earl of Tyrone 1550–1616* (1942; repr. 1947).

O'GRADY, S. H., *The flight of the eagle* (Dublin, n.d.).

RENEHAN, Rev. L. F., *Collections on Irish church history*, ed. D. MacCarthy, i: *archbishops* (Dublin, 1861).

SCHENK, W., *Reginald Pole: cardinal of England* (1950).

WALSH, Micheline, *The O'Neills in Spain* (O'Donnell Lecture, Dublin, 1960).

WALSH, Rev. Paul, 'Scots Clann Domhnaill in Ireland', in *I.E.R.*, ser. 5, lxviii (1936), 23–42.

—— *The will and family of Hugh O'Neill* (Dublin, 1930).

—— 'James Blake of Galway', in *I.E.R.*, ser. 5, l (1937), 382–97.

INDEX

adelantado, office of, 31 n

Adelantado Mayor of Castile, *see* Padilla, Don Martín de

Africa, 9, 18, 45

Aguado Bleye, Pedro, cited, 39 n

Águila, Don Juan del, *maestre de campo*, 3, 4, 7, 26–7, 32, 105–7, 135, 145, 147, 153–4, 156–9, 175, 178; his career, 96–97; prefers landing in north, 98–103, 108–9, 120; opposed by captains, 109, 120, 128, 164, 169; at Kinsale, 3, 7, 110–152, 160, 176–7; subject of inquiry, 163–5, 167–74; death of, 172

Aguilar y Castro, Diego de, captain, 181

Alba, duke of, *see* Álvarez de Toledo y Pimentel, Fernando

Albert of Austria, Cardinal Archduke, sovereign of Netherlands, 6, 32–3, 38, 43–4, 49–50, 58–9, 62–5, 72, 85, 89, 161–2, 173; defeated at battle of Dunes, 6, 89; offered Irish crown, 28, 31

Albornoz, Juan de, captain, 96, 113, 178, 180

Alcalá, Irish college at, 29

Aldobrandini, Cinzio (Passeri), cardinal, joint secretary of state, 63 n, 66

Algiers, 16; *see also* Berbers

Alsace, 9

Álvarez de Toledo y Pimentel, Fernando, duke of Alba, 4, 17–19

America, 9–10, 14, 45, 48, 73; emigration to, 48; market of, 33, 47; *see also* Indies

Andalusia, 4, 96, 148, 178

Anglo-Flemish state, 14

Anglo-Irish, *see* England, settlers in Ireland, Old English

Anjou, duke of, *see* Francis of Valois

Annals of the Four Masters, cited, 123, 142, 173

Aquaviva, Rev. Claude, S.J., general of Jesuit order, 67, 94

Aragón, admiral of, *see* Hurtado de Mendoza, Don Francisco

Aragon, kingdom of, 9–11, 14, 38; council of, 37

Aramburu, Marcos de, general, 59–60

Arbe, Andrés de, captain, 110, 132, 179, 181

Archer, Rev. James, S.J., 54–5, 98, 106, 150, 155; his mission to Rome, 83–4

Arias de Bobadilla, Don Fernando, count of Puñoenrostro, assistant of Seville, 138, 172–3

armada, 'invincible' (1588), vii, 2–3, 24, 30, 55; 'invisible' (1599), 58

Armagh, garrison at, 28, 120

Arostegui, Antonio de, secretary of state, 42

Artois, county of, 9, 28

Asia, Portuguese colonies in, 44

Asturias, 149, 181; prince of, *see* Philip IV

Athy, co. Kildare, 54

Atlantic, conflict, vii, 1–2, 15–30, 44–5, 49–50, 138, 175; discoveries, *see* America; trade, 33, 45

Atlantic Ocean, 3, 11, 15, 31

Austria, duchy of, 9; territorial power, 10–11, 14

Ávila, province of, 96–7, 167

Ayala, Don Christóbal de, captain, 155, 180

Azores Islands, 4, 31

Babington (Anthony) plot, 24

Bagenal, Sir Henry, marshal, 28

Bagshawe, Rev. Dr Christopher, 62 n

Bagwell, Richard, cited, 57

Balearic Islands, 45

Ballecilla, Martín de, sea-captain, 148–9, 181

Ballesteros y Beretta, Antonio, cited, 40

Ballinacubby Hill, co. Cork, 112

Ballinacurra Creek, co. Cork, 111

Ballincollig, co. Cork, 126

Ballymote castle, co. Sligo, 54, 121

Ballyshannon castle, co. Donegal, 125, 163